International Trade Policies

STUDIES IN INTERNATIONAL TRADE POLICY

Studies in International Trade Policy includes works dealing with the theory, empirical analysis, political, economic, legal relations, and evaluations of international trade policies and institutions.

General Editor: Robert M. Stern

John H. Jackson and Edwin A. Vermulst, Editors. *Antidumping Law and Practice: A Comparative Study*

John Whalley, Editor. *Developing Countries and the Global Trading System,* Volumes 1 and 2

John Whalley, Coordinator. *The Uruguay Round and Beyond: The Final Report from the Ford Foundation Project on Developing Countries and the Global Trading System*

John S. Odell and Thomas D. Willett, Editors. *International Trade Policies: Gains from Exchange between Economics and Political Science*

International Trade Policies

Gains from Exchange between
Economics and Political Science

Edited by John S. Odell
and Thomas D. Willett

Ann Arbor
The University of Michigan Press

Copyright © by The University of Michigan 1990
All rights reserved
Published in the United States of America by
The University of Michigan Press
Manufactured in the United States of America

1993   1992   1991   1990   4   3   2   1

Library of Congress Cataloging-in-Publication Data

International trade policies : gains from exchange between economics
   and political science / edited by John S. Odell and Thomas D.
   Willett.
      p.   cm. — (Studies in international trade policy)
   Includes bibliographical references.
   ISBN 0-472-10153-6 (alk. paper)
   1. Commercial policy.   2. International trade.   I. Odell, John
S., 1945–   .   II. Willett, Thomas D.   III. Series.
HF1411.I558   1990
382'.3—dc20   90-32073
                                                                   CIP

Acknowledgments

The project that produced this book originated with the warm encouragement of Thomas O. Bayard and Enid C. B. Schoettle of the Ford Foundation's International Affairs Program. With the Foundation's generous support, the Claremont Center for Economic Policy Studies at the Claremont Graduate School and the Center for International Studies at the University of Southern California hosted two major conferences in 1987 and 1988. The general purpose was to foster and speed the development of better-integrated basic knowledge of international political-economic phenomena. Over sixty economists and political scientists interested in international trade policies and in economic policy more generally debated most of the present chapters in 1987. The second set of meetings concentrated on international financial topics; a number of the works discussed there appeared together as a 1988 special issue of the *Journal of Public Policy*, entitled *International Monetary Cooperation, Domestic Politics, and Policy Ideas.*

These conferences proved to be quite successful in stimulating cross-disciplinary dialogue. Few (if any) participants left without gaining insights into how they could make use of knowledge and research methodologies generated by the other discipline. A major purpose of this volume is to make some of this experience available to a wider group.

We are grateful to the Ford Foundation, the Claremont Graduate School, Claremont McKenna College, and the University of Southern California for their assistance. Cecilia Cicchinelli and Lori Harnack, at USC and Claremont respectively, also helped us carry out the project from start to finish. We also thank Colin Day, director of the University of Michigan Press, for his generous efforts in bringing the book to publication. Several of the papers presented at our conference and included in this volume have been previously published during the interim. We gratefully acknowledge permission from *Economics and Politics,* the International Finance Section, Princeton University, and *World Politics* to reprint essays previously appearing in these sources.

Contents

x   Contents

CHAPTER 1

Gains from Exchange: An Introduction

John S. Odell and Thomas D. Willett

International trade policies are having an increasingly important influence on the operation of the world's economic and political systems. The trend toward trade liberalization that characterized most of the postwar period has come to a halt, and in recent years more trade barriers have been erected or raised than have been removed or reduced. Trade issues now frequently attract considerable attention in the political arena, with substantial consequences for international trade, national economic performance, international political relations, and elections.

While most discussions focus on the normative question of which trade policies should be adopted, another important field of inquiry considers the positive question of what factors influence the trade policy choices that governments make. In addition to its inherent academic interest, better knowledge about these processes is of obvious practical importance both to those who may be affected by changes in trade policies and to those recommending policy strategies. For example, a particular strategy might be implemented quite differently depending on whether or not the policy process is dominated by special interest groups. Questions about the operation of the policy process clearly require a rich understanding of both political and economic considerations. As is well known, however, the intellectual disciplines specializing in those two subjects have been separated since the mid-nineteenth century. Our knowledge has been largely compartmentalized into "economics" and "political science," each of which has developed significantly in its own direction. In recent years important efforts have begun to reintegrate major aspects of economic and political analysis as applied to a range of important policy issues, both domestic and international. Still, while a minority of political scientists and a minority of economists have begun to write about political economy, many others in each discipline have yet to explore it. Even those working this terrain have often limited themselves largely to approaches most familiar to their home discipline, without having investigated fully the possible value of the other's research traditions.

What is new is that such cross-investigation is becoming more common and more profound. This volume on trade policies seeks to demonstrate that analysts are realizing more fully the potential gains from exchange between the two disciplines—more fully than is often recognized—and that as a result a subfield of international political economy that genuinely represents both political science and economics is gradually developing. While we have far to go, economists are increasingly exploring and contending with the insights of political science, and political scientists are similarly deepening their use of economics. Potential gains from exchange are not limited to adopting or agreeing with ideas from other fields. In some cases analysts seriously consider objections from other disciplines and conclude that they are not valid, or are valid under more restricted conditions than was thought. Confronting such debates and their implications more explicitly also contributes to significant progress on both sides.

One effective way to see this evolution concretely is to disaggregate contemporary research and delve sequentially into different traditions or different approaches to the same subject. In practice analysts from the two disciplines are bumping into each other intellectually in the vicinity of certain focal points, and in the process are learning from and disputing with each other.

This volume offers a rich sample of work at the frontiers of research on the political economy of international trade policies. It is not designed to support a single thesis or theory about trade policies, or to produce a common empirical conclusion. Any contemporary effort to produce such a convergence encompassing both economists and political scientists would still be premature, necessarily ending in either platitudes or agreement to disagree over familiar fundamental issues.

The book should be useful, nonetheless, both to specialists in the trade area and to those interested in political economy more generally. This introduction provides a guide to, and the chapters illustrate, these basic schools of analysis. Mainly, however, the book is not a review of literature but a report of new research, mostly using concrete empirical evidence, which goes beyond earlier generations of political-economy work and suggests ideas that could be used in other applications as well. The volume is not intended to settle any of these theoretical or empirical questions conclusively, but is offered most of all in the hope of enticing additional scholars to explore possible gains from exchange in their own work. It illustrates a menu of possibilities. Bearing in mind especially the interests of readers new to political economy, this first essay introduces the broad issue of disciplinary divergence and summarizes how recent trade policy analyses, including the subsequent chapters, deal with it.

Scholars in international political economy differ greatly in the emphasis they place on various considerations that influence the determination of coun-

tries' national policies and their international interactions. The realist paradigm adopted by many international relations scholars views countries as
highly centralized rational decision makers concerned with maximizing some
combination of national power, security, and economic well-being in an interdependent world. This emphasis on a centralized policy process is similar in
political structure to the assumption, implicit in much of traditional economic
policy analysis, that governments pursue aggregate economic efficiency.

While this unified rational actor model is useful for many purposes, a full
understanding of the formulation of domestic and international economic
policies requires recognition that governments are subject to a wide array of
pressures and that there are sometimes multiple focal points of power within
the policy process. Public choice analysis demonstrates how in a decentralized setting the pursuit of individual interests can lead to outcomes that
are not efficient in the aggregate. In other words, in many institutional en-
vironments Adam Smith's invisible hand does not function for political
markets.

Recognition of such considerations has led many scholars from both
economics and political science to focus on the role of interest groups in the
policy process. Recent research has illustrated, however, that concerns with
societal pressures, especially rent seeking by interest groups, should not cause
analysts to overlook the importance of the legal and institutional environment
in influencing the relative power of such interest groups and the ways in which
their pressures are channeled. Likewise, while analysis of the domestic influences on international economic policies has undercut the assumption that
governments always behave as unified rational actors free of domestic pressures, neither is there a basis for assuming that governments cannot play an at
least partially independent role in the political process. The papers in this
volume illustrate how for some purposes considerable insight can be gained
from analysis that treats nations as unified rational actors, while for other
purposes the adoption of more complex views of the political process is
essential.

The volume also illustrates how a wide array of types of analysis can be
used to shed light on political-economy questions. The essays contain examples of both qualitative analysis and more formal mathematical modeling
(including game theory). With respect to evidence, we have included examples of both statistical (econometric) testing and carefully constructed historical case studies. While, unfortunately, there is sometimes a tendency for
academics to devote considerable attention to disputes over the alleged superiority of one method over another, we believe this volume provides numerous
examples of how a wide range of types of analysis can be highly productive.
In forming a more comprehensive picture of the operation of the policy
process, there are substantial gains from the exchange of the results from

studies using different methodologies. Unlike many earlier political-economic treatments that viewed orthodox economic analysis as fundamentally flawed, and unlike much analysis by economists that assumed that political considerations are irrelevant, the diverse contributors to this volume share the view that mainstream economic analysis is a useful (but not the exclusive) ingredient for good analysis of policy issues. It must be supplemented with explicit political analysis.

The essays in this book do not purport to offer detailed surveys of the literature, but each author has provided references to relevant literature and has attempted to provide sufficient background to make his or her analysis understandable to readers from the other discipline. We are particularly pleased at the extent to which most papers have drawn upon contributions from both the economics and political science literatures.

In the following sections of this introduction, we briefly discuss the traditional separation and the recent efforts at reintegration of economics and political science within political-economy analysis. We conclude this introduction with discussion of the individual contributions to the volume.

Traditional Separation of the Disciplines

Prior to the twentieth century, most writings on what are today called economic policy issues appeared under the label "political economy." Adam Smith was representative of his time in regarding political economy as "a branch of the science of a statesman or legislator" (1937, bk. 4, 397). But beginning in the nineteenth century, the professional disciplines of economics, political science, and sociology diverged, developing along distinct lines and losing contact with each other to a significant extent.[1]

This division of labor made a crucial contribution toward the rapid growth of social science knowledge. Many issues, however, do not fall neatly into the purview of a single discipline. Subfields drawing upon two or more major disciplines have developed, such as economic history, political psychology, political sociology, and a number of branches of political economy.

In the United States, with the exception of Marxist analysis, one of the least explored of these cross-cutting subfields has been political-economy studies.[2] Journal articles by international economists and world politics specialists often diverge in fundamental respects. Frequently, they ask different

---

1. Reviews and critiques of these developments are voluminous. For a sampling, see Mill 1844, Myrdal 1965, Heilbroner 1970, Chattopadhyay 1974, Gilpin 1977, and Staniland 1985, as well as works cited below.

2. There have been some important non-Marxist exceptions, including such economists as Schumpeter, Viner, and Hirschman, and political scientists such as Schattschneider and Haas.

questions, make different analytical assumptions, and use different methods and evidence. They rarely address colleagues in the other discipline.

Where contact has been established, greater familiarity has sometimes provoked more hostility or contempt than interest. Economists have often found political scientists' discussions of economic matters lacking an elementary understanding of modern economics. Similarly, political scientists are frequently amazed to find economists venturing into political matters without even undergraduate-level knowledge of modern political science. The two have been known to disagree over the rationality assumption and over the relative importance of individuals and institutions or of the market and the state. Some political scientists have found little value in models that assume away or distort aspects of reality they consider decisive. Some economic theorists have disdained political scientists' work for analytical weakness and lack of theoretical and technical rigor. Each may have been reluctant to use the concepts of the other out of concern that this necessarily implied importing an unwelcome ideology in the process.

Political Economy Revival

Growing attention to economic matters (including trade) in international relations and increasing politicalization of both domestic and international economic policies have made it increasingly awkward for the two disciplines to ignore their interrelationships. These developments joined with dynamics internal to the disciplines to generate broader interest in political economy on both sides of the fence. For instance, specialists on economic development and political development both probed connections between economies and political institutions. Formal modeling, quantitative methods, and rational choice assumptions became more widespread in political science. An interdisciplinary subfield of public choice helped stimulate greater interest among economists in political processes and in distributional effects, to complement the traditional emphasis on aggregate economic efficiency. The increasing internationalization of national economies has helped push specialists on international economic relations to the forefront of these efforts.

For us, political economy is best defined not by theoretical or methodological perspective but by subject matter.[3] In a broad sense, political economy at the international level is the study of the reciprocal effects of the pursuit of wealth, security, and power in international relations. At its core is a

---

3. Coase (1978) underlines the value of this orientation. Our use of the term "political economy" excludes much of today's economics and political science. In that sense this usage departs from nineteenth-century precedent, but it is more useful in differentiating contemporary studies.

quest to explain, and sometimes to improve, governments' economic policies by paying explicit attention to both political and economic conditions and the interactions between the two. Some political economists emphasize the sources of policy while others concentrate on the effects. Clustered around this core are closely related subjects, including international and national institutions, the operation of competitive and not-so-competitive world markets for goods and capital, and national macroeconomic conditions. Also related are studies not analyzing political and economic conditions simultaneously but using concepts or techniques from one discipline to answer policy questions located traditionally in the other.[4]

During the past two decades a great deal of useful work has been produced on the political economy of international economic relations, but we have so far only scratched the surface of the field's potential. Lack of awareness of relevant work by scholars outside one's discipline is still a major problem. Even when this barrier is broken, the difficulties of understanding and mastering the contributions from another field can be daunting. Barriers are also serious between subfields within each discipline. For example, while most political scientists writing specifically on international economic affairs today have an understanding of basic economic theory, this is far from sufficient to follow the intricacies of much current economic literature on trade theory. Indeed, some of this literature is hard to follow for nonspecialist economists. With these difficulties in mind, this book attempts to present all its analyses in ways which are as accessible as possible to readers from other disciplines, and to discuss antecedent literatures briefly.

Four Evolving Research Traditions

Much scholarship that is relevant for a political-economic understanding of international trade policies has been developed within one of four research traditions. Major intellectual strands would certainly include modern trade theory, international realism, interest group analysis, and studies of national political institutions.[5] Each of these traditions is itself evolving, and links are being built among them. Subsequent chapters of this book present new works that collectively both illustrate and criticize each school of thought and simultaneously push beyond their boundaries. In this chapter we introduce these

---

4. Other recent definitions of the subfield are found in Frey 1984, Staniland 1985, Wade 1983, Gilpin 1987, and Frieden and Lake 1987.

5. We have not attempted to include all fruitful analytical perspectives in this one volume. Omitted, for example, is the study of policy beliefs and perceptions. Nor is this categorization the only possible one. See, e.g., Gilpin 1987.

four strands or schools of thought and highlight examples of potential gains from exchange and criticism to be found in subsequent chapters.

Modern Trade Theory

Recently critics have leveled strong charges against liberal trade theory. Chapter 2 considers these charges and provides a new assessment of its usefulness and limitations as a component of political-economy analysis. In replying, economists Patricia Dillon, James Lehman, and Thomas D. Willett suggest respects in which other disciplines can use trade theory more effectively. They maintain that many recent denunciations, including some by prominent political scientists, are based on outdated understandings of the theory's contemporary content. For example, they object to the claim that economics is concerned exclusively with efficiency, and they argue that relaxing simplifying assumptions of the perfect competitive textbook model does not necessarily diminish the case for free trade. After dissecting specific published attacks, they conclude that no legitimate support remains for the view that trade theory should be discarded. They acknowledge, however, that not every free trade argument is correct or useful. Attempting to bridge the gap between positive and normative analysis, they suggest important distinctions to keep in mind in deciding which propositions can be applied to different policy problems. With respect to predicting policy outcomes, they argue that trade theory can be useful but only if coupled with explicit analysis of the political process.

International Realism

Political scientists do not subscribe, as a group, to any single body of theory having the wide acceptance of modern trade theory among international economists. Many, however, do consider themselves adherents of "realism," which assumes that the international system is fundamentally anarchic and points therefore to the enduring importance of state security and relative power. Applying this perspective to international trade policies has meant assuming that they too will depend on the nature of the world political system of which they are a part. This tradition, like modern trade theory, assumes rationality, but a rationality having a different substance, which may imply quite different policies. From this standpoint, states may be expected to adopt policies that are less than optimal in trade theory terms, if necessary in order to weaken military adversaries or strengthen allies. Furthermore, apart from its military goals, a state may set its policies primarily to increase its economic and competitive power relative to that of its economic rivals, to a degree not captured by standard trade theory.

During the 1970s and 1980s political scientists devoted much attention to the hegemony hypothesis, the broad argument that only in a special international power structure—one dominated by a single overwhelming leader— has free trade been stable or is it likely to be so. The hegemony notion derived from economic historians and from the theory of public goods as well. Subsequent debates over hegemony and trade raised important questions about both the meaning of the concepts and their empirical validity in history.[6]

In chapter 3, political scientist Joanne Gowa outlines the hegemonic theory of open trade, and then dissects three recent lines of attack against its theoretical foundations—assaults launched from the home territories of both economics and political science. She finds each of these charges wanting and argues that neither the theory of optimal tariffs, nor the complaint that free trade is not in fact a public good, nor the possibility of a small-group solution to hegemonic decline, seems fatal to the hegemonic theory. Gowa does contend, however, that this theory is highly vulnerable if it confines itself to states' economic interests, forgetting their security rivalries. The most durable barrier to free trade, she maintains, may be an eternal desire on the part of each state for power gains at the expense of other states, which may inhibit their participating in trade-liberalizing agreements, even in the presence of a hegemon.

In this conclusion Gowa joins many others in affirming that nations' security and economic interests are linked empirically, so analysis of behavior in either realm in isolation from the other may be perilous. Perhaps the most common version has been that the linkage is a negative one, whereby security rivalries disrupt or distort what would otherwise be beneficial economic exchange.[7] We also hear the opposite argument, that alliance ties reinforce trade at least among the allies, perhaps encouraging more liberalization than would be adopted otherwise. Some historians attribute commercial agreements at least in part to strategic realignments or desires to cement political partnerships or send a peaceful signal. For example, such interpretations have been offered for the 1860 Cobden-Chevalier treaty liberalizing trade between France and Britain, the financial opening between France and Russia in the 1890s, and Britain's turn toward currency collaboration with Washington in 1936. Even better known are the historic American shift toward liberalization in this century and the creation of the GATT and related bilateral relations with Japan during the height of the Cold War and thereafter. Making an analogous point, free-traders opposing new import protection sometimes warn that imposing it might damage military alliance ties. But for all the commen-

---

6. Chapter 3 presents many references to this literature.

7. On the national security argument for protection, see the analysis and references in Willett and Jalalighajar 1983–84.

tary on economic-security linkage in diplomacy, analysts have made surprisingly little progress in developing more precise empirical and theoretical knowledge about the matter.[8]

Chapter 4 develops new analytical apparatus for treating such problems, and illustrates its ideas by reference to links between NATO spending and gas trade in Europe. Like others, political scientist James E. Alt and economist Barry Eichengreen assume that nations are unitary rational actors. Using game theoretic techniques, they go beyond previous game theory applications in both economics and political science, which have tended to concentrate on strategic behavior in either business or national security but not both. In order to bridge the divide, they develop formal concepts for "parallel games" and "overlapping games," representing two different types of linkage, and they deduce implications for international cooperation. Parallel games are those in which a common set of actors plays on two different issues simultaneously. Overlapping games represent situations in which a single actor plays on one issue simultaneously against two others who experience no direct interaction between themselves.

Alt and Eichengreen suggest that analyzing European behavior in either NATO or gas trade as though it were isolated from the other can lead to misleading conclusions on both issues. The NATO contribution game played in isolation ought to be debilitated by free-riding, yet Norway seems to invest significantly in defense. This they attribute to a parallel game in gas trade, where West Germany is in a position to make a side payment to induce Norwegian military cooperation. The consequence in the gas market is reduced German purchases from the Soviet Union, higher prices, and greater Norwegian income than if the gas game were played alone. These game concepts are general and could illuminate cross-issue links other than those between security and trade. The notion of overlapping games might also help clarify complex negotiations in which a government deals simultaneously with a domestic industry seeking protection and overseas trading partners.

Interest Group Studies and the Public Choice Approach

A third research tradition differs from international realism by relaxing the assumption that nation-states are unitary actors and emphasizing the varied

---

8. Substantial subliteratures have, however, investigated the relationship between military spending and economic growth, long historical cycles of war and production, East-West trade, and the use of economic sanctions for political purposes. For windows into each of those topics, respectively, see Cappelen, Gleditsch, and Bjerkholt 1984, Faini, Annez, and Taylor 1984, Goldstein 1988, and Holzman and Legvold 1975. Regarding economic sanctions, see the citations in chapter 7.

interests of particular industries in determining trade policies. Typically, international security and power influences on policies are absent here, as are the effects of different national political institutions. This approach also differs from modern trade theory by virtue of the questions it emphasizes; it is concerned in the first instance with why policies are adopted rather than primarily with their effects on the economy. Here too, other like-minded economists and political scientists have been working common terrain, and in the process surpassing previous work in each discipline.

Attention to the role of interest groups has been one of the important aspects of public choice analysis, which emerged as a subfield in the 1960s and in recent years has been applied with much success to trade policy, especially as international issues have become of greater concern to Americans. Many such public choice studies have national rather than global focuses, asking, for example, why a particular country's tariff levels vary across industries as they do. Rent seeking and vote and revenue seeking by politicians and other special interests are important motivations in the political market for protection. The public choice approach applies traditional economic assumptions of individual rationality to newer problems.[9] This school of analysis, like that concerned with international hegemony, has confronted testable hypotheses with extensive empirical evidence. Interestingly, these two literatures have paid little attention to each other.

In chapter 5 economists Stephen V. Marks and John McArthur review public choice studies of political activity at the national level (concentrating on trade issues), concluding that they have made useful progress in identifying industrial and macroeconomic conditions that are favorable and unfavorable for protection, but have shed less light on the process by which policy makers decide to intervene on behalf of domestic producers. Marks and McArthur advance this work with an empirical study of U.S. policy applied to the automobile industry in the form of Congressional voting on the domestic content legislation in 1982. While accepting some traditional public choice premises, this chapter also takes seriously political science's traditional emphasis on the importance of political institutions, and on goals other than self-interest.

Rather than assuming the U.S. government is a single actor, Marks and McArthur concentrate on the Congress in particular, emphasizing the importance of members' ideologies. Many observers believe that members of Con-

---

9. While many early public choice studies of trade policy concentrated on industry characteristics, this tradition is moving into additional dimensions, as evidenced by this book. Moreover, public choice generally has never been limited to analyzing interest groups. It considers a much wider range of issues, including the roles of alternative voting rules and other institutional arrangements. For an additional example, see Kaempfer and Willett 1989.

gress vote on trade policy issues simply according to their constituents' economic interests. In contrast, Marks and McArthur find that legislators' own ideological beliefs also affect their trade votes. Those who are more left-of-center on the economic issues are more likely to vote for protection (at least they were in this case) than are the more conservative, even controlling for constituency interests.

Additionally, they reason that if fear of constituency retribution pushes legislators to vote for protectionist policies, then legislators would be more likely to support liberal trade policies if they were free of reelection concerns. Comparing lame-duck legislators with their reelected colleagues confirms that lower political opportunity cost leads to greater resistance to protectionist pressures. This chapter illustrates ways to broaden simple rent-seeking models, as well as possible contributions of statistical methods to trade policy analysis.

Overlapping with this public choice school is the even older tradition of interest group studies in sociology and political science, which dates from the early twentieth century.[10] One of the best known works in this tradition is Schattschneider's (1935) study of the process that produced the 1930 U.S. Smoot-Hawley tariff. As far as trade policies are concerned, this literature has followed Schattschneider's lead, as well as political reality, in concentrating on the groups seeking protection.[11]

This interest-group research tradition has (especially since the 1960s) shown the increased influence of economic concepts. After the publication of Mancur Olson's *The Logic of Collective Action* (1965) and the development of exchange theories in sociology, some analysts began explaining both group formation and their interactions with governments in a basically economic framework, including activities of noneconomic groups.

Chapter 6 by political scientist Helen Milner goes beyond previous studies in this tradition to deepen knowledge of the U.S. trade policy process. She focuses on explaining industries' policy preferences and pressures, rather than policies themselves, and unlike most of her predecessors, she concentrates on groups that lose from protection and bring pressure against it. Milner uses changes in world industrial markets to derive insights into U.S. industries' policy stands. As a national industry becomes more internationalized, she expects it to reduce its political demand for protection and to fight for liberalization. Her evidence shows that even firms facing strong import penetration

---

10. Key references in American political science include Truman 1971, Lowi 1979, and Wilson 1973. Also see Moe 1980 and Cigler and Loomis 1986. For an influential related comparative study, see Gourevitch 1986.

11. Bauer, Pool, and Dexter (1972) question both the power of organized groups and the degree to which their trade interests are fixed.

spoke publicly against protection if they also depended heavily on exports or global production, both in the 1920s and in the 1970s. The U.S. did not slide nearly as far down a slippery slope of protectionism in the 1970s as it did during the interwar period (even though the two periods were similar in important respects) because many more of today's industries are internationalized. Milner maintains that well-known political science arguments (like that of Joanne Gowa) attributing trade policies to informal power structures or to formal international regimes are incomplete without this focus on economic variables.

Milner's new evidence is also relevant for empirical conclusions reached by economists using different research designs and data, such as the studies reviewed by Marks and McArthur. Where these have typically worked at the industry level and used published statistical data, Milner goes to case studies at the company level, sometimes revealing different degrees of internationalization within the same industry, with interesting political consequences. And while many previous studies have not been based on direct observation of industry policy preferences, relying instead on the assumption that they corresponded to observed government policy, Milner's conclusions are based on direct evidence of companies' political activities, such as testimony before Congress. This new political science study therefore offers partial confirmation for some of the work by economists, as well as a more discriminating account of how factors they discuss actually operate to affect firms' political preferences.

The public choice approach can also make an important contribution to understanding international political-economic sanctions, including trade measures, according to economists William H. Kaempfer and Anton D. Lowenberg in chapter 7. Recent work in both disciplines has been developing more rigorous comparative and empirical knowledge about sanctions.[12] After discussing earlier approaches to the subject in political science as well as in their own field, Kaempfer and Lowenberg propose a formal model that shows how one state's economic sanctions will affect a target country's political decision-making process. They apply this model to the case of international economic sanctions against South Africa. The core of the analysis is a bold attempt to model the South African apartheid policy itself. Coming full circle, the Kaempfer and Lowenberg model, growing originally out of economics, predicts that under some conditions economic sanctions will change politics even when the sanctions have little economic effect. They argue that sanctions may have a broader set of objectives and may operate through a broader set of mechanisms than has been assumed in the economics and political science literatures. This chapter emphasizes the compatability of a formalized public

---

12. See the many citations in chapter 7.

choice account with those developed by political scientists using other methods.

National Political Institutions: Bringing the State Back In

Another branch of political science and sociology, reacting precisely against both interest-group pluralism and traditional economic thinking, has been reviving interest in the state and political institutions themselves as central influences on the character of trade and economic policies. In this view, the postwar behavioral movement in social science had obscured valuable insights of earlier institutionalist writers, and it was important to "bring the state back in."[13] Here the primary interest is in the state's relation to other elements within its own society, as distinct from its relations with other states in the international system.

Several works of the 1970s articulated this point of view and illustrated how institutional features could help explain differences in trade and other foreign economic policies.[14] More recent studies have traced enduring patterns (in U.S. trade policies and those of other nations) to political and social institutions inherited from very different earlier decades. Others show that activist presidents or secretaries of state have substantial scope for shaping the political struggle to their ends and are not necessarily mere responders to interest-group initiatives.[15]

Such analysis has been applied mostly to the United States, occasionally to other industrial democracies, and only rarely to policies of developing countries. Chapter 8 by political scientist David R. Mares breaks ground in the latter direction. His empirical puzzle is why Colombia, unlike most of Latin America, shifted from an inward- to an outward-oriented trade and development strategy in the late 1960s, and was able to maintain this new strategy. He considers prominent economic interpretations and finds them useful but insufficient. "Society-centered" arguments concerning rent-seeking interest groups are powerful for the period of the 1950s before the shift, but lose their force over time. Mares contends that major changes in central Colombian political institutions preceding the policy shift were necessary conditions, and that the president's bold political initiatives in 1966–68 to

13. See Evans, Rueschemeyer, and Skocpol 1985 and March and Olsen 1984.

14. See Destler 1974, Katzenstein 1977, Krasner 1978, and Pastor 1980.

15. See Destler 1986, and *The State and American Foreign Policy*, a special issue of *International Organization* 42 (Winter 1988), especially chapters by Goldstein, Haggard, Ikenberry, and Lake. Also representative is Peter Hall's (1986) comparative study.

forge a supportive group coalition and even risk his presidency may have also been essential in putting Colombia on a path to more liberal trade policy.

Exchange between Traditions: Domestic Regulation and International Trade

Further gains can be realized by exchanges between these four traditions themselves. The case study of Colombia, for instance, illustrates the possible power of what is sometimes called statist thinking in political science, but does not limit itself to that approach; it also incorporates lessons from public choice analysis.

There is also considerable scope for gains from combining analyses of international and domestic policies. In the macroeconomic arena, for example, domestic policies affecting national inflation and recession clearly intersect with international monetary negotiations, at least over the longer term.[16] International trade policies are a subset of regulatory policies more generally, and the study of national regulation has also been attracting attention.[17] There has been relatively little arbitrage, however, between this literature and international trade studies.[18]

In chapter 9, political scientist Peter Cowhey makes the case for the primacy of domestic electoral politics as a determinant of regulatory policies including those affecting external trade. Upon that fundamental insight Cowhey begins to construct a "political choice" theory of policy, which also illustrates possible gains from related work by economists. This variant of the "new institutionalism" assumes that policy making in these areas is plagued with collective action problems and that politicians respond to such problems by designing political institutions in ways which will further their electoral goals. He draws on illustrations from the United States and the internationally significant and highly regulated oil and telecommunications industries.

This model begins with a demand side, but differentiates itself from many public choice and interest group approaches, by insisting that interest groups make a difference only to the extent that they influence politicians' electoral calculations. Politicians also structure political institutions in ways

---

16. See Odell and Willett 1988, based on our companion conference on the political economy of international financial policies, for illustrations.

17. Recent major contributions include Pelzman 1976, Wilson 1973, and Wilson 1980. For a useful survey see Mitnich 1980.

18. A major exception is the emphasis placed in some of the trade literature on the Pelzman-Stigler hypothesis on why protectionism is likely to increase during economic downturns and fall during upswings. Recent theoretical analysis of this issue include Cassing, McKeown, and Ochs 1986 and Hillman 1982. For empirical evidence for the U.S., see Baldwin 1985 and Feigenbaum, Ortiz, and Willett 1985.

that favor some groups over others. On the supply side, politicians as political entrepreneurs provide regulation and deregulation. Cowhey emphasizes that electoral politics leads them to package even collective goods with distributional consequences in mind. Here the model is differentiated from realist and statist political science, which concentrate on the international system and resulting national interests as the molds for foreign economic policy.

Cowhey sees institutional structures as the "production function" of regulatory policy, and argues that they themselves shape the substance of policies and outcomes. In the United States the Congress and President have delegated authority to agencies like the Federal Trade Commission and Federal Communications Commission in ways that freeze the terms of a political bargain reached at the time of delegation. Political choice theory also expects politicians to delegate in a way that allows them to escape electoral costs of unpopular decisions while still maintaining some means for oversight and influence over outcomes. Aspects of oil and telephone deregulation, including international trade effects, are attributed to these institutional properties. This chapter, like the others, merges selected ideas from both economics and political science, and it uses its model to criticize other works in both disciplines.

Recently some economists concerned primarily with domestic economic policies have been developing an interesting intermediate view, in contrast to two familiar and sharply contrasting views in their discipline. One of the two is that governments adopt optimal policies; the other sees governments as both too interventionist in the economy and inefficient in how they intervene. The intermediate, public choice view sees government as highly responsive to domestic pressure groups and, hence, frequently engages in redistributive policies that reduce aggregate economic efficiency. The novel assumption is that while engaging in such costly redistributive policies governments will tend to do so in efficient ways which minimize these costs. Thus, instead of being full of bungling bureaucrats, governments are depicted as competent participants in the game of pressure politics.

Economist Keith Acheson, writing in chapter 10, develops aspects of this view and shows how it can help explain changes in Canadian policies toward the large transnational automobile industry. His theory predicts frequent adjustments in policies as circumstances change. He discusses conditions that influence the enforceability of "exchanges" between government and private sector groups, and the ability of governments to fine tune policies. Acheson analyzes both cases of unilateral policies adopted by the Canadian government toward its auto industry and others where interactions between the Canadian and U.S. governments have importantly influenced Canadian policy. He also discusses some of the key differences between the Canadian and U.S. political economies that give rise to differences in policy objectives and measures between the two countries. He shows how his political-economy analysis can explain important effects of the U.S.-Canadian auto pact, which would not be predicted by standard economic theory.

Conclusion

Professional knowledge of policy making on international trade has generally developed on two separate tracks, as part of the different disciplines of economics and political science. Calls for greater integration have run up against fundamental intellectual disagreements and the high costs to the individual of mastering more than one field.

The political economy revival has nevertheless proceeded gradually, though for some time with economists primarily reading other economists and the same to some extent among political scientists. Now it has reached a point where mutual criticism and learning across disciplines are becoming more profound and productive. Analysts are discovering ways to continue working within some of the familiar premises of their home disciplines while also relaxing other assumptions and incorporating fruitful ideas from others. Some long-standing political science complaints about economics are becoming less valid, and the same is so with respect to traditional economics doubts about political science.

In fact a genuine joint subfield of the two, or joint "invisible college," is in the process of forming itself. Its members are individuals from the two fields who cite each other's work. They are greatly reducing entry costs for both sides by engaging in joint research and participating in meetings like the conference where these papers were initially debated. At that conference, many references were exchanged between economists and political scientists, new points were discovered, and some misunderstandings were clarified. A few individuals have become essentially "bilingual," while other experts new to political economy as such are developing greater interest.

During this project one of our major surprises has been the extent to which the methodological differences and difficulties of communication parallel each other and are almost as great within as they are between the two disciplines. For example, game theorists from economics and political science may often have much more in common with each other than with colleagues in their own disciplines who are primarily interested in historical studies. While there are substantial differences in the relative frequencies with which various types of methods of investigation are used in economics and political science, these matters are in general more of degree than of kind. Our conference appeared to stimulate considerable excitement and cross-fertilization among the participants. Some scholars undoubtedly have imperialist views about the need to colonize the opposing discipline and convert it to the correct way of thinking about political economy; but most participants seemed to discover a solid basis for mutual gains from exchange of information and approaches, both across and within disciplines.

One of the principal conclusions to be drawn from the contributions to this volume is that a complex array of factors may influence the formulation of trade and other international economic policies over time. In the concluding paper in this volume, written in collaboration with Patricia Dillon, we offer suggestions for attempting to deal with such complexity and the wide array of possible research methods available without abandoning a theoretical orientation. While we see considerable scope for methodological pluralism, we certainly do not endorse "a soggy ecumenicalism."[19] We propose that greater attention be given to the interrelationships among hypotheses and that efforts be made to develop higher level theory about the factors which influence the relative importance of different primary level hypotheses. Thus, for example, we have a basis in public goods and public choice theory to expect that private interest groups typically will be more heavily involved in lobbying for economic policy changes which have concentrated as opposed to widely spread economic effects. This helps explain why such lobbying is generally more prevalent in the international trade than in the international monetary area.

There should be scope for the development of potentially powerful hypotheses that examine how differences in issues, institutional structures, and the environment affect the behavior and relative importance of key actors in the policy process and in turn affect policy outcomes. In our view the search for and testing of such higher level hypotheses should be at the heart of the research agenda of modern positive political economy analysis.

REFERENCES

Baldwin, Robert. 1985. *The Political Economy of U.S. Import Policy.* Cambridge, Mass.: MIT Press.

Bauer, R. A., I. de Sola Poole, and L. A. Dexter. 1972. *American Business and Public Policy: The Politics of Foreign Trade.* Chicago: Aldine Atherton.

Cappelen, Adne, Nils Peter Gleditsch, and Olav Bjerkholt. 1984. "Military Spending and Economic Growth in the OECD Countries." *Journal of Peace Research* 21:361–73.

Cassing, James, Timothy J. McKeown, and Jack Ochs. 1986. "The Political Economy of the Tariff Cycle." *American Political Science Review* 80:843–62.

Chattopadhyay, Paresh. 1974. "Political Economy: What's in a Name?" *Monthly Review* 25:23–33.

---

19. Downs (1989) uses the phrase in discussing an analogous debate concerning rational deterrence theory.

Cigler, A. J., and B. A. Loomis, eds. 1986. *Interest Group Politics.* 2d ed. Washington, D.C.: CQ Press.

Coase, Ronald H. 1978. "Economics and Contiguous Disciplines." *Journal of Legal Studies* 7:201–11.

Destler, I. M. 1974. *Making Foreign Economic Policy.* Washington, D.C.: Brookings Institution.

Destler, I. M. 1986. *American Trade Politics: System Under Stress.* Washington, D.C.: Institute for International Economics.

Downs, George. 1989. "The Rational Deterrence Debate." *World Politics* 41 (January): 225–38.

Evans, Peter B., Dietrich Rueschemeyer, and Theda Skocpol, eds. 1985. *Bringing the State Back In.* Cambridge: Cambridge University Press.

Faini, Riccardo, Patricia Annez, and Lance Taylor. 1984. "Defense Spending, Economic Structure and Growth: Evidence Among Countries Over Time." *Economic Development and Cultural Change* 32 (April): 487–98.

Feigenbaum, Susan, Henry Ortiz, and Thomas D. Willett. 1985. "Protectionist Pressures and Aggregate Economic Conditions: Comment on Tackacs." *Economic Inquiry* 23:175–82.

Frey, Bruno. 1984. *International Political Economics.* New York: Basil Blackwell.

Frieden, Jeffrey, and David A. Lake, eds. 1987. *International Political Economy.* New York: St. Martin's Press.

Gilpin, Robert. 1977. "Economic Interdependence and National Security in Historical Perspective." In *Economic Issues and National Security,* ed. Klaus Knorr and Frank Trager. Kansas: Allen Press.

Gilpin, Robert. 1987. *The Political Economy of International Relations.* Princeton: Princeton University Press.

Goldstein, Joshua. 1988. *Long Cycles: Prosperity and War in the Modern Age.* New Haven: Yale University Press.

Gourevitch, Peter. 1986. *Politics in Hard Times.* Ithaca: Cornell University Press.

Hall, Peter. 1986. *Governing the Economy: The Politics of State Intervention in Britain and France.* New York: Oxford University Press.

Heilbroner, Robert. 1970. "On the Possibility of a Political Economics." *Journal of Economic Issues* 4:1–22.

Hillman, Arye L. 1982. "Declining Industries and Political-Support Protectionist Motives." *American Economic Review* 72:1180–87.

Holzman, Franklyn D., and Robert Legvold. 1975. "The Economics and Politics of East-West Relations." In *World Politics and International Economics,* ed. C. Fred Bergsten and Lawrence B. Krause. Washington, D.C.: Brookings Institution.

Kaempfer, William H., and Thomas D. Willett. 1989. "Combining Rent-seeking and Public Choice Theory in the Analysis of Tariffs versus Quotas." *Public Choice* 63:79–86.

Katzenstein, Peter, ed. 1977. *Between Power and Plenty.* Madison: University of Wisconsin Press.

Krasner, Stephen D. 1978. *Defending the National Interest.* Princeton: Princeton University Press.

Lowi, Theodore J. 1979. *The End of Liberalism*. 2d ed. New York: W. W. Norton.

March, James, and Johan Olsen. 1984. "The New Institutionalism: Organizational Factors in Political Life." *American Political Science Review* 78:734–50.

Mill, J. S. 1844. "On the Definition of Political Economy and on the Method of Investigation Proper to It." *Essays on Some Unsettled Questions of Political Economy*. Aldwych, London: Reprinted by the London School of Economics and Political Science. Originally published 1844.

Mitnick, Barry M. 1980. *The Political Economy of Regulation*. New York: Columbia University Press.

Moe, Terry M. 1980. *The Organization of Interests*. Chicago: University of Chicago Press.

Myrdal, Gunnar. 1965. *The Political Element in the Development of Economic Theory*. Cambridge, Mass.: Harvard University Press. Originally published 1929.

Odell, John S., and Thomas D. Willett, eds. 1988. "International Monetary Cooperation, Domestic Politics, and Policy Ideas." Special issue of *Journal of Public Policy* 8 (July–December).

Olson, Mancur. 1965. *The Logic of Collective Action*. Cambridge, Mass.: Harvard University Press.

Pastor, Robert. 1980. *Congress and the Politics of U.S. Foreign Economic Policy*. Berkeley: University of California Press.

Pelzman, Sam. 1976. "Toward a More General Theory of Regulation." *Journal of Law and Economics* 14:109–48.

Schattschneider, E. E. 1935. *Politics, Pressures, and the Tariff*. New York: Prentice-Hall.

Smith, Adam. 1937. *An Inquiry into the Nature and Causes of the Wealth of Nations*, ed. Edwin Cannan. New York: Modern Library. Originally published 1776.

Staniland, Martin. 1985. *What is Political Economy?* New Haven: Yale University Press.

Truman, David. 1971. *The Government Process*. 2d ed. New York: Alfred Knopf.

Wade, Larry, ed. 1983. *Political Economy*. Boston: Kluwer-Nijhoff Publishing.

Willett, Thomas D., and Mehrdad Jalalighajar. 1983-84. "U.S. Trade Policy and National Security." *Cato Journal* 3:717–28.

Wilson, James Q. 1973. *Political Organizations*. New York: Basic Books.

Wilson, James Q., ed. 1980. *The Politics of Regulation*. New York: Basic Books.

CHAPTER 2

Assessing the Usefulness of International Trade Theory for Policy Analysis

Patricia Dillon, James Lehman, and Thomas D. Willett

1. Introduction

As trade problems mount, it has become increasingly common to see arguments that international trade theory is fundamentally flawed as a guide for analyzing policy issues. This is a frequent theme in the popular press and has for some time been used by organized labor and some industrialists as a rationale for protectionist policies. The view has even been put forward by some economists. None of those economists wrote this paper.

We believe that most of these criticisms are based on misunderstandings about the nature and content of modern trade theory and on a failure to appreciate its richness. This paper is directed at those who are interested in trade policy, but who are not research economists specializing in the area. Although there are a number of excellent surveys of trade theory,[1] they are typically addressed to economic specialists and can be quite inaccessible to others. In fact, another barrier to clear and widespread understanding of the theory is that much of modern trade research takes the form of sophisticated mathematical modeling and/or highly technical quantitative analysis. Such work is often difficult for other economists to read and understand, and is much more so for practitioners and scholars who are not economists. Our purpose is to characterize in a nontechnical manner major elements of modern trade theory and to evaluate them in light of some of the most common criticisms raised by noneconomists.[2]

---

1. For the international economics specialist, there is a valuable recent survey of developments in modern trade theory in Jones and Kenen 1985. A useful guide to current developments for the nonspecialist may be found in Greenaway 1985. Earlier surveys by Haberler (1961) and Corden (1965) remain quite useful and do not require knowledge of advanced economics on the part of the reader.

2. We stress that while a number of the examples of criticisms that we evaluate come from prominent political scientists, such views are far from dominant among the political scientists

We will argue that trade theory is both robust and useful; but even when a body of theory is basically sound, it must be handled with care—theory can easily be misapplied. For example, one trade model may be used where another would be more appropriate. Likewise, economic efficiency is sometimes treated as if it were the sole objective where other considerations are important as well. Enthusiasts with some simple vision of trade theory are as wrong in believing that as long as free trade is maintained there can be no legitimate trade policy issues, as are protectionists who do not understand the possibility of mutual gains from trade and believe that, on balance, all imports cause net harm.

The adequacy of a theory must be judged in terms of the particular uses to which it is put. We believe that much of the criticism of trade theory stems from a failure to appreciate the scope of its modern formulations. Critics frequently focus on the relevance of specific trade models, especially the classical Ricardian and the neoclassical Heckscher-Ohlin factor proportions models, without recognizing that modern theories encompass a much broader range of analysis.

One major source of misunderstanding is the tendency of many to equate trade theory with free trade policies and (not infrequently) with complete laissez faire. Thus, one sees criticisms of a particular trade theory or of laissez faire in general taken as if each were logically an argument against free trade. Such association by assumption is a non sequitur.

Modern trade theory analysis considers the implications of a wide range of assumptions and models about the behavior of an economy including factor immobility, monopoly power, and dynamic considerations involving government activity. Contrary to frequent popular assertions, modern trade theory does not show that free trade is always the best policy. But it does show that relaxing many of the assumptions of the simplified textbook trade model does not diminish (and in some cases even strengthens) the case for free trade.[3] Thus one of our points is that popular debate over the relevance of trade theory

---

now working most actively in the field of international political economy. Indeed, much recent political science literature makes considerable use of modern economics such as public goods analysis and public choice theory, as well as trade theory. See, for example, the contribution by Gowa in this volume and the analysis and references in Keohane 1984.

3. By the "simplified textbook trade model" we mean the typical exposition in the international section of introductory economics texts; it is usually this level of theory that is criticized by noneconomists such as Calleo and Rowland, Kuttner, and Jones. Most elementary level undergraduate texts in international economics include some discussion of the issues addressed in this article, for example, Kreinin 1983, Meier 1980, and Richardson 1980. More advanced texts treat in greater depth most of the complications we discuss in this article, for example, Caves and Jones 1985, Ethier 1983, Williamson 1983, Krugman and Obstfeld 1988, and Markusen and Melvin 1988.

is often put in seriously oversimplified and fundamentally misleading terms. Such is sometimes the case in scholarly writings as well.

It is perhaps not surprising that misunderstanding of modern trade theory is so widespread. A cynical interpretation, which we find at times persuasive, is that some authors may engage in deliberate misrepresentation to strengthen their advocacy of specific policies. If one is advocating protection, for example, it is often more politically effective to argue against an oversimplified picture of "academic" trade theory than to attempt to show that the situation meets one of the limited sets of conditions under which modern theory suggests that trade restrictions may make economic sense.

In considering the interrelationships between theory and policy, it is important to be clear on the distinction made by economists between positive and normative analysis. The former refers to the part of economics which aspires to be a science; that is, to be descriptive and predictive. It attempts to predict, for example, what the effects of a change in policy will be. Normative analysis involves value judgments about the objectives to be sought by policy. Differences in policy recommendations may reflect differences in (normative) objectives, or differences in (positive) analysis of how a given set of objectives can best be pursued. Economists do display a strong normative preference for efficiency (discussed in section 3 below), but this need not imply a view that economic goals dominate social and political goals. Whatever the objective, economic analysis is useful in determining how the objective can be achieved at the lowest cost in terms of other objectives. Whether or not a particular economist personally favors policies to protect domestic workers from import competition, his economic analysis can still be used to determine the most effective and least costly way of pursuing this goal.

The question of how conflicting objectives are weighted within the political process is at the heart of political economy. Here again it is useful to distinguish between the positive political economy analysis of how policies are in fact formulated, and the normative political economy analysis of how policies should be formulated. Normative analysis in this case refers not to what particular policies should be, but instead to what the process by which they are chosen should be. Although this paper's focus is the use of trade theory for positive analysis, we shall along the way illustrate its applicability to a range of normative issues.

The following section reviews a number of conceptual distinctions that should be kept in mind when evaluating the usefulness of trade theory. We feel that they are important enough to be emphasized before moving on to evaluation and criticism. In section 3 we evaluate trade theory as a guide to normative analysis, set in the context of criticisms that have appeared in recent literature.

In section 4 we review the main arguments promoted as exceptions to the rule that free trade will maximize national economic welfare: infant industries and terms-of-trade arguments, and the related concern that free trade policies are disadvantagous to us if others do not also follow free trade policies. Interest in these arguments has recently revived, but nowadays is expressed as a concern with strategic trade and industrial policy and with reciprocity. It is true that each of these arguments involves legitimate problems for public policy. Trade intervention, however, will rarely be the most efficient policy response and can run a serious risk of stimulating trade warfare. In other words, while these concerns raise relevant issues, it does not automatically follow that a good case for trade restriction exists.

Current policy debates reflect differences of opinion about the operation of political processes as much as differences about economic issues, a conclusion that highlights the importance of political economy analysis. In section 5 we consider the role of trade theory in positive political economy analysis of governments' trade policies.

We shall argue that for both positive and normative analysis trade theory by itself is inadequate, but that modern trade theory, blended with political and other considerations, is part of a broader and more satisfactory political economy analysis.

2. Some Important Conceptual Distinctions

The Case for Free Trade Does Not Require Complete Laissez Faire

Although the principle of laissez faire implies free trade, free trade does not necessarily imply laissez faire. The arguments for free trade and for laissez faire are not one and the same; the impression that they are is understandable, but quite incorrect.[4] Modern economic analysis does stress the power of the market as a mechanism for creating incentives and for coordinating resource allocation, but it does not argue that the market always generates acceptable results or that free trade is always the best policy. Indeed, a considerable portion of economic analysis is devoted to delineating the conditions under which laissez faire or the unbridled market will not work well. These include situations where externalities are present or where activities display aspects of public goods.[5] Even Adam Smith pointed to instances where laissez faire was unlikely to be a good idea. He argued that protection of certain industries

---

4. For an example of discussion suggesting that the case for free trade is the same as the case for laissez faire, see chapter 6 of Calleo and Rowland 1973.

5. For further discussion, see Alt and Chrystal 1983, Amacher, Tollison and Willett 1976, and Rhoads 1985.

might be called for if they were "necessary for the defense of the country." More surprisingly, in cases where foreign countries introduce protectionist policies, he suggested the potential usefulness of a policy of reciprocity; in his words, "revenge in this case generally dictates retaliation."[6] A considerable amount of work has been undertaken by modern international trade theorists to analyze such situations.[7] One of the powerful insights they have generated is that in most cases which call for deviations from laissez faire on economic efficiency grounds, the forms of government intervention implied do not include restricting international trade. This is consistent with one of the basic propositions in modern applied welfare economics, that distortions or market failures in the economy are best dealt with by policies aimed directly at the sources of the market failure.[8] Consider, for example, a situation where the infant-industry argument legitimately can be invoked to support government intervention in an industry's behalf, that is, where some market failure precludes the creation of the industry. In this standard example, intervention might take the form of a direct subsidy to the industry (making financing available if the failure is in capital markets) or of insulation from foreign competition through an import tariff. The subsidy generates no byproduct distortions and so is superior to the tariff, which "protects" the fledgling domestic industry but increases consumer prices as well, creating another distortion.

Theories Should Not Be Judged Independently of Their Applications

The adequacy of a theory should not be judged independently of the purpose to which it is being applied. A theory quite useful for one purpose may be seriously deficient for another; failure of one part of the theory to explain certain phenomena may not be an indictment of either that part of the theory in particular or trade theory in general. An example of how judgments about

---

6. The quotes are from pages 429 and 434 of Book IV of *An Inquiry into the Nature and Causes of the Wealth of Nations* (1937 Modern Library edition), and we are grateful to Bell (1980) for highlighting them on page 166.

7. See, for example, Corden 1974.

8. See, for example, Bhagwati 1971, Corden 1985, and Johnson 1965. Today the only first-best arguments for trade restrictions commonly considered valid by economists are based on national security concerns (discussed later) and on the nationalist terms-of-trade argument. (Of course many economists argue on normative grounds that such nationalistic behavior is inappropriate.) Even here the imposition of a tariff to improve the terms of trade is not as efficient as a bribe to keep the tariff from being imposed. A less nationalistic argument with some validity is that where taxation is costly efficient public finance suggests equating the marginal costs of revenue raising across different sources; this could make it optimal to refrain from reducing tariffs to zero. For a recent analysis of this issue, see *World Development Report* 1988.

theories may vary depending on the purpose for which the theory is used is the analysis of the gains from trade. Textbook treatments of the gains from trade based on simple models are, in our judgment, valuable in demonstrating the possibilities of gains and illustrating how they can come about. It is quite a different matter to take such illustrations as proof that free trade is always optimal. To the extent that economists make such a leap, they are open to valid criticism. To the best of our knowledge, such misuse is not common practice.

Another source of confusion and disagreement in evaluating theories concerns whether the theory in question is being judged as a virtually complete explanation of how the world works, or instead as a partial explanation that provides useful but incomplete insight into an issue. Often advocates and critics are not clear on the criteria being applied. Economists undoubtedly tend at times to write as if their theories explain a much higher proportion of behavior than is in fact the case, while critics often unduly minimize the usefulness of economics by succumbing to the fallacy that if a theory does not explain everything, then it explains nothing.

Consider, for example, the usefulness of the standard Heckscher-Ohlin-Samuelson (HOS) factor proportions theory of international trade. Critics quite correctly point out that a substantial proportion of trade flows (such as intra-industry trade) cannot be explained by the natural factor endowments emphasized in this theory. As a complete explanation of trade flows, the HOS model is clearly a failure.[9] On the other hand, a considerable portion of trade flows are, in fact, explained by relative factor endowments, especially when the simple two-factor labor-capital model is expanded to include such considerations as land and human capital within a multifactor framework.[10]

Necessary Versus Sufficient Conditions

It is important to distinguish clearly between necessary and sufficient conditions when evaluating theory. Simple textbook treatments are typically designed to illustrate particular points. This is often best done under quite strong sets of assumptions that are sufficient to obtain the conclusion being illustrated; many of these assumptions may not be necessary for the conclusion to hold. For example, simple trade models assume perfect competition, which (as discussed in section 3) has caused many critics to interpret the assumption

---

9. The limitations of the HOS model are readily acknowledged in standard textbook treatments. See, for example, Krugman and Obstfeld 1988, 84–86.

10. Such a broadening of the factor endowments theory was quite important in explaining the Leontief paradox—that the United States appeared to be exporting labor-intensive and importing capital-intensive products. On the current state of empirical research on the determinants of trade flows, see Leamer 1984 and Deardorf in Jones and Kenen 1985.

of perfect competition as a necessary condition for free trade to increase efficiency. Such a conclusion does not logically follow, however.[11] The existence of imperfect competition may either strengthen or weaken the case for free trade depending upon its particular form and location; this point will be amplified in section 3 in the discussion of appropriateness of assumptions.

Impact Versus General Equilibrium Effects

Another important distinction is that between initial impact (partial equilibrium) effects and final (general equilibrium) effects. The belief that imports cost jobs is one of the most politically powerful arguments for trade restrictions. Yet this typically is true only when analysis is limited to initial impact effects. Increased imports will certainly reduce the demand for domestic production of similar products and this can lead, in turn, to reductions in employment, ceteris paribus. However, this greatly overstates the net loss of jobs. Most of these workers will find new jobs, albeit often lower-paying ones.[12] Furthermore, trade restrictions are likely to lead to reductions in employment in export industries. Thus, exclusive focus on impact effects can generate seriously misleading conclusions. (This issue is explored further in section 3, in the discussion of adjustment costs and unemployment.) Taking a more general equilibrium perspective does not necessarily lead to the conclusion that there are no significant problems of adjustment costs associated with free trade, but it does help to put issues in a more appropriate perspective.

3. The Relevance of Trade Theory: A Review of Criticisms

Most policy-oriented criticisms of international trade theory focus either on the lack of realism of the theory's basic assumptions or on the alleged narrowness of the efficiency criterion. For example, in his international political economy survey, R. J. Barry Jones (1983, 175) argues that "the corpus of liberal [trade] theory rests not upon sound simplifying assumptions about reality but upon simplifications which require evasions, or even distortions, of reality if they are to be useable, or a priori assumptions which are quite simply unwarranted"; while Robert Kuttner (1983, 16) argues that trade theory

---

11. See Richardson 1989 for a survey of four empirical studies of imperfectly competitive situations showing that free trade is still welfare-improving.

12. Where the increase in imports is due primarily to a domestic boom, domestic employment is likely to rise, although by less than if there were no increase in imports. Typically such a reduction in the rate of growth of domestic employment causes fewer political problems than do absolute reductions in employment. For a survey of the debate over changing job quality in the United States, see Loveman and Tilly 1988.

"doesn't fit a world of learning curves, economies of scale, and floating rates." Kuttner does limit his critique to classical and factor endowments theory, but gives the reader no indication that trade theory has developed beyond that.

Although we cannot hope to offer in this paper a detailed summary and evaluation of modern trade theory, we will attempt to evaluate briefly some of the most common criticisms and to answer them with examples from modern theory. Our interest in criticizing the critiques flows from a belief that modern economic analysis provides a useful approach to a wide range of issues; we do not believe that it has all of the answers.

In the first part of this section, we discuss the role of trade theory in a world where our objectives go beyond the maximization of physical production. We concur in spirit with Strange's (1985, 237) comment that economic efficiency is "only one of the four basic values that any politically organized society seeks to achieve for its members . . . wealth, order, justice, and freedom." However, we believe that economic analysis has much to say about how to pursue these objectives efficiently, in ways that minimize the amounts of one objective which must be given up to achieve more of another. The assertions of writers such as Calleo and Rowland (1973, 134) that "the case for freer trade is . . . in its essentials a case for achieving a maximum of consumption" are grossly misleading if consumption is used in the narrow sense implied by these authors. The case for freer trade is a case for increasing real income for citizens of trading nations.

In later parts of this section, we deal with a number of the charges that trade theory is based on highly unrealistic and/or faulty assumptions.

Do Economists Define the Objectives of Trade Too Narrowly?

"Sometimes economists write and speak as if they thought that economic optimality was either the normal or the only desirable objective of public policy. They really know better" (Diebold 1983, 338). Economists are routinely accused of being concerned only with efficiency (Strange 1985, 237), or with the maximization of production and income (Calleo and Rowland 1973, 136–37), or with those actions that occur in the marketplace. For example, Barry Jones (1983) describes the concept of economic rationality as an evasive and distorting assumption before going on to characterize rationality as confining "rational choice to the maximization of only those objectives which can be satisfied through market exchanges and which therefore ignores (and ultimately illegitimizes) all those other needs, wants, and desires which an individual may well seek to satisfy through his actions and choices" (175). This statement is in itself a serious distortion; the economic approach draws no such conclusions and indeed gives extensive consideration to situations (for example, public goods, issues of taxes, and externalities like pollution) where market exchanges are unlikely to produce efficiency. The concept of efficiency argues for minimizing the costs—including all costs to society—of achieving society's objectives. As Diebold has observed (1983, 337), the analysis of trade-offs is one of the main contributions that economics can make.

Another misinterpretation of economic theory holds that it is concerned only with maximizing consumer well-being and ignores producer interests (Calleo and Rowland 1973, 137–38). Some critics correctly stress that economic policy should be concerned with producer as well as consumer values, but fail to understand how a competitive market system achieves this. The market mechanism—the point of interaction between consumers and producers—depends on maximizing behavior by *both* agents; and all producers are also consumers. Prices and levels of production are determined by the interaction of supply and demand. Together consumer preferences and alternative sources of supply determine the demand for domestic production, while domestic supply is generated by the combination of cost considerations and producer preferences. Nonmarket considerations are often important aspects of these consumer and producer preferences. For example, it is common (even for economists) to choose jobs other than those that pay the highest money wages because of nonpecuniary considerations such as desirable location or stimulating colleagues.

Calleo and Rowland go so far as to argue (referring to neoclassical economic theory) that ". . . a system which focuses on the welfare of consumers and expects producers to shift for themselves has its priorities backwards . . . a more rational system would orient itself toward production . . . . Consumption would then take care of itself" (134). While such ideas certainly underlie some of the more grandiose of the recent proposals for a new industrial policy in the United States, we believe there is considerable evidence that the typical result of sacrificing consumer interests to protect jobs and output in a particular industry is a policy designed for special interests, and ironically one that may well lead to employment losses elsewhere.

Critics also raise serious issues of possible trade-offs between economic efficiency and security, both national and domestic (the latter referring to social and political stability) (Strange 1985, 237–38). Strange notes that economists have paid considerable attention to national defense arguments for trade restrictions. As in the case of infant-industry arguments (discussed below), economic analysis accepts that national defense considerations can present valid reasons for departures from laissez faire. Furthermore, the most efficient responses to such concerns may involve restrictions on trade. Economic analysis has also shown, however, that (depending upon the particular type of national defense issue under consideration) trade restrictions may be less efficient than alternatives such as the stockpiling of strategic materials and the offering of direct subsidies for the maintenance of essential job skills and productive capacity. Policies adopted in the past in the name of national defense have often been inefficient and at times even counterproductive as means of securing these objectives; a good example is the system of oil import quotas in force in the United States in the 1960s.[13]

Economic analysis per se has much less to offer in considering the concern, which goes back at least to Plato, that international trade leads to political conflict among nations. Liberal economics does argue for the possibility of mutual gains from trade and hence suggests more benign social and political consequences of economic activity than do some approaches that see exchange primarily as a zero-sum activity leading to exploitation and alienation (as do Culbertson 1984 and Hager 1986). However, demonstrating that there are mutual gains from trade is quite different from showing that everyone gains from trade; and there is no implication that all of those who gain from trade gain equally. Any observer of recent economic history can see that international economic relations can generate conflict. Developing countries' proposals for a New International Economic Order provide a clear case in point. We believe that most of their complaints against the industrial countries and a more liberal international economic order have much more to do with the distribution of mutual gains than with instances of absolute harm;[14] but this does not counter the argument that economic relationships may generate conflict. So may policies that substantially reduce trade. The imposition of trade restrictions is often a source of international tensions. There appears to be no strong negative correlation between the low level of integration of some developing countries into the world economy and the militancy of their representatives in the United Nations. Furthermore, a notable element of the trade literature, associated particularly with the name of Cordell Hull,[15] argues that liberal trade relations develop good neighbors and reduce the likelihood of war. Although Hull overstated his case, the experiences of the European Economic Community suggest that there is some merit to this view. Today a war between France and West Germany seems inconceivable despite their long history of military disputes.

Economic analysis has little to say about the effects of trade on social stability. That changes in trade patterns can have significant social consequences is undeniable, but Calleo and Rowland (1973) carry their discussion of the "moral poverty" of the economists' assumption of consumer sov-

---

13. For further analysis and references to the literature on national security and trade policies, see Willett and Jalalighajar 1983–84.

14. On these issues see the contributions and references in Amacher, Haberler, and Willett 1979.

15. For a useful discussion of Hull's views, see Calleo and Rowland 1973.

ereignty too far when they conclude that "its trade theory's basic assumptions would—if they prevailed—mean the collapse of modern civilization" (138). However, considerations of equity and concern for social stability may imply policies to ease the adjustment burdens imposed on individuals by the operation of market forces (and actions by governments). Issues of adjustment assistance programs (to be revisited later) have been a major topic of economic analysis.

It is important to note that there is little difference in the economic and social effects of increased competition from abroad and increased competition among domestic producers. While questions of political strategy can help explain why government policies have often differentiated between the consequences of foreign and domestic competition, there is little basis on efficiency grounds or on grounds of moral principle for this distinction. Structural unemployment generated by domestic innovation is seen as an inevitable byproduct of continuing growth and change; such unemployment generated by imported products is typically characterized as unfair and destructive (AFL-CIO 1986).

Is Trade Theory Based on Inappropriate Assumptions?

A common criticism of orthodox trade theory is that it holds only under the assumption of certain ideal conditions.[16] This charge can usually be traced to a failure to distinguish clearly between the conditions necessary to produce ideal efficiency on the one hand and the case for free trade on the other, much like the confusion between the case for laissez faire and that for free trade discussed in section 2. It is certainly true that under an ideal set of market conditions free trade is economically efficient. Deviations from ideal conditions do lower the achievable levels of utility or well-being, but they do not necessarily weaken the case for free trade. We argue that the absence of ideal conditions does not necessarily strengthen the case for government intervention in the economy; rather, cases where government intervention *is* indicated typically involve a second-best argument for trade restrictions. For example, to return to the infant-industry case examined above in section 2, if there are cogent reasons why direct intervention cannot be undertaken, a tariff to protect the fledgling industry may still be superior to no intervention, provided the gains from fostering the new industry exceed the associated distortion in consumer prices.

We agree with the observation by Tyson and Zysman (1983) that analytical forays moving beyond simple textbook-level assumptions do not always yield clear-cut conclusions. However, we disagree with their argument that

---

16. Jones 1983, 176–77; Calleo and Rowland 1973, 130–33; and Tyson and Zysman 1983, 26–27.

there are policy issues "that the traditional theory is powerless to grapple with. These questions arise as soon as one moves away from the static orientation and the assumption of perfect competition that characterize traditional trade theory. Once dynamics and market imperfections are allowed to enter the picture, both the theoretical models and their implied policy prescriptions become confused" (26). Tyson and Zysman correctly point out that there exists no single and simple valid generalization about policy questions and that the current trade literature fails to reach unambiguous conclusions about all policy questions. However, neither of these points is a sound reason for characterizing this literature as confused, as opposed to the issues involved being complex.[17]

Barry Jones (1983, 175–76) argues that prominent among the "absurd" assumptions necessary to liberal economic theory is that of perfect information. This assertion is an example of the failure to distinguish between necessary and sufficient conditions. It may also reflect a still widespread reliance on Pigovian welfare economics combined with an assumption of ideal government;[18] from this perspective, any deviation from perfect information on the part of consumers and/or producers is grounds for government intervention. Modern public choice analysis, however, asks whether it is plausible to assume that the government has good information when producers and consumers do not; and whether when the government does have better information, it is likely to intervene in an efficient manner.[19] We do not argue that the answers to these questions will always be in the negative, but the recognition of their importance undercuts the argument that the existence of less than perfect information in the private sector is a sufficient condition for government intervention. Indeed, one of the major arguments for the market system has been its perceived ability to economize on the need for costly information (see, for example, Hayek 1945 and Friedman and Friedman 1980). Markets do work more efficiently when information is better; but their operation also generates information, and we cannot assume that the public sector will always do so more efficiently.

As with imperfect information, it is also often argued that the existence of imperfect competition undercuts the case for free trade (Jones 1983, 176–77). Calleo and Rowland (1973, 133) argue that while trade produces more specialization and hence greater economic efficiency, "for the efficiency to be realized, perfect market conditions must prevail." This statement is simply not true (as Richardson's 1989 survey clearly demonstrates). Deviations from

---

17. Of course we are not arguing that there are no confusions in any of the modern trade theory literature.

18. See Pigou 1932.

19. For applications of public choice analysis to trade issues, see Baldwin 1985, Frey 1984, and Willett 1980.

perfect competition do not necessarily imply that trade cannot increase efficiency (although less than would be the case under ideal conditions). The analysis of this question depends importantly on whether one is considering the effects of oligopoly or monopoly in the domestic or foreign economies. Where domestic monopoly power exists, the case for free trade is generally strengthened rather than weakened. Haberler (1950) argued long ago that free trade is probably the most effective antitrust policy ever devised.

The case of monopoly power abroad is more complicated; it may present a valid terms-of-trade argument for active trade policy, but (as will be discussed later) such issues must be analyzed with care. Ill-conceived policy responses may worsen rather than improve domestic economic welfare. For example, while a tariff will lower the profit-maximizing price of a foreign monopolist, the imposition of a quota, by creating an inelastic demand curve over a particular range, may raise the monopolist's profit-maximizing price.[20]

Does Trade Theory Ignore Unemployment, Adjustment Costs, and Factor Mobility?

A common objection to trade theory is that it ignores the problem of unemployment and other adjustment costs which may result from free trade (Strange 1985, 238–39). Kuttner (1983, 19) is quite correct when he argues that classical trade theory assumes full employment, but he fails to note that modern trade theory has gone well beyond this simple assumption. Decades ago Haberler (1950) clarified the roles of domestic factor immobility and wage and price rigidities in modifying the gains from international trade. He showed that domestic factor immobility in itself will limit the gains from trade but does not negate the proposition that there are net gains. Wage and price rigidities, on the other hand, may cause unemployment, which reduces the net benefits from free trade and could even make them negative. Such analysis has contributed to economists' emphasis on the possible roles of greater wage and price flexibility, adjustment assistance, and perhaps even temporary protection as superior alternatives to permanent protection (see Cline 1983b).

It is common in criticisms of trade theory to jump from showing the existence of unemployment costs to claiming that they outweigh the benefits of free trade. It is true that introductory textbook expositions of the gains from trade generally depict costless readjustments along the country's production possibility or transformation curve; for example, from A to B along the frontier in figure 1.[21] This clearly oversimplifies reality. In figure 1, point A

---

20. For analysis of this point in relation to the U.S. response to OPEC, see Willett 1976; 1979.

21. Krugman and Obstfeld (1988, ch. 5) and other textbooks in international economics discuss this model in greater detail; see the additional references in footnote 1.

GOOD *y*

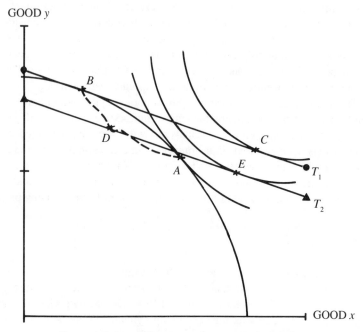

Fig. 1. Adjustments to changing trade conditions

(where the domestic production possibility curve is tangent to a consumption indifference curve) yields the most efficient allocation of resources in a closed economy. Opportunities for international trade can be represented by a terms-of-trade line, T_1 (showing the ratio of price of X to price of Y). Where relative prices on the world market differ from those in the domestic market, efficiency gains are possible by reallocating domestic resources (in fig. 1, from point A to point B). The country now (at point B) produces more of good Y, but is able via international trade to move along T_1 to consume at point C, where T_1 is tangent to a new higher indifference curve. In reality, the reallocation of resources from A to B may be costly. This can be reflected by movement along the dotted line within the production possibility frontier. During this transition the net benefits from liberal trade are lessened and could be negative. Note, however, that gains to consumers from the opportunity for international trade offset the costs of reallocating productive resources. In order for net benefits from liberal trade to be negative, the adjustment costs would have to exceed the gains to consumers. Figure 1 illustrates the case where the production loss (of producing at point D within the production possibility curve) is more than offset by the consumption efficiency gains, so point E lies on a higher indifference curve than the closed-economy equilibrium at point A, although on a lower curve than the costless adjustment equilibrium at point C. (The price ratio is the same on any line parallel to T_1.) It should be remembered that the unemployment costs of trade-related adjustments, while quite real, are generally temporary. Thus over time the equilibrium would approach point C. While the conceptual possibility exists, available estimates of adjustment costs suggest that cases where costs outweigh benefits of trade are extremely rare.[22] It is interesting to note that studies on this topic are seldom mentioned by critics of trade theory.

Another popular source of concern is that classical trade theory assumes factor immobility between countries, whereas multinational corporations nowadays account for an increasing proportion of international production and exchange.[23] These points are correct, but they ignore the contributions of a substantial modern literature on the role of foreign investment and international factor mobility. One of the major insights offered by traditional trade theory is the role that international trade can play as a substitute for factor mobility. Modern analysis treats national advantage arguments for restrictions on foreign investment as analogous to the traditional terms-of-trade national advantage arguments for restrictions. There are certainly reasons for concern with such issues as the tax effects of multinational corporations, but the existence of foreign investment and multinationals has not undermined the usefulness of trade theory. Instead, these areas have been the subjects of extensive analysis in the modern trade theory literature and have been sources of a number of useful insights.[24]

Does Trade Theory Depend on Fixed Exchange Rates?

Kuttner's previously quoted statement (1983) that trade theory does not hold in a world of floating exchange rates is incorrect, but his mistake is an understandable one. Classical economists generally thought in terms of a system of fixed exchange rates (typically a gold standard),[25] and textbook treatments are often not clear about the balance of payments assumptions underlying their presentations of trade theory. It is therefore not surprising to hear claims that trade theory depends upon the assumption of fixed exchange rates. This is not in fact the case. The necessary assumption is that there is an

---

22. See, for example, Glenday and Jenkins 1984, Wachter and Eascher 1983, Richardson in chapter 12 of Cline 1983b, and Hufbauer and Rosen 1986.

23. Jones 1983, 177–78; Strange 1985, 245–46; and Tyson and Zysman 1983, 26–27.

24. For a nontechnical discussion of these issues and references to the literature, see Tollison and Willett 1982. For a review of the technical literature, see Ruffin 1985.

25. See, for example, Ricardo 1973, 83; or Smith 1937, 284.

efficiently operating international adjustment process so that market exchange rates are at equilibrium levels, which balances the demand for and supply of foreign exchange. This can be achieved either by well-functioning systems of flexible rates with stabilizing speculation, or by fixed rates with wage and price flexibility (the textbook versions of floating rates and/or the gold standard, respectively).

In reality, neither floating rates nor the gold standard have performed ideally, nor have compromise systems such as the adjustable peg system adopted at Bretton Woods. The pegged exchange rates of the Bretton Woods system were often disequilibrium rates that had to be maintained by heavy official intervention in the foreign exchange market, and often by capital and trade controls as well. These led at times to substantial distortions of resource allocation.

The concept of disequilibrium under freely floating exchange rates is more complex; but modern analysis emphasizes that market clearing rates can also be disequilibrium rates if they are generated by speculative forces which do not adequately reflect underlying economic fundamentals. Such rates would not be expected to be sustainable indefinitely and would eventually generate substantial resource misallocations.

Where exchange rates are at disequilibrium levels, domestic and foreign prices are not efficiently translated into one another and a potentially policy-relevant externality exists.[26] Indeed, it is only with disequilibrium exchange rates that there is limited validity to the (generally fallacious) popular concern with absolute rather than comparative advantage, expressed in the fear that foreign competition can undercut domestic producers. The maintenance of equilibrium exchange rates will keep the magnitude of trade imbalances limited and as a consequence assures that domestic producers cannot be outcompeted across the board.[27] There has developed a substantial literature devoted to analyzing the implications of exchange rate volatility and disequilibrium exchange rates for alternative exchange rate systems.[28] Likewise there has been a long-standing and inconclusive debate about whether fixed or flexible exchange rates are more conducive to lowering trade barriers.[29] In general, the answer depends on which system is seen as generating less disequilibrium. Those who have argued that pegged rates make the adoption of liberal trade policies more likely tend to assume that the pegged rates are approximately

---

26. See Willett 1971 and Cooper 1975.

27. Note that equilibrium exchange rates do not require a zero trade balance. For example, with net capital inflows a trade deficit is required for overall payments balance. The requirements for equilibrium, however, would normally prevent a trade imbalance from growing indefinitely.

28. On this issue and for discussion and references to the literature on the effects of fixed versus floating rates on resource allocation, see Arndt, Thursby, and Willett 1985 and Willett 1986.

29. For discussion and references to the literature, see Flacco et al. 1984.

equilibrium ones, while floating rates display considerable instability generated by destabilizing speculation. Those who argue that flexible rates contribute to trade liberalization, on the other hand, tend to believe that floating rates are dominated by stabilizing speculation, while pegged rates tend fairly quickly toward disequilibrium levels.

The lack of convergence on this issue reflects both a multiplicity of views about relevant concepts of equilibrium and the difficulties of finding measurable counterparts to these concepts. As in the case of imperfect competition, such considerations give rise to complications that in our current state of knowledge leave room for disagreements among knowledgeable people of good will.[30] For example, there is still considerable disagreement among experts about how much of the observed instability in our current system of floating exchange rates has reflected destabilizing speculation versus efficient market responses to economic and financial shocks and instabilities in national economic policies.[31]

Still we believe that recent economic analyses of various aspects of the interrelationships of exchange rates and trade policy have generated a number of useful contributions to sensible policy analysis.[32] One such contribution is the notion common in mainstream economic analysis that the large U.S. trade deficit of the 1980s is as much or more a reflection of domestic economic policies (primarily of U.S. budget deficits) as it is of deficiencies in the operation of flexible exchange rates or of increases in unfair trade practices abroad.[33] A second useful conclusion is that across-the-board import restrictions, particularly under flexible exchange rates, are unlikely to be a very effective method of reducing the trade deficit, because of the corresponding discouragements to exports which would result.[34]

Does Trade Theory Assume Static Comparative Advantage?

The argument is advanced by some that, because comparative advantage is so fluid and so susceptible to manipulation, trade models derived from it are not

---

30. For recent discussions of concepts of equilibrium in the context of the strong dollar of the early and mid-1980s, see Willett 1985a, 1985b; and John Williamson 1985; and for a still useful earlier analysis, see Machlup 1955.

31. For recent analysis of this issue and extensive references to the literature, see Arndt, Sweeney, and Willett 1985.

32. See, for example, Bergsten and Williamson 1983 and Richardson 1983a, 1983b; in addition to the papers already cited.

33. It should be noted that this posited causal linkage between the twin deficits is not accepted by all economists; in particular, it is rejected by many supply-side and rational expectations economists. For further discussion and references see Willett 1985b.

34. For discussion and references see Kaempfer and Willett 1987.

relevant. Comparative advantage therefore may be illusory—or at least the free trade prescription rendered invalid.

Most trade models are static. Thus such charges are quite understandable. There has, however, been considerable attention by trade economists to issues of dynamic comparative advantage. In fact, work on this topic goes back decades.[35] It is true, nonetheless, that such dynamic considerations make policy analysis much more difficult and can present a case for ideal government intervention in the economy. It is even possible, as Tyson and Zysman (1983, 30) point out, that "in these dynamic conditions, there are no longer automatic mutual gains from exchange."

That the pattern of production is changing across countries is clear.[36] The more important point, however, concerns what Cline (1983a) calls "arbitrary comparative advantage." For a number of manufactured goods, highly similar relative endowments in trading partners may fail to reveal a basis for specialization. In fact, for such goods the actual trade flow may be arbitrarily determined by, for example, government intervention. Strategic government behavior might well include an array of tariffs, quotas, subsidies, etc., marshalled to extract some market share in some instances or to prevent its erosion in others.[37] It is entirely likely that such strategic behavior by countries or firms will inflict losses on others.

Yeager and Tuerck (1983–84, 662) are appropriately skeptical of the ability of governments to choose the "national pattern of production and consumption," whether it is the case of attempting to control a market economy through optimal interventions or the case of a planned economy. Furthermore, arbitrary comparative advantage may describe certain kinds of manufactures but is not characteristic of a majority of trade. Thus rejecting more traditional theories of sources of comparative advantage out of hand because arbitrary comparative advantage exists in some sectors seriously overstates the generality of new methods of analysis and ignores the continuing validity of the traditional explanations for much of world trade.[38]

---

35. See, for example, Chenery 1960.

36. For examples of studies describing the changing pattern of U.S. production, see Lawrence 1983 and Pugel 1980.

37. It is worth noting that some examples of "successes" in industrial targeting may not be so convincing under further scrutiny. See, for example, Krugman 1983. For a useful discussion of the difficulties of applying the theory to a specific industry, see Pugel 1987.

38. There is in addition a danger of confusing product cycle transitions with arbitrary comparative advantage shifts. The product cycle theory of trade implies that innovation and initial product development and market development occur in higher per capita income countries with higher relative endowments of skilled labor and higher research and development commitments. As product standardization occurs, the comparative advantage in production shifts toward relatively labor-abundant countries. Failure to distinguish between these two types of shifts may well be a source of domestic welfare loss, not gain.

Of course, implementation of policies that target certain industries is fraught with difficulty. The information needed to implement such policies is often extremely hard (if not impossible) to obtain and the intrusion of special interest pressures may be difficult to avoid.[39]

4. Protectionism Revisited

The New International Economics and Strategic Intervention

The past decade has seen the emergence of a stream of theoretical and policy analysis that focuses on the existence of imperfect competition in international trade and its implications for strategic behavior by firms as well as governments. Much of this literature is written for an audience of specialists; however, Krugman's (1986a) book and a survey article by Stegemann (1989) are explicitly aimed at nonspecialists. Some of the early work by Krugman (1979), Lancaster (1979; 1980), Dixit and Norman (1980), and Helpman (1981) was stimulated by the need for models to explain the prevalence of intra-industry trade among countries, an outcome not generated by the standard neoclassical model. Relaxing assumptions to entertain differentiated products, economies of scale in production, and less-than-perfectly-competitive markets yielded results that accounted for both intra-industry and intersectoral (Heckscher-Ohlin type) trade.[40] Following this initial work, a variety of lines of exploration have been pursued, especially spillover effects, rent capture, and the "new" reciprocity. These are discussed, respectively, in the next three subsections.

Infant-Industry Arguments: Old and New

It has long been asserted that the infant-industry case is one of the few valid arguments for protection. This argument continues to appear, both in its older version and in a newer one, the former having been addressed in the economics literature and found wanting, and the newer forming the focus of some of the industrial policy debate. Two aspects of the criticism of protection for infant industries are particularly important. First, the call for protection is based on a presumed market failure—that is, domestic business interests for some reason are not creating productive capacity, which once in place would (it is argued) be self-sustaining. Given a "running start," the industry would

---

39. See, for example, the arguments in Krugman 1983 and Richardson 1983a.
40. Greenaway and Milner (1986) provide a comprehensive treatment of the literature on intra-industry trade.

be sufficiently profitable to survive the removal of protection. But if there is a market failure here, it is in the capital market, which overlooks an apparently obvious opportunity. Second, even acknowledging that such a failure is possible, we must nevertheless address the issue of the appropriate response.[41] If the failure is a divergence between the market discount rate and some agreed-on social discount rate, then is protection an efficient response? In the context of first-best/second-best responses, a direct solution (such as a financing subsidy) is more efficient than trade restriction. Trade restriction, the equivalent of a tax on consumption and a subsidy to production, represents a second-best response that may nonetheless be optimal if the first-best response in economic terms is not feasible politically. Thus Kuttner's (1983, 17) statement that free trade "as an economic paradigm . . . denies us a realistic appraisal of second bests" gets the logic backward. It is a realistic appraisal of second bests that leads to a clear-eyed assessment from an efficiency standpoint of calls for protection.

Extensions of the infant-industry argument include what Corden (1985, 92) terms dynamic external economies. In one version, firms generate new knowledge in their workers but cannot keep their workers, once trained. Here again, in the context of perfect markets, firms would be rewarded for the training. In the case of market failure, that is, of persistence of the externality, the first-best response is a subsidy linked to knowledge creation.

Krugman (1986b, 13) makes the case as follows: "External economies present a different justification for activist trade policies. By an external economy, economists mean a benefit from some activity that accrues to other individuals or firms than those engaging in the activity. The most plausible example is the diffusion of knowledge generated in one area to other firms and other sectors." Although this externality argument may be persuasive from the standpoint of national economic welfare, determining the form of the policy response to the externality again brings us to the matter of first-best and second-best policies, with no presumption that trade restriction is a first-best response.

Is There a Modern Terms-of-Trade Argument for Protection?

The traditional terms-of-trade argument for protection (Johnson 1965) holds that where a country has market power as a consumer in the market for an important good, there may be net gains in domestic welfare from introducing a tariff which effectively lowers the world price of the good. In effect, the tariff improves domestic welfare at the expense of foreign welfare. As men-

---

41. See Baldwin 1969 and Johnson 1965.

tioned above, however, there are a number of issues that detract from the simple appeal of such a move. First, on straightforward efficiency grounds, the traditional "optimal tariff" of this type is, in fact, a second-best tariff since the trading partner who would incur losses has an incentive to bribe the domestic government not to impose the tariff. Second, retaliation and tariff warfare are possible outcomes that are disturbingly likely.

Brander and Spencer (1985) and Krugman (1984) have provided a modified version of this motivation for intervention. Krugman (1986b) describes the modern basis for activist trade policy as residing in the ability of the government to extract a portion of economic rent. Rent here means payment to a factor of more than it could earn in its best alternative use. Typically, rent is assumed to be a temporary phenomenon, dissipated by the entry of additional units of those factors receiving rents in that activity. Barriers to entry provide the key to the argument in support of strategic trade policy. If it is true that major industries in tradable goods production are characterized by barriers to entry (economies of scale or learning curves, for example),[42] then entry into the industry by new firms may be unprofitable despite the existence of rents. Government policies of protection and subsidy may be used to secure a share of the rent in the industry for domestic firms at the expense of foreign firms.[43]

The existence of this line of inquiry renders moot such criticisms as that by Jones (1983, 176): "Prominent among such absurd assumptions are . . . the general absence of barriers to entry. . . ." Modern trade theory does, indeed, grapple with such questions. In the Brander and Spencer (1985) analysis, the industry consists of two firms, one in each of two countries, providing a homogeneous export to a third country. Brander and Spencer assume Cournot duopoly behavior (each firm takes the other's output and exports as given) and examine three cases of strategic behavior as the two firms vie for the export market. In the first case, if one firm makes a credible commitment to expansion, the other contracts accordingly. Of course, if, as they assume, the two firms are very similar, it would require some kind of external support, such as a government subsidy, to make the expansion credible. In this first case, only one of the firms is able to mount such support and in consequence it expands, the other contracts, and the subsidizing government has effectively assisted in rent capture. In their second case, both firms are able to secure government support, and so neither is inclined to contract its output as the other seeks to expand. The result is a kind of prisoner's dilemma in which both the exporting nations could

42. For a survey of the recent technical literature incorporating such characteristics, see Helpman 1985.

43. Note also that this result (that is, domestic gains from intervention) is very sensitive to model specification. See, for example, the critical assessment by Greenaway and Milner 1986, especially chapters 10 through 12.

be better off if they could agree not to subsidize. The importing nation is of course enjoying the benefits of lower import prices. In their third case, the two exporting nations are able to act cooperatively to generate joint rent-maximizing results. In this instance, because of the peculiarities of the standard Cournot solution,[44] the optimal response is for the two nations to *tax* exports so that their firms produce the level of exports equivalent to that generated by a rent- or profit-maximizing cartel.

That strategic circumstances and behavior are treated in the international trade literature is clear. However, the treatments do not reveal any clear policy prescriptions, short of careful modeling of the particulars of each specific case. The policy implications of the Brander and Spencer (1985) rent-capture model change markedly with different assumptions about the rival's behavior and the gains rely on no retaliation. This is an important assumption since the intervention is explicitly predatory. The probability of retaliation is likely to be high.

Foreigners Violate Free Trade Rules; So Should We: Arguments for Reciprocity

According to Calleo and Rowland (1973, 140), ". . . free trade should be demoted from its central position in American international economic policy. . . . Modern nation-states have long ago abandoned laissez faire for welfare mercantilism. There is no reason why trade alone should be exempted from the general progress of modern civilization." The AFL-CIO (1985, 28) contends that "U.S. trade law must be modernized to reflect contemporary realities in a world where the United States is the only country which exposes its industrial foundation to unlimited erosion from imports." And again, Kuttner (1983, 17): "The seductive fallacy that pervades the hand-wringing about protectionism is the premise that free trade is the norm and that successful foreign exporters must be playing by the rules."

That we live in a neomercantilist world is not in dispute. That our trading partners violate free trade norms is not in dispute. In recognizing that others have violated these norms, however, it is important to distinguish between cases where the foreign government has restricted trade and cases where they have subsidized their home producers. Trade restrictions abroad are harmful to us. This has been the major rationale for emphasis on negotiations for multilateral tariff reductions. It is important to note, however, that where our trade policy actions do not influence those abroad, the case for allowing

---

44. See Nicholson (1989, 563) or other microeconomic theory textbooks.

foreign trade policy actions to influence our own is substantially weakened. While trade barriers abroad harm our economic interests, raising our own trade barriers is likely to make a bad situation even worse.

If there are no externalities and if competitive conditions exist, foreign subsidies may, in fact, generate a transfer to us. In the case of subsidies, the Yeager and Tuerck (1983–84, 184) argument may hold: It should make no difference to us what is the source of the gains from trade, provided only that they exist. Furthermore, ". . . American workers are no better or worse off if displaced by subsidized imports than if displaced by imports actually produced at low cost, displaced by competition at home, displaced by new and better products, or displaced by changes in the tastes of consumers" (59).

Nevertheless, there may be circumstances when foreign subsidies to their exporters are not welfare-improving for us. First, such support may give rise to dumping. Conceptually, predatory pricing has the possibility of worsening our overall economic welfare. The conditions for this to occur are seldom met in reality, however. Probably a more important reason for antidumping laws is that such pricing seems to offend a general public sense of fairness.

As is emphasized in the recent literature on strategic trade policy, if imperfect competition and externalities are present, there is a potential case for home government intervention on efficiency grounds. Such home government response presents two problems: *a*) what form of intervention should be chosen and *b*) what outcome will ensue after the form has been chosen and implemented. As Richardson (1983a) notes, uncertainty about outcomes is not necessarily a justification for a passive stance. After all, "our policy may be able to improve for us *their* calculation of optimal policy" (emphasis added) (285). A retaliatory stance may well be welfare-improving for the home country. Richardson emphasizes, however, that policies of this type should "be predictable, nondiscretionary, and temporary (contingent on foreign behavior)" (285).

Cline (1983a) provides a careful treatment of the shortcomings of a bilateral, aggressive approach to reciprocity. Among the cautionary notes he sounds is the considerable danger that although reciprocity as a trade strategy may be effective, it may also degenerate into tariff warfare. Threats of intervention in response to barriers may be an effective response, but are less likely to be effective when applied as ad hoc responses. If reciprocity is embedded in a framework of multilateral international agreements, it appears to come closest to the type of policy Richardson describes above. It is certainly not the case that trade theory has ignored the neomercantilist character of modern trading relations. Modern trade theory does point out that free trade is not necessarily optimal and that the choice of intervention and the results of intervention are often ambiguous.

5. Trade Theory and Positive Political Economy

Trade theory alone cannot provide a complete positive theory for trade policy formulation, nor can it provide a complete normative theory of desirable trade policies. In the first case, positive economic analysis must be combined with value judgments about the objectives of policy. In the second, even if economic considerations were the only concerns of policy, economic analysis must be coupled with theories of the operation of the political process. Traditionally, economists have not been altogether clear about this; even normative policy disagreements among economists have often had at least as much to do with differences in views about the operation of the policy process as with differences about economic analysis. These differences in political judgment have typically been implicit rather than explicit. When views about the political process are made explicit, acceptance of some particular one is often treated as being virtually self-evident, with little concern devoted to alternative views of the operation of the political process. The spread of public choice analysis has helped to reduce this lacuna to some extent, although some of the leading contributors to the public choice movement have themselves at times fallen prey to this tendency.[45]

Most economists need a greater awareness of the assumptions about the operation of the political process underlying discussion of policy formulation. The development of greater familiarity with the work of political scientists should be a major priority for economists interested in policy. Among economists who have paid relatively little explicit attention to the political assumptions underlying their analysis, several contradictory perspectives have been adopted. One approach assumes that the political process operates in a way which encourages the adoption of economically efficient policies. In literature on international political economy, this approach corresponds to the liberal or "sovereignty at bay" school.[46] This tendency toward economically efficient policies is perceived to be the result of the decisions of experts motivated by the public interest, who operate with considerable freedom from the pressure of the general public and from the outcome of vigorous electoral competition. Although this efficiency view enjoyed a good deal of support during the days of progressive trade liberalization among the industrial countries in the 1950s and 1960s, the slowing down and eventual reversal of this trend in the 1970s seemed to demonstrate the limitations of this approach, at least as applied to international trade issues.

---

45. For further discussion of this set of issues with particular reference to macroeconomic policies, see Willett and Banaian 1988.

46. For discussions of this and the major alternative approaches, see Gilpin 1975, Jones 1983, and Willett 1980.

The other commonly held view is nearly an opposite one. Long before the advent of formal public choice analysis, many trade economists explained protectionism in terms of the political clout of well-organized special interest groups. In this view not only does the combination of concentrated power and poor information under which the political process operates lead to the adoption of excessive protection, but the forms of protection adopted tend themselves to be inefficient. For example, while trade theory suggests that for a given level of trade restrictions a tariff will impose lower inefficiency costs on the economy than quotas and "voluntary" export restraints, the trend has been toward greater use of the latter relative to the former.

An interesting intermediate view, recently emerged from the University of Chicago, emphasizes the importance of the political process and sees rent-seeking activities by interest groups leading to government redistribution policies (see Becker 1983). Such policies will generate deviations from aggregate economic efficiency, but in the new Chicago view the methods of transfer adopted will tend to be efficient in the sense that they will minimize the marginal deadweight costs of redistribution. In other words, while rent seeking may generate an excessive level of trade barriers, the forms of trade protection (for example, tariffs versus quotas) will be efficient. Theoretical and empirical analysis of this view is just beginning to be applied to trade policies. (See, for example, Kaempfer, Marks, and Willett 1988; Kaempfer, McClure, and Willett 1989; and Kaempfer, Tower, and Willett 1989.)

Each of these views offers useful insights but is far from a complete explanation of the operation of the policy process. Trade theory, we believe, offers a useful and essentially correct view of the economic effects of alternative trade policies, but analysis of the formulation of trade (or of any other economic) policy must deal explicitly with the ability of interest groups to influence policy outcomes. Even this is still an incomplete basis for analysis, however, for the proposition that economic interest groups have an important effect on trade policy formulation is far different from the proposition that economic interests are the only important influence. We believe that it is useful to undertake formal modeling on the basis of the former assumption to see what insights may be gained.[47] But these insights must then be integrated into a broader analysis that takes into account such factors as ideology, foreign policy considerations, and public perceptions of fairness.[48]

The possible influence of ideology on economic policy outcomes has become a topic of debate among economists interested in regulation and trade

---

47. See Kaempfer 1989, for example.

48. See the paper in this volume by Marks and McArthur. On the need for public choice analysis to go beyond concern with the aggregation of narrowly conceived economic interests, see also Kindleberger 1975, North 1984, and Willett 1980.

policy. It should be noted that public opinion polls commonly show considerable public support for trade restrictions. We believe that this reflects both a
lack of appreciation of the full effects of trade restrictions (poll questions
often take forms such as "should we restrict imports in order to save American jobs?") and concern with concepts of fairness on the part of citizens and
legislators who see little direct stake in the issues in question.[49]

It is also important to recognize that the analysis of the economic effects
of alternative trade policies should not be limited to simple two-factor trade
models. A considerable amount of the analysis of the income distribution
effects of trade policies has taken place in terms of the conflict between
aggregate labor and capital shares. Ironically, while the underlying economic
theories are quite different, these traditional two-factor trade theory models
focus on capital-labor conflicts, just as does Marxist analysis. Some trade
policy issues have had a strong component of aggregate labor-capital conflict.
More often, however, trade policy pressures result from labor and capital in
particular industries operating together with similar interests. The public
choice critique of Marxist political theory applies as well to the use of two-
factor trade theory as a guide to the analysis of trade policy formulation.[50] For
this purpose, trade analysis based on industry-specific adjustment costs is
quite important.[51]

As with our discussion of trade theory as a guide for normative analysis,
we conclude that modern trade theory is useful in the positive analysis of trade
policy formulation. It is only one of several important elements, however.
Casual observation is sufficient to show that governments do not always seek
simply to maximize economic efficiency. This does not mean that efficiency
considerations are irrelevant to positive political economy analysis. Furthermore, trade theory is useful in analyzing the economic impacts of trade
policies on various important interest groups, considerations that are certainly
important (although not always dominant) in trade policy determination.

6. Concluding Remarks

We conclude with a blunt statement of the point emphasized and illustrated
throughout this paper: we find no legitimate support for the view that trade
theory is so flawed that it should be discarded as a basis for political economy

---

49. For an interesting recent analysis of the influences of concepts of fairness on economic
behavior and references to earlier literature, see Kahneman, Knetsch, and Thaler 1986. For
discussion of self-interest versus public-interest voting on macroeconomic issues, see Kiewiet
1983 and Willett and Banaian 1988.
50. See Olson 1965.
51. See, for example, Magee 1980.

analysis. For political economy purposes, however, trade theory must be combined with explicit political analysis.

The assumption often (but not universally) made by economists that whatever policy is most economically efficient will be adopted does not hold up well in the face of empirical scrutiny. Failure of the prediction of the pure economic efficiency approach can occur both because of the pursuit of broader social objectives and because of failures in political markets that allow particular actors to dominate outcomes even when the benefits they receive are not as great as the costs imposed on others.

Modern trade theory reflects an approach to analysis and provides a set of tools for analyzing particular situations. It is not one monolithic theory which implies that laissez faire is economically efficient under all circumstances. Debates over the virtues or lack thereof of trade theory in the abstract are pointless and display a lack of understanding of the requisites of constructive policy analysis. The important questions concern which particular theories are useful for particular purposes. The issues are complex and provide ample scope for disagreement among people of intelligence and good will, but this is the appropriate arena for debate and analysis.

We do not believe that trade theory has all the answers; there are many areas crying out for further research, both theoretical and empirical.[52] For example, the development of strategic trade theory is still in an early stage and our understanding of its likely empirical applicability to various types of industries is more rudimentary still.[53] Analysis of adjustment costs and optimal strategies for liberalization are additional topics where a great deal of useful work remains to be done.[54] The increasing use of computable general equilibrium (CGE) models holds great promise for practical applications.[55] The effects of the growing use of counter trade is another important topic for research.[56]

At least equally exciting are the many possibilities for combining trade theory with political analysis. For example, while there has been a great deal of analysis by economists comparing the economic efficiency effects of alternative types of trade restrictions, only recently has attention begun to focus

---

52. For suggestions complementary to our own, see Dixit's 1986 article.

53. In proposing areas for further research, Dixit (1986) notes that the existence of rents remains to be demonstrated in each instance where policy intervention is proposed; further, it remains to be shown that domestic firms cannot capture these rents themselves.

54. Some of the existing work on adjustment costs includes that by Glenday and Jenkins 1984, Wachter and Eascher 1983, Richardson 1983b, and Hufbauer and Rosen 1986. Liberalization considerations are treated in Edwards 1989 and Kreuger 1986.

55. On the design of CGE models, see, for example, Robinson 1989 or Tower 1984. For an interesting application of CGE, see Loo and Tower 1989.

56. See, for example, the article by Banks 1983.

on the comparative political efficiency of such measures under alternative assumptions about the operation of the political process. Paying explicit attention to political considerations opens up a vast area of interesting research for trade theories.[57] The gains from greater interaction between economic and political analysis run in both directions.

BIBLIOGRAPHY

AFL-CIO. *The National Economy and Trade, AFL-CIO Policy Recommendations for 1986*. Pamphlet reprinted from The National Economy section of the report of the Executive Council of the AFL-CIO to the Sixteenth Convention, Anaheim, California, October 1985.

Alt, James, and Alex Chrystal. 1983. *Political Economics*. Berkeley: University of California Press.

Amacher, Ryan, Gottfried Haberler, and Thomas D. Willett, eds. 1979. *Challenges to a Liberal International Economic Order*. Washington, D.C.: American Enterprise Institute.

Amacher, Ryan, Robert D. Tollison, and Thomas D. Willett, eds. 1976. *Economic Approaches to Public Policy*. Ithaca: Cornell University Press.

Arndt, Sven, Marie Thursby, and Thomas D. Willett. 1985. "Flexible Exchange Rates and International Trade: An Overview." In *Exchange Rates, Trade, and the U.S. Economy,* ed. Sven Arndt, Richard J. Sweeney, and Thomas D. Willett. Cambridge, Mass.: Ballinger Publishing Co.

Baldwin, Robert. 1969. "The Case Against Infant Industry Protection." *Journal of Political Economy* 77:295–305.

Baldwin, Robert. 1985. *The Political Economy of U.S. Import Policy*. Cambridge, Mass.: MIT Press.

Banks, G. 1983. "The Economics and Politics of Countertrade." *The World Economy* 6:159–89.

Becker, Gary. 1983. "A Theory of Competition Among Pressure Groups for Political Influence." *Quarterly Journal of Economics* 98:371–400.

Bell, John Fred. 1980. *A History of Economic Thought*. 2d ed. New York: Ronald Press Co.

Bergsten, C. Fred, and John Williamson. 1983. "Exchange Rates and Trade Policy." In *Trade Policy in the 1980s,* ed. William Cline. Cambridge, Mass.: MIT Press for the Institute for International Economics.

Bhagwati, J. N. 1971. "The Generalized Theory of Distortions and Welfare." In *Trade Balance of Payments and Growth,* ed. J. Bhagwati, R. Jones, R. Mundell, and R. Vanek. Papers in International Economics in honor of Charles P. Kindleberger. Amsterdam: North-Holland Press.

---

57. For a recently published survey of the formal literature on the political economy of trade policy, see Hillman 1989.

Brander, James A., and Barbara J. Spencer. 1985. "Export Subsidies and International Market Share and Rivalry." *Journal of International Economics* 18:83–100.

Calleo, David P., and Benjamin M. Rowland. 1973. *America and the World Political Economy*. Bloomington: Indiana University Press.

Caves, Richard, and Ronald W. Jones. 1985. *World Trade and Payments*. 4th ed. Boston: Little, Brown.

Chenery, H. B. 1960. "Patterns of Industrial Growth." *American Economic Review* 50:624–54.

Cline, William. 1983a. "Reciprocity: A New Approach?" In *Trade Policy in the 1980s*, ed. William Cline. Cambridge, Mass.: MIT Press for Institute for International Economics.

Cline, William. ed. 1983b. *Trade Policy in the 1980s*. Cambridge, Mass.: MIT Press for the Institute for International Economics.

Cooper, Richard N. 1975. "Economic Assumptions of the Case for Liberal Trade. In *Toward a New World Trade Policy: The Maidenhead Papers*, ed. C. Fred Bergsten. Lexington: Lexington Books.

Corden, W. Max. 1965. *Recent Developments in the Theory of International Trade*. Special Papers in International Economics No. 7, International Finance Section, Department of Economics, Princeton University.

Corden, W. Max. 1974. *Trade Policy and Economic Welfare*. London: Oxford University Press.

Corden, W. Max. 1985. "The Normative Theory of International Trade. In *Handbook of International Economics*, vol. 1, ed. Ronald W. Jones and Peter Kenen. New York: North-Holland Press.

Culbertson, John M. 1984. *International Trade and the Future of the West*. Madison: 21st Century Press.

Deardorff, Alan V. 1985. "Testing Trade Theories and Predicting Trade Flows." In *Handbook of International Economics*, vol. 1, ed. R. W. Jones and P. B. Kenen. New York: North-Holland Press.

Diebold, William. 1983. "Overview." In *Industrial Change and Public Policy*, a Symposium Sponsored by the Federal Reserve Bank of Kansas City.

Dixit, Avinash K. 1986. "Trade Policy: An Agenda for Research." In *Strategic Trade Policy and the New International Economics*, ed. Paul Krugman. Cambridge, Mass.: MIT Press.

Dixit, A. K., and V. D. Norman. 1980. *Theory of International Trade*. Cambridge: Cambridge University Press.

Edwards, Sebastian. 1989. "Debt Crisis, Trade Liberalization, Structural Adjustment and Growth: Some Policy Considerations." *Contemporary Policy Issues* 7:30–41.

Ethier, Wilfred. 1983. *Modern International Economics*. New York: W. W. Norton.

Flacco, Paul, Leroy O. Laney, Marie C. Thurby, and Thomas D. Willett. 1984. "Exchange Rates and Trade Policy." *Contemporary Policy Issues* 4:6–18.

Frey, Bruno. 1984. "The Public Choice Approach to International Political Economy." *International Organization* 38:199–223.

Friedman, Milton, and Rose Friedman. 1980. *Free to Choose: A Personal Statement*. New York: Harcourt Brace Jovanovich.

Gilpin, Robert. 1975. "Three Models of the Future." In *World Politics and International Economics*, ed. C. Fred Bergsten and Lawrence Krause. Washington, D.C.: Brookings Institution.

Glenday, Graham, and Glenn P. Jenkins. 1984. "Industrial Dislocation and the Private Cost of Labor Adjustment." *Contemporary Policy Issues* 4:23–36.

Greenaway, David, ed. 1985. *Current Issues in International Trade Theory and Policy*. New York: St. Martin's Press.

Greenaway, David, and Chris Milner. 1986. *The Economics of Intra-Industry Trade*. New York: Basil Blackwell.

Haberler, Gottfried. 1950. "Some Problems in the Pure Theory of International Trade." *Economic Journal* 60:223–40.

Haberler, Gottfried. 1961. *A Survey of International Trade Theory*. Special Papers in International Economics No. 1, International Finance Section, Department of Economics, Princeton University, New Jersey.

Hager, Wolfgang. 1986. "Free Trade: A Threat to World Economic Stability and Socio-Economic Autonomy." In *Free Trade–Managed Trade*, ed. Gunnar Sjostedt and Bengt Sundelilus. Boulder: Westview Press.

Hayek, Friedrich A. 1945. "The Use of Knowledge in Society." *American Economic Review* 35:519–30.

Helpman, Elhanan. 1981. "International Trade in the Presence of Product Differentiation, Economics of Scale and Monopolistic Competition." *Journal of International Economics* 11:305–40.

Helpman, Elhanan. 1985. "Increasing Returns, Imperfect Markets, and Trade Theory." In *Handbook of International Economics,* vol. 1, ed. Ronald W. Jones and Peter Kenen. New York: North-Holland Press.

Hillman, Arye L. 1989. *The Political Economy of Protection*. New York: Harwood Academic Publishers.

Hufbauer, Gary Clyde, and Howard F. Rosen. 1986. *Trade Policy for Troubled Industries*. Washington: Institute for International Economics.

Johnson, Harry G. 1965. "Optimal Trade Intervention in the Presence of Domestic Distortions." In *Trade, Growth, and the Balance of Payments: Essays in Honor of Gottfried Haberler,* ed. Robert Baldwin et al. Chicago: Rand McNally.

Jones, Ronald W., and Peter Kenen. eds. 1985. *Handbook of International Economics,* vol. 1. New York: North-Holland Press.

Jones, R. J. Barry. 1983. "Perspectives on International Political Economy." In *Perspectives on Political Economy,* ed. R. J. Barry Jones. New York: St. Martin's Press.

Kaempfer, William. 1989. "Explaining the Form of Protection: A Public Choice Perspective." Working Paper, The Claremont Center for Economic Policy Studies.

Kaempfer, William H., and Thomas D. Willett. 1987. "Why An Import Surcharge Wouldn't Help America's Trade Deficit." *The World Economy* 10:27–37.

Kaempfer, William H., Stephen V. Marks, and Thomas D. Willett. 1988. "Why Do Large Countries Prefer Quantitative Trade Restrictions?" *Kyklos* 41:625–46.

Kaempfer, William H., J. Harold McClure, Jr., and Thomas D. Willett. 1989. "Incremental Protection and Efficient Political Choice Between Tariffs and Quotas." *Canadian Journal of Economics* 22:228–36.

Kaempfer, William H., Edward Tower, and Thomas D. Willett. 1989. "Performance-Contingent Protection." *Economics and Politics* 1, no. 3 (November): 261–75.

Kahneman, Daniel, Jack L. Knetsch, and Richard Thaler. 1986. "Fairness as a Constraint on Profit Seeking." *American Economic Review* 76:728–41.

Keohane, Robert. 1984. *After Hegemony: Cooperation and Discord in the World Political Economy.* Princeton: Princeton University Press.

Kiewiet, Roderick D. 1983. *Macroeconomics and Micropolitics: The Electoral Effects of Economic Issues.* Chicago: University of Chicago Press.

Kindelberger, Charles. 1975. "The Rise of Free Trade in Western Europe." *Journal of Economic History* 35:20–55.

Kreinin, Mordechai E. 1983. *International Economics: A Policy Approach,* 4th ed. New York: Harcourt Brace Jovanovich.

Kreuger, A. O. 1986. "Problems of Liberalization." In *Economic Liberalization in Developing Countries.* Oxford: Basil Blackwell.

Krugman, Paul. 1979. "Increasing Returns, Monopolistic Competition and International Trade." *Journal of International Economics* 9:469–79.

Krugman, Paul. 1983. "Targeted Industrial Policies: Theory and Evidence." In *Industrial Change and Public Policy.* A symposium sponsored by the Federal Reserve Bank of Kansas City.

Krugman, Paul. 1984. "Import Protection as Export Promotion." In H. Kierzkowski. *Monopolistic Competition and International Trade.,* ed. Oxford: Oxford University Press.

Krugman, Paul, ed. 1986a. *Strategic Trade Policy and the New International Economics.* Cambridge, Mass.: MIT Press.

Krugman, Paul. 1986b. "Introduction: New Thinking About Trade Policy." In *Strategic Trade Policy and the New International Economics,* ed. Paul Krugman. Cambridge, Mass.: MIT Press.

Krugman, Paul R., and Maurice Obstfeld. 1988. *International Economics: Theory and Policy.* Glenview: Scott, Foresman and Company.   •

Kuttner, Robert. 1983. "The Free Trade Fallacy." *New Republic* 28:16–21.

Lancaster, K. 1979. *Variety, Equity and Efficiency.* New York: Columbia University Press.

Lancaster, K. 1980. "Intra-industry Trade under Perfect Monopolistic Competition." *Journal of International Economics* 10:151–75.

Lawrence, Robert Z. 1983. "Changes in U.S. Industrial Structure: The Role of Global Forces, Secular Trends, and Transitory Cycles." In *Industrial Change and Public Policy,* a symposium sponsored by the Federal Reserve Bank of Kansas City.

Leamer, Edward E. 1984. *Sources of International Comparative Advantage: Theory and Evidence.* Cambridge, Mass.: MIT Press.

Loo, Tom, and Edward Tower. 1989. "Agricultural Protectionism and the Less Developed Countries: The Relationship Between Agricultural Prices, Debt Servicing Capacities and the Need for Development Aid." In *Macroeconomic Consequences of Farm Support Policies,* ed. Andrew Stoeckel, David Vincent, and Sandy Cuthbertson. Durham: Duke University Press.

Loveman, Gary W., and Chris Tilly. 1988. "Good Jobs or Bad Jobs: What Does the Evidence Say? Federal Bank of Boston *New England Economic Review* (January/ February): 46–65.

Machlup, Fritz. 1955. "Equilibrium and Disequilibrium: Misplaced Concreteness and Disguised Politics." *Economic Journal* 68:1–24. Reprinted in F. Machlup. 1964. *International Payments, Debts, and Gold*, chap. 5. New York: Charles Scribner's.

Magee, S. P. 1980. "Three Simple Tests of the Stolper-Samuelson Theorem." In *Issues in International Economics*, ed. P. Oppenheimer. London: Routledge and Kegan Paul.

Markusen, James R., and James R. Melvin. 1988. *The Theory of International Trade*. New York: Harper and Row.

Meier, Gerald M. 1980. *International Economics, The Theory of Policy*. New York: Oxford University Press.

Nicholson, Walter. 1989. *Microeconomic Theory, Basic Principles and Extensions*. 4th ed. Chicago: Dryden Press.

North, Douglas C. 1984. "Three Approaches to the Study of Institutions. In *Neoclassical Political Economy, The Analysis of Rent-Seeking and DUP Activities*, ed. D. Colander. Cambridge, Mass.: Ballinger Publishing Co.

Olson, Mancur. 1965. *The Logic of Collective Action*. Cambridge, Mass.: Harvard University Press.

Pigou, A. C. 1932. *The Economics of Welfare*, 4th ed. London: Macmillan.

Pugel, Thomas A. 1980. "The Changing Position of U.S. Industries in the Global Pattern of Industrial Production." In *Special Study on Economic Change*, vol. 9, *The International Economy: U.S. Role in a World Market*, Joint Economic Committee, U.S. Congress.

Pugel, Thomas A. 1987. "Limits of Trade Policy Toward High Technology Industries: The Case of Semiconductors." In *Trade Friction and Economic Policy*, ed. R. Sato and P. Wachtel. New York: Cambridge University Press.

Rhoads, Steven E. 1985. *The Economist's View of the World*. New York: Cambridge University Press.

Ricardo, David. 1973. *The Principles of Political Economy and Taxation*. London: J. M. Dent and Sons, Ltd. Originally published 1821.

Richardson, J. David. 1980. *Understanding International Economics: Theory and Practice*. Boston: Little, Brown.

Richardson, J. David. 1983a. "International Trade Policies in a World of Industrial Change." In *Industrial Change and Public Policy*, a symposium sponsored by the Federal Reserve Bank of Kansas City.

Richardson, J. David. 1983b. "The New Nexus Among Trade, Industrial, and Exchange-Rate Policies." Working Paper No. 1099. National Bureau of Economic Research.

Richardson, J. David. 1989. "Empirical Research on Trade Liberalization with Imperfect Competition: A Survey." OECD Economic Studies Number 12.

Robinson, Sherman. 1989. "Multisectoral Models." In *Handbook of Development Economics*, vol. 2, ed. H. Chenery and T. N. Srinivasan. Amsterdam: North-Holland Press.

Ruffin, Roy J. 1985. "International Factor Movements." In *Handbook of International Economics*, vol. 1, ed. Ronald W. Jones and Peter Kenen. New York: North-Holland Press.

Smith, Adam. 1937. *An Inquiry into the Nature and Causes of the Wealth of Nations.* New York: Modern Library, Random House. Originally published 1776.

Stegemann, Klaus. 1989. "Policy Rivalry Among Industrial States: What Can We Learn From Models of Strategic Trade Policy?" *International Organization* 43:73–100.

Strange, Susan. 1985. "Protectionism and World Politics." *International Organization* 39:233–59.

Tollison, Robert D., and Thomas D. Willett. 1982. "Power, Politics, and Prosperity: Alternative Views of Economic Interdependence. In *The Internationalization of the World Economy, Annals* of the American Academy of Political and Social Science, 460: 21–28.

Tower, Edward. 1984. "Effective Protection, Domestic Resource Cost and Shadow Prices: A General Equilibrium Perspective." Working Paper No. 664. World Bank Staff.

Tyson, Laura, and John Zysman. 1983. "American Industry in International Competition." In *American Industry in International Competition,* ed. J. Zysman and L. Tyson, 26–31. Ithaca: Cornell University Press.

Wachter, Michael L., and William L. Eascher. 1983. "Labor Market Policies in Response to Structural Changes in Labor Demand. In *Industrial Change and Public Policy,* a symposium sponsored by the Federal Reserve Bank of Kansas City.

Willett, Thomas D. 1971. "International Trade Theory Is Still Relevant." *Banca Nazionale del Lavoro Quarterly Review* 98:3–19.

Willett, Thomas D. 1976. "Oil Import Quotas Are Not the Answer." *Journal of Energy and Development* 1 (Spring): 240–48.

Willett, Thomas D. 1979. "Structure of OPEC and the Outlook for International Oil Prices." *World Economy* 2:51–64.

Willett, Thomas D. 1980. "Some Aspects of the Public Choice Approach to International Economic Relations. Working Paper, The Claremont Center for Economic Policy Studies.

Willett, Thomas D. 1985a. "Modern Exchange Rate Analysis." In *Exchange Rates, Trade, and the U.S. Economy,* ed. S. Arndt, R. J. Sweeney, and T. D. Willett. Cambridge, Mass.: Ballinger Publishing Co.

Willett, Thomas D. 1985b. "The Dollar and the Deficit." In *Exchange Rates, Trade, and the U.S. Economy,* ed. S. Arndt, R. J. Sweeney, and T. D. Willett. Cambridge, Mass.: Ballinger Publishing Co.

Willett, Thomas D. 1986. "Exchange Rate Volatility, International Trade, and Resource Allocation: A Perspective on Recent Research." *Journal of International Money and Finance* 5 (Supp.): S101–12.

Willett, Thomas D., and King Banaian. 1988. "Models of the Political Process and Their Implications for Stagflation: A Public Choice Perspective." In *Political Business Cycles,* ed. T. D. Willett. Durham: Duke University Press for Pacific Institute for Public Policy Research.

Willett, Thomas D., and Mehrdad Jalalighajar. 1983–84. "U.S. Trade Policy and National Security." *Cato Journal* 3:717–28.

Williamson, John. 1983. *The Open Economy and the World Economy, A Textbook in International Economics.* New York: Basic Books.

Williamson, John. 1985. *The Exchange Rate System,* 2d ed. Washington, D.C.: The Institute for International Economics.

World Development Report. 1988. Washington: The World Bank.

Yeager, Leland B., and David G. Tuerck. 1983–84. "Realism and Free Trade Policy." *Cato Journal* 3:645–66.

Zysman, John, and Laura Tyson. 1983. *American Industry in International Competition.* Ithaca: Cornell University Press.

CHAPTER 3

An Epitaph for Hegemonic Stability Theory?: Rational Hegemons, Excludable Goods, and Small Groups

Joanne Gowa

The political correlates of a stable world market economy remain unclear. Early in the 1970s, a burst of scholarly interest in this subject produced what at the time appeared to be a compelling thesis: the world was safe from tariff wars and great depressions only if a single state or hegemonic power dominated the international political system. Defining international free trade as a public good, "hegemonic stability theory" concluded that its reliable supply depended upon a distribution of international power analogous to that within a privileged group.

In relatively short order, however, critics challenged three assumptions fundamental to hegemonic theory. They argued that: (1) rational hegemons, according to standard international trade theory, adopt an optimum tariff rather than free trade; (2) small groups, as public-good theory itself claims, are close substitutes for privileged groups; and (3) the provision of open international markets implies the supply of excludable rather than public goods. Thus, they concluded, hegemony is not necessary for, and indeed may be antithetical to, a stable world economy based on market exchange.

The potential power of these criticisms is considerable: a persuasive

---

The first version of this essay was presented at the Conference on Blending Political and Economic Analysis of International Trade Policies, University of Southern California, March 1987. I am grateful to participants at that conference for comments, particularly Jeff Frieden, Stephan Haggard, Stephen Marks, John S. Odell, J. David Richardson, and Thomas D. Willett. I am also grateful to Benjamin J. Cohen, Youssef Cohen, John A. C. Conybeare, Avery Goldstein, Richard J. Herring, Robert O. Keohane, Timothy J. McKeown, and Kenneth A. Oye for comments on later versions of the essay. Reprinted from Joanne Gowa, "Rational Hegemons, Excludable Goods, and Small Groups: An Epitaph for Hegemonic Stability Theory?" *World Politics* 41, No. 3 (April 1989). Copyright © 1989 by Princeton University Press. Reprinted with permission of Princeton University Press.

argument on their behalf would destroy the analytic foundations of a theory that is already the target of attack on empirical grounds.[1] In this paper I argue, however, that these attacks are not fatal to the theory: on economic grounds alone, a *nonmyopic* rational hegemon may reject an optimum tariff; exclusion from a free-trade accord is itself a public good; and hegemons enjoy a clear advantage relative to small groups with respect to the supply of international public goods. Strategic interdependence, incomplete information, and barriers to "*k*" group formation are the core elements of the argument presented here.

I conclude that the most significant flaw in hegemonic theory is its neglect of the essence of the domain to which it applies: the politics of interstate trade in an anarchic world. Because the security externalities that inevitably accompany the removal of trade barriers can shift the balance of power among states, any analytic representation of international free trade must model these effects explicitly. In short, hegemonic stability theory must include security as an argument in the utility functions it assigns to states opening their borders to trade.

Several important limitations of this analysis should be stated at the outset. Because the public-good variant of hegemonic theory is cast at the systemic level, this paper also focuses exclusively on the incentives to trade freely that arise at the level of international system. As a result, it does not consider the influence of domestic factors on the pursuit of these incentives: neither the organization of domestic exchange via hierarchies instead of markets nor the role of special interest groups, for example, is considered.[2]

The argument also assumes as given the conditions under which standard international trade theory applies, and the paper contains only illustrative rather than systematic empirical referents.[3] These restrictions are appropriate in view of the essay's objectives: (1) to demonstrate that the assumptions about rational hegemons, public goods, and privileged groups actually allow hegemonic stability theory to represent analytically several critically important barriers to free trade among states, and (2) to make clear that any theory of international trade in an anarchic world must explicitly model its security externalities.

After a brief explanation of hegemonic stability theory, a careful review of the arguments of its most persuasive critics is presented. The paper concludes with the suggestion that hegemonic theory is problematic largely because it neglects the political consequences of agreements to trade freely.

---

1. McKeown 1982; McKeown 1983; Conybeare 1983.
2. Ruggie 1982; Frieden 1988.
3. Ethier 1983.

Hegemonic Stability Theory

In 1973, Charles P. Kindleberger laid the foundations of what Robert O. Keohane, almost a decade later, labeled "hegemonic stability" theory.[4] The term is also frequently applied to the arguments of both Robert G. Gilpin and Stephen D. Krasner, although Kindleberger's emphasis is on the stability of the international system, and Gilpin's and Krasner's is on the self-interest of the dominant state.[5] Common to all three, however, is the claim that, because a stable system of international free trade involves the supply of a public good, it has a political prerequisite: the existence of a hegemonic power. As Kindleberger puts it, "for the world economy to be stabilized, there has to be a stabilizer, one stabilizer."[6]

The analytics of hegemonic theory are drawn from the literature on public goods. Unlike private goods (cookies or Big Macs), public goods (nuclear deterrence or clean air) are joint in supply and nonexcludable. That is, any individual's consumption of these goods does not preclude their consumption by others, and no individual can be excluded or prevented from consuming such goods whether or not he has paid for them.

As a consequence, Prisoner's Dilemma (PD) preferences characterize each member of a large group or of any short-lived group facing a public good or collective-action problem. The corresponding payoff matrix is found in figure 1. Confronting these payoffs, the dominant strategy of each player is to refuse (defect) rather than to contribute (cooperate) to the supply of the public good: $DC > CC > DD > CD$. A Pareto-inferior equilibrium outcome (DD) results: no one contributes, no public good is produced, and another—albeit unstable—outcome (CC) exists in which all would be better off.[7]

Kindleberger argues that, if states locked into an international free trade PD are to be able to escape their dilemma, a hegemon must exist. Because of its relative size in the international system, Kindleberger's hegemon is the equivalent of what public-good theory calls a "privileged" group: that is, a group "such that each of its members, or at least some one of them, has an incentive to see that the collective good is provided, even if he has to bear the full burden of providing it himself."[8]

Casual empiricism appears to confirm Kindleberger's argument. British hegemony in the nineteenth and U.S. hegemony in the mid-twentieth century

---

4. Kindleberger 1973; Keohane 1980, 132.
5. Gilpin 1975; Gilpin 1987; Krasner 1976.
6. Kindleberger 1973, 305.
7. A Pareto-superior equilibrium is one in which at least one individual would be better off and no individual would be worse off than at the existing outcome.
8. Olson 1971, 50.

COLUMN

ROW		Cooperate	Defect
	Cooperate	2,2	4,1
	Defect	1,4	3,3

Fig. 1. Payoffs are ranked from 1 (best) to 4 (worst); Row's payoffs are listed first.

coexisted with relatively open international markets. The inability of Britain and the unwillingness of the United States to lead coincided with the construction of "beggar-thy-neighbor" trading blocs in the interwar period.[9] The apparent decline in U.S. hegemony in recent decades and the simultaneous increase in trade barriers among the industrialized countries also appear to support Kindleberger's assertion. Whether a correlation between hegemony and free trade actually exists or represents a causal relationship has become extremely controversial.[10]

Much ink has also been spilled over three analytic issues: (1) Do rational hegemons have an interest in free trade? (2) Is free trade necessarily nonexcludable? and (3) Does a hegemon provide the only solution to whatever public-good problems exist? Although analyses of these issues appear to damage hegemonic theory irreparably, the critics have in fact chosen boomerangs as their weapons.

Rational Hegemons and Free Trade

Some observers contend that the attribution of free-trade preferences to a hegemon violates the principles of standard international trade theory.[11] According to the latter, they note, any state large enough to influence its terms of

---

9. Kindleberger 1973, 28.
10. For examples of the large literature that violently and sometimes persuasively objects to every historical interpretation in this paragraph, see McKeown 1983; Oye 1985b; Russett 1985.
11. Conybeare 1984.

trade—the relative price of its exports on world markets—will maximize its real income by imposing an optimum tariff: that is, a tax on trade set at the point that maximizes the net gain which accrues from the resulting improved terms and reduced volume of trade. Thus, they suggest, only an irrational hegemon would conform to the behavioral prescriptions of hegemonic theory.[12]

Flawed premises undercut the power of this argument. It implicitly assumes that the hegemon's influence over its terms of trade is the most efficient source of leverage available to it. More importantly, the argument ignores strategic variables that can affect a hegemon's choice of tariff levels. As a result, it effectively violates the logic of game-theoretic models of price setting by domestic monopolists, thereby inflating the costs an economic hegemon incurs when it abandons its trade barriers for political reasons.

The possession of power in the trade-theory sense, for example, necessarily implies the use of a tariff only if the hegemon cannot find a more efficient way to redistribute income from its trading partners to itself. Because other states lose more than the hegemon gains, a tariff "is an inferior way to redistribute income between countries."[13] In its *own* long-run interest in enhancing its revenue base, therefore, the dominant state has an incentive to pursue either of two potentially Pareto-superior alternatives to trade barriers: bribes or taxes.[14]

In practice, the transaction costs associated with both alternatives are likely to exceed the deadweight loss produced by a tariff. In the case of small states engaged in a collective effort to bribe the hegemon to adopt free trade, a public-good problem arises: each small state that is potentially a party to such bribery has an incentive to let the others assume its costs. Free riding can be prevented only in the unlikely event that the hegemon can cheaply discriminate among the exports of a large number of small countries.

Designing, implementing, and enforcing a system to tax other states is likely to be prohibitively costly to the hegemon. Although the international equivalent of a lump-sum tax may leave small states better off than would an optimum tariff, these states may recognize that they would be even better off as free riders: the hegemon's threat to sanction tax evaders may not be credible to them. The situation of the hegemon is analogous to that of the incumbent firm in the chain-store paradox: it confronts a trade-off between the short-term costs to it if it punishes defiance and the longer-term costs to its reputation if it

---

12. This argument is intended to apply only to single-minded hegemons. Critics acknowledge that hegemons that pursue political as well as economic goals may prefer free trade for political reasons. See, for example, Conybeare 1984.

13. Caves and Jones 1973, 244.

14. For a brief discussion of bribery as an alternative to tariff retaliation in the context of two states of equal size, see Conybeare 1984, 14–15.

does not do so.[15] In any case, unilateral imposition of an optimum tariff is likely to be less costly to the hegemon than the theoretically Pareto-superior alternative of taxation.

Despite the dearth of alternative means to redistribute income in its favor, a clear-thinking, nonmyopic hegemon may still reject the optimum tariff recommended to it by standard trade theory. Its interest in doing so would be the preservation of its monopoly power. Thus, it would act on the same logic that motivates a domestic monopolist to set prices below their short-run maximizing levels: the incumbent firm thereby attempts to deter entry into its markets. By "limit" pricing, the monopolist seeks to signal potential entrants that its costs of production are lower than they are in reality.[16] Its ability to sacrifice short-run gains in order to earn higher long-run returns depends on the existence of costs to entry as well as asymmetric information about the monopolist's costs of production.[17]

A rational, nonmyopic hegemon may set its tariff at less than the short-run optimum level under analogous conditions—if, for example, it has some private information about the elasticity of global demand and supply curves, and if small countries organizing to exert countervailing power in world markets incur some costs in doing so.[18] A hegemon may indeed have private information about global markets because of its incentives to become informed about them; a small country, by contrast, has little incentive to acquire such information because it cannot influence its terms of trade. Significant transaction costs may be incurred in the process of forming customs unions because of the distributional effects both within and across the potential members that result from the setting of uniform external trade barriers.[19]

The trading practices of both Britain and the United States suggest that the analogy to limit pricing is of more than just analytic interest. Mid-nineteenth century Britain, according to one observer, maintained its tariffs at less than optimum levels in order to fix its "monopoly of manufactures on the rest of the world for a few more decades than its natural term."[20] The logic of limit pricing apparently impressed itself on the United States when it attempted, in the 1930 Smoot-Hawley tariff, to turn the terms of trade in its favor. This

---

15. For a formal analysis of the chain-store paradox, see Kreps and Wilson 1982.

16. Milgrom and Roberts 1982.

17. Since potential entrants are aware of the incentives of established firms to engage in limit pricing, the established firm's strategy may not work. See Milgrom and Roberts 1982.

18. In his most recent work, Conybeare notes that heavy export taxes may induce substitution that, in turn, dictates the use of lighter taxes in the interest of maximizing long-run profits. Conybeare dismisses this argument unpersuasively: he maintains that "long-term elasticity . . . arguments merely assert that the hegemon is not really a hegemon." See Conybeare 1987, 72.

19. McMillan 1986, 67.

20. Cunningham, as cited in McCloskey 1980, 304; but also see note 23 below.

effort provoked the construction of trading blocs abroad,[21] and apparently induced the United States to try to lower global barriers to trade after the war.[22]

In short, because an attempt to exploit its power in the short run may undermine that power over time, a nonmyopic, rational hegemon may reject an optimum tariff. Although the limit-pricing argument does not support an inference that free trade—the international analogue of competitive prices at the domestic level—will prevail, it does suggest that unilateral restrictions on the use of an optimum tariff can be in the strictly economic self-interest of a far-sighted, clear-thinking hegemon.

Because the limit-pricing analogue suggests that it may be cheaper to forgo an optimum tariff than standard trade theory implies, it also suggests that the incidence of decisions to do so for political reasons may be higher than would otherwise be expected. Thus, for example, the introduction of long-term elasticities into empirical estimates of the welfare losses incurred by Britain as a consequence of its unilateral adoption of free trade in the mid-nineteenth century suggests that the magnitude of these losses was "extremely small."[23] Although Britain's repeal of the Corn Laws is conventionally attributed to domestic politics, the British case nevertheless suggests that a hegemon does not need very strong political incentives to adopt free trade: the economic losses it incurs by doing so may be insignificant.

In sum, even the exclusively economic self-interest of a rational hegemon may not persuade it to adopt the optimum tariff of standard trade theory. Its preferences will depend on the relative costs of bribery, taxation, and tariffs, and on its ability to deter entry through the strategic use of its monopoly power. It is certainly possible that, under some circumstances, a hegemon

---

21. For an analysis that suggests that the Great Depression would have led to the same outcome even without this provocation by the United States, see Eichengreen 1986.

22. The present analysis seems to suggest that the American encouragement of what became the European Economic Community was illogical. Even without introducing security factors, however, the U.S. action can be interpreted as taking control of, rather than waiting for, the inevitable: in promoting the formation of the EEC when it did, the United States had an opportunity to exert significant leverage over the direction of the union. Thus, it could successfully demand, for example, that the EEC treat foreign direct investment as it did national investment, thus ensuring that U.S. firms would be able to circumvent EEC tariffs, albeit at some cost to those firms. See Gilpin 1975.

23. McCloskey has argued that Britain lost "at most" 4 percent of national income when it chose free trade rather than an optimum tariff (1980, 305). Bhagwati notes that McCloskey's analysis relies on "intuition"; he observes that Douglas Irwin has "estimated British foreign trade elasticities for that period and calculated the welfare loss of unilateral tariff reduction at about 0.5 percent of national income in the very short run. As Irwin points out, though, longer-run elasticities imply an extremely small welfare loss, and if foreign tariff reductions are factored in (resulting from Britain's demonstration effect promoting free trade) Irwin finds that Britain was made better off" (Irwin, as cited in Bhagwati 1988, 29–30).

will choose an optimum tariff as conventionally defined. Under different circumstances, however—even in situations in which political factors do not influence its choice—it may not do so.

Free Trade and Public Goods

The public-good premise of hegemonic theory has also become controversial. Arguing that the "benefits of free trade are largely excludable," John A. C. Conybeare asserts, for example, that "countries may, individually or collectively, penalize a country that attempts to impose a nationally advantageous tariff at the expense of the international community."[24] Thus, Conybeare contends that free trade is not a public good because it fails to fulfill the nonexcludability attribute of such goods.

Arguing that free trade is, instead, a Prisoner's Dilemma, Conybeare notes that an optimum tariff maximizes the gains of a large state. If all states employ tariffs, however, the outcome is inferior to a free-trade truce, as it reduces the volume but does not change the terms of trade.[25] The mutually preferred outcome of free trade is difficult to achieve because it is not a stable or Nash equilibrium of the one-shot game: each state has an incentive to deviate to an optimum tariff if others adhere to free trade. Thus, Conybeare observes, trade theory effectively assigns PD preferences to large states (where C represents free trade and D an optimum tariff).

Conybeare is correct: free trade *is* excludable, and his argument is an important modification of hegemonic theory. But implicit in this argument is an assumption that each state benefits from sanctioning would-be free riders. If, however, the policing of a cooperative agreement is costly, enforcement itself becomes a public good.[26] As Michael Laver observes, costly exclusion "simply replaces one collective action problem with another, the problem of raising exclusion costs."[27]

Whenever defection is either ambiguous or easily concealed, sanctioning is likely to be costly.[28] Ambiguity threatens to make punishment appear as provocation, thus initiating a feud that will not eliminate the alleged offense, but will impose costs on the would-be enforcer. Ambiguity is virtually indigenous to PDs because incentives to conceal cheating are strong; as George

---

24. Conybeare 1984, 6.

25. This assumes that states possess similar degrees of market power. If they do not, it is possible for one state to be better off, even after the cycle has been completed, than if it had pursued free trade. See Johnson 1953–54.

26. Axelrod and Keohane 1985.

27. Laver 1980, 200.

28. Oye 1985a, 15.

Stigler observes of industrial cartels, "the detection of secret price-cheating will of course be as difficult as interested people can make it."[29]

Informational asymmetries pervade trade agreements, arising from the varied sources of ambiguity inherent in them. Among these sources are: the need to translate international agreements into domestic law; the difficulty of determining if conditions of breach have occurred; the inability to specify illegal behavior precisely; and the possibility of currency manipulation as a substitute for overt action on trade.[30] Would-be free riders may also conceal cheating by shipping their exports through third countries.

Thus—as is true of many PDs—monitoring, assessing, and punishing attempts to cheat are crucial but costly aspects of international trade agreements. As a result, it becomes individually rational but collectively suboptimal for states to free ride on the enforcement efforts of others: whenever incomplete information exists, exclusion of deviants from a trade agreement itself becomes a public good.[31]

In short, while technically excludable, free trade nonetheless presents public-good problems under realistic assumptions about the costs of sanctions. Even if the public-good problems that may inhere in other regimes ancillary to the trade regime are set aside, therefore, open international markets do involve the supply of a public good. Although, as the next section demonstrates, a variety of game-theoretic solutions to enforcement problems exist that do not require the presence of either a privileged *or* a small group, their relevance in the context of international politics is considerably less than is their abstract analytic appeal.

Privileged and Small Groups

Following Thomas C. Schelling, small-group critics of hegemonic theory contend that even large-number systems can successfully resolve collective action problems if there exists a k or subgroup of actors who would profit by doing so even if they alone absorbed its costs.[32] Small-group theory, however, does not satisfactorily confront two issues that are critical to the ability of a group of states to substitute for a hegemon: the theory addresses neither the origins nor the enforcement mechanisms of the group adequately. Although game-theoretic solutions to both problems exist, their assumptions provide a

---

29. Stigler 1964, 47.

30. Yarbrough and Yarbrough 1987, 7–9.

31. Thus, the supply of information assumes a central role in recent analyses of international regimes. See, for example, Keohane 1984, 259; Russett 1985, 222.

32. Schelling 1978.

poor fit to the situation of states that are engaged in trade in an anarchic political structure.

Origins

The origin of small groups is typically approached as an empirical rather than as an analytic issue: the legacy of hegemony explains the creation of k groups.[33] In some respects, the neglect of k-group genesis is unimpeachable: proponents of small-group theory themselves readily acknowledge that they do not systematically address the issue,[34] and no theory of international cooperation should be indicted simply because it cannot explain completely the evolution of inter-state cooperation.

The reliance on hegemony, however, remains troubling for several reasons. First, it implies that the international system evolves peacefully from a hegemonic to a nonhegemonic structure, despite evidence that such power transitions can be potent sources of war.[35] Second, its recourse to history leaves small-group theory mute before a problem that is central to the field of international political economy: because the great powers are always few in number, the theory cannot explain why wide variations exist in the capacity of different systems to support market exchange among their constituent states.

The role attributed to history also dismantles axiomatically a formidable barrier to entry that a small group would otherwise confront: the need to agree on the cooperative equilibrium it will thereafter enforce. The literature on oligopolistic supergames has been strongly criticized for its silence on this aspect of collusion:[36] this criticism applies *a fortiori* to discussions of free-trade k groups.[37] If neither oligopolies nor would-be international k groups can reach agreement on what is to be enforced, it is, as James Friedman observes in the industrial context, "cold comfort to know that the firms, should they ever find themselves at the equilibrium, would never seek to deviate from it."[38]

Agreement on any single equilibrium is problematic because different equilibria imply different distributions of the net benefits of cooperation.[39] Although several game-theoretic solutions to this problem exist, no single

---

33. Keohane 1984, Snidal 1985, 603; cf. Haggard and Simmons 1987, 506.
34. Keohane's book (1984) is titled, after all, *AFTER Hegemony* (emphasis added).
35. See, for example, Organski and Kugler 1980.
36. Shapiro 1987, 56–58 (cited by permission).
37. Snidal, however, provides a good discussion of the distributional problems that small groups encounter with respect to collective action generally. See Snidal 1985, 604–12.
38. Friedman 1977, 15.
39. Luce and Raiffa 1958, 121.

solution currently commands general acceptance.[40] Moreover, insofar as they assume that the utility functions of all players are common knowledge, these solutions tend to assume away rather than confront directly what R. Duncan Luce and Howard Raiffa refer to as the "real" bargaining problem: the existence of strategic incentives to conceal preferences.[41]

Apart from abstract game-theoretic solutions, several solutions exist that are arguably more feasible. As is true of firms attempting to form cartels, states can readily agree to maximize their joint profits or gains from trade either if the distribution of profits that results will benefit all equally, or if side-payments are possible. It is unlikely that collusion on the joint maximum will lead to a symmetrical distribution of benefits. This will occur within an industrial cartel only in the highly improbable event that all firms are "absolutely" identical to each other.[42] In the context of international trade, it will occur only if reciprocal demand curves are identical in the negotiating countries—an equally improbable event.

The joint maximum theoretically retains its appeal if side-payments are possible. Side-payments redistribute the net benefits of cooperation among the relevant actors precisely in order "to equalize any inequities arising from their cooperation."[43] Significant impediments to their use exist, however: utility must be transferable; the contracting parties must agree on a redistributive mechanism;[44] and, most importantly, recipients must accept the potential threat that inheres in their reliance on what is, in effect, the extension of subsidies to them from others. Oliver Williamson's assessment of the risks to subsidized firms applies to states as well:

> Firms which are authorized to expand relatively as a result of the agreement will be powerfully situated to demand a renegotiated settlement at a later date. Wary of such opportunism, firms for which retrenchment is indicated will decline from the outset to accept a full-blown profit-pooling arrangement.[45]

If neither natural nor induced symmetry of profit distribution renders the joint maximum a workable point of agreement, the "intrinsic magnetism of particular outcomes" may yet single out one from among the set of Pareto-

---

40. Friedman 1986, 170.
41. Luce and Raiffa 1958, 134.
42. Friedman 1977, 28.
43. Luce and Raiffa 1958, 180; see also Snidal 1985, 605.
44. Young 1975, 32 note 40.
45. Williamson 1975, 224.

optimal points.[46] The "egalitarian nature" of the Swiss tariff-reduction proposal at the Tokyo Round negotiations, for example, reportedly led to its general acceptance.[47] Yet this example only serves to illustrate how difficult it may be for a unique focal point to emerge: behind agreement on equity as the standard for the Tokyo Round formula stood the relatively equal power of the four principal parties to that negotiation, a long history of tariff cuts and a relatively low level of tariffs among them, and no discernible security ramifications to the accord.

In the absence of any of these facilitating conditions, would-be international k groups may face insuperable obstacles to organization. Moreover, if the play of the game violates the "heroic" assumption of supergame analysis that the payoff matrix does not change over time,[48] this problem will arise not only at the initial but at *every* stage of the iterated game in which change occurs. The international context poses particularly difficult problems in this respect, as any distribution of the gains from trade can affect not only the economic but also the military balance of power among participating states. In the international system, therefore, small groups are poor substitutes for privileged groups.

Enforcement

Despite their emphasis on enforcement, small-group advocates have not yet addressed adequately the deterrence and punishment of cheating. The discussion that follows focuses on the three hostages to good behavior in any single regime that are prominent in the small-group literature: linkage to existing regimes and, through reputation, to future regimes, and the breakdown of the regime in which the defection occurs.[49]

What is not explained, however, is why exclusion from other existing regimes is a credible threat: the literature does not specify either the excludable goods they supply or the cooperators' interests in punishing those who free ride on a *different* regime. As both theoretical and empirical analyses suggest, linkage may as easily torpedo as reinforce cooperation in any specific issue area: the interests of states in linking cooperation on one to cooperation on other issues can as easily diverge as converge.[50] Analytically, then, there is no reason to assume that linkages stabilize cooperation.

Analogously, in order to attribute significant explanatory weight to reputation, small-group advocates must show that: (1) extrapolations from past to

46. Thomas C. Schelling, cited in Baldwin 1987, 30.
47. Chan 1985, 463.
48. McGinnis 1986, 164.
49. Keohane 1984, 100, 104–5.
50. For discussion, see Sebenius 1983; Tollison and Willett 1979; Oye 1979.

future behavior are reliable because the interests of states are the same in both the past and the present situations, *and* (2) informational asymmetries exist between the contracting parties.[51] Theoretical and empirical work on strategic deterrence, however, suggests that state interests and behavior vary widely across time and place.[52] As a consequence, states tend to discount the past heavily as a predictor of the behavior of other states in later situations.

In addition, the regime context suggests that informational asymmetries will be rare: regimes are created specifically to correct the "market for lemons" problem.[53] Because regimes supply information to states about the behavior of others, they do not provide opportunities for states to develop a reputation for honesty. As Robert H. Frank observes,

> if people act rationally, . . . we [cannot] discover that someone is honest by observing what he does in situations where the detection of cheating is not *unlikely*. . . .These are situations in which we frequently discover how a person has acted. For precisely this reason, however, it will not be rational to cheat in these cases. To observe that someone does not cheat would tell us only that he is prudent, not honest. . . .The kinds of actions that are likely to be observed are just not very good tests of whether a person is honest.[54]

That states understand the logic of Frank's argument is nicely illustrated by Lord Salisbury's comment about Prussian intentions. He noted "that they should have been pacific when they were weak is not unnatural, but if we wish to know the character of their disposition when left to itself, we must ask what they were when they were strong."[55]

In the abstract, at least, it may not matter much that these two hostages do not adequately secure cooperation. Sufficient power to deter free riding

---

51. It is this combination that motivates the role of reputations in such games as the chainstore paradox and formal analysis of cooperation in finite PDs. See Kreps and Wilson 1982; Kreps, Milgrom, Roberts, and Wilson 1982.

52. Lebow 1985.

53. Moreover, any government known to put stock in past behavior invites others to cheat it. L. G. Telser observes:

The accumulation of a fund of goodwill of a buyer toward a seller that depends on past experience stands as a ready temptation to the seller to cheat the buyers and convert their goodwill into ready cash. It is the prospect of the loss of future gain that deters and the existence of past goodwill that invites cheating. Therefore, rational behavior by the parties to an agreement requires that the probability of continuing their relation does not depend on their past experience with each other.

See Telser 1980, 36.

54. Frank 1988, 74–75.

55. Salisbury 1870, 546.

inheres in the one mechanism to which the existing literature generally gives relatively short shrift: each state's recognition that, "because regimes are difficult to construct, it may be rational to obey their rules if the alternative is their breakdown. . . ."[56] Endowed with additional structure, this recognition alone renders the cooperative a Nash or self-enforcing equilibrium. If each state realizes that its attempt to free ride will lead to the collapse of the regime, it has no incentive to defect, and the problem of enforcement does not arise. A critical omission in existing analyses, however, is how such a self-destruct mechanism might be built into a regime.[57]

A credible threat that the response to any attempt to free ride will be the collapse of the entire regime creates just such a self-destruct mechanism. Existing work on tacit collusion among oligopolists relies on precisely this threat in order to stabilize cooperation: all firms agree to revert to the Cournot or noncooperative equilibrium for some period if *any* firm attempts to free ride.[58] The threat is credible because it is in every firm's interest to execute it provided all others do so: by definition, if one firm believes that all other firms will, after any deviation, begin to produce their Cournot outputs, that firm cannot do better than do so itself.[59] Thus, no firm has an interest in deviating from the collusive equilibrium: sanctions need never be implemented.

In effect, this solution generalizes the two-person Tit-for-Tat solution to the n-person game, with analogous restrictions on the discount rate relative to the payoffs, and on the information available to each player about the others.[60] Unlike the two-person game, however, the n-person situation confronts the nondefecting players with the temptation to respond to any defection in either of two ways that return short-term profits higher than those of the noncooperative equilibrium: to offer the defector a second chance or to recontract among themselves in order to maximize their profits in light of the defection. The fact, however, that both alternatives tend to unleash a chain of defections strengthens incentives to execute the original threat.[61] Thus, this solution is a self-enforcing agreement that sustains cooperation without the need for linkage to other PDs or to reputations.

The relevance of this solution in the context of international politics is considerably smaller than is its abstract analytic appeal, however. Its application requires agreement among the contracting states that a deviation has

---

56. Keohane 1984, 100. One article that *does* briefly discuss this solution is Yarbrough and Yarbrough 1986.

57. Snidal 1985, 610–11.

58. Bendor and Mookherjee 1987.

59. Friedman 1983, 131.

60. For a discussion of these limits, see Friedman 1983; also Bendor and Mookherjee 1987, 133–34.

61. Friedman 1983, 133–34.

occurred; it also requires a consensus on the response. Yet, not only the economic but also the political interests of states influence their judgments on these issues: incentives to perceive and sanction a deviation can vary widely as the identity of the alleged deviant varies. Kindleberger observes that free riding can result when "the police are politically opposed to a rule . . . or to its application in a given case . . .": he points out that the United Nations and the League of Nations before it demonstrate that attempts to protect the international collective good are highly vulnerable to the tendency of states to interpret any alleged threat to that good in a highly self-interested fashion.[62] Thus, in enforcing a cooperative equilibrium, any small group of states encounters political problems that do not confront hegemonic states.

Conclusion

Although critics of hegemonic stability theory have not destroyed its analytic foundations, they have achieved several less ambitious objectives. They have, for example, argued persuasively that a hegemonic preference for free trade cannot be assumed: a more discriminating analysis is essential to establish the conditions under which a rational hegemon will, in its *own* interests, act benevolently rather than coercively toward others. In addition, the critics have forced a rigorous examination of the assumed public character of free trade. Moreover, they have successfully challenged the assumption that international public goods can, under *all* conditions, be provided only by a privileged group.

They have not, however, deprived hegemonic stability theory of its analytic base: hegemons can reject the prescriptions of standard trade theory; whenever asymmetrical information prevails, open international markets do present public-good problems; and privileged groups enjoy a stronger advantage than small-group advocates acknowledge.

More importantly, its critics have not challenged the public-good variant of hegemonic theory at its point of maximum vulnerability. Focusing exclusively on the real income gains that accrue to a state which opens its borders to trade, the theory analyzes economic exchange in a political vacuum. Yet, national power is engaged in free-trade agreements because such agreements inevitably produce security externalities: the removal of trade barriers affects not only the real income but also the security of the contracting states.[63]

---

62. Kindleberger 1976, 24.

63. More generally, an external economy "is said to be emitted when an activity undertaken by an individual or firm yields benefits to other individuals or firms in addition to the benefits accruing to the emitting party." External diseconomies inflict injury rather than confer benefits. See Boadway and Wildasin 1984, 60.

The security externalities of trade arise from its inevitable jointness in production: the source of gains from trade is the increased efficiency with which domestic resources can be employed, and this increase in efficiency itself frees economic resources for military uses.[64] Thus, trade enhances the potential military power of any country that engages in it.[65] In doing so, free trade can disrupt the preexisting balance of power among the contracting states.[66]

Thus, the most durable barrier to open international markets may not be the trade preferences of a rational hegemon, the effectively public character of free trade, or the inability of small groups to substitute easily for privileged groups. Instead, it may be the anarchic international system that makes two facts common knowledge among states: (1) each seeks to exploit the wealth of others to enhance its own power, and (2) trade is instrumental to this end.[67] The structure of international politics, in short, may lead a state to prefer the status quo ante because it fears that any change may benefit others more than itself.[68]

In a first-best world, of course, these fears would not paralyze states. A two-step process would neutralize them: states would first maximize their absolute gains from trade, and would then adjust their defense strategies to compensate for any changes in the balance of power that occur as trade barriers fall. In a more realistic, less than first-best world, however, the time lag that intervenes between these two steps may open a window of vulnerability that can allow one state to threaten the existence of another.

As a consequence, states may prefer the conservative course. Open markets thus become victims of the primacy of security concerns in an anarchic international political structure. The failure of hegemonic stability theory to acknowledge this barrier to trade constitutes the theory's most profound flaw. Progress toward a more powerful theory of the political economy of international trade must begin with an explicit recognition of the influential role played by security concerns in the determination of national trade policies.

---

64. Root 1984.
65. Baldwin 1985.
66. McKeown 1982, 225.
67. As Baldwin (1985, 116), observes, trade "is by far the most [cost-] effective . . . way for one country to acquire the goods or services of another."
68. In theory, it is possible for states negotiating with each other to conclude an agreement that improves the absolute welfare of each while it preserves the preexisting balance of power between them. The prerequisites of such an agreement are formidable, however: the utility functions of the states must be common knowledge, and the contracting states must agree on a utility scale that will determine both the status quo ante and the division of benefits from cooperation (Rapoport 1974, chap. 11). In practice, it seems unlikely that these conditions will be fulfilled.

REFERENCES

Axelrod, Robert, and Robert O. Keohane. 1985. "Achieving Cooperation under Anarchy: Strategies and Institutions." *World Politics* 38:226–54.
Baldwin, David A. 1985. *Economic Statecraft.* Princeton: Princeton University Press.
Baldwin, David A. 1987. "Politics, Exchange, and Cooperation." Paper prepared for delivery to the 28th Annual Convention of the International Studies Association, Washington, D.C.
Bendor, Jonathan, and Dilip Mookherjee. 1987. "Institutional Structure and the Logic of Collective Action." *American Political Science Review* 81:129–54.
Bhagwati, Jagdish. 1988. *Protectionism.* Cambridge, Mass.: MIT Press.
Boadway, Robin W., and David E. Wildasin. 1984. *Public Sector Economics,* 2d ed. Boston: Little, Brown.
Caves, Richard E., and Ronald W. Jones. 1973. *World Trade and Payments: An Introduction.* Boston: Little, Brown.
Chan, Kenneth S. 1985. "The International Negotiating Game: Some Evidence from the Tokyo Round." *Review of Economics and Statistics* 67:456–64.
Conybeare, John A. C. 1983. "Tariff Protection in Developed and Developing Countries." *International Organization* 37:441–68.
Conybeare, John A. C. 1984. "Public Goods, Prisoners' Dilemmas and the International Political Economy." *International Studies Quarterly* 28:5–22.
Conybeare, John A. C. 1987. *Trade Wars: The Theory and Practice of International Commercial Rivalry.* New York: Columbia University Press.
Eichengreen, Barry. 1986. "The Political Economy of the Smoot-Hawley Tariff." NBER Working Paper No. 2001. Berkeley, Calif.: University of California, Department of Economics.
Ethier, Wilfred. 1983. *Modern International Economics.* New York: W. W. Norton.
Frank, Robert H. 1988. *Passions Within Reason: The Strategic Role of the Emotions.* New York: W. W. Norton.
Friedan, Jeff. 1988. "Sectoral Conflict and U.S. Foreign Economic Policy." *International Organization* 42:59–90.
Friedman, James W. 1977. *Oligopoly and the Theory of Games.* Amsterdam: North-Holland.
Friedman, James W. 1983. *Oligopoly Theory.* New York: Cambridge University Press.
Friedman, James W. 1986. *Game Theory with Applications to Economics.* New York: Oxford University Press.
Gilpin, Robert. 1975. *U.S. Power and the Multinational Corporation.* New York: Basic Books.
Gilpin, Robert. 1987. *The Political Economy of International Relations.* Princeton: Princeton University Press.
Haggard, Stephan, and Beth A. Simmons. 1987. "Theories of International Regimes." *International Organization* 41:491–517.
Irwin, Douglas. 1987. "Welfare Effects of British Free Trade: Debate and Evidence from the 1840s." Presented to Midwest International Economics Meetings, Ann Arbor, Michigan.
Johnson, H. G. 1953–54. "Optimum Tariffs and Retaliation." *Review of Economic Studies* 21:142–53.

Keohane, Robert O. 1980. "The Theory of Hegemonic Stability and Changes in International Regimes, 1967–1977." In *Change in the International System,* ed. Ole Holsti. Boulder: Westview Press.

Keohane, Robert O. 1984. *After Hegemony: Cooperation and Discord in the World Political Economy.* Princeton: Princeton University Press.

Kindleberger, Charles P. 1973. *The World in Depression, 1929–1939.* Berkeley: University of California Press.

Kindleberger, Charles P. 1976. "Systems of International Economic Organization." In *Money and the Coming World Order,* ed. David P. Calleo. New York: New York University Press.

Krasner, Stephen. 1976. "State Power and the Structure of International Trade." *World Politics* 28:317–47.

Kreps, David M., Paul Milgrom, John Roberts, and Robert Wilson. 1982. "Rational Cooperation in the Finitely Repeated Prisoners' Dilemma." *Journal of Economic Theory* 27:245–52.

Kreps, David M., and Robert Wilson. 1982. "Reputation and Imperfect Information." *Journal of Economic Theory* 27:253–79.

Laver, Michael. 1980. "Political Solutions to the Collective Action Problem." *Political Studies* 28:195–209.

Lebow, Richard Ned. 1985. "Conclusion." In *Psychology and Deterrence,* ed. Robert Jervis, Richard Ned Lebow, and Janice Gross Stein. Baltimore: The Johns Hopkins University Press.

Luce, R. Duncan, and Howard Raiffa. 1958. *Games and Decisions: Introduction and Critical Survey.* New York: John Wiley and Sons.

McCloskey, Donald N. 1980. "Magnanimous Albion: Free Trade and British National Income, 1841–1881." *Explorations in Economic History* 17:303–20.

McGinnis, Michael D. 1986. "Issue Linkage and the Evolution of International Cooperation." *Journal of Conflict Resolution* 30:141–70.

McKeown, Timothy James. 1982. "The Rise and Decline of the Open Trading Regime of the Nineteenth Century." Ph.D. diss., Stanford University.

McKeown, Timothy James. 1983. "Hegemonic Stability Theory and 19th-Century Tariff Levels in Europe." *International Organization* 37:73–91.

McMillan, John. 1986. *Game Theory in International Economics.* New York: Harwood Academic Publishers.

Milgrom, Paul, and John Roberts. 1982. "Limit Pricing and Entry Under Incomplete Information: An Equilibrium Analysis." *Econometrica* 50:443–59.

Olson, Mancur. 1971. *The Logic of Collective Action.* Cambridge, Mass.: Harvard University Press.

Organski, A. F. K., and Jacek Kugler. 1980. *The War Ledger.* Chicago: University of Chicago Press.

Oye, Kenneth A. 1979. "The Domain of Choice: International Constraints and the Carter Administration." In *Eagle Entangled: U.S. Foreign Policy in a Complex World,* ed. Kenneth A. Oye, Donald Rothchild, and Robert J. Lieber. New York: Longman.

Oye, Kenneth A. 1985a. "Explaining Cooperation under Anarchy: Strategies and Institutions." *World Politics* 38:1–24.

Oye, Kenneth A. 1985b. "The Sterling-Dollar-Franc Triangle: Monetary Diplomacy 1929–1937." *World Politics* 38:173–99.

Rapoport, Anatol. 1974. *Fights, Games and Debates.* Ann Arbor: University of Michigan Press.

Root, William A. 1984. "Trade Controls that Work." *Foreign Policy* 56:61–80.

Ruggie, John Gerard. 1982. "International Regimes, Transactions, and Change: Embedded Liberalism in the Postwar Economic Order." *International Organization* 36:379–415.

Russett, Bruce. 1985. "The Mysterious Case of Vanishing Hegemony." *International Organization* 39:207–32.

Salisbury, Lord. 1870. "The Terms of Peace." *Quarterly Review* 129:540–56.

Schelling, Thomas C. 1978. "Hockey Helmets, Daylight Savings, and Other Binary Choices." In *Micromotives and Macrobehavior,* ed. Thomas C. Schelling. New York: W. W. Norton.

Sebenius, James K. 1983. "Negotiation Arithmetic: Adding and Subtracting Issues and Parties." *International Organization* 37:281–316.

Shapiro, Carl. 1987. "Theories of Oligopoly Behavior." Discussion Papers in Economics, No. 126. Princeton University: Woodrow Wilson School.

Snidal, Duncan. 1985. "The Limits of Hegemonic Stability Theory." *International Organization* 39:579–614.

Stigler, George. 1964. "A Theory of Oligopoly." *Journal of Political Economy* 72:44–61.

Telser, L. G. 1980. "A Theory of Self-enforcing Agreements." *Journal of Business* 53:27–44.

Tollison, Robert D., and Thomas D. Willett. 1979. "An Economic Theory of Mutually Advantageous Issue Linkages." *International Organization* 33:425–49.

Williamson, Oliver. 1975. *Markets and Hierarchies: Analysis and Antitrust Implications, A Study in the Economics of Internal Organization.* New York: Free Press.

Yarbrough, Beth V., and Robert M. Yarbrough. 1986. "Reciprocity, Bilateralism, and Economic 'Hostages': Self-enforcing Agreements in International Trade." *International Studies Quarterly* 30:7–22.

Yarbrough, Beth V., and Robert M. Yarbrough. 1987. "Cooperation in the Liberalization of International Trade: After Hegemony, What?" *International Organization* 41:1–26.

Young, Oran R. 1975. "Introduction." In *Bargaining: Formal Theories of Negotiation,* ed. Oran R. Young. Urbana: University of Illinois Press.

CHAPTER 4

Parallel and Overlapping Games: Theory and an Application to the European Gas Trade

James E. Alt and Barry Eichengreen

1. Introduction

"Trade policy is foreign policy" is both the title and the message of one of Richard Cooper's well-known articles.[1] Cooper's point can be generalized: economic policy is foreign policy in the sense that negotiations among countries over economic issues and the impact of each country's economic policies on foreign economic outcomes have foreign policy repercussions. Realistic analyses of international economic and political relations should acknowledge and build upon the interdependence of issue areas. Equally, foreign policy is domestic policy: foreign policy decisions have immediate repercussions on the domestic standing of the governments involved. Realistic analyses of foreign policy debates should acknowledge and build upon the interdependence of domestic and international issue areas.

While narrative accounts of international relations and of the formulation of international economic policy traditionally have acknowledged both types of interdependencies, recent work building on game-theoretic foundations has tended to analyze each type of strategic interdependence in isolation from the others. For example, while one strand of research in international monetary economics has analyzed international economic policy coordination as a strategic game between domestic and foreign governments, an entirely separate

Earlier versions of this essay were presented to interdisciplinary conferences co-sponsored by the National Bureau of Economic Research and Harvard University, and by the University of Southern California and the Claremont Colleges, respectively. We thank our discussants, Kenneth Oye, Andrew Hughes-Hallett, Dave Richardson, and Arthur Stein, and conference participants for their suggestions. Lisa Martin, John Odell, Bob Powell, Ken Shepsle, and Thomas Willett also provided extremely helpful comments. Professor Alt gratefully acknowledges the assistance of the National Science Foundation under grant SES86-40444. Professor Eichengreen acknowledges support from the Institute of Business and Economic Research at the University of California at Berkeley. Reprinted from *Economics and Politics* 1, no. 2 (July 1989): 119–40. Reprinted by permission of Basil Blackwell.

1. Cooper 1986.

strand in closed-economy macroeconomics has analyzed the formulation of domestic monetary and fiscal policies as a noncooperative game between an incumbent government and a constituency with different preferences.[2] Contributors make little more than passing reference to linkages between these strategic games arising from the fact that a domestic government may be playing simultaneously against a domestic interest group and a foreign rival.[3] Similarly, while one strand of research in international relations has used the noncooperative game paradigm to analyze international negotiations over economic issues such as trade liberalization and monetary policy harmonization, a wholly separate strand has applied a virtually identical framework to the analysis of diplomatic and military issues such as arms control and NATO contributions, neither group making more than passing mention of the linkages between issue areas.[4]

In this paper we attempt to bring these disparate strands together, first developing some analytic concepts and then illustrating their applicability. The core concepts we label "parallel" and "overlapping" games. Parallel games arise when the same opponents play against one another at the same time in more than one arena. Overlapping games arise when a particular player is engaged at the same time in games against distinct opponents, and when the strategy pursued in one game limits strategies available in the other. The question upon which we focus is how increasing the range of simultaneous or overlapping games affects the prospects for cooperation.

In the first half of the paper (sections 2 and 3), we formalize these concepts. We keep the exposition as nontechnical as possible, since to a considerable extent the central points can be demonstrated without mathematical apparatus. In the second half of the paper (sections 4 and 5), we then apply this framework to a case study of European trade in natural gas and European security issues. This turns out to be a useful illustration of a complex of games with both parallel and overlapping elements.

We are not the first to argue that governments in their international relations interact strategically with several rivals, that governments simultaneously consider multiple issues, or that governments may be engaged at the same time in domestic and foreign games. Haas (1980) has suggested that "issue-linkage"—the notion that strategies utilized in different issue areas are often linked to one another—may be conducive to the emergence of cooperative behavior. Keohane and Nye (1977, 1987) coined the term "complex interdependence" to denote this same phenomenon but were more skeptical that multiple interdependencies were necessarily conducive to cooperation.

---

2. See Buiter and Marston 1985 and Tabellini 1983, respectively.
3. An important exception to this generalization is Rogoff 1985.
4. See Gowa 1984 and Nye 1987 for examples of the respective applications.

Denzau, Riker, and Shepsle (1985) have suggested that several paradoxes in voting behavior dissolve once politicians are seen as being engaged in two games, one against fellow legislators, another against the electorate. A related perspective is taken by Putnam (1988), who views international negotiators as playing one game against each other and a second game against domestic legislators responsible for ratification, and by Axelrod (1987), in whose model domestic ratification is replaced by maximization of domestic support. Tsebelis (1987, 1988) has developed the related notion of "nested" games to capture the dynamics of coalitional politics.[5] In addition to this work, there is an extensive theoretical literature on games with more than two players, reviewed recently by Shepsle (1985). Finally, there is a direct analogy with the literature in economics on multimarket oligopoly, in which an imperfect competitor is engaged in games against rivals in a number of distinct product markets. In the analysis to follow, we draw extensively on this last literature.

2. Parallel Games

A. Preliminaries

Consider a scenario in which players or agents are confronted by more than one strategic situation. We refer to players or agents as "governments."[6] Each of these strategic situations is characterized by the standard features of a noncooperative game. There is a strategy space: in each game, each government chooses among a range of alternative plays. There is a payoff matrix of returns associated with alternative strategies. Payoffs to strategies are interdependent: the returns to the strategy adopted by one government depend on the strategies adopted by the others.

We define parallel games as two or more strategic situations in which common players or agents interact. One may think of the United States and the Soviet Union as engaged in one game whose goal is to secure a strategic

---

5. In Tsebelis's model, political parties are seen as pursuing strategies in two distinct but connected arenas. Each party to the coalition is simultaneously engaged in a game against other coalition members to determine the balance of power within the coalition, and in a second game in which coalition members play jointly against the opposing coalition. While there is a parallel with our notion of overlapping games in the sense that each party plays simultaneously against allied parties and opposing ones, there are differences in the sense that Tsebelis focuses explicitly on the special case where rivals in the first game act collusively in the second, and implicitly on the case where a particular sequence of plays occurs (the game among coalitional partners first, the game between coalitions second).

6. While the unitary-actor assumption—that governments can be represented as single, unified agents—is not without consequence, the implications of conflicts between branches of government or between elected officials and their constituencies for the conduct of foreign policy are better treated in the overlapping-game framework considered below.

advantage in the Middle East and another game the goal of which is to secure a strategic advantage in Central America. Or one may think of U.S. and European governments as engaged in one game whose goal is to secure a contract to sell some portion of their domestic agricultural surplus to the Soviet Union on the most favorable terms possible, alongside a second game the goal of which is for each exporting country to secure a contract to sell commercial aircraft to Japan. These games are parallel by virtue of the fact that the same players—the United States and the Soviet Union in the first example, U.S. and European governments in the second—interact in both arenas.

Industrial organization theorists will recognize the analogy with multi-market oligopoly. In a multimarket oligopoly, the same firms are imperfect competitors in several markets. IBM and Olivetti, as rivals in both computers and typewriters, are surely aware of their strategic interdependence in each market. They recognize both that their profits depend not just on their own marketing strategy but in addition on that of their rival, and that they are engaged in rivalry with the same competitor in each of these markets. The literature on multimarket oligopoly analyzes the potential for conglomerates and mergers among firms active in different markets to act as competition-restraining devices. A substantial empirical literature has examined the statistical relationship between multimarket contact and competitive behavior (see the review in Scott 1982). Two recent theoretical analyses are Bulow, Geanakoplos, and Klemperer (1985), who analyze markets linked directly by demand- and supply-side spillovers, and Bernheim and Whinston (1986), who focus on the implications of multimarket contact for the sustainability of collusive allocations. The analogy between firms' abilities to sustain collusive allocations and governments' abilities to sustain cooperation is direct. Hence our task in this paper is greatly facilitated by the important work of the last-cited authors. Most of the insights of this section are drawn from Bernheim and Whinston.

The question with which we are concerned here is whether linkage among games is conducive to the emergence of cooperative behavior. A common conjecture is that a proliferation of contact points strengthens the tendency toward cooperation (Haas 1980; Hardin 1982). When governments are simultaneously engaged in games with one another in a number of distinct arenas, informal reasoning goes, they will be less inclined to deviate (to renege on a pledge to behave cooperatively) because of the increased scope for retaliation. To return to our examples, the argument is that the Soviet Union will be deterred from escalating military tensions in the Middle East, even if this would be to its advantage despite any retaliatory steps taken by the United States to strengthen its military presence there, if the United States could escalate in Central America in response. Analogously, the argument is that the United States is less likely to undercut its European competitors to secure a larger share of Soviet grain purchases when it realizes that European governments can retaliate by undercutting U.S. firms attempting to sell aircraft to Japan. This intuition presumably underlies the notion, current at least since the time of Cordell Hull, that countries which trade with one another are less likely to go to war. It underlies the central argument of Edwards (1955) in his analysis of multimarket oligopoly, to wit "when one large conglomerate enterprise competes against another, the two are likely to encounter each other in a considerable number of markets. The multiplicity of their contacts may blunt the edge of their competition."

Unfortunately, this logic is flawed. Although a proliferation of points of contact increases the cost of defection, it can also increase the benefits. A Soviet or U.S. government reneging on an understanding not to escalate tensions can maximize the benefits by defecting in each of its parallel games. A U.S. or European government reneging on an agreement not to undercut its rival in shared export markets can maximize the benefits by defecting in each market in which it competes. The benefits of defection, like the costs, can be an increasing function of the number of parallel games. Without additional structure, it is impossible to say whether the existence of several points of contact has a greater impact on the costs or benefits of cooperation.

We can begin to develop that structure by distinguishing among parallel games that are "symmetrical," "exclusive," and "inherently linked." By symmetrical games we mean those which are mirror images of one another. By exclusive games we mean those played exclusively by a common set of players; our example of superpower rivalries in the Middle East and Central America will not be exclusive if additional military powers (Israel? Saudi Arabia?) play a role in the Middle East but not in the Western Hemisphere. (We shall refer to players present only in a subset of parallel games as "extraneous.") By inherently linked games we mean games connected not only by the fact that common players participate in both but also by spillovers from choice of strategy in one to range of feasible strategies or payoffs in the other. (The terminology is from Bulow, Geanakoplos and Klemperer 1985). For example, if the instrument available to the U.S. and Soviet governments in their parallel Middle Eastern and Central American games is the location of a fixed number of battleships, a decision to escalate in the Middle East by moving battleships there directly affects the balance of power in Central America by reducing the number of battleships in the Caribbean; these games would be inherently linked. Bulow, Geanakoplos, and Klemperer consider inherently linked games in which a common set of firms are rivals in more than one market. If the amount a firm produces for sale in one market affects its cost of production for another market, then the two markets are said to have inherent technological linkages. Similarly, if the price a firm charges in one market affects price and profitability in another market, due for example to substitution between commodities by consumers, then the two markets have inherent demand linkages. (The example of Olivetti and IBM competing in both the computer and typewriter markets illustrates this inherent linkage, since personal computers and typewriters are imperfect substitutes in demand.)

We proceed in the manner of Bernheim and Whinston, focusing on infinitely repeated, full-information games. A first difficulty that must be faced is the indeterminacy of noncooperative games and the problem of choosing among the multitude of solution concepts that have been offered. We narrow the range of alternatives by assuming that at every point in time the strategies selected comprise a Nash equilibrium. (In a Nash equilibrium, no player has an incentive to alter its strategy, given the strategies of its rivals.) Since there may be multiple Nash equilibria, we restrict our attention to those which are subgame perfect. (In a subgame perfect Nash equilibrium to a repeated game, strategies form a Nash equilibrium in every subset of repetitions; see Selten 1975.) We further narrow the range of alternatives by focusing exclusively on optimal collusive Nash equilibria. (The optimal collusive Nash equilibrium to a repeated game is that subgame perfect Nash equilibrium in which the expected welfare of the players is highest.) The rationale for focusing on this solution is the same as in any application of the assumption of optimizing behavior.[7] Optimal collusive Nash equilibria satisfy the requirement of dynamic consistency: players act in their own best interest under all circumstances, thereby ruling out incredible threats. In the following, we focus on the optimal collusive Nash equilibrium identified by Abreu (1988): governments adopt the simple strategy of retaliating against deviations by their foreign counterparts with the most severe punishments feasible. The severity of the punishment is limited by the requirement that it too be a subgame perfect Nash equilibrium.[8]

---

7. The assumption of optimality is not uncontroversial; see Bernheim, Peleg and Whinston 1985 and Fudenberg and Tirole 1986. For asymmetric settings where players disagree about which payoff is "highest," one might assume that the payoff chosen is the Nash Bargaining Solution (the product of payoffs which is highest).

8. Intuitively, the most severe punishment possible is optimal since it minimizes the probability that other governments will deviate and hence maximizes the likelihood of cooperation. Some readers may find this assumption of "grim trigger strategies"—that players retaliate as severely as possible against any infraction and never forgive—implausibly draconian, especially in light of Axelrod's (1984) finding that more forgiving strategies tend to dominate in experimental settings. An important difference between our framework and many of those experimental settings is that we have not allowed for uncertainty due to randomness or mistakes on the part of players. In the presence of such uncertainty, a more forgiving strategy may in fact dominate. Players may prefer to renegotiate after new information about their opponents or about the state of the world is revealed. See Crawford 1987. An appealing analogy is with the ultimate grim trigger

It may clarify the concept of optimal retaliation to consider it in a single (in contrast to a parallel) game, using one of the examples introduced above. Consider two national aircraft producers attempting to secure third-market sales in competition with one another. They are engaged in an infinitely repeated game with discounting (just as in all the examples that follow). Assume further that they compete exclusively in terms of price. While in equilibrium they must charge the same price, a continuum of prices will clear the market. Which price prevails under the assumption of optimal retaliation? Optimal retaliation, like any other strategy, must satisfy the conditions for a Nash equilibrium: given the price charged by one country, the other country has no incentive to undercut it. The worst possible Nash equilibrium is that in which both firms charge the competitive price and earn zero profits (assuming constant marginal cost). If either firm set a lower price, the other would exit; optimal retaliation cannot yield negative profits, since negative profits cannot obtain in a Nash equilibrium with exit. If either firm set a higher price, it would sell zero units and make losses; hence the zero-profit competitive price is a Nash equilibrium. (It is also the static Nash equilibrium—the Bertrand solution—to the one-shot game.)

The optimal collusive equilibrium to the repeated game is that in which the players charge the monopoly price and share the monopoly profits in the absence of any deviation. If one player deviates, the other(s) retaliate by permanently cutting prices to the competitive level.

B. Cooperation in Parallel Games

Consider now parallel games in which players move simultaneously. The most severe punishment possible involves retaliation in all parallel games. To maximize the likelihood of compliance, governments respond to any deviation by retaliating in all arenas in which the rivals are simultaneously engaged. This has implications for the form defection takes: knowing that retaliation will be maximal and will be felt in all games, if a government chooses to deviate it will do so in all arenas in which it is engaged.

With these assumptions in hand, we can consider the possibilities for cooperation. A number of points can be made with the base case of two players and two games. Consider first two (exclusive) parallel games that are

---

strategy: capital punishment. Capital punishment for minor offences can be viewed as an efficient solution to the game between criminals and law enforcement officials if verdicts of guilt or innocence are never mistaken and acts in violation of the law are never inadvertent. In the presence of either source of uncertainty, one may prefer sentences that provide an opportunity for a new hearing if additional evidence comes to light. Here, however, we consider only full information, nonstochastic games with which the "grim-trigger strategy" assumption is consistent.

without inherent linkages (strategies adopted in one do not directly affect payoffs in the other). Here parallelism cannot reduce the likelihood of cooperation. If both games would have been played cooperatively had it been possible to consider them in isolation, then there is no incentive for either player to defect in either game (and hence in both games, given our assumption of grim trigger strategies) when they are played in parallel. But the observation that parallelism does not impede the maintenance of cooperation that would otherwise emerge is a far cry from the commonplace assertion that it facilitates cooperation where it would not otherwise obtain.

It is also clear that, when the games involved are symmetrical, exclusive and without inherent linkages, parallelism has no implications for the emergence of cooperation. If their parallelism went unrecognized, the two players would consider each game independently when deciding whether to cooperate. Since the two games are identical, the same outcome obtains in each. Now assume that the parallelism is suddenly recognized.[9] Equilibrium strategies are unaffected by this recognition. If one government contemplates deviating in one arena, it anticipates that it will incur retaliation in both arenas; knowing this it will choose between continuing to cooperate in both arenas or deviating in both. Whichever strategy dominated prior to the recognition of parallelism continues to dominate thereafter.

Removing either symmetry or exclusivity may be sufficient to overturn this neutrality result. Consider first a particular asymmetry, namely response lags that differ across games. Retaliation, which still takes the form of the severest possible punishment in both arenas, will be swift if it is elicited by deviation in one game, slow if caused by deviation in the other. If, for example, the prices at which Japan buys foreign aircraft are widely published while the prices at which the Soviet authorities buy grain from the West are not, U.S. and European governments may be quicker to respond when aircraft prices rather than grain prices are cut. If the parallelism of games is not recognized, cooperation between the United States and European authorities will be easier to sustain in the aircraft than the grain trade. The exporter who cuts prices reaps benefits until retaliation occurs and suffers costs thereafter; the longer the response lag the greater the present value of the benefits relative to the costs. The incentive to cut prices is greater in the market with the longer response lag. The two exporters may cooperate in aircraft trade but not in grain.

Suppose that the governments previously played these games without acknowledging their parallelism, cooperating in one but not in the other. Then

---

9. In games of incomplete information, we could think of bringing this "sudden recognition" within the model as a signalling or learning process, with quite different results for the impact of parallelism on cooperation. For the rest of this chapter, we retain the complete information assumption.

their parallel nature is recognized. From the assumptions of optimal collusive equilibria, it follows that failure to cooperate in one game will lead to retaliation in both. Although each rival previously had an incentive to play the game with the long response lag noncooperatively, parallelism raises the stakes by increasing the scope for retaliation. That the U.S. and European governments are also engaged in an aircraft export game, which they already are playing in cooperative fashion, may increase the likelihood that they will behave cooperatively in the grain export game in which they are simultaneously engaged. Parallelism serves to "pool the incentive constraints" in the two arenas. Rather than comparing the costs and benefits of defection for each individual game and choosing strategies accordingly, governments pool costs and benefits across games before deciding whether to cooperate or defect across the board.

Removing exclusivity similarly may alter the scope for cooperation. Consider a situation in which the United States and Canada are engaged simultaneously in a pair of negotiations, one revolving around a North American convention regulating acid rain, the other around the financing of their national defense through NATO contributions. In the case of acid rain, both countries produce more than the optimal quantity because some costs are incurred across the border. While both will be rendered better off by an agreement under which they trade reductions in acid rain generation, both have an incentive to shirk in the absence of retaliation. In the case of NATO, there is a classic free-rider problem since all participants benefit from the contribution of any one to their common defense. Each has an incentive to undercontribute to NATO in the hope that the others will make up the shortfall, and each will be rendered better off by an agreement under which they match increases in budgetary contributions (Olson and Zeckhauser 1966).

Now assume that the United States and Canada are the only two countries affected by one another's acid rain, but that other players participate in NATO. Holding constant other features of the games, it is generally the case that the larger the number of players, the less the likelihood of cooperation. It is harder to hold together large coalitions than small ones, or to cartelize markets with many firms than those with few, since the larger the number of players the smaller the share of the costs suffered by the player who deviates. If two identical countries contribute equally to their common problem of acid rain, they each suffer half the consequences of either one's decision to deviate from their restrictive agreement. But if ten identical countries contribute equally to the provision of their collective defense, each suffers only ten percent of the consequences of the decision to deviate from their collective agreement.

If when considered in isolation the acid rain game was played cooperatively while the mutual defense game was not, then recognition that these games were proceeding in parallel will alter the likelihood of a cooperative outcome in each. The countries involved in both games (in the current example, Canada and the United States) realize that they are rivals in both arenas. If they fail to cooperate in either game, then optimal retaliation dictates noncooperation in both. Hence if the countries are better off when cooperating with one another in both games than when playing both noncooperatively, parallelism without exclusivity increases the likelihood of cooperation in the game previously played noncooperatively. Recognizing that shirking rather than making their full contributions to NATO may lead their neighbor not just to reduce its own NATO contributions but to violate the agreement to restrict acid rain generation as well, the United States and Canada may increase their NATO contributions even if, taken in isolation, the costs of increased contributions exceed the benefits. To put the point another way, if the benefits of cooperation in the acid rain game, when analyzed in isolation, exceed the returns to deviating in the collective defense game when analyzed in isolation, deviation in the latter is discouraged.

What of the extraneous players? Whether recognition of parallelism encourages them to cooperate depends on the nature of the spillovers involved. In the case of positive externalities in the game with extraneous players, as when the countries of Europe are affected positively by increased U.S. and Canadian NATO contributions, if the United States and Canada internalize the benefits to one another of their individual defense expenditures and increase their outlays, the incentive for the other participants to undercontribute is reinforced. Hence the movement toward cooperation is not general. Since the United States and Canada recognize this under the assumption that the outcome is a Nash equilibrium, this reduces, other things equal, the likelihood that parallelism causes them to cooperate where they otherwise would not. From the viewpoint of the governments engaged in both parallel games, the benefits of cooperation are attenuated by the costs of further deviation by the extraneous players.

In the case of negative externalities in the game with extraneous players, recognition of parallelism may encourage cooperation even among third parties. Take the example where the United States and Europe export both grain to the Soviet Union and aircraft to Japan, but now assume that Australia is added as a third grain exporter. The externalities in the grain game are negative: any exporter undercutting the monopoly price in an effort to capture additional market share reduces the profits of its rivals by more than it increases its own. Assume that, in the absence of acknowledgment of their parallel nature, the aircraft game would be played cooperatively but the grain game would not. Then if the United States and Europe recognized the parallelism, they might have an incentive to cooperate with one another in the grain game in order not to endanger their monopoly profits in the aircraft game. By raising their grain export prices toward the monopoly level, they would shift market share and profits toward Australia. But now possessing a larger market share, there is a smaller residual market for Australia to capture through price cutting, while the lost profits from lower prices on inframarginal sales are increased. The benefits to Australia of playing noncooperatively are reduced while the costs are increased. The recognition of parallelism by players involved in both games may induce even the extraneous participants to cooperate.[10]

To this point, inherent linkages have not been considered. We can illustrate inherent linkages by extending our U.S.-Canadian example to assume that an increased national defense contribution requires additional steel production, a consequence of which is to increase the cost of limiting acid rain. If raising contributions to their common defense also requires that the United States and Canada increase their steel production, the costs of adhering to a bilateral agreement to limit acid rain will be increased. Here the spillovers between games, as distinct from spillovers between players, are negative. Other things equal, negative spillovers between games reduce the likelihood that cooperative outcomes will obtain in either. Acknowledging parallelism reduces the slack in the incentive constraint in the acid rain game, so the pooling of incentive constraints reduces the likelihood of cooperation. One can think also of counterexamples in which the spillovers between games are positive, increasing the likelihood of cooperation. We have more to say about this issue of intergame spillovers in the next section.

3. Overlapping Games

A. Preliminaries

Overlapping games may be treated at less length, since in a full information setting an overlapping game is analytically indistinguishable from a standard three-player noncooperative game. An overlapping game is a situation in which one player is engaged in two games each involving a distinct rival. Although the payoff accruing to one rival is not directly affected by the strategy of the other, their payoffs are linked indirectly by the fact that their common opponent is constrained to adopt the same strategy against both of them. The two rivals are concerned about one another's actions insofar as they influence those of their common rival, not because of any direct impact those

---

10. One can think of equally plausible examples that work the other way. For example, if output restriction by the United States and Europe, rather than expanding the market share of a third large exporter, leads to entry by a large number of smaller grain producers, this would reduce rather than increase the likelihood of cooperation.

actions have on one another. At the same time, the fact that their common rival has two opponents may profoundly affect the prospects for a cooperative solution.

This situation differs from a general three-player noncooperative game by the fact that direct interdependencies between two of the players are absent. Analytically, the two games are indistinguishable. Each rival of the player involved in both overlapping games must be concerned about the likely response of the other rival because that reaction will affect the behavior of their common opponent and therefore the entire vector of payoffs.[11]

This point can be illustrated by considering a noncooperative game in extensive form. The example presented here is a simple three-country extension of a two-country game from Eichengreen (1989). We proceed by reviewing the two-country case and then by introducing a third country and analyzing the fully interdependent three-country case, moving finally to an overlapping game.

Consider two countries (a and b) faced with the decision of whether to continue to adhere to an established international monetary system. One may think of each country, having previously maintained a fixed exchange rate, as deciding whether to devalue. To avoid the complications introduced by the "nth country" problem, we concentrate on gold-standard-like systems in which each country declares a parity against a common numeraire (gold).[12]

By assumption, countries derive benefits from participation in the international monetary system and incur costs upon defection. These might be thought of as transactions costs associated with the existence of more than one currency (analogous to extra costs of interstate trade in the United States if there existed 50 state monies floating against one another). All countries incur a cost with any one country's defection, so systemic stability has the character of an international public good. A country will choose to incur the cost of systemic instability when it is less than the stimulus to exports to be obtained through currency devaluation.

Each country (indexed i) is assumed to choose between the current exchange rate E_i and a devaluation of size dE. Assume a constant world output

---

11. Thus, an overlapping game is a general form of the "two-level" or "gamma" games discussed by Putnam (1988) and Axelrod (1987). In each of those cases, the overlapping player, generically a national executive or agent negotiator, plays against a foreign counterpart and also against a domestic opponent, either a legislature with subsequent ratification rights and thus an ex post veto or a public whose support is required for reelection and thus appears as a maximand in the executive's utility function. In both cases the salient feature of the model is that the two separated players interact only through their strategic interactions with the overlapping player.

12. The nth country problem is that only $n - 1$ exchange rates link the currencies of n countries, since the exchange rate is the *relative* price of two national currencies.

Q divided equally between the two countries at the start of play.[13] Each country can use beggar-thy-neighbour exchange rate policy to increase its share of world output, where α is the response of output to exchange rate changes:

Two player symmetrical game

$$Q = Q_a + Q_b \tag{1}$$

$$Q_a = (1/2)Q + \alpha(E_a - E_b) \tag{2}$$

$$Q_b = (1/2)Q - \alpha(E_a - E_b). \tag{3}$$

In addition, traders are assumed to incur a cost p when either country changes its exchange rate, defecting from the international monetary system. International monetary stability is assumed to be a pure public good. Each individual, regardless of country, suffers equally if one country devalues. The cost to each country totals $(1/2)p$. If both countries devalue, each suffers a penalty of p.

Countries move in alphabetical order. The game repeats infinitely to eliminate the arbitrary incentive to defect that would otherwise be offered the last to play. Country a first decides whether to devalue, raising its exchange rate by dE. Country b then decides whether to retaliate with a competitive devaluation of equal size.

There are two cases depending on the sign of $\alpha dE - (1/2)p$. This term can be interpreted as the benefits of devaluation αdE without retaliation net of the costs $(1/2)p$. If the costs exceed the benefits, neither country devalues. If the term is positive, the benefits of unilateral retaliation exceed the costs. Devaluation without retaliation improves the payoff to the devaluing country, while devaluation with retaliation leaves it worse off. But whenever $\alpha dE - (1/2)p$ is positive, the home country also prefers to retaliate, because the benefits to the country that moves second of reversing its initial loss of competitiveness are greater than the costs of additional monetary instability. Since retaliation is guaranteed, neither country has an incentive to defect, and cooperation results.

We now introduce a third identical country c. The case with most in common to the two-country example is that of full interdependence, in which

---

13. We focus throughout on the case of countries of equal size. Eichengreen (1989) and Alt, Calvert, and Humes (1988) explore the implications of differences in size for the strategies adopted.

each country plays against the other two. Each country loses output when either of its trading partners devalues and gains output from both when retaliating. Residents of each country suffer a "public bad" p when one of the three changes its exchange rate.

Three player symmetrical game

$$Q = Q_a + Q_b + Q_c \qquad (1')$$

$$Q_a = (1/3)Q + \alpha[E_a - (1/2)E_b - (1/2)E_c] \qquad (2')$$

$$Q_b = (1/3)Q + \alpha[E_b - (1/2)E_a - (1/2)E_c] \qquad (3')$$

$$Q_c = (1/3)Q + \alpha[E_c - (1/2)E_a - (1/2)E_b]. \qquad (4')$$

Players move in alphabetical order. The critical condition is the sign of $\alpha dE - (1/3)p$, which differs from the two player game only by the substitution of $1/3$ for $1/2$ (the reciprocal of the number of countries). If $\alpha dE - (1/3)p$ is negative, devaluation without retaliation does not pay. If positive, devaluation without retaliation pays but so does retaliation. Since retaliation will be elicited by defection, leaving the defector worse off, no one has an incentive to defect. As before, cooperation results.

B. Cooperation in Overlapping Games

We are finally prepared to analyze the overlapping game in which a and c both are directly affected by the actions of b but not by those of one another. One can think of this as an exchange-rate or tariff game in which two countries have a common trading partner but do not trade with one another.

Three player overlapping game

$$Q = Q_a + Q_b + Q_c \qquad (1'')$$

$$Q_a = (1/3)Q + \alpha[E_a - E_b] \qquad (2'')$$

$$Q_b = (1/3)Q + \alpha[E_b - E_a] + \alpha[E_b - E_c] \qquad (3'')$$

$$Q_c = (1/3)Q + \alpha[E_c - E_b]. \qquad (4'')$$

a and c incur the cost p only when they themselves or b defect, while b incurs p when any of the players defect. The decision facing c is the same as in the three-player game above: if $\alpha dE - (1/3)p$ is negative, then the costs of retaliation exceed the benefits; but if $\alpha dE - (1/3)p$ is positive, defection by b elicits retaliation.

Knowing c's response, what does b do? And given b's choice, what does a prefer? There are three cases to consider.

Case 1. $\alpha dE > 1/3p$. Knowing that c will retaliate against b, will b retaliate against a? Yes, since b gains twice as much from devaluation as either of her trading partners while incurring the same costs. By devaluing her exchange rate, b can capture exports previously belonging to both a and c. But knowing that both b and c will retaliate, a realizes that devaluation will elicit retaliation that leaves all the players worse off. Similarly, b realizes that both a and c have an incentive to retaliate, leaving b worse off. In this case, moving from a fully interdependent to an overlapping game has no implications for cooperation.

Case 2. $(1/6)p < \alpha dE < (1/3)p$. Since $\alpha dE - (1/3)p$ is negative, a has no incentive to defect and c no incentive to retaliate. But b, which can beggar both of its neighbors, still has an incentive to defect. Since b is engaged in two overlapping games where the incentives to defect are reinforcing, overlap makes cooperation less likely.

Case 3. $\alpha dE < (1/6)p$. In this case, the costs of devaluation, unaccompanied by retaliation, exceed the benefits even for b. a and c have the same incentive as before to adhere to the system, while now even b has no incentive to defect. In this range, moving to the overlapping game has no implications for cooperation.

To summarize this example, moving from a simple to an overlapping game can induce a fundamental change in outcomes, in this instance reducing the incentive for the overlapping player to cooperate (here, if $(1/6)p < \alpha dE < (1/3)p$). The specification, intended to analyze international monetary relations, is readily reinterpreted as a noncooperative tariff game, suggesting that similar conclusions would emerge from a variety of international economic applications.[14] Yet it is also possible to develop counterexamples in which the existence of overlapping games increases the costs of defection, enhancing the incentive to cooperate.[15] The message of this section is that overlapping

---

14. In this context, our conclusion regarding overlapping games confirm the results of Johnson (1954) and Conybeare (1987), who found that large countries who are likely to be the central players in overlapping tariff games are the most likely to defect from a free-trade system.

15. Consider a defense game among three symmetric NATO countries:

Three player symmetrical game

$Q_a = (1/3)Q - [E_a - (1/2)E_b - (1/2)E_c]$
$Q_b = (1/3)Q - [E_b - (1/2)E_a - (1/2)E_c]$
$Q_c = (1/3)Q - [E_c - (1/2)E_a - (1/2)E_b]$

games can profoundly affect the strategy adopted by the overlapping player, in directions that hinge on the structures of the component games.

4. An Application: The European Gas Trade

In this section we show how the analysis of linkage can be used to analyze trade and strategic policy in Europe. The case we study is one in which several political allies, the NATO countries Norway, the Netherlands, Germany, and the United Kingdom, play a contribution game subject to the free-rider problem. However, some of those NATO countries (Germany, United Kingdom) depend on a rival, the Soviet Union, for supplies of natural gas while competing with each other as consumers. The other NATO countries (Norway, Netherlands) compete directly with each other and the Soviet Union as producers of gas and have a buyer-seller relationship with their political allies.

Leaving aside for the moment the role of the United States, we can treat the European gas and security games as two asymmetric parallel games among five nations. In one, the security game, four members of an alliance play a contribution game to provide the common good of mutual defense. In the other, the gas trade, two allies compete with a third rival outside the NATO framework as suppliers of natural gas to the remaining two allies. The question is what difference the existence of these parallel games makes for the prospects of cooperative outcomes in each. Specifically, how does the existence of the gas trade affect the abilities of the alliance members to guarantee contribution and secure defense? How do alliance politics affect the possibilities for collusion and contracting among trading partners and competitors in the gas game?

Taking first the simplest possible subset of the larger game, imagine that two countries—say, the Netherlands and Norway—are involved in parallel games of gas trade (as competing suppliers) and security (where they seek common defense through mutual contribution). Assume that if played in isolation the gas game would be played cooperatively but the NATO game would not. Then, as in the acid rain example of section 2, cooperation in the gas game could spill over into the NATO game, enabling them to reach a mutually advantageous agreement over contributions. Alternatively, it is possible that the incentives not to cooperate in the NATO game could spill over to

---

where Q_i is an index of country i's national security net of cost paid by domestic citizens, and E_i is security expenditures by country i. To make the analogy with the game in the text transparent, a country is assumed to reap \$0.50 of security benefit from each \$1 expenditure by an ally. In addition, each country is assumed to feel more secure by $(1/3)p$ if it pays for (controls?) more than one-third of the alliance's *defense* expenditure. This game is a mirror image of that in the text. Hence moving from the three-player symmetric game to its overlapping counterpart can increase the incentive of the overlapping player to cooperate.

the gas game, discouraging the Netherlands and Norway from coordinating their supply contracts.

Since the Soviet Union is not one of the NATO allies, we can treat it as an extraneous player in the gas game, analogous to Australia in the aircraft and grain trade example of section 2. From that example, we know that the introduction of an extraneous player will either increase or decrease the tendency for parallelism to produce cooperative spillovers depending on the exact structure of the game, and in particular on the externalities created by cooperation among players in both parallel games. Assume that Norway and the Netherlands have incentives to cooperate in the gas trade but wish to avoid contributing to NATO. Cooperation over gas could take the form of agreements to restrict output and raise prices, reducing the burden of NATO contributions. To determine the likely extent of spillovers in that case it is essential to recognize the existence of the extraneous player, since the Soviet Union as well can choose to expand sales (raising its market share) or reduce them (cooperating in taking advantage of the higher price). If the Soviet Union were inclined to increase sales, this would discourage any cooperative spillover to security from gas, and the incentives for Norway and Holland to cooperate in the gas game would be reduced. Alternatively, if by raising prices Holland and Norway shift market share toward the Soviet Union, it may have less to gain by undertaking price cuts (there being less of a residual market to capture) and so the extraneous player may be induced to cooperate as well.

The rest of this section extends this model to an empirical analysis of gas trade and alliance politics in Europe. It shows how the desirability of cooperating over gas can provide incentives to cooperate in security. It shows how institutions in the gas game—public corporations, enforceable long-term contracts—have effects that spill over into the security game, making it possible to provide the public good of defense more effectively. Thus, this game illustrates the possibility that linkage allows sanctions and selective benefits to be carried over from one arena into another.

Until now we have spoken of cooperation as though it were a "yes-no" sort of thing, without considering the extent and distribution of the gains from cooperation. Empirically, we shall see that a range of feasible prices and quantities are cooperative equilibria of the gas game. In what follows we also attempt to show how parallelism affects which of a variety of cooperative equilibria will emerge. In other words, we argue that not only does linkage affect incentives to cooperate, but it can affect the *distribution* of benefits from cooperation.

In order to say both what effects the parallel existence of a security game has on the outcomes in the gas trade, and whether cooperation in the gas trade carries over into the security game, we proceed as follows. We first offer a brief stylization of the security game. We then present a game-theoretic treatment of the gas trade and speculate about what degree of cooperation might emerge in the absence of security considerations. (There would probably be some, though the asymmetry of size of the competing European producers will affect its form.) Finally, we consider how the existence of a parallel security game along the lines we stylize would affect the outcome of the gas game, in terms not only of cooperation among the allies, but also of the distribution of benefits among the players.

A. The Security Game

The various European buyers and sellers of gas play a parallel game of international security. Alliance politics are complicated by the presence of an extraneous player, the United States, which does not appear directly in the European gas trade, but for whom the extent of Soviet involvement in the gas trade, and of European dependence on Soviet energy supplies, is a foreign policy concern.[16]

A defensive alliance is a contribution game among the allies. Games like these frequently fail to produce cooperative outcomes through free-riding consequent upon lack of enforcement.[17] We consider three players: Norway,

---

16. The United States was involved throughout the late 1970s and early 1980s in the alliance politics of the gas trade, trying to dissuade alliance partners from participating in pipeline construction with the Soviet Union and trying to persuade them to accept a voluntary ceiling on imports from that source. The history of the alliance politics, and particularly of the relationship between American domestic politics and American success in persuading its allies to go along with anti-Soviet energy initiatives, is carefully chronicled in Jentleson 1986. His analysis makes it clear that the United States was increasingly unable to impose its wishes, either because the Cold War threat had receded, its prestige had declined, or because Congress would not go along with costly sanctions. Jentleson's analysis thus treats the United States as playing a Putnam/Axelrod type of overlapping game in alliance politics, trying to persuade its allies to accept initiatives which subsequently require Congressional approval (or public support), which frequently turn out not to be forthcoming.

In fact, complex interdependencies of the energy market limit the ability of the United States to formulate clear alliance strategies. Naturally, if there were no Soviet "threat," increased Soviet gas imports to Europe at low prices would be a means to increase overall trade. However, increased US-Soviet tension could make West European governments agree on a ceiling on the share of Soviet gas in their markets, for reasons of foreign policy, but this creates expanded market shares for Algeria and/or Norway and invites the Soviet Union to maximize revenues by increasing prices rather than volumes. Moreover, the American strategy of trying to restrict Soviet imports by maintaining tension in East-West relations is also limited by a foreign policy game among US–USSR–Middle East. Any increase in tension in the Middle East produces European reluctance to buy Algerian gas and promotes the demand for Soviet gas since either Algeria or the USSR must supply Europe or leave the field to the price-inelastic North Sea suppliers. This interdependency—that is, that Middle East tension would increase demand for Soviet gas in Europe—presents further strategic alternatives to the USSR.

17. In addition, each nation can be thought of as involved in two overlapping games over contributions, one with alliance partners (where all agree on the desirability of mutual contribu-

the USSR, and West Germany. To represent the idea that these three players are engaged in two parallel games, imagine that Germany and Norway are allies A_1 and A_2, both of which are "small" countries capable of defending themselves but incapable of seriously threatening the other countries. These two small allies are threatened by a larger country, the Soviet Union *(H)*. Both small countries will thus be prepared to invest in their own defense, and their fates depend both on their investments and on the extent to which the larger country invests in its military strength. Let us stylize one round of the game as follows. Ally 1 decides whether to pay one unit for defense or pay nothing; then the large country decides whether to increase military spending by one unit or not, and then the second ally decides. If H invests, then any ally *not* investing forfeits three units to H while any ally who *does* invest forfeits nothing. If H does not invest, there are no forfeits regardless of the A's behavior. (Payoffs to H from the case where both allies do not invest could be made larger without altering the results below, at least in the one-shot case.)

Consider one play of such a game, whose normal form appears in table 1. There is a Nash equilibrium in which A_1 invests while H and A_2 do not. If A_1 invests, then H has nothing to gain by investing, since if H invests, A_2 will as well, and there will be no gain to H from investing. Were A_1 not to invest, H would, since some net benefit is guaranteed. But A_1 always loses by not investing, and so A_1 will always prefer to invest. Nevertheless, the result is that A_1 bears all the costs of defense. Its financial commitment thus grows as the game is repeated. Assume that it will ultimately be unable to afford its defense. This of course will leave A_2 in the undesirable situation of facing a wealthier H alone, but, within this noncooperative security game structure there is nothing much it can do about it. Thus A_2 faces the prospect of having to match investments with H in a financial war of attrition.

This outcome is not implausible in the European security game. Were it to obtain, neither Germany nor Norway would be likely to fare well in the security alliance. Whichever has to decide to invest first cannot prevent subsequent free-riding by the other ally. The question is whether parallelism with the gas game, in which the players are firms and legal enforcement and long-term contracting is possible, offers the possibility of spillovers ameliorating

tions) and one with domestic interest groups (where the cost of contributions and/or side payments will be compared with other political concerns beside security). Thus, looking for instance at Norway's security dilemma, it involves the Norwegian government both in its relations with NATO partners and in relation to the USSR, at the same time involving domestic interests in an overlapping game. The domestic game needs to incorporate complex interactions in the Norwegian Parliament, where investment plans formulated by bureaucrats and proposed by ministers are reviewed by multi-party committees on which regional representation is strong. North and South, military and economic demands collide here. The only consensus is that the outcome is very expensive. We will abstract from the domestic game, restricting our attention to the international side.

TABLE 1. Security Game in Normal Form

Strategies			Payoffs		
A_1	H	A_2	$(A_1,$	$H,$	$A_2)$
I	I	I	(0,	0,	0)
I	I	N	(0,	1,	−2)
I	N	I	(0,	−1,	0)
I	N	N	(0,	1,	1)
N	I	I	(−2,	1,	0)
N	I	N	(−2,	6,	−2)
N	N	I	(1,	1,	0)
N	N	N	(1,	1,	1)

Note: Strategies are to Invest or Not. Payoffs are normalized to the (I, I, I) case.

the noncooperative play of the security game. If it does, then similarly we need to see whether the desire for cooperation in defense affects the disposition to cooperate in gas. To resolve these questions, we first have to look at the gas game in isolation, and then consider the effect of linkage.

B. A Model of the European Gas Game

The European natural gas market has grown considerably over the last thirty years. In 1985, the total consumption of natural gas in Western Europe was approximately 216 bcm (billion cubic meters), of which 34 percent was delivered from the Netherlands, 14 percent from the USSR, 12 percent from Norway, and 9 percent from Algeria. Details of sales, consumption, and reserves are given in table 2. The large consumers are West Germany, the Netherlands, Italy, France, and the United Kingdom, who together account for about 90 percent of West European consumption. In most countries the wholesale gas trade is at least partly nationalized, with distribution companies exercising near-monopoly power. With the exception of British Gas, European wholesale buyers frequently negotiate purchase agreements jointly. With a declining domestic resource base, these companies rely increasingly upon external gas supplies and derive an advantage from bargaining together.

On the supply side, three countries, Algeria, Norway, and the Soviet Union, each have reserves with lifetimes of at least 70 years at current replacement rates, which enable them to supply the entire substitution (buyers' domestic shortfall) market as well as a large part of any expansion market.[18]

---

18. The Netherlands has recently reentered the export market, apparently to provide limited volumes of gas above existing contracts until the year 2000, probably on a peak-load basis. They, like the UK, which could conceivably become a small-scale exporter, have reserves likely to last about twenty years at present rates.

TABLE 2. Production and Consumption of Natural Gas in Europe

Production and Reserves

	Reserves 1/83	% World Reserves	Product 1982	R/P	Exports '82 (Europe)	
USSR	34,500	40	500	69	58	(28)
Norway	1,440	2	25	57	24	(24)
Netherlands	1,515	2	68	22	35	(35)
UK	633	1	38	17	0	(0)
	Reserves 1/85	% World Reserves	Product 1985	R/P	Exports '82 (Europe)	
USSR	42,500		650	65		(28)
Norway	2,900		27	107		(24)
Netherlands	1,900		74	26		(35)
Germany	176	—	17	10	2	(2)

Consumption and Imports

		Imports and Source				
	Consumption	Total	NL	Norway	USSR	Algeria
1979						
Germany	57	36	23	6	9	
UK	45	8		8		
Oth. Eur.	175	50	30	6	11	5
1982						
Germany	49	31	14	7	10	
UK	47	11		11		
Oth. Eur.	114	54	19	6	18	9
1985						
Germany	47	35	16	7	12	
UK	54	13		13		
Oth. Eur.	115	59	19	7	18	10

Note: Units are bcm. Some data from Hoel, Holtsmark, and Vislie 1987, 4, quoting BP *Review of World Gas.*

Negotiations on prices and quantities are controlled by government or government-owned companies. Since only four countries export on a large scale (the three above plus the Netherlands, which has smaller reserves[19]), there is scope for cooperation and collusion among sellers.

---

19. As the importance of Dutch gas diminishes, USSR and Norway should dominate the supply side, especially in West Germany, unless Algerian gas is brought in. Reduced tension between Western Europe and the Islamic world would make Algerian gas a better substitute for Norwegian and Soviet supplies, whereas continued unrest in the Middle East and concerns about oil supplies will make Algerian gas a less acceptable substitute. At the moment, however,

However, the difference in costs and reserves among the producers is considerable. The consumption-weighted average retail price for gas consumed by Continental Europe in 1984 was $5.70/mcf (thousand cubic feet), corresponding to a wholesale import price averaging somewhere between $3.60 and $4.00/mcf. Norway's gas production costs may be as much as four times those of the USSR. Thus, even allowing for transportation, the minimum marketable price for the USSR is about $1.50/mcf, while Norway's approaches $4.00. Such differences have led some to suggest that cooperation may take place under the "hegemonic" leadership of the Soviet Union, the largest, lowest-cost, most price-elastic supplier.[20] We return to such considerations below.

The gas game explicitly analyzes the strategies of three (or more) players—at a minimum the United Kingdom, Continental Europe, and Norway. Such models in fact have been proposed by Lorentsen and Roland (1985) and Hoel, Holtsmark, and Vislie (1987). Assuming that bargaining among a small number of players results in enforceable long-term contracts for delivery of gas, Hoel, Holtsmark, and Vislie formulate the game as a two-buyer, two-seller cooperative game, for which they identify the core of Pareto-efficient solutions. They model the demand and supply of gas to the year 2000 as follows. Demand is approximated, at the current real price, by assuming an annual real growth rate of 2.5 percent and an income elasticity of demand for gas of 0.8 (lower in France and the Netherlands because of more intensive competition from other fuels). Price is a function of the estimated demand for gas, exogenously given domestic supplies, and gas imported from other sources. The game is assumed to take place between two sets of players, buyers N_b and sellers N_s. Sellers' profit function is of the form $\Pi_i = \Sigma(p_{ij} - q_{ij})x_{ij} - C_i(\Sigma x_{ij})$ where p is price per unit from seller i to buyer j, q is a constant unit transportation cost, and x is the quantity delivered, so that total production of seller i is $P_i = \Sigma_j x_{ij}$ and the total cost of extraction is $C_i P_i$, with extraction costs constant regardless of destination and a capacity ceiling assumed. Buyers by contrast have payoffs $P_j = B^j(\Sigma x_{ij}) - \Sigma p_{ij} x_{ij}$ where the

---

Algerian gas is piped to France and Italy, and thus affects Norwegian calculations only through the joint decisions of the European gas buyers. Even though it thus constitutes an overlapping game—and there is an asymmetric, directly dependent parallel game in oil—we shall omit concerns about Algerian gas from the rest of this analysis, and focus only on the Soviet-Dutch-Norwegian producers' interaction.

20. Demand for supplier differentiation plus a small price elasticity of demand will tend to produce high prices, low volumes, and the threat of entry against the USSR. This gives an incentive to cooperate on the supply side. Incentives to cooperate are lessened by gas' higher price elasticity, though price may not be sensitive to volume changes, which implies incentives toward volume competition. Oil by contrast is less elastic and price is highly responsive to volume changes, so there are stronger incentives to cooperate to stabilize the market.

benefit function B is the area under the linear demand curve (a quadratic in x_{ij}). The core then contains all feasible outcomes in which a coalition of buyers and sellers receives at least as much as they could without cooperating.

The Hoel-Holtsmark-Vislie analysis is restricted to four players, the two buyers ("Continent" and UK) and two sellers (USSR and Norway). While Norway sells to both Continent and UK, USSR sells only to Continent. In our terminology this is an overlapping game, since all the players do not trade with each other. This is because there is no pipeline from USSR to UK: thus USSR adds nothing to the interaction of Norway and UK, while UK adds nothing to the interaction of Continent and USSR.[21]

The core of the gas game contains a range of price vectors. Outcomes in the core are more or less those in which the USSR produces up to its capacity constraint and sells the output to the Continent, with Norway picking up residual trade on the Continent, at a minimal profit, while trading to mutual benefit with UK but on a small scale. The majority of benefits of the gas trade accrue to the USSR and the Continent. The first three columns of table 3 give an example of results calculated from the Hoel-Holtsmark-Vislie model. They show the midpoints of the vectors of prices and payoffs in the core, under the assumption of a binding capacity constraint on the USSR. The USSR sells 70 bcm on the Continent at $140 million/bcm, or about $4.00/mcf, making $3.8 billion after production and transport costs. Norway sells 17 bcm on the Continent but makes very little profit on the sale. It is able to sell a further 21 bcm to the UK at a higher price, taking in a total of about $600 million.[22] UK also derives little benefit from the gas trade. Within the core, USSR could get from $2.40 to $4.50/mcf for its gas, and the price is not greatly affected by Norway's assumed capacity production level. Continent on the other hand benefits from increased Norwegian capacity but also from increasing access to (potentially cheaper) Soviet gas. In any case the main rents are shared by USSR and Continent though the net payoffs to each depend on what prices result from bargaining over contracts.

C. The Role of Linkages

Recall that when the stylized security game was played in isolation, in equilibrium whichever ally—Germany or Norway—had to contribute first would

---

21. For simplicity, the Netherlands is assumed to take on the role of a residual producer which does not enter the market strategically; that is, the game models the gas market net of Dutch exports.

22. We have not calculated the integral under the demand curve to evaluate the rents to the Continent under this outcome, but they are probably on the order of $6 billion, and, since Germany imports 1/3 of the gas imported from USSR on the Continent, we place its rents at $2 billion.

TABLE 3. Quantities, Prices, and Payoffs in the Gas Game

	q	p	Π	q	p	Π
USSR	70	140	3.8	48	165	3.8
Norway	17	140	0.1	39	165	1.1
to						
UK	21	170	0.6	16	175	0.5
Continent	87	140	6.0	87	165	4.0

Note: Quantities are in bcm, prices in $millions/bcm. Payoff calculations ($billions) are explained in the text.

be unable to guarantee alliance contributions from the other. Most likely Germany would have to "go first" and would end up financing the alliance alone, since Norway, with smaller resources, would be unable to sustain NATO alone. In fact, however, Norway has recently made considerably expensive investments in the military security of the high North, where Norway comes closest to Russian military installations, at least in part owing to its NATO commitments (Jervell 1987). The question is whether the parallel play of these two games allows the allies to avoid the destructive war of attrition which could be a result of the security game.

Consider the situation in which the gas game described above is played in parallel with the security game. Define a unit investment in defense as the commitment to spend $1 billion. We may place either Norway or Germany in the role of A_1, with the USSR as H. In the cooperative framework of the security game, A_2 will not wish to provide assistance to A_1.[23]

How would the parallel existence of the gas game affect this result? The structure of the gas trade, dominated by public corporations with a large degree of central control permits governments to take initiatives unavailable to them in the security game.[24] Parallelism means that free-riding in the security game produces retaliation in the gas game as well. Thus, free-riding by Norway as A_2 can be punished by Germany's freezing Norway out of the Continental gas trade. Similarly, Norway as A_1 can invest in security only when Germany has contracted for enough gas to make Norway's domestic defense affordable.

Essentially, recognition of parallelism permits governments to choose a gas price cooperatively, which alleviates the financial problems inherent in the

---

23. For instance, even if A_2 "wished" to assist A_1, one could assume that any alliance commitment made by A_2 would be subject to subsequent ratification and thus could not be guaranteed at the time A_1 must commit to making defense investments.

24. For example, the French Government in 1981 took the initiative in the gas deal with Algeria in order to improve political relations between the countries.

noncooperative security game. Furthermore, reliance on public firms in the gas trade brings in courts and the possibility of enforcement of multiyear contracting, so that the security "negotiator" gains the ability to make side payments without going back to the legislature for ratification and without the problem of dealing with potential political fallout from actions of private firms. So in this way the institution of dominant public firms in the gas trade creates enforcement and agency possibilities without which the security game would be played noncooperatively.[25]

How is the play of the gas game affected by recognition of parallelism? The solution to the parallel gas game would have the Continental buyers restrict their purchases of gas from the Soviet Union in order to induce greater Norwegian gas production and sales to the Continent.[26] This would cause the price of gas to rise, but would create greater profits for the Norwegians, financing their security investments. We simulate the Hoel-Holtsmark-Vislie model under the assumption that Continent restricts itself to purchasing about 25 percent of its gas from the Soviet Union. Table 3, columns 4–6 show the resulting prices and quantities under this assumption, again taken from midpoints of the respective vectors.

The price of gas on the Continent has risen to $165 million/bcm, or $4.71/mcf. At this price, under the quantity restriction, USSR can sell 48 bcm, again taking home $3.8 billion. Notice that this gives the Soviet Union the same rent as before: since these equal rents are obtained at a lower depletion rate, the USSR should favor this outcome, ceteris paribus. Norway sells 39 bcm at the same price, earning $1.1 billion, though in consequence its sales and profits from the UK trade have to fall owing to the binding Norwegian supply constraint. At this higher price, Continental rents are reduced by quantity times price difference, or $25 million times 87, a reduction of about $2 billion, of which again Germany's share is about one-third. The assumption of parallel play results in an outcome in which the USSR is no worse off, West Germany pays about $0.7 billion in foregone rents vis-à-vis the gas game played in isolation, and Norway takes in an extra $1.5 billion in rent, sufficient to pay for its defense policy. Presumably, if Continental buyers behaved this way, it would be because the cost in foregone rents is less than

---

25. If the energy trade contained only private firms, incentives might be structured which would allow the requisite side payments to take place. But reliance on private firms would create formidable agency problems for governments, who would be unable to observe all private actions, or to know firms' balance sheets, and thus could not observe the actual distribution of rents.

26. Clearly, such a ceiling need not have its origins in international politics. Regardless of alliance relations, to reduce the risk of seller collusion and to avoid dependence on a single supplier, buyers have an interest in keeping a large number of suppliers in the market, even at higher short-term cost.

the long-run costs of losing an alliance partner threatened by the security game in isolation.

The parallel game analysis could be taken a step further, though we lack the necessary data. The 25 percent ceiling on Soviet gas imports modeled above was an example of a possible choice. But if the security game is being played in parallel, and the price of gas is actually chosen by Continental players in order to eliminate Norway's free-riding by financing its security problem, then recognition of parallelism restricts the equilibrium outcomes within the core of feasible prices which the gas bargainers can reach. The outcome should be at the price where Continent makes the minimum contribution consistent with Norway's just financing its defense commitment, at no further cost to the USSR. If the Continental buyers recognize the parallelism between gas and security, a smaller contribution would serve no purpose and thus be wasted. Given our assumptions about the origins of the linkage between games, there is also no reason other than Norway's bargaining success for Continent to choose a price above that at which Norway survives the security game. We don't have the data on defense costs necessary to solve the Hoel-Holtsmark-Vislie model for this outcome, but it seems likely to be a point between the two sample outcomes listed in table 3.

Play in two parallel games in this case has two consequences. First, the cooperative play of the gas game permits spillovers into the noncooperative play of the security game. If governments could make enforceable international bargains at will, problems like the security dilemma would not arise. In this case the widespread presence of public corporations in gas enables central control and ameliorates the agency problem that dealing with private firms would create. Second, parallelism constrains the equilibrium solution to the gas game. While the gas game would probably be played cooperatively in any case, recognition of the parallel security game gives bargainers reason to choose particular cooperative outcomes in the core. Thus, in general, analysts of linkage can not only find that it permits cooperation to occur where it otherwise might not, but also how much cooperation might appear and what form it would take.

5. Conclusions

In this essay we have tried to give substance to the notion of issue linkage and to apply the concepts of parallel and overlapping games to the European natural gas industry. Both parallel and overlapping games are simplified representations of the more complex underlying game among many players, which is rendered tractable by the imposition of restrictions or limitations on the set of available strategies. In parallel games, the restriction is on the number of players rather than the number of games. In overlapping games, the restriction is on the dimensions along which the players interact.

In the case of the European gas trade, the underlying game involves five players, US–USSR–Continent–Norway–Middle East, and is played over two arenas, defense and energy, one of which, the energy game, itself is played over two commodities, oil and gas. This detail would imply a game of formidable complexity. But we can stylize the overlap in defense as the absence of direct interaction between Middle East on the one hand and Norway and the Continent on the other, and utilize the concept of an overlapping game. Similarly, in the gas game there is no direct play between US and the other players, and—at least until the pipelines envisaged to connect Norway and France under the Troll deal are complete—no direct play between Norway and Middle East. Without this sort of simplification through restriction, which produces a set of smaller, linked three- and four-player parallel and overlapping games, there would be no hope of making the gas/defense game analytically tractable.

The implication of our analysis is that a conventional economic treatment of the West European gas market, focusing on supply, demand, and price elasticities, risks conveying a static and incomplete picture. It ignores decision makers' awareness of long-term strategic interests and risks, and overlooks the political dimension of international gas trade. Thus, a benefit of considering linkage in this arena is to take steps to integrate the security problem with the energy game. It would be equally erroneous, however, to rely exclusively upon a political analysis of the West European gas market, for important economic interests are at stake for both buyers and sellers. Thus, our perspective complements Jentleson's analysis by increasing the role of explicit interdependencies derived from the gas trade. Indeed, "the development of the West European gas market should be seen as the outcome of a bargaining game, where economic interests and political factors interact and where long-term considerations interact with more immediate preoccupations" (Noreng 1987, 18).

Our analysis has been built on an array of simplifying assumptions, for the most part including complete information and a static structure. Once one moves beyond complete information, the possibilities for analysis multiply rapidly. The "grim-trigger strategy" assumption is no longer a compelling way of modelling retaliation, and the investigator must choose from among a wide range of "more forgiving" alternatives. Linkages can take on the characteristic of one-way mirrors: a player's moves in one arena may be observable by players outside that arena (whose own counter-moves may or may not be reciprocally observable), allowing learning to take place between plays. Such repeated overlapping games of incomplete information can be characterized by informational "linkage" or "isolation," depending on whether the results of one iteration become common knowledge to all players on all subsequent plays or remain the knowledge only of the player involved (Fudenberg and Kreps 1987).

Models of this sort allow the gas example to be extended to considerations of hegemonic advantage based on reputation or leadership in the sense of asymmetries of size and information (Alt, Calvert, and Humes 1988). All solutions to the linked game in section 4 involved significant rents to the Soviet Union, which has by far the largest gas reserves in Europe. Indeed, in spite of low costs, Soviet gas has recently been imported in West Germany at a premium vis-à-vis the price received by the Norwegians (Austvik 1986).[27] Modeling the Soviet presence in both the gas trade and the security arena might cast light on the relative importance of structural advantages (reserves, price elasticity of supply) versus political alliances (for example, Norway's position in NATO) in producing price premiums in the gas trade.

Finally, it is important to acknowledge that the parallel and overlapping structure of games is not simply a datum to which countries react. If, for example, the pooling of incentive constraints due to the parallelism of games increases the probability of cooperation in a particular instance, then governments may invest in the creation of structures or institutions of parallelism in order to increase the scope for cooperation. What strategies would dominate when structures are endogenous we cannot even begin to speculate.

REFERENCES

Abreu, Dilip. 1988. "Infinitely Repeated Games with Discounting: A General Theory." *Econometrica* 56:383–96.
Alt, J., R. Calvert, and B. Humes. 1988. "Reputation and Hegemonic Stability: A Game-Theoretic Analysis." *American Political Science Review* 81:445–66.
Austvik, O. 1986. "Political Gas Pricing Premiums: The Development in West Germany 1977–1985." Norwegian Institute of International Affairs, No. 359.
Axelrod, Robert. 1984. *The Evolution of Cooperation*. New York: Basic Books.
Axelrod, Robert. 1987. "The Gamma Paradigm for Studying the Domestic Influence on Foreign Policy." Manuscript.
Bernheim, B. Douglas, Dan Peleg, and Michael D. Whinston. 1985. "Coalition-Proof Nash Equilibria, I: Concepts." Manuscript.

---

27. While up to 1978 Soviet gas was imported into Germany at a 25 percent discount compared to Norwegian gas, since 1980 it has sold at par or at a premium approaching 25 percent.

Bernheim, B. Douglas, and Michael D. Whinston. 1986. "Multimarket Contact and Collusive Behavior." Manuscript.

Buiter, Willem, and Richard Marston, eds. 1985. *International Economic Policy Coordination.* Cambridge: Cambridge University Press.

Bulow, Jeremy I., John D. Geanakoplos, and Paul D. Klemperer. 1985. "Multimarket Oligopoly: Strategic Substitutes and Complements." *Journal of Political Economy* 93:488–511.

Conybeare, John. 1987. *Trade Wars.* New York: Columbia University Press.

Cooper, Richard. 1986. "Trade Policy is Foreign Policy." In *Trade Policy in the United States,* ed. Robert Stern. Cambridge, Mass.: MIT Press.

Crawford, Vincent P. 1987. *International Lending, Long-term Credit Relationships and Dynamic Contract Theory.* Princeton Studies in International Finance No. 59. Princeton: Princeton University Institute of Financial Economy.

Denzau, Arthur, William Riker, and Kenneth Shepsle. 1985. "Farquharson and Fenno: Sophisticated Voting and Home Style." *American Political Science Review* 79:1117–34.

Edwards, Corwin D. 1955. "Conglomerate Bigness as a Source of Power." In *Business Concentration and Price Policy,* NBER Conference Report. Princeton: Princeton University Press.

Eichengreen, Barry. 1985. "International Policy Coordination in Historical Perspective: A View from the Interwar Years." In *International Economic Policy Coordination,* ed. Willem Buiter and Richard Marston. Cambridge: Cambridge University Press.

Eichengreen, Barry. 1989. "Hegemonic Stability Theories of the International Monetary System." In Richard Cooper, Barry Eichengreen, C. Randall Henning, Richard Holtham and Robert D. Putnam, *Can Nations Agree? Issues in International Cooperation.* Washington D.C.: The Brookings Institution.

Fudenberg, Drew, and David Kreps. 1987. "Reputation in the Simultaneous Play of Multiple Opponents." Manuscript.

Fudenberg, Drew, and Jean Tirole. 1986. "Noncooperative Game Theory for Industrial Organization: An Introduction and Overview." Department of Economics, University of California, Discussion Paper No. 8613. Berkeley: University of California.

Gowa, Joanne. 1984. "Hegemons, IOs and Markets: The Substitution Account." *International Organization* 38:661–84.

Haas, Ernest B. 1980. "Why Collaborate? Issue-Linkage and International Regimes." *World Politics* 32:357–405.

Hardin, Russell. 1982. *Collective Action.* Baltimore: Johns Hopkins University Press.

Hoel, M., B. Holtsmark, and J. Vislie. 1987. "The Market for Natural Gas in Europe: The Core of the Game." Department of Economics, University of Oslo, Memorandum No. 13. Oslo.

Jentleson, Bruce. 1986. *Pipeline Politics.* Ithaca: Cornell University Press.

Jervell, S. 1987. "The Military Buildup in the High North." Manuscript.

Johnson, Harry G. 1954. "Optimal Tariffs and Retaliation." *Review of Economic Studies* 21:142–53.

Keohane, Robert, and Joseph Nye. 1977. *Power and Interdependence*, Boston: Little, Brown.

Keohane, Robert, and Joseph Nye. 1987. "Power and Interdependence Revisited." *International Organization* 41:725–53.

Lorentsen, L., and K. Roland. 1985. "Norway's Export of Natural Gas to the European Gas Market: Policy Issues and Model Tools." In *Macroeconomic Prospects for a Small Oil Exporting Country*, ed. O. Bjerkholt and E. Offerdal. Dordrecht: Martinus Nijhoff.

Noreng, O. 1987. "The West European Gas Gamble." Manuscript.

Nye, J. 1987. "Nuclear Learning and U.S. Soviet Security Regimes." *International Organization* 41:371–402.

Olson, M., and R. Zeckhauser. 1966. "An Economic Theory of Alliances." *Review of Economics and Statistics* 48:226–79.

Ordeshook, P. 1986. *Game Theory and Political Theory*. Cambridge: Cambridge University Press.

Putnam, Robert. 1988. "Diplomacy and Domestic Politics: The Logic of Two-Level Games." *International Organization* 42:427–61.

Rogoff, Kenneth. 1985. "Can International Monetary Policy Coordination be Counterproductive?" *Journal of International Economics* 18:199–217.

Scott, J. T. 1982. "Multimarket Contact and Economic Performance." *Review of Economics and Statistics* 64:368–75.

Selten, R. 1975. "Re-examination of the Perfectness Concept for Equilibrium Points in Extensive Games." *International Journal of Game Theory*. 4:25–55.

Shepsle, Kenneth. 1985. "Cooperation and Institutional Arrangements." Manuscript.

Stern, J. 1984. *The International Gas Trade in Europe: The Policies of Exporting and Importing Countries*. London: Gower.

Tabellini, Guido. 1983. "Accommodative Monetary Policy and Central Bank Reputation." Manuscript.

Tsebelis, George. 1987. "Nested Games: Political Context, Political Institutions, and Rationality." Manuscript.

Tsebelis, George. 1988. "Nested Games: The Cohesion of French Coalitions." *British Journal of Political Science*. 18:145–70.

CHAPTER 5

Empirical Analyses of the Determinants of Protection: A Survey and Some New Results

Stephen V. Marks and John McArthur

Empirical analyses of the political economy of protection in the United States and other countries have multiplied dramatically over the past twenty years, spurred by breakthroughs in the measurement of rates of protection and by progress in theoretical political-economy or public choice analyses of policy-making processes. This paper evaluates the various approaches to the empirical analysis of the determinants of the level and incidence of protection. It focuses mostly on work done by economists, but considers related contributions from political scientists.

The primary contention of this paper is that although these analyses of foreign trade interventions have provided useful descriptions of the factors associated with a higher rate or incidence of protection, few have been able to shed much light on the nature of the process by which policy makers decide to intervene on behalf of domestic producers. We argue that there is a need for more focused analyses of the policy process that provide insights about the objective functions held by policy makers, and the constraints upon their actions. In an effort to provide a new and useful perspective along these lines, we present original results in one of the more recent areas of inquiry.

Three general approaches to analysis of the determinants of protection can be identified. The earliest analyses of the political economy of protection in the United States examined cross sections of industries in an effort to link the level or incidence of protection to arrays of industry characteristics. More recent studies have looked at the macroeconomic determinants of the overall amount of protectionist pressure or protection provided over time in a single country, or at the structural determinants of the level of protection across

We thank Keith Acheson, David Card, Karen Hult, Miles Kahler, Daniel Mazmanian, Edward Ray, Rodney Smith, Thomas Willett, and Mark Zupan for helpful comments and discussions, and Jung-Sik Kim for efficient research assistance.

countries at a given point of time. Even more recently there have been efforts to identify the determinants of patterns of votes in the U.S. Congress on trade policy legislation. Each of these areas of inquiry offers potential insights and pitfalls that we will try to identify in this essay.

Though the focuses of these efforts have varied considerably, many can be placed within a general public choice framework: (1) The main goal is to explain the level or incidence of import protection provided by governments. (2) The decision-making unit is the individual. For simplicity individual behavior is sometimes aggregated into a net outcome, just as the net demands of consumers in a market may be represented by a market demand function. Such aggregation may result in the loss of detail, but this loss is assumed to be of a lower order of importance than are the forces represented explicitly. (3) A critical concern is with the process by which competing pressures get translated into policy. In the absence of direct measures of the pressures that interests are able to bring to bear on trade policy makers, these studies employ proxies for the basic socioeconomic determinants of these pressures. (4) There is some variation in the implicit or explicit assumptions about the objective functions of the relevant actors. This is especially important for the objectives of policy makers. Do policy makers seek only to maximize their chances of remaining in power, or do they put weight on other objectives as well? Are these other objectives narrow and self-interested, or broader and based on some conception of the public interest? (5) Institutional structures and constraints are viewed as inherently important. Indeed, one of the newer fields of microeconomics is concerned with the reasons for the emergence of both public and private institutions. However, economists have typically put much less emphasis on the role of institutions than have political scientists. (6) Many, but not all, of these studies focus on domestic political economy, and thus tend to attach less importance to the effects of alliances or national security considerations, international norms like those embodied in the General Agreement on Tariffs and Trade (GATT), or the behavior of other states.

The first part of this paper reviews the previous literature in the three major areas we have identified. We first survey in very general terms the literature on cross-industry determinants of protection. Since many of these works are less recent and have been reviewed elsewhere, we will examine only a few important contributions and make some rather broad generalizations. Next, we examine more closely the literature on the sources of aggregate protectionist pressure or levels of protection. Finally, we survey in detail the recent empirical literature on the determinants of congressional voting behavior on trade policy legislation. Along the way, we critically evaluate each of these three strands of literature, partly as motivation for the original analysis that follows.

The second part of this paper applies the economic approach to analysis of congressional voting behavior to the vote on automotive products domestic content legislation in the U.S. House of Representatives in 1982. We first describe the domestic content bill and review the results of an earlier analysis of the House vote. We then present estimation results based upon a more complete characterization of the constituent interests relevant to congressional voting on trade policy. Specifically, we take into account the roles of exporters and other interests opposed to protectionist trade policies. We also compare the predictive power of alternative measures of the ideological positions of members of the House. Finally, we exploit an unusual opportunity provided by the 1982 domestic content vote, which was held during a lame-duck session of the Congress. It can be argued that lame ducks and returnees are exposed to different levels of political opportunity cost, so there is a basis for a natural experiment on the effect of opportunity cost on legislator voting. This is important because it provides us with a perspective on the actual process by which trade policy is determined and, in particular, on the nature of the objectives of legislative policy makers.

Determinants of Protection Across Industries

The earliest empirical works on the determinants of protection across industries in the United States were concerned with the question of whether U.S. import policies tended to favor labor or capital.[1] These works rested on the intuition of the Stolper-Samuelson theorem of the distributional effects of trade policy—that protection of an industry from import competition tends to favor the factor of production used relatively intensively by the industry. Some studies found a significant link between labor intensity and the rate of tariff protection for the output of the industry. Travis (1964) cited this result as one explanation of the famous Leontief paradox: U.S. import substitutes could tend to be more capital-intensive than U.S. exports because trade barriers systematically kept labor-intensive products from the U.S. market.

A voluminous literature that followed tried to identify the more general influences on the rate or incidence of protection across industries.[2] Within much of this literature, a variety of alternative models of the political

---

1. See Vaccara 1960; Balassa 1965; Basevi 1966; Ball 1967; Travis 1964, 1968; Balassa, Guisinger, and Schydlowsky 1970; Constantopoulos 1974; Cheh 1976; Stone 1978; and Clark 1980.

2. See Cheh 1974; Pincus 1975, 1977; Baldwin 1976; Caves 1976; Fieleke 1976; Bale 1977; Helleiner 1977; Riedel 1977; Saunders 1980; Ray 1974, 1981a, 1981b, 1987; Finger 1981; Finger, Hall, and Nelson 1982; Baack and Ray 1983; and Ray and Marvel 1984. Pugel and Walter (1985) survey corporate positions on recent trade policy decisions, and relate these to characteristics of the firms and industries in which they reside. Milner (1988) draws upon qualitative evidence on firms in a variety of U.S. industries in the 1920s and 1970s, and argues that the extent of international economic ties is one influence on the trade policy preferences of individual

economy of trade policy have been implicitly or explicitly pitted against each other. Two general sets of questions can be identified:

1. Do policy outcomes favor private interests, some notion of the public interest, or a combination of the two? Specifically does protection tend to be higher for industries that meet reasonable efficiency or equity criteria for support, or for those that are able to wield political clout to their advantage?

Pincus (1975) poses this issue in particularly sharp terms. He questions the casual historical observation that tariffs in the United States have commonly been levied on infant industries, a result that can be at least partly rationalized in efficiency terms. Pincus proposes the alternative hypothesis that interest group pressures determined historical patterns of tariffs. He finds support for his alternative from evidence on the pattern of tariff rates in 1824, but does not rule out the more traditional view.

2. Given a private interest view of the world, does the capacity of an industry to gain protection rest simply on its capacity to deliver votes from its own ranks, or does it reflect a more general set of determinants of the political influence of the relevant interest groups?

The empirical analysis of Canadian tariffs by Caves (1976) marks the start of debate on this issue. He considers two general political-economy models. The first is an "adding-machine" model that assumes maximization of voter support to be the dominant policy motive. The second is an "interest-group" model that stresses the costs and benefits of collective action by industry groups, relative to their opponents, as well as their ability to elicit favor from the political process because of public sympathy or other inherent advantages. Caves finds generally greater support for the interest group model.

Baldwin (1984) provides a detailed taxonomy of models and of the general empirical results in this cross-industry literature. We will summarize this literature simply by looking at the kinds of variables that may influence the pressures for protection and the willingness of a government to provide it.

---

firms. Much of this literature is focused on the United States. However, the World Bank published a series of applications to other industrial countries. Among these are the works by Cable and Rebelo 1980, Glismann and Weiss 1980, Tharakan 1980, Verreydt and Waelbrock 1980, Anderson and Baldwin 1981, Lundberg 1981, and Grilli and La Noce 1983. Cline (1984, appendix C) provides a detailed chronological survey of many of the contributions to this literature, along with a summary of the stylized facts obtained.

Industry Variables Associated With Protection

Comparative Advantage. The greater the inherent comparative advantage of an industry temporarily threatened by imports, the greater is the likelihood that it will eventually regain its competitive position internationally. Thus we should expect industries with stronger comparative advantage to demand less protection. Variables that have been used to reflect comparative advantage include value added per worker, the quantity of physical or human capital per worker, and average wages in the industry.

Import Penetration. The higher the share of imports in total consumption of the products of an industry, or the lower the industry trade balance, the more likely is it that import competition will be identified as the source of its difficulties, and thus the more likely is it that the industry will seek protection. A potential problem is that high import shares based primarily on geographical comparative advantage are natural for many U.S. industries like cocoa and chromium. This suggests that *changes* in import shares over time may be most relevant in political-economy terms.

Export Dependence. The higher the share of industry output produced for export, the more likely is the industry to fear foreign retaliation against its exports, and thus the less likely is it to demand protection.

Labor Adjustment Costs. The greater are the adjustment costs anticipated for an industry confronted by dislocation, the more likely are policy makers to grant it protection from import competition. Industries that enjoy inherent comparative advantage will eventually tend to regain their competitive edge, which suggests a prospect of lower adjustment costs if temporary dislocation occurs. Similarly, industries with high growth rates should be more able to absorb displaced workers, which also implies lower adjustment costs. On the other hand, industries that are labor intensive, or that have high proportions of unskilled and older workers, may experience greater adjustment costs.

Political Potency. Larger industries should be more powerful politically, in terms of the votes and dollars that can be mustered in support of their positions. The more concentrated the industry, the more readily should it be able to overcome the free-rider problems inherent in organizing for political action. Thus we should expect more concentrated industries to exert more effective pressure for protection. More concentrated industries may be less likely to command broad geographical support, however, and may be less likely to be viewed sympathetically by the public. Industries with labor-intensive production may wield more votes relative to total industry size. On the other hand, the lower are the wages of workers in the industry, the more likely is it to enjoy public sympathy. Similarly a decline in employment in an industry could generate greater public sympathy. Finally, if the buyers of its products are highly concentrated and can overcome their own free-rider problems in wielding political influence, there could be strong political resistance to protection of the industry.

Common Empirical Issues

The cross-industry literature has wrestled, with mixed success, with a variety of difficult conceptual and empirical issues.

(1) How to define industries at a level that is appropriate politically and economically, and for which data exist.

(2) Whether to measure the rate of protection as a nominal or effective rate. The nominal rate is simply the tariff rate that applies to the output of an industry, while the effective rate measures the rate of protection on value added, and thus accounts for any differences between the nominal tariff rate and tariff rates on inputs used by the industry. Effective rates are more relevant to the resource-allocation implications of an overall structure of protection, but nominal rates could be more relevant politically. It is hard for legislators to observe or understand effective rates of protection, and there are asymmetries in the sense that it may be more difficult politically to remove tariffs on inputs than simply to impose tariffs on the output of the industry.

(3) How to measure the effects of nontariff barriers to trade (NTBs), given the difficulties of identifying NTBs or of calculating their implicit tariff equivalents. The increasing importance of NTBs in the packages of protection provided, especially in ways that do not mirror the pattern of tariff levels across industries, makes this an especially serious problem. Earlier studies tended to use tariff rates and sometimes added the tariff-rate equivalents of quantitative restrictions and other NTBs. Other studies finessed this issue by using zero-one dependent variables to indicate the presence of substantial policy barriers to imports in an industry. Ray (1981b), Lavergne (1983), and others have separate equations for tariff and nontariff barriers, but this misses the determination of the overall level of protection for an industry and the possibilities for substitution of one form of protection for others.[3]

(4) How to account for inertia in the political process, given that tariff levels across industries depend to a very great extent on past tariff levels. Cheh (1974), Riedel (1977), and Marvel and Ray (1983) address this problem by looking at changes in tariff rates following the Kennedy Round of multilateral trade negotiations. Similarly Baldwin (1985) examines the determinants of the U.S. tariff rate reductions following the Tokyo Round of multilateral negotiations. Lavergne (1983) examines U.S. tariff changes in the

---

3. For a survey of works on the mode of protection, see the essay by William H. Kaempfer in this volume.

Kennedy and Tokyo Rounds, but also looks at the determinants of recent tariffs levels. He finds 1930 Smoot-Hawley tariff levels to be the main determinant of variations of levels of protection across industries. Lavergne suggests that economic and administrative adjustment costs, uncertainty about the effects of policy changes, and respect for the existing pattern of political property rights may create a bias in favor of the status quo. As he points out, however, his results may also simply mean that important omitted variables or industry-specific factors that influenced levels of protection in 1930 continue to do so today.

(5) How to avoid multicollinearity among the explanatory variables. Studies that have included a number of factors in eclectic fashion have generally ended up with weak results due to this problem. For example, the import penetration and export dependence of an industry tend to be correlated with direct measures of its comparative advantage. If all of these factors are included as explanatory variables, their estimated coefficients will tend to have high standard errors due to multicollinearity.

(6) How to sort out the causal relationships between import protection and variables like import penetration or industry wages, size, or growth. For example, not only will import penetration affect the capacity of an industry to obtain protection, but protection granted in the past will bear on the current level of import penetration. Past protection is in turn related to protection granted in the present, perhaps due to the systematic effects of economic and political variables omitted from the analysis.

(7) A number of economic analyses have viewed trade policy formation as a political market for protection, with the relevant interest groups on the demand side and public officials on the supply side.[4] However, the conceptual distinction between the demand and supply sides of the market has not carried over to the econometric analyses, which generally estimate a single equation relating trade policy outcomes to industry characteristics. Demand and supply behavior are thus convoluted in the coefficients estimated. Determinants of protection like industrial concentration, for example, could easily act on both sides of the market and with different signs: higher concentration might mean that an industry could organize more effectively for political action, but might also mean that the policy makers would be less sympathetic with its plight. The fundamental econometric problem is that there are few direct quantitative measures of the level of political activity undertaken by the interests most directly affected by trade policy. If measures of effort on the demand side were available, then there would be a much better opportunity to sort out the various demand and supply factors.

---

4. Hayes (1981) provides an insightful survey and critique of economic models of legislatures as markets, from the perspective of a political scientist.

General Evaluation

The works in this cross-industry literature have in general provided a useful and relatively consistent description of the industry characteristics that apparently favor protection. There has been less success, however, in identifying the nature of the political economy process that converts these factors into trade policy outcomes. One of the important issues about this process is whether policy makers simply react to competing interests so as to maximize their own probability of remaining in power, or whether they put weight on their own ideological views or on public-interest considerations that stand apart from their objective of remaining in power.

The cross-industry studies to this point have generally not been able to provide an answer. One reason is that there is considerable overlap in the empirical implications of alternative models. For example, labor adjustment costs could be important because the government is truly trying to minimize *economic* adjustment costs. On the other hand, the government could be trying to minimize the *political* costs of adjustment: higher economic adjustment costs would provide an industry with stronger incentives to seek protection, and labor could be a well-organized and influential interest group, or labor-intensive industries could simply have the votes. The typical proxies for labor adjustment costs, like the age of the work force and the percentage of unskilled workers, have their own liabilities. These proxies could reflect the public sympathy that an industry can generate rather than its adjustment costs per se.

In a provocative exception to this general limitation of the literature, Finger, Hall, and Nelson (1982) examine the dual process of less-than-fair-value (LFV) pricing and injury determinations by the U.S. government from 1975 through 1979. In response to an LFV petition by a domestic producer, the Treasury Department first determined whether the foreign product had been sold at less than fair value in the United States. (This determination is now made by the Commerce Department.) For cases in which there was an affirmative pricing determination, the U.S. International Trade Commission then determined whether such pricing had caused injury to the domestic producer. If the injury determination was affirmative, a duty to offset the subsidization or dumping was automatically imposed.

LFV pricing determinations were made on the basis of clearly defined technical criteria and could be appealed by the petitioner in federal court. In contrast, LFV injury determinations relied on much more ambiguous criteria and were not appealable. We thus might expect political considerations to be important, but only in injury determinations. This process provides a natural experiment on the role of institutional constraints on policy outcomes. The authors find substantial empirical evidence that technical factors dominate

LFV pricing determinations, but that both domestic and international political factors dominate LFV injury determinations. We could fuss over their proxies for politically and technically relevant industry characteristics.[5] However, their results are strongly suggestive that both institutional constraints and political factors play a role in LFV decisions.

Variations in Overall Levels of Protection

The apparent intensification of protectionist pressures in the United States and other industrial countries in response to macroeconomic turbulence over the past two decades created new interest in the relationship between trade policy and economic conditions. In addition dramatic changes in the international distribution of economic power in the 1970s led international relations theorists to examine the connection between the nature of the international regime and the overall pattern of protection across countries. Two general kinds of questions can be identified.

1. Within a country is foreign competition the main source of pressures for protection, or does the domestic business cycle independently cause additional variations in the pressure for protection? Is the extent to which protection is provided mainly sensitive to external pressures, or to the business cycle as well?
2. Do changes in the nature of the international system as a whole cause worldwide changes in the average level of protection? Can variations in the average level of protection across countries be better explained by their position in the international system, or by domestic factors? Of the domestic factors, are public, private, or bureaucratic interests more important?

Variations in Protection Within a Country Over Time

Takacs (1981, 1985) relates pressures for protection in the United States to the domestic business cycle and the international competitive position of the economy. She measures protectionist pressure as the total number of escape clause petitions filed with the U.S. International Trade Commission per year over 1949–79. The level of real GNP, the unemployment rate, and the capacity utilization rate are used to measure cyclical factors. The merchandise trade balance and the ratio of imports to GNP reflect international factors.

---

5. For example, the average wage rate of the industry is interpreted as one of the technical variables. However, it could also relate to political factors like public sympathy or the ability of workers in the industry to afford political action. The authors provide a spirited defense against these interpretations.

She controls for changes in U.S. trade law by using dummy variables to indicate changes in 1962 and 1974 in the stringency of the requirements for protection under the escape clause. She also includes the lagged success rate to reflect a potential "demonstration effect" that would encourage additional petitions.[6]

Due to the high degree of multicollinearity among the cyclical variables and among the trade-related variables, Takacs includes only GNP, one of the other cyclical variables and one of the international variables in each regression. She finds that the pressure for protection is negatively related to the level of GNP, the capacity utilization rate, and the stringency of the escape clause criteria; it is positively related to the unemployment rate and the level of imports relative to exports or relative to national output.

Takacs then examines how the number of *successful* escape clause petitions relates to economic conditions, and finds that the position in the business cycle does not affect the incidence of successful petitions for protection. On the other hand, the estimated effects of the trade-related variables turn out as expected. Changes in the stringency of the requirements for escape clause protection also had the expected effects on the number of successful petitions. Takacs concludes that although macroeconomic stress increased the pressure for protection over the sample period, it did not necessarily cause more protection to be provided.

Feigenbaum, Ortiz, and Willett (1985) criticize Takacs on two grounds. First, the *level* of GNP is not an appropriate indicator of cyclical changes and may act more as a indicator of the passage of time. In the protectionist pressure equation, if real GNP is replaced by a time trend, it turns out that the explanatory power of the model does not change significantly. If GNP is included in addition to the time trend, there is no significant gain in explanatory power. They conclude that there has been a significant tendency for protectionist pressure to decline over the postwar period, though this trend might have been reversed in recent years outside of the sample. Second, the trade legislation dummies are highly correlated with underlying economic variables and should not be viewed as strictly exogenous. Indeed, including both of these dummies robs all other explanatory variables of their significance.

The authors do not point out a related conceptual difficulty: if there is a sound reason to account for each of these changes in trade law individually, then *both* must be included in the equation in order to avoid omitted variables bias. In addition, although Takacs finds the lagged success rate to have a

---

6. Frey (1984) reports similar work by Magee (1982) on the determinants of U.S. aggregate protectionist pressure, measured by the number of dumping cases filed with the U.S. Customs Bureau from 1933 to 1979.

positive and significant effect on protectionist pressure, this could simply reflect autocorrelation in economic conditions rather than a demonstration effect per se.

Feigenbaum and Willett (1985) extend this work on protectionist pressures to account for the level of the real exchange rate, on the presumption that this will reflect the competitiveness of U.S. industries. It turns out that none of the international variables remains a consistently significant factor, although their signs are generally as expected. Since the domestic business cycle variables prove significant in almost all cases, their results suggest that domestic economic conditions are the dominant determinants of the overall pressure for protection.

These results should not be considered a definitive refutation of Takacs. First, the time period used by Feigenbaum and Willett is only 1963–81 due to limited data availability. Second, though it is reasonable to expect the real exchange rate to affect the competitive position of industries, using both *price* and *quantity* measures of international competitiveness seems to stack the deck against finding either one significant.

The dependent variable in these analyses—the number of escape clause petitions filed with the ITC each year—must equal zero or a positive integer no matter how weak protectionist pressures may be. Under these circumstances ordinary least squares estimates are inconsistent. This latter problem is addressed in recent work by Coughlin, Terza, and Khalifah (1989), who note that Poisson regression is the proper estimation technique in this case. For the period 1948–84, their estimation on this basis shows that protectionist pressure is significantly increased by cyclical downturns or by deterioration of the trade balance, and is significantly reduced if the inflation rate goes up. Both of the changes in U.S. trade law have significant effects and the expected signs: the stricter 1962 criteria led to a decrease in the number of petitions filed, while the weaker 1974 criteria led to an increase. The authors show that their results are sensitive to the econometric technique used and are highly supportive of the original results obtained by Takacs.

Economists have done most of the work in this area so far, but political scientists have also made recent contributions. Gallarotti (1985) develops a business-cycle model of tariff changes, which rests on the proposition that industries find the expected utility of getting protection to be higher during a contraction than during an expansion. The microeconomic foundations of this theory are rather weak.[7] However, Gallarotti does obtain empirical results

---

7. For example, Gallarotti (1985) draws upon the argument of McKeown (1984) that the abundance of entrants into an industry during an expansion will cause producer surplus generated by protection to be bid away rapidly, while the paucity of entrants during a contraction will cause it to be bid away more slowly. These assertions rely upon some sort of unmentioned inertia in the

generally consistent with the model. Historical data for Germany, the United States, the Great Britain show legislated tariff increases to be preponderant during periods of generally slow growth, tariff decreases during periods with higher growth rates. His detailed historical analysis of political economy in these three countries suggests that variations in growth rates provided at least a partial explanation of changes in tariff levels.

Finally, Magee and Young (1987) survey the political economy of protection in the United States in the twentieth century. Their main focus is on the determinants of the level of and change of the average tariff rate on U.S. imports across presidential administrations from 1900 to 1984. Their results suggest the importance of cyclical factors, like the unemployment rate, and of the terms of trade in manufactured goods, which reflects the international price competitiveness of U.S. producers.

Magee and Young also argue that inflation may rouse the opposition to protection: and they find a negative and significant relationship between the rate of inflation and the average tariff rate, and between the change in inflation and the change in the tariff rate. However, these results may be in part an artifact of their data. Many industries were protected by *specific* duties (a fixed dollar amount per unit) rather than by *ad valorem* duties (a percentage of the price) throughout the sample period. Given the infrequency of congressional passage of trade legislation and given the absence of automatic inflation adjustments for specific duties, inflation would *directly* erode the average tariff rate.[8] For example, decreases in the average tariff rate after passage of the Underwood-Simmons Tariff Act of 1913 were due in part to inflation brought on by World War I. Similarly increases in the average tariff rate after passage of the Smoot-Hawley Tariff Act of 1930 were due to deflation caused by the Great Depression.[9]

Magee and Young also examine the outcomes of antidumping cases filed with the U.S. government from 1954 to 1981. Their dependent variable is the annual proportion of cases decided in favor of the petitioner seeking protection. Magee and Young find that its determinants are generally similar to those of the average tariff rate. However, the effect of inflation is significant, but its sign is opposite the one predicted by their theory.

---

entry and exit process: economic theory suggests that entry (or exit) should continue if and only if it is profitable, whether conditions have changed due to the business cycle or due to changes in the rate of import protection.

8. This average rate is equal to total tariff duties divided by the total value of imports. See Lavergne (1983) for an analysis of the roles of inflation and specific tariffs in the determination of nominal and effective tariff rates across industries in recent years.

9. See Taussig 1931 or Ratner 1972 for details on U.S. tariff history.

Variations in the Level of Protection Across Countries

Krasner (1976) generated considerable interest with his theoretical and historical analysis of the connection between state power and the structure of international trade. He tests the hypothesis that the overall openness of international trade is positively related to the existence and ascendancy of a hegemonic power. Using both tariff levels and direct measures of the openness of international trade, he finds generally strong support for his hypothesis.

Conybeare (1983) adopts an ambitious alternative strategy to explain variations in aggregate levels of protection: he uses average nominal tariff rate data for 35 countries in 1971 to examine the causes of variations in the average level of tariff protection across countries.[10] Conybeare posits four alternative political-economy models. (1) In an "international system" model, the level of protection is related to national power and size. (2) In a "rational governmental economic actor" model, it is related to the level of economic development and to the rate of growth.[11] (3) In an "intragovernmental politics" model, it is related to government expenditure relative to GDP, the extent of reliance on indirect taxation for revenue, and the degree of fiscal federalism. (4) In an "interest group politics" model, it is related to the ability of interest groups in the export- and import-competing sectors to take collective action.

Conybeare is careful to point out many of the problems of interpretation and simultaneity that arise in estimation of these models. Nevertheless, there is a general problem with his methodology. He does not formally test the validity of each model versus the others. On the other hand, his detailed interpretations of the signs of the coefficients of the explanatory variables suggest that the estimation results for each model are to be taken seriously. However, if a variable shown relevant in one model is not included in the others, serious omitted variable biases may result, though it may be hard to make sense of a comprehensive model due to multicollinearity problems.

For example, Conybeare concludes that the level of economic development, measured by GDP per capita, is the most important of the explanatory factors. In his interest group model, however, the level of protection is shown to be significantly negatively related to the commodity diversification of ex-

---

10. The time frame is actually 1958–71. He also examines similar data for 16 countries in 1902, and looks at changes in average worldwide tariff rates for manufactures between 1902 and 1971.

11. Conybeare (1983) argues that governments of nations at low levels of economic development may adopt infant-industry strategies in order to develop and diversify their manufactured goods production, and that instability of export revenues may create additional incentives to turn inward.

ports. He interprets this as evidence that the more highly concentrated national export sectors have difficulties in mustering broad support among voters to oppose protection, even if their free-rider problems for collective action are lessened.[12] An alternative interpretation is that countries at low levels of economic development tend to have exports concentrated in relatively few commodities *and* higher tariff levels.

This problem is compounded by his assumption that variations in tariffs across countries accurately reflect variations in protection of all sorts, including nontariff barriers to trade. This assumption seems to merit further empirical investigation, since, as Conybeare points out, there are substantial differences between developed and developing countries in the incidence of tariff and nontariff barriers to trade.[13] This implies that there could be serious biases in his results, if they are interpreted as applying to overall levels of protection rather than to rates of tariff protection alone.

General Evaluation

These general results on overall levels of protectionist pressure or on protection over time and across countries are useful as predictive tools and for descriptive purposes. However, the link between economic conditions and trade policy outcomes is presented at too high a level of aggregation to say much about the policy process. A variety of casual models of this link appear consistent with the limited empirical evidence available. For example, Takacs (1981) finds that policy rules are important, in the sense that the stringency of escape clause criteria seems to affect expectations about the probability of success of a petition, and indeed seemed to influence the actual success rate. But we could argue instead that changes in the rules were themselves endogenous responses to pressure, in which case the causation argument may be invalid.

Congressional Voting on Foreign Trade Legislation

In recent years, some empirical analyses have set their focus at a very different level, that of the individual policy maker. Specifically a number of studies by political scientists and economists have examined the voting behavior of members of the Congress on single votes or on bundles of votes. These studies

---

12. Conybeare (1983) concedes that the commodity diversification of trade is not an ideal measure of the collective action problem: more important is the extent of concentration within these traded-goods industries.

13. This could be explained by the heavy use of tariffs for revenue collection in developing countries; developed countries tend to rely more on NTBs that are less likely to incite negative reactions at home and abroad.

have emphasized the basic principal-agent relationship between legislators and their constituents.

In a world in which the political market worked perfectly, legislators would never be able to vote in opposition to the interests of a majority of their constituents. However, the existence of a variety of imperfections in electoral markets may allow legislators to put some weight as well on their own ideological views. Kalt and Zupan (1984) survey the theoretical public choice analysis of these market imperfections and provide a comprehensive set of references to earlier empirical works in this area.

In the analysis of congressional voting on protectionist policies, at least three general sets of questions emerge.

1. Do legislators make trade policy decisions only based on the pocket-book and ideological interests of their constituents, or do their votes also reflect their own ideological beliefs or other interests? If legislators do express their own views, is their willingness to do so sensitive to the perceived opportunity cost?
2. Are legislators influenced by monetary or other contributions from interest groups, or only by the interests of voters in their district or state?
3. How important is log-rolling within Congress on trade policy issues? Does political party affiliation play an important role in these voting decisions?

The first two questions roughly parallel those posed in the cross-industry literature. Since ideology might be defined as a view of the ideal society and of the best means to attain it, the first question can be viewed as a variant of the public interest versus private interest debate. The second question is pertinent to the debate over the nature of the pressures brought to bear on policy makers, and more generally to the technology of getting reelected.

Survey of Recent Works

Recent studies of the determinants of the pattern of votes on trade policy legislation in the U.S. Congress have provided mixed results, due in part to differences in the nature of the votes examined and to differences in the explanatory variables included.

Baldwin (1985) tries to identify the determinants of the pattern of votes in Congress on the Trade Act of 1974, which authorized the president to participate in the Tokyo Round of multilateral trade negotiations. A yes vote for the bill was interpreted as a vote generally in favor of trade liberalization. Baldwin uses probit analysis to relate opposition to the bill among members of the House and Senate to their party affiliation, campaign contributions from labor organizations opposed to the bill, and the percentage of employment in the district or state in import-sensitive and export-sensitive industries. For the House, he finds opposition to the bill related significantly to political party (+ [positively related] for Democrats relative to Republicans), union contributions (+), and import-sensitive employment (+). For the Senate, he does not include union contributions, but obtains otherwise similar results.[14]

Baldwin finds for both the House and the Senate that the percentage of district or state employment in export-sensitive industries is insignificant, and does not have the expected sign. This may be in part a function of his definition of export-sensitive (or import-sensitive) industries as those whose workers or managers testified in favor of (or against) the liberalization provisions of the trade act. Under this definition, only two export-sensitive industries were identified; this outcome might be expected, given the free-rider problems entailed in such lobbying efforts.

Tosini and Tower (1987) examine the determinants of the patterns of votes in the House and Senate on the Textile Bill of 1985. Their probit estimation relates voting for the bill to constituent interests, campaign contributions, and party affiliation. For the House, the statistically significant factors were the percentage of state employment in textiles and apparel (+), the percentage of state employment related to exports (− [negatively related]), the state unemployment rate (+), campaign contributions from companies and labor unions in the textiles and apparel industries (+), and the political party of the member (+ for Democrats relative to Republicans). All of these signs were as expected. For the Senate, the statistically significant factors were state employment in textiles and apparel (+), the state unemployment rate (+), and political party (+).[15]

General Evaluation

These two studies show a clear association between proxies for the prominence of interests in favor of protection and patterns of votes in the House and Senate. We would be surprised were this connection not to exist. We also see associations between campaign contributions, political party, and voting behavior. These results are generally supportive of an interest group model of political influence and are useful for predictive purposes. On the other hand, the link between congressional voting and campaign contributions or political

14. In the House these variables are significant at the one percent level, in the Senate at the five percent level. Baldwin (1985) also reports results of estimation in which the import-sensitive industries are included individually rather than in an aggregate.

15. All variables were significant at the five percent level, and some at the one percent level.

party affiliation is not totally clear in theoretical terms, and these results do not add to our understanding. Moreover, showing that private interests were apparently influential in the trade policy-making process does not imply that broader concerns were not important as well. Indeed, Baldwin explicitly admits of a role for such concerns in his theoretical analysis.

   In contrast to some other empirical analyses of congressional voting, the two studies do not use measures of the prior ideological positions of the members of Congress as predictors of their votes on the specific issues examined. However, as the next sections try to make clear, the existence of an empirical association between such past measures and specific votes cannot by itself demonstrate a role for ideology or public interest considerations. One way to verify the existence of such factors, however, is to examine how legislator voting responds to changes in political opportunity cost. If we find that members put less weight on constituent interests as opportunity costs fall, then we can argue that some objectives in addition to electoral support are being addressed.

The Domestic Content Vote of 1982

We now apply empirically the economic model of legislator behavior to the 1982 vote in the House of Representatives on automotive products domestic content legislation. The 1982 domestic content bill specified a schedule of minimum percentages of U.S. labor and parts costs required of firms selling passenger cars and light trucks in the United States. The House passed the bill—HR 5133, "The Fair Practices in Automotive Products Act"—by a 215 to 188 vote on December 15, 1982. Including those paired for and against the bill, the totals were 219 for and 192 against.[16]

   Coughlin (1985) performed a useful empirical analysis of this vote. As a benchmark for comparison with his results, given some minor differences in our data, McArthur and Marks (1988) replicate his probit estimation.[17]

   In his analysis, the dependent variable *vote* equals 1 for yes votes, and 0 for no votes. Three variables reflect constituent interests—the percentages of *auto employment* and *steel employment* in total employment in the district, and the state *unemployment rate*. These variables should have positive effects

---

16. This vote was largely symbolic. The bill faced an uphill fight in the Senate, and at a minimum would have had to be reintroduced in the next Congress. Even if it passed Congress, there was a virtual certainty of presidential veto. However, the vote had a high profile with the public, and members had to be concerned with its electoral implications, and we are confident that there are no *systematic* biases due to its symbolic nature.

17. The differences in the results are probably due to differences in our treatment of PAC contributions data. A complete description of all the data used in this paper, and of the sources from which they were obtained, is presented in an appendix.

on the likelihood that a member would vote for this bill. Included as control variables are *labor contributions*, the percentage of the member's political action committee (PAC) contributions made by labor PACs, and *political party*, a dummy variable that is 1 for Democrats, 0 for Republicans. Finally, to get at the role of legislator ideology, Coughlin includes the 1981 rating of each member by the Americans for Democratic Action (*ADA*). His estimation shows *auto employment, steel employment*, the *unemployment rate, labor contributions, political party*, and *ADA* all to have positive and significant effects on the probability that a member would vote for the bill.

In related work, McArthur and Marks (1988) emphasize the aspects of this vote related to the role of legislator ideology in voting decisions. In this paper we stress the most important aspects for U.S. trade policy, including the influence of exporters and other opposition interests on the policy process and the effect of political opportunity cost on voting decisions on trade policy by members of Congress. We examine the latter by means of an unusual opportunity presented by the domestic content vote: the vote was held during a lame-duck session of the Congress, and we observe significant differences in the behavior of lame ducks and returnees.

Voter Interests Versus Legislator Ideology

Coughlin (1985) adopts a parsimonious specification of voter interests, and omits several potentially important determinants of voting patterns for the domestic content bill. For example, he includes measures of interests in favor of the bill, but not of interests opposed to it. In the hearings held on the bill by the House Ways and Means Committee and Energy and Commerce Committee, however, the bill was strongly supported by the UAW and the AFL-CIO, but was opposed by almost all others who made statements about it.[18]

The big winners from the bill would have been workers not only in the automobile industry, but also in supplier industries that would have been protected by the bill.[19] To reflect more fully the extent of labor influence, we include the percentage of employees in the state who are labor union members. This variable reflects not only variations in labor interests across states, but is also indicative of the degree of union organization. We expect the sign of the coefficient of *union membership* to be positive.

The constellation of interests opposed to the bill was much more diffuse.

---

18. For details see U.S. Congress 1982a and 1982b. For coverage of the legislative history of the bill, see *Congressional Quarterly Weekly Report*, September 11, 1982, and December 18, 1982.

19. Grossman (1981) and Findlay and Wellisz (1986) analyze the effects of domestic content policies of the sort proposed in this bill.

It included farmers, manufactured good producers, auto dealers, consumers, and longshoremen. Representatives of each of these groups testified against the bill in committee hearings. However, their overall lobbying effort in opposition to the bill fell far short of the effort made in favor of it by the UAW and the AFL-CIO. Public choice theory suggests that these more diffuse interest groups should have a limited influence on the policy formation process due to the free-rider problems inherent in information gathering and lobbying.[20] It is conceivable, therefore, that their interests were not taken into account by legislators for the domestic content vote. We consider in detail three opposition interests: farmers, manufactured good exporters, and consumers.[21]

As high-profile exporters who have been subject to foreign retaliation in recent years, U.S. farmers strongly opposed the bill. A major concern was that passage of the bill would hinder progress in negotiations on Japanese farm import barriers and on European Community farm export subsidies and other agricultural policies. In addition, manufactured goods producers lobbied against the bill. The prospect of foreign retaliation was cited, as was the potential effect on labor costs. Representatives of the Reagan administration noted that a measure like the domestic content bill that substantially limited U.S. imports would in the long run necessarily harm export industries.

Baldwin (1985) suggests that exporters view the likelihood of retaliation as highest for measures that support "generalized protectionism" rather than for ones that would protect specific industries. One could argue the reverse, however. General measures that allow greater scope for protectionism in the process of trade policy formation have no clear victims. In contrast, a measure that actually protects a particular industry will have identifiable losers abroad. If the industry is sufficiently large and the import barrier substantial, the measure can have repercussions throughout the economy.

To account for the interests of exporters, we have included two variables: *export employment* is the percentage of the state civilian labor force directly involved in production of manufactures for export, and *farm employment* is the percentage of the district labor force employed in farming, fisheries, or forestry. The more important are export industries to a state or district, the lower should be the probability that the legislator will vote for the bill, all else equal. Thus we expect the coefficients of these two variables to be negative. Note that these measures of export interests are more direct than those used by Baldwin, who only included industries that lobbied for the 1974 trade bill. We find the broader measure more attractive since lobbying is only one of the

---

20. See, for example, Downs 1957, Olson 1965, or Stigler 1971.
21. Destler and Odell (1987) examine the role of free-trade interests in the United States in recent years.

ways that industries express their positions: their support via campaign contributions and at the polls can be important as well.

Finally, to allow for the possibility that members of the House responded to objective measures of automobile consumption by their constituents, we include the number of *auto registrations* per 1000 residents of the state. We expect the coefficient of this variable to be negative. However, consumers were the most diffuse of the interest groups that would have been affected by this bill and, therefore, might be expected to have the least influence on the Congress.

We employ two alternative measures of the ideological positions of the members of the House in 1981. The *ADA* rating is the classic measure of ideological stance along a traditional right-left spectrum, and reflects votes on key social, economic, and foreign policy issues. On the other hand, McArthur and Marks (1988) argue that these dimensions of the issue space may not all map consistently into voting on trade policy issues.[22] Thus as an alternative we use the ratings compiled by the *National Journal* on votes in the House on economic issues, *NJE*. This rating in 1981 was determined mostly by votes on general federal expenditure and tax policies. Therefore, it can be defended as being relatively well insulated from the special interests that would be affected by foreign trade legislation.

Results of estimation using *ADA* appear in column 1 of table 1, results using *NJE* in column 2.[23] The estimated coefficients and t-statistics of the constituency variables are remarkably similar in the two equations, and all have the expected signs. The signs of the constituency variables included originally by Coughlin are stable, but the effects of the state *unemployment rate* no longer appears significant. Of the variables we have added, the coefficients of *union membership* and *export employment* are significantly different from zero at the five percent level, but the coefficients of *farm employment* and *auto registrations* are not significantly different from zero.

The apparent significance of *export employment* is striking, given the public-choice prediction that diffuse opposition interests should tend to be less influential than interests that gain from trade intervention.[24] This is consistent

---

22. See Poole and Daniels 1985 for an exhaustive list of the interest groups that have rated members of the Congress, and the time spans for which these ratings are available.

23. The statistics shown in the table include the maximized value of the log-likelihood function and the percentage of votes correctly predicted. A yes vote is "predicted" if the predicted probability of a yes vote by a member exceeds 0.5.

24. We have examined some alternative proxies for state export employment. All were measured relative to the civilian labor force in the state. (This stands in contrast to Tosini and Tower [1987], who look at employment directly related to manufactured exports relative to total manufacturing employment in the state, contrary to their own assertion. We find their measure

TABLE 1. Determinants of Domestic Content Votes (1 = Yes, 0 = No); Probit Coefficients and t-Statistics

Independent Variables	1 (ADA)	2 (NJE)	3 (ADA)	4 (NJE)
Constant	−1.95613	−2.37748	−2.53177	−3.00662
	(−1.89450)	(−2.25576)*	(−2.37273)*	(−2.75034)**
Auto employment	0.11663	0.10935	0.12047	0.11425
	(2.87908)**	(2.69135)**	(2.94532)**	(2.78117)**
Steel employment	0.06846	0.07118	0.08227	0.08727
	(2.25852)*	(2.34729)*	(2.60170)**	(2.76075)**
Unemployment rate	0.05114	0.06378	0.05962	0.07570
	(1.12847)	(1.40100)	(1.29767)	(1.63107)
Union membership	0.03897	0.03467	0.04064	0.03547
	(2.55923)*	(2.27981)*	(2.62933)**	(2.28186)*
Export employment	−0.36307	−0.37625	−0.39066	−0.41129
	(−2.11612)*	(−2.16676)*	(−2.23752)*	(−2.31609)*
Farm employment	−0.04244	−0.03046	−0.04960	−0.03801
	(−1.47587)	(−1.03442)	(−1.70215)	(−1.27402)
Auto registrations	−0.00019	−0.00011	−0.00028	−0.00024
	(−0.10927)	(−0.06165)	(−0.16292)	(−0.13808)
Labor contributions	0.01563	0.01299	0.01596	0.01290
	(3.01959)**	(2.65797)**	(3.05799)**	(2.61749)**
Political party	0.95747	0.35056	0.90641	0.24428
	(4.07072)**	(1.18449)	(3.82263)**	(0.80909)
Ideological rating	0.00673	0.02114	0.00665	0.02239
	(1.58146)	(3.75359)**	(1.54827)	(3.90460)**
Reelected to House			0.67453	0.73563
			(2.85717)**	(3.07732)**
Number of observations	411	411	411	411
Percent correctly predicted	81	82	82	84
Log likelihood function	−168.80	−162.65	−164.50	−157.66

* Significant at the 5 percent level
** Significant at the 1 percent level

less than ideal, since in some states manufacturing employment is a very small percentage of total employment.) We find that if manufacturing employment devoted to production of goods for ultimate export from other states is added to our original measure, there is apparently not as strong an effect on votes by the members of the House. If non-manufacturing employment related to manufactured exports is added as well, the link becomes even weaker. One might conjecture that the most directly involved workers have the strongest stake in the outcome and may be more highly visible to the legislators.

with the view that exporters are concerned about, and influential opponents of, trade restrictions that apply to specific industries, counter to the conjecture of Baldwin (1985).

The apparent insignificance of unemployment compared to the estimates by Coughlin can be readily explained. In 1982 the effects of recession were felt especially strongly in traditional industries with large labor unions, and state unemployment rates could have reflected the importance of rust-belt industries to the states. Moreover, economists have long rejected the claim that protection can yield sustained increases in employment overall, but emphasize instead that gains in protected industries tend to be outweighed by losses in other sectors of the economy. Thus, although members of Congress could have been concerned about employment, imposition of import protection might not have been viewed as a particularly good way to increase it. On the other hand, one of the objectives of the sponsors of the bill was to send a message that further Japanese investment in production facilities in the United States would be appreciated. Some members could have been pushing for new automobile plants to be built in their districts.

The signs of the coefficients of labor contributions, political party, and *ADA* are all plausible, given our casual priors. However, political party is significant in column 1, but not in column 2. In econometric terms this suggests that multicollinearity between *NJE, labor contributions,* and *political party* is reflected in smaller coefficients and *t*-statistics for the latter two in column 2. In more general terms, *NJE* may provide a better representation than *ADA* of the differences between the economic views of members of the two political parties.

Finally although the correlation between *ADA* and *NJE* for the members in this sample is a substantial 0.8558, it turns out that their usefulness as predictors for the pattern of votes on the bill is dramatically different. Using *NJE* rather than *ADA* raises considerably the overall predictive power of the equation, as indicated by the maximized values of the log likelihood, and suggests that ideology could be an explanatory factor of some importance.[25] Thus, if prediction of trade policy votes is our main concern, the economic ideology measure appears to be much more useful than the more general

---

25. Since the domestic content bill would have strongly favored labor, or at least the members of the UAW and of the industrial unions of the AFL-CIO, we have also performed this estimation using the 1981 AFL-CIO ratings compiled by *Congressional Quarterly*. The correlation between this measure and *ADA* is 0.8273; the correlation between it and *NJE* is 0.9269. Use of the AFL-CIO rating improves the ex post predictive power of the equation even more than does use of *NJE:* the percentage of votes correctly predicted is 84 percent, the value of the log-likelihood function is -153.33, and the *t*-statistic for the measure of ideology is 5.59231. However, use of the AFL-CIO rating is problematic on the grounds that it may represent "capture" by a special interest group more than "ideology" per se.

rating. However, both of our measures of ideology can be viewed at least in part as functions of unmeasured voter interests or of capture by special interest groups, and the issue-specific measure of ideology may simply be mirroring omitted factors that are especially relevant. Therefore, the role of ideology per se cannot be determined simply by reference to the significance of these coefficients.

This issue of the role of legislator ideology has generated recent debate among economists. Peltzman (1984) argues that if constituent interests are given an appropriate empirical representation, econometric analysis will show them to play a dominant role in congressional voting, while party affiliation and ideology will play small roles. However, Peltzman (1985) finds persistent regional differences in congressional voting in the twentieth century, even after controlling for regional economic differences. He argues that one must be "agnostic" about whether the implied ideological component of congressional voting generates utility for voters or legislators or both.

Political Opportunity Costs and Voting Behavior

Peltzman (1984) and Kalt and Zupan (1984, 1990) adopt the perspective that political constraints affect legislator voting primarily on bundles of issues, rather than on specific votes, and are enforced at the time of reelection. For issues as prominent as the domestic content bill, however, political constraints can be important at the time of the vote itself. Along these lines, Nelson and Silberberg (1987) compare the voting decisions of members of the U.S. Senate on 12 defense expenditure bills in 1982. They assume that the cost of voting against constituent interests is higher for specific defense expenditure bills than for general ones in which the winners and losers are not as easily identified. Their estimation results suggest that ideology exerts a greater influence on voting for general bills than it does for specific ones. Nelson and Silberberg argue that this supports the hypothesis that senators vote more ideologically the lower is political opportunity cost.[26]

We analyze the role of political opportunity costs in legislative voting based on an experiment of a different sort. Table 2 reveals significant differences in the patterns of votes cast by returnees and by lame ducks on the domestic content bill. Of the 347 returnees, 194 (57 percent) voted for domestic content; of the 64 lame ducks, only 22 (34 percent) voted for it. Using a

---

26. Similarly Schneider and Frey (1988) argue that the democratic governments will focus on staying in power only if their reelection prospects are low or if the election is near, but will otherwise pursue their ideological goals.

TABLE 2. Domestic Content Voting by Returnees and Lame Ducks

	Number of Votes		
Vote	Returnee	Lame Duck	Total
No	150	42	192
Yes	197	22	219
	347	64	411

chi-square test, we can easily reject the hypothesis that electoral status and voting behavior were independent.[27]

Public choice analyses have long recognized that there are a variety of political biases that favor the imposition of protection. For example, the benefits of import protection are concentrated, and the recipients of these benefits tend to be well organized. The costs are more diffuse, and those who are hurt by protectionist policies tend to have limited incentives or capacity to organize for collective action or to find out how their representatives voted.[28] Therefore, we tend to observe higher levels of protection for particular industries and a greater incidence of protection in the economy overall, than if all interest groups had identical capacities for collective action.

Analysis of decision making at the level of individual legislators rests on rather different considerations, however. Specifically it is reasonable to posit that the opportunity cost of voting on criteria other than electoral advantage is higher for those who have been reelected than it is for lame ducks: returnees will in general have a higher probability of wanting voter support in the future.[29] However, if there are behavioral differences between returnees and lame ducks—if those with higher political opportunity costs are more likely to vote for import protection—then there must be some factor or factors pulling members of Congress away from voting for the bill. Otherwise all legislators would simply seek the maximum electoral advantage, and we would not expect any systematic differences between returnees and lame ducks.

One such deterrent factor is the interest of the legislator as consumer. Since the bill had little chance of becoming law and the vote was mainly symbolic, this narrow pocketbook interest probably did not carry much

---

27. The chi-square statistic is 10.01, with one degree of freedom. The probability that this value could have occurred randomly in the contingency table is well below one percent.

28. For classic expositions of this problem, see Downs 1957, Olson 1965, or Stigler 1971.

29. The lame-duck problem can be viewed as a special case of the problem of electoral control in a political process in which politicians are finite-lived. For more elaborate models of the general problem, see Davis 1987 or Lott and Reed 1989.

weight. Logrolling factors could have been at work as well, and are considered below in some detail. Other factors could include the acceptance of the economic logic of freer trade or of the traditional broader foreign policy arguments against increased protection. In a statement to the House Ways and Means Committee, U.S. Trade Representative William E. Brock called the domestic content bill "the worst threat to our own prosperity and the international trading system to be put before Congress in a decade" (U.S. Congress 1982b, 25). Perhaps this message was appreciated by members of Congress. In that case, even a roll call that was acknowledged to be mostly symbolic could provide an important way for members to register their preferences for or against protectionism, given the background of interests of their constituents or financial contributors.

Political scientists have suggested that such considerations have had an important influence on Congress. Recent works by Pastor (1980) and Goldstein (1986) are especially supportive of this view. Destler (1980) analyzes in detail how Congress managed to include strong freer-trade provisions and to resist protectionist pressures in the Trade Act of 1974. Kindleberger (1975) asserts the importance of free trade ideology for the liberalization of trade policies in Western Europe in the nineteenth century. See Destler (1986) for further institutional evidence on recent congressional behavior in the trade policy area.

To examine the role of political opportunity cost in a way that controls for all other factors, we repeat our probit estimation with a dummy variable included to indicate whether the member had been reelected to the House in November 1982.[30] The results for *ADA* and *NJE* appear in columns 3 and 4 of table 1. Having been reelected is a significant, positive determinant of the probability of voting for the bill.[31] In both columns the coefficients and t-statistics of the constituency variables are stable. There are small shifts in the apparent significance of *political party* and *ideological rating*.

There is a potential causality problem with our interpretation of the role of lame-duck status in voting behavior: being a lame duck lowers the political

---

30. This variable equals 1 for reelected members, and is 0 otherwise. Three of the members who were not reelected won other statewide offices in November 1982. (One was elected governor of his state, one was elected state attorney general, and one was elected to the Senate.) Because these individuals would continue to be subject to local political pressures, we treated them as if they had been reelected to the House.

31. One could argue that lame ducks are in effect no longer politicians and are not subject to political constraints at all, so their behavior does not shed light on legislator behavior in general. We would respond that it may be useful simply to view lame ducks and returnees as being at two extremes in terms of political opportunity costs. We also take comfort that our result on the effect of lame-duck status is similar to one obtained by Tosini and Tower (1987), who find that the probability that members of the Senate would vote for the 1985 textile bill was negatively related (though not significantly) to the length of time remaining until their next election bid.

opportunity cost of ideological behavior, but being a lame duck and voting against domestic content could have both been characteristics of members who systematically failed to act in the interest of their constituents. Edward J. Ray suggests the term "lemons problem" to describe this phenomenon.

We can make an effort to evaluate the seriousness of this problem. First of all, the 1982 congressional elections were unusual for several reasons. New congressional district boundaries based on the 1980 census were imposed by state legislatures for the first time in the 1982 elections. In many states incumbents were forced to run against each other or found themselves in much less secure districts. The country was also in the midst of its deepest postwar recession, and the economic policies of the Reagan administration were under fire. Moreover, many Republican candidates who were swept into office by the Reagan landslide in 1980 saw their districts swing back to the Democratic party in 1982. Finally various scandals forced several members from office. For these reasons there was high turnover in the House in 1982.[32]

Of the 64 lame ducks who voted on the domestic content bill, 21 retired, 10 were defeated in bids for higher office, and 33 were beaten in reelection bids. Some of those who retired did so because the new district boundaries put them at a disadvantage, but in none of these cases was their own behavior in office a major issue. Of those who were beaten in their reelection bids, we can identify 15 whose own political positions were at issue; many of these were harmed at the polls by their steadfast support of Reaganomics.[33]

To determine whether this causality problem could have imparted an upward bias to the estimated effect of being reelected, we have rerun the equations shown in columns 3 and 4 of table 1 using two alternative samples: one that excludes the 15 members who were apparently beaten for ideological reasons, and one that excludes all 33 members who were defeated in their reelection bids. For both samples and for both ADA and NJE, the coefficients and t-statistics for being reelected turn out to be higher than in the full sample. Thus we conclude that reverse causality was not a serious problem in this case.

As an alternative measure of the effect of lame-duck status on voting behavior, we have derived the mean predicted probability that lame ducks would have voted for the bill, had they behaved as returnees did. Specifically we have estimated the voting equation for returnees only, and then formed mean predicted probabilities using these coefficients and the data for lame ducks. Using both ADA and NJE, we find that the actual probability that lame ducks would have voted for the bill is significantly below the probability

---

32. Jacobson (1987) emphasizes that losses by Republican incumbents in 1982 House elections would have been much higher, however, in the absence of the superior damage control carried out by the national Republican party.

33. These assessments are based primarily on the analyses in *Politics in America, 1984* (Washington, D.C.: Congressional Quarterly Press).

predicted by all other factors.[34] This suggests that lame ducks systematically voted against interests that returnees responded to.

Our potential explanations for these behavioral differences so far include only items that are in the objective functions of legislators and not in the objective functions of voters. Indirect electoral pressures could have played a role, however. Legislators who engage in logrolling may vote against the short-run interests of their constituents in order to provide them with a net long-run benefit. Only returnees would be able to obtain a future payoff from vote trading of this sort. Thus our result could reflect that returnees put more weight on long-run voter interests, rather than that lame ducks put more weight on their own ideologies.[35]

However, if we make the plausible assumption that the preponderance of logrolling pressure among Democrats was in support of the bill but among Republicans was in opposition, then we can make a stronger statement about the role of legislator ideology per se.[36] Table 3 presents separate estimates for the two parties, using the two measures of ideological position. From these estimates, we get t-statistics for being reelected of 2.73183 (with *ADA*) and 2.82121 (with *NJE*) for Democrats, and of 1.71468 (with *ADA*) and 1.73703 (with *NJE*) for Republicans. If our logrolling assumption is valid, then reelected Republicans would have extra incentives to vote against the bill, and reelected Democrats to vote for it. This suggests that the significance of ideology per se lies between these bounds. In any case legislators with lower political opportunity costs were better able to resist protectionist pressures.

The 1982 domestic content vote thus provided an unusual opportunity to examine the role of political opportunity cost in legislative voting. The apparent significance of political opportunity cost implies that members of Congress addressed objectives in addition to electoral support. We find it plausible that their behavior in the domestic content vote reflected at least in part the potency of free trade ideology in Congress.

Conclusions

Earlier studies of legislative votes have interpreted ideology broadly, as a residual determinant of voting behavior once constituent interests have been

---

34. The actual percentage of lame ducks voting for the bill was 34 percent. For *ADA* the predicted probability is 50 percent, and the t-statistic for the difference between actual and predicted is -2.57500. For *NJE* the predicted probability is also 50 percent, and the t-statistic is -2.60754.

35. See Kau and Rubin 1979 for further indirect evidence on logrolling in the Congress.

36. We assume that members of the two parties had identical tastes for shirking. The basis for the political party logrolling assumption is that the sponsors of the bill were mostly Democrats, while the Reagan administration led the opposition to it. Of the 233 Democrats who voted on the bill, 175 (75 percent) were for it; of the 178 Republicans, 44 (25 percent) were for it.

TABLE 3.   Determinants of Domestic Content Votes by Party (1 = Yes, 0 = No); Probit Coefficients and t-Statistics

Independent Variables	Democrats		Republicans	
	1 (ADA)	2 (NJE)	3 (ADA)	4 (NJE)
Constant	-0.55747	-1.83662	-4.67377	-5.57433
	(-0.37516)	(-1.15363)	(-2.36713)*	(-2.67321)**
Auto employment	0.26173	0.25050	0.09564	0.07528
	(2.15581)*	(2.15835)*	(1.96075)*	(1.63648)
Steel employment	0.44896	0.57032	0.04151	0.04337
	(1.95948)	(2.24878)*	(1.12655)	(1.19706)
Unemployment rate	0.02736	0.04741	0.09449	0.06622
	(0.41311)	(0.70307)	(1.26885)	(0.91593)
Union membership	0.03144	0.01763	0.06219	0.07105
	(1.40403)	(0.76807)	(2.08429)*	(2.30203)*
Export employment	-0.44734	-0.49772	-0.43173	-0.40108
	(-2.08512)*	(-2.26054)*	(-1.21754)	(-1.11667)
Farm employment	-0.06802	-0.04978	-0.02860	-0.02640
	(-1.66170)	(-1.17185)	(-0.63782)	(-0.58024)
Auto registrations	-0.00202	-0.00230	0.00177	0.00313
	(-0.85169)	(-0.93947)	(0.52420)	(0.91324)
Labor contributions	0.01884	0.01229	0.02310	0.02092
	(2.79097)**	(1.97209)*	(2.21921)*	(2.03703)*
Ideological rating	0.00318	0.02858	0.01932	0.02391
	(0.57057)	(2.97857)**	(2.41501)*	(2.99325)**
Reelected to House	1.09680	1.13907	0.53783	0.54168
	(2.73183)**	(2.82121)**	(1.71468)	(1.73703)
Number of observations	233	233	178	178
Percent correctly predicted	87	87	81	80
Log likelihood function	-83.14	-78.29	-72.16	-70.43

* Significant at the 5 percent level
** Significant at the 1 percent level

accounted for. In practice ideological positions are typically represented as a single-dimensional index along a right to left spectrum. The results of the previous sections suggest that a single scale may not be sufficient. The predictive power of alternative ideological ratings can differ substantially, and even if we control for past ideological positions with the *ADA* rating or the *NJE* rating, we indirectly see the effects of other factors that influence the voting behavior of members of Congress. We therefore have evidence that legislator ideology embodies multiple dimensions.[37]

---

37. For a sophisticated empirical analysis of the issue of the dimensionality of legislator voting behavior, see Poole and Daniels 1985.

Much remains to be done on the determinants of legislator voting behavior. The technology of getting reelected needs to be understood in greater detail in order to isolate the roles of campaign contributions and other kinds of interest-group support versus direct support in the voting booth. The various dimensions of political parties as logrolling coalitions or as ideological labels must be better understood as well. It will be inherently difficult to achieve these goals through econometric analysis alone. Detailed analysis of the legislative histories must be carried out as well. At least in the past, political scientists have shown themselves to have a comparative advantage in this area.

More generally, much remains to be done on the determinants of protection. There is a great need for more precise specifications of the interaction of the demand and supply sides of the market for protection, for individual congressional votes, across industries, and for national economies overall. The empirical literature on the political economy of protection is too often guilty of simply including in estimatable equations a mishmash of variables consistent with a variety of political-economy models. Further efforts must be made in the future to test formally these various models against each other. We must learn more about the ways that the institutional framework of the trade policy formation process shapes the outcomes of that process. We have tried in this paper to highlight some fruitful steps that have already been taken in that direction.

Finally it is apparent that further fruitful empirical analysis of the determinants of protection will come to a virtual standstill unless improved measures of the levels of nontariff trade barriers become available. Tariff rates are now typically low in the major industrial countries, but there is tremendous variation in the coverage and severity of quantitative restrictions and less visible barriers. Recent work by Hufbauer, Berliner, and Elliott (1986) is a step in the right direction. However, given the prominence of the free-rider problem in our society, the agencies of the U.S. government or international institutions will without doubt have to bear much of the costly burden of that effort in the future.

APPENDIX: DESCRIPTIONS AND SOURCES OF THE DATA

Vote: A dummy variable that equals one if the member voted for (or was paired in favor of) the domestic content bill (HR 5133), zero otherwise. Source: *Congressional Quarterly Almanac, 1982,* 16-C.

Auto Employment: Percentage of district employment in motor vehicles and equipment. Source: Economic Information Systems, *Congressional District Business Patterns,* 1981.

Steel Employment: Percentage of district employment in steel. Source: See *Auto Employment.*

Unemployment Rate: State unemployment rate. Source: U.S. Bureau of Labor Statistics, *Employment and Earnings,* January 1983, table E-1.

Union Membership: Union membership as a percentage of state nonagricultural employment in 1980. Source: U.S. Department of Commerce, Bureau of the Census, *Statistical Abstract of the United States, 1984,* table 728.

Export Employment: Percentage of civilian labor force in the state directly involved in manufactured export production. Export-related employment data are from *Statistical Abstract of the United States, 1986,* table 1349. State civilian labor force data are from U.S. Department of Commerce, Bureau of the Census, *State and Metropolitan Areas Data Book, 1986,* table C, Items 775-790.

Farm Employment: Percentage of the employed persons in the district working in farming, fisheries, or forestry. Source: U.S. Bureau of the Census, Summary Tape File 3C, *1980 Census of Population and Housing,* Congressional Districts of the 96th and 97th Congresses.

Auto Registrations: State automobile registrations per 1000 persons. Source: *Statistical Abstract of the United States, 1984,* table 1062.

Labor Contributions: Labor PAC contributions to candidates as a percentage of their total PAC contributions. Source: U.S. Federal Election Commission, *FEC Reports on Financial Activity, 1979–1980, Final Report, U.S. Senate and House Campaigns,* January 1982.

Political Party: A dummy variable that takes a value of one if the member was a Democrat, zero if a Republican. Source: *Politics in America, 1982.* Washington, D.C.: Congressional Quarterly Press.

ADA: The percentage of times the member voted for (or was paired in favor of) the position of the Americans for Democratic Action for 20 selected votes in 1981. Source: *Congressional Quarterly Weekly Report,* July 3, 1982, 1616–7.

NJE: A rating of liberalness on economic issues compiled by the *National Journal,* based on 12 selected votes in 1981. Source: *National Journal,* May 7, 1983, 940–7.

Reelected: A dummy variable that takes a value of one if the member was reelected to the House in November 1982, zero otherwise. Source: *Politics in America, 1984.* Washington, D.C.: Congressional Quarterly Press.

REFERENCES

Anderson, Kym, and Robert E. Baldwin. 1981. "The Political Market for Protection in Industrial Countries: Empirical Evidence." World Bank Staff Working Paper 492, World Bank, Washington, D.C.

Baack, Bennett D., and Edward John Ray. 1983. "The Political Economy of Tariff Policy: A Case Study of the United States." *Explorations in Economic History* 20:73–93.

Balassa, Bela. 1965. "Tariff Protection in Industrial Countries: An Evaluation." *Journal of Political Economy* 73:573–94.

Balassa, Bela, Steven E. Guisinger, and Daniel M. Schydlowsky. 1970. "The Effective Rate of Protection and the Question of Labor Protection in the United States: A Comment." *Journal of Political Economy* 78:1150–62.

Baldwin, Robert E. 1976. "The Political Economy of Postwar U.S. Trade Policy." *The Bulletin* 4:5–37. New York University Graduate School of Business.

Baldwin, Robert E. 1984. "Trade Policies in Developed Countries." Chap. 12 of *Handbook of International Economics,* vol. 1, ed. Ronald W. Jones and Peter B. Kenen. Amsterdam: North-Holland.

Baldwin, Robert E. 1985. *The Political Economy of U.S. Import Policy.* Cambridge, Mass.: MIT Press.

Bale, Malcolm D. 1977. "United States Concessions in the Kennedy Round and Short-Run Labour Adjustment Costs: Further Evidence." *Journal of International Economics* 7:145–48.

Ball, David S. 1967. "United States Effective Tariffs and Labor's Share." *Journal of Political Economy* 75:183–87.

Basevi, Giorgio. 1966. "The United States Tariff Structure: Estimates of Effective Rates of Protection of U.S. Industries and Industrial Labour." *Review of Economics and Statistics* 48:147–60.

Cable, Vincent, and Ivonia Rebelo. 1980. "Britain's Pattern of Specialization in Manufactured Goods with Developing Countries and Trade Protection." World Bank, Staff Working Paper 425, World Bank, Washington, D.C.

Caves, Richard E. 1976. "Economic Models of Political Choice: Canada's Tariff Structure." *Canadian Journal of Economics* 9:278–300.

Cheh, John H. 1974. "United States Concessions in the Kennedy Round and Short-Run Labour Adjustment Costs." *Journal of International Economics* 4:323–40.

Cheh, John H. 1976. "A Note on Tariffs, Nontariff Barriers, and Labor Protection in United States Manufacturing Industries." *Journal of Political Economy* 84:389–94.

Clark, Don P. 1980. "Protection of Unskilled Labour in the United States Manufacturing Industries: Further Evidence." *Journal of Political Economy* 88:1249–54.

Cline, William R. 1984. *Exports of Manufactures from Developing Countries: Performance and Prospects for Market Access.* Washington, D.C.: Brookings Institution.

Constantopoulos, Maria. 1974. "Labour Protection in Western Europe." *European Economic Review* 5:313–28.

Conybeare, John A. C. 1983. "Tariff Protection in Developed and Developing Countries: A Cross-Sectional and Longitudinal Analysis." *International Organization* 37:441–63.

Coughlin, Cletus C. 1985. "Domestic Content Legislation: House Voting and the Economic Theory of Regulation." *Economic Inquiry* 23:437–48.

Coughlin, Cletus C., Joseph V. Terza, and Noor Aini Khalifah. 1989. "The Determinants of Escape Clause Petitions." *Review of Economics and Statistics.* 71:341–47.

Davis, Michael. 1987. "Why is There a Seniority System?" Paper presented at the annual meeting of The Public Choice Society, March 27–29, Tucson, Arizona.

Destler, I. M. 1980. *Making Foreign Economic Policy.* Washington, D.C.: Brookings Institution.

Destler, I. M. 1986. *American Trade Politics: System under Stress.* Washington, D.C.: Institute for International Economics.

Destler, I. M., and John S. Odell. 1987. *Anti-protection: Changing Forces in United States Trade Politics.* Washington, D.C.: Institute for International Economics.
Downs, Anthony. 1957. *An Economic Theory of Democracy.* New York: Harper and Row.
Feigenbaum, Susan, Henry Ortiz, and Thomas D. Willett. 1985. "Protectionist Pressures and Aggregate Economic Conditions: Comment on Takacs." *Economic Inquiry* 23:175–82.
Feigenbaum, Susan, and Thomas D. Willett. 1985. "Domestic versus International Influences on Protectionist Pressure in the United States." In *Exchange Rates, Trade, and the U.S. Economy,* ed. Sven W. Arndt, Richard J. Sweeney, and Thomas D. Willett. Cambridge, Mass.: Ballinger.
Fieleke, Norman S. 1976. "The Tariff Structure for Manufacturing Industries in the United States: A Test of Some Traditional Explanations." *Columbia Journal of World Business* 11:98–104.
Findlay, Ronald, and Stanislaw Wellisz. 1986. "Tariffs, Quotas and Domestic-Content Protection: Some Political Economy Considerations." *Public Choice* 50:221–42.
Finger, J. M. 1981. "The Industry-Country Incidence of 'Less Than Fair Value' Cases in U.S. Import Trade." *Quarterly Review of Economics and Business* 21:259–79.
Finger, J. M., H. Keith Hall, and Douglas R. Nelson. 1982. "The Political Economy of Administered Protection." *American Economic Review* 72:452–66.
Frey, Bruno S. 1984. "The Public Choice View of International Political Economy." *International Organization* 38:199–223.
Gallarotti, Giulio M. 1985. "Toward a Business-Cycle Model of Tariffs." *International Organization* 39:155–87.
Glismann, H. H., and F. D. Weiss. 1980. "On the Political Economy of Protection in Germany." World Bank Staff Working Paper 427, World Bank, Washington, D.C.
Goldstein, Judith. 1986. "The Political Economy of Trade: Institutions of Protection." *American Political Science Review* 80:161–84.
Grilli, Enzo, and Mauro La Noce. 1983. "The Political Economy of Protection in Italy: Some Empirical Evidence." World Bank Staff Working Paper 567, World Bank, Washington, D.C.
Grossman, Gene M. 1981. "The Theory of Domestic Content Protection and Content Preference." *Quarterly Journal of Economics* 96:583–603.
Hayes, Michael T. 1981. *Legislators and Lobbyists: A Theory of Political Markets.* New Brunswick, N.J.: Rutgers University Press.
Helleiner, Gerald K. 1977. "The Political Economy of Canada's Tariff Structure: An Alternative Model." *Canadian Journal of Economics* 10:318–26.
Hufbauer, Gary Clyde, Diane T. Berliner, and Kimberly Ann Elliott. 1986. *Trade Protection in the United States: 31 Case Studies.* Washington, D.C.: Institute for International Economics.
Jacobson, Gary C. 1987. "Running Scared: Elections and Congressional Politics in the 1980s." In *Congress: Structure and Policy,* ed. Mathew D. McCubbins and Terry Sullivan. Cambridge: Cambridge University Press.
Kalt, Joseph P., and Mark A. Zupan. 1984. "Capture and Ideology in the Economic Theory of Politics." *American Economic Review* 74:279–300.
Kalt, Joseph P., and Mark A. Zupan. 1990. "The Apparent Ideological Behavior of

Legislators: Testing for Principal-Agent Slack in Political Institutions." *Journal of Law and Economics.* Forthcoming.

Kau, James B., and Paul H. Rubin. 1979. "Self-Interest, Ideology, and Logrolling in Congressional Voting." *Journal of Law and Economics* 22:365–84.

Kindleberger, Charles P. 1975. "The Rise of Free Trade in Western Europe, 1820–1875." *Journal of Economic History* 35:20–55.

Krasner, Stephen. 1976. "State Power and the Structure of International Trade." *World Politics* 28:317–47.

Lavergne, Réal P. 1983. *The Political Economy of U.S. Tariffs: An Empirical Analysis.* Toronto: Academic Press.

Lott, John R., Jr., and W. Robert Reed. 1989. "Shirking and Sorting in a Political Market with Finite-Lived Politicians." *Public Choice* 61:75–96.

Lundberg, Lars. 1981. "Patterns of Barriers to Trade in Sweden: A Study in the Theory of Protection." World Bank Staff Working Paper 494, World Bank, Washington, D.C.

Magee, Stephen P. 1982. "Protectionism in the United States." Manuscript, Department of Finance, University of Texas at Austin.

Magee, Stephen P., and Leslie Young. 1987. "Endogenous Protection in the United States, 1900–1984." In *U.S. Trade Policies in a Changing World Economy,* ed. Robert M. Stern. Cambridge, Mass.: MIT Press.

Marvel, Howard P., and Edward J. Ray. 1983. "The Kennedy Round: Evidence on the Regulation of International Trade in the United States." *American Economic Review* 73:190–7.

McArthur, John, and Stephen V. Marks. 1988. "Constituent Interest vs. Legislator Ideology: The Role of Political Opportunity Cost." *Economic Inquiry* 26:461–70.

McKeown, Timothy. 1984. "Firms and Tariff Regime Change: Explaining the Demand for Protection." *World Politics* 36:215–33.

Milner, Helen. 1988. "Trading Places: Industries for Free Trade." *World Politics* 40:350–76.

Nelson, Douglas, and Eugene Silberberg. 1987. "Ideology and Legislator Shirking." *Economic Inquiry* 25:15–25.

Olson, Mancur. 1965. *The Logic of Collective Action.* Cambridge, Mass.: Harvard University Press.

Pastor, Robert. 1980. *Congress and the Politics of U.S. Foreign Economic Policy: 1929–1976.* Berkeley: University of California Press.

Peltzman, Sam. 1984. "Constituent Interest and Congressional Voting." *Journal of Law and Economics* 27:181–210.

Peltzman, Sam. 1985. "An Economic Interpretation of the History of Congressional Voting in the Twentieth Century." *American Economic Review* 75:656–75.

Pincus, Jonathan J. 1975. "Pressure Groups and the Pattern of Tariffs." *Journal of Political Economy* 83:757–78.

Pincus, Jonathan J. 1977. *Pressure Groups and Politics in Antebellum Tariffs.* New York: Columbia University Press.

Poole, Keith T., and R. Steven Daniels. 1985. "Ideology, Party, and Voting in the U.S. Congress, 1959–1980." *American Political Science Review* 79:373–99.

138   International Trade Policies

Pugel, Thomas A., and Ingo Walter. 1985. "U.S. Corporate Interests and the Political Economy of Trade Policy." *Review of Economics and Statistics* 67:465–73.
Ratner, Sidney. 1972. *The Tariff in American History*. New York: Van Nostrand.
Ray, Edward J. 1974. "The Optimum Commodity Tariff and Tariff Rates in Developed and Less Developed Countries." *Review of Economics and Statistics* 56:369–77.
Ray, Edward J. 1981a. "The Determinants of Tariffs and Nontariff Trade Restrictions in the U.S." *Journal of Political Economy* 89:105–21.
Ray, Edward J. 1981b. "Tariff and Nontariff Barriers to Trade in the United States and Abroad." *Review of Economics and Statistics* 63:161–8.
Ray, Edward J. 1987. "The Impact of Special Interests on Preferential Tariff Concessions by the United States." *Review of Economics and Statistics* 69:187–93.
Ray, Edward J., and Howard P. Marvel. 1984. "The Pattern of Protection in the Industrialized World." *Review of Economics and Statistics* 66:452–8.
Riedel, James. 1977. "Tariff Concessions in the Kennedy Round and the Structure of Protection in West Germany: An Econometric Assessment." *Journal of International Economics* 7:133–43.
Saunders, Ronald S. 1980. "The Political Economy of Effective Tariff Protection in Canada's Manufacturing Sector." *Canadian Journal of Economics* 13:340–8.
Schneider, Friederich, and Bruno S. Frey. 1988. "Politico-Economic Models of Macroeconomic Policy: A Review of the Empirical Evidence." Chap. 9 of *Political Business Cycles: The Political Economy of Money, Inflation and Unemployment*, ed. Thomas D. Willett, Durham, N.C.: Duke University Press.
Stigler, George J. 1971. "The Theory of Economic Regulation." *Bell Journal of Economics and Management Science* 2:3–21.
Stone, Joe A. 1978. "A Comment on Tariffs, Nontariff Barriers, and Labor Protection in United States Manufacturing Industries." *Journal of Political Economy* 86:959–62.
Takacs, Wendy E. 1981. "Pressures for Protectionism: An Empirical Analysis." *Economic Inquiry* 19:687–93.
Takacs, Wendy E. 1985. "More on Protectionist Pressure and Aggregate Economic Conditions: A Reply." *Economic Inquiry* 23:183–5.
Taussig, Frank W. 1931. *The Tariff History of the United States*. New York: G. P. Putnam's Sons.
Tharakan, P. K. M. 1980. "The Political Economy of Protection in Belgium." World Bank Staff Working Paper 431, World Bank, Washington, D.C.
Tosini, Suzanne C., and Edward Tower. 1987. "The Textile Bill of 1985: The Determinants of Congressional Voting Patterns." *Public Choice* 54:19–25.
Travis, W. P. 1964. *The Theory of Trade and Protection*. Cambridge, Mass.: Harvard University Press.
Travis, W. P. 1968. "The Effective Rate of Protection and the Question of Labour Protection in the U.S." *Journal of Political Economy* 76:443–61.
U.S. Congress. 1982a. House Committee on Energy and Commerce. Subcommittee on Commerce, Transportation, and Tourism. *Hearing on the Fair Practices in Automotive Products Act.* 97th Cong., 2d sess., 1982.
U.S. Congress. 1982b. House Committee on Ways and Means. Subcommittee on

Trade. *Hearings on the Fair Practices in Automotive Products Act.* 97th Cong., 2d sess., 1982.

Vaccara, Beatrice N. 1960. *Employment and Output in Protected Manufacturing Industries.* Washington, D.C.: Brookings Institution.

Verreydt, E., and J. Waelbrock. 1980. "European Community Protection Against Manufactured Imports from Developing Countries: A Case Study in the Political Economy of Protection." World Bank Staff Working Paper 432, World Bank, Washington, D.C.

CHAPTER 6

Trading Places:
Industries for Free Trade

Helen Milner

In the United States today, protectionism is a central political issue once again. In this century, pressures for protectionism have captured the national attention several times. One such time was in the 1920s. During this decade U.S. trade policy made a U-turn. From the Dingley tariff bill in 1897 until the Fordney-McCumber tariff law of 1922, protectionism declined, as the average value of tariffs on dutiable goods fell from 45 percent to 28 percent.[1] But in the 1920s this downward trend was reversed. Between 1922 and 1930, the United States closed its market dramatically, with tariffs attaining an ad valorem average of 53 percent.[2] This level, set by the 1930 Smoot-Hawley tariff, was one of the highest ever and the highest for the twentieth century. American protectionism thus ascended to its zenith during the 1920s.

Beginning in the early 1930s, protectionism in the United States once again abated. The Reciprocal Trade Acts Agreement (RTAA), introduced in 1934 and serving as a model for future trade acts, initiated this opening of the American market. Between 1934 and 1972, average U.S. tariff levels declined by some 70 percent.[3] By 1972, tariffs averaged a mere 9.9 percent in the United States.[4] The American market had been opened widely in these forty years.

In the early 1970s, the course of U.S. trade policy again became a source of heated debate. Many questions were raised about the future of American trade policy. What direction would trade policy take in the 1970s and beyond?

I would like to thank David Baldwin, Jeff Frieden, Stephen Haggard, Robert Keohane, Ken Oye, the participants at the Ford Foundation Conference on Blending Political and Economic Analysis of International Trade Policies, and the anonymous referees at *World Politics* for their helpful comments. Reprinted from Helen Milner, "Trading Places: Industries for Free Trade," *World Politics* 40, No. 3 (April 1988): 350–76. Copyright © 1988 by Princeton University Press. Reprinted with permission of Princeton University Press.

1. Pastor 1980, 78, table 3; Lake 1983, 534, table 2, tells a similar story.
2. Lake 1983.
3. U.S. Tariff Commission 1974, 81–82.
4. Pastor 1980, 119, table 6.

Many casual observers and scholars feared the resurgence of rapidly rising protectionism and international trade wars.[5] Extrapolating from previous historical periods of rising and falling protectionism, these observers saw the 1970s and beyond looking much more like the 1920s than the period between 1934 and 1970. In fact the 1920s were adduced often as the example for the decade after 1973. For many a significant closure of the U.S. market in the 1970s and 1980s threatened a repeat of the dismal interwar years.

This article challenges this view of the current period. I argue that there were sizable differences in trade policy outcomes between the 1920s and 1970s, and that these differences are puzzling because they belie predictions of other theories. I maintain that the one reason for these different policy outcomes was the growth of international economic interdependence in the post–World War II period. By the 1970s, the expansion of these international economic ties helped damp pressures for trade barriers by shifting firms' preferences against protectionism. Using evidence from a number of industries in the 1920s and 1970s, I show how the internationalization of firms reduced their interest in protection even in difficult economic times, and thus helped the United States resist turning protectionist in the 1970s.

The Puzzle

What similar features of the 1920s and 1970s drew observers to this comparison between their trade policies? Two common elements, which distinguish the two periods from the intervening years, seem central.

First, both the 1920s and 1970s were times of serious economic distress and instability. Economists have seen such difficult conditions as a key precondition for rising protectionist activity. As one economist notes,

> It is generally agreed that in a modern industrial economy the cyclical state of the economy and the country's competitive position internationally are the principal determinants of the degree of protectionist pressure. Low levels of economic activity, high unemployment, unused capacity, trade deficits, rapid increases in imports, and increases in import penetration all operate to increase the temptation to protect domestic industries from import competition.[6]

---

5. Examples are Malmgren 1970, Bergsten 1971, and Kronholz 1979. Hegemonic stability theorists also predict this. See Kindleberger 1973, esp. 307–8; and Gilpin 1975, esp. 258–62. For more skeptical views, see Krasner 1976 and Keohane 1980.

6. Takacs 1981, 687. In general, see McKeown 1984, Gallarotti 1985, Strange and Tooze 1980.

Many theories of protection would predict that periods of economic downturn would provoke rising protectionist demands. In fact economic difficulties were similar in the two periods, marked by relatively high unemployment rates and sizable agricultural and industrial overcapacity. In the 1920s, the U.S. economy suffered two major downturns—one in 1920–23 and one in 1929–33. In addition, price deflation, labor unrest and international monetary problems created further economic instability.[7] In the 1970s, the U.S. economy experienced deep recessions between 1973–75 and 1978–82. Sparked by the oil "shocks," these recessions were aggravated by rapidly shifting trade patterns, price instability, and a confused international monetary situation. In sum these high levels of economic distress and instability felt in the 1920s and 1970s might be expected to generate similar widespread protection.

Indeed given the absolute levels of economic distress in the two periods, the 1970s might have seen even greater levels of market closure than the 1920s.[8] The averages for three major economic indicators are worse in the 1970s than in the 1920s, as table 1 indicates. The even worse performance of the U.S. economy in the 1970s suggests that if economic difficulty is a precursor to protectionism, the 1970s should have experienced protectionism with a vengeance.

A second similarity between the 1920s and 1970s, which has been linked to protectionism, is the declining power of the world's hegemonic state. This change in the international distribution of power has been cited as a major factor leading to the closure of the world's markets. As Gilpin (1975, 258–59) states,

Today, . . . the dominant economy is itself in relative decline and is being challenged by rising centers of economic power. With the decline of the dominant economic power, the world economy may be following the pattern of the late nineteenth century and of the 1930s: it may be fragmenting into regional trading "blocks", exclusive economic alliances, and economic nationalism.[9]

In the 1920s, the hegemon of the nineteenth century, Great Britain, was

---

7. Lewis 1949; U.S. Department of Commerce 1919–30; U.S. Department of Commerce 1975; Kindleberger 1973, esp. chap. 5–8; League of Nations 1942; Feldstein 1980, 12.

8. Ratner, Soltow, and Sylla 1979, 482, 502. The worst economic difficulties of the Great Depression followed, rather than preceded, the tariff increases, occurring in the early 1930s. For instance, unemployment averaged 3 percent in 1930, the year Smoot-Hawley was passed, but rose to 25 percent by 1933, the year before the Reciprocal Trade Agreements Act.

9. Others are Kindleberger 1973, esp. 307–8; Krasner 1976; Keohane 1980; Lake 1988; Kindleberger 1981; and Gilpin 1981.

144   International Trade Policies

TABLE 1. Averages of Three Major Economic Variables, 1920s and 1970s, in Percentage

	1923–29	1973–79
Average annual growth in real GNP	3.1	2.3
Average mean value of unemployment rate	3.5	6.8
Average value of nonresidential fixed investment to GNP	11.2	10.2

Source: Data from Martin Feldstein, ed., *The American Economy in Transition* (Chicago: NBER, 1980), 104–5.

losing its status. From a peak of 24 percent in 1870, Great Britain's share of world trade fell to 14 percent before World War I.[10] Additionally its share of the world's manufacturing output tumbled from a dominant 32 percent in 1870 to a third rate level of 14 percent by 1913.[11] Germany and the United States overtook it in industrial competitiveness in certain critical, advanced sectors.[12] Moreover Britain's control over the international monetary system was declining. Its problems returning to and maintaining the gold standard in the 1920s, as well as its final abandonment of that system in 1931, all signaled this loss of influence.[13] By the 1920s then, Britain's hegemony had eroded, while the strength of other industrial countries, especially Germany and the United States, had grown.

A similar situation existed by the 1970s. By the early part of the decade, the global dominance once exercised by the United States in the 1950s and 1960s had been reduced, as other nations challenged the United States. The U.S.'s share of world trade dropped from 18.4 percent in 1950 to 13.4 percent in 1977.[14] More tellingly its share of the world's manufactured exports plummeted from a peak of nearly 30 percent in 1953 to about 13 percent by the late 1970s.[15] From a dominant 62% in 1950, its share of the world's manufacturing output also lost ground, dropping to 44 percent by 1977.[16] Many American industries had lost their economic advantage and faced bitter competition both at home and abroad by the 1970s. In addition American hegemony in the international monetary system was somewhat diminished. By 1973, it had scuttled the monetary system it had created earlier and found itself unable to fashion a new, stable system. U.S. hegemony in monetary

10. Lake 1983, 525, table 1.
11. Ratner, Soltow, and Sylla 1979, 385.
12. Lake 1983; Gerschenkron 1962, chaps. 1–2; and Hays 1957, chaps. 1,7,8.
13. Keohane and Nye 1977, 70; Kindleberger 1973, 63–68, 146–70.
14. Lake 1983, 541, table 3; Keohane and Nye 1977, 141.
15. Feldstein 1980, 193.
16. Feldstein 1980, 191.

relations in the 1970s, however, was not as reduced as was Britain's in the 1920s and early 1930s.[17] But American hegemony, especially in trade and production, had declined substantially by the 1970s, leaving the international distribution of power in the 1970s more similar to that of the interwar period than to that of the immediate post–World War II period. This eclipse of hegemony might have been expected to produce widespread protectionism, as it had in the 1920s.

While both periods were characterized by the decline of a hegemon, this may be less important to U.S. policy than the relative position the United States held. The striking fact about the U.S.'s relative international position is how similar it appears in the late 1920s and late 1970s, and how different it is in the 1950s and 1960s from these two times. The U.S.'s share of the world's manufacturing output reached 42 percent in 1929 and had leveled off at 44 percent in 1977.[18] In contrast the U.S. dominated in the 1950s and 1960s, holding 62 percent in 1950 and 51 percent in 1960.[19] Moreover in the trade area the United States was more dominant in the 1920s than the 1970s, but nowhere near as dominant as in the 1950s. In the 1920s, it was the world's largest exporter and biggest foreign investor and ranked second only to Britain in its imports.[20] By the late 1970s, it had become the world's second largest exporter of manufactures—West Germany led with almost 16 percent compared to the United States's 13 percent—and was being challenged for that spot by Japan, which held 11 percent.[21] In contrast in 1953 the United States reigned supreme in trade, controlling nearly 30 percent of all manufactured exports.[22]

A similar story is told by changes in its relative economic size and productivity. According to Lake, who uses these two measures in his analysis of international economic structures, the U.S.'s position was almost identical in 1929 and 1977.[23] This contrasts with its clear predominance in 1950. Moreover, in both 1929 and 1977, the United States appeared similarly situated relative to its nearest rivals. In 1929, it led all countries on these two indicators, barely edging out Britain while retaining a substantial lead over France and Germany. In 1977, its relative position was comparable: it was almost even with West Germany but still outdistanced Japan and France.

---

17. U.S. hegemony in money was much less diminished than in trade. Its ending of the Bretton Woods system was more an act of power than of weakness, according to many analysts. See Keohane and Nye 1977, 141, 165–86; and Odell 1982, chap. 4, esp. 219.

18. Ratner, Soltow, and Sylla 1979, 402, 464; Feldstein 1980, 191.

19. Feldstein 1980, 191.

20. Ratner, Soltow, and Sylla 1977, 464.

21. Feldstein 1980, 21.

22. Feldstein 1980, 21.

23. Lake 1984, figures 5 and 6.

Hence two strong similarities in the international distribution of economic power existed in the 1920s and 1970s. In both a hegemon was in decline, and in both the U.S.'s relative position was slightly superior to all others, but most importantly was being challenged by several nations. These conditions in the international economic structure have been linked to rising protectionism and thus might have been expected to engender similar protectionist responses in the two periods.[24]

The argument here is *not* that in all respects the 1920s and the 1970s were alike. Two important differences, at least, may attenuate the comparison made. First, the United States was a rising hegemon in the 1920s and a declining one in the 1970s. While hegemonic stability arguments provide no theoretical reason to expect this difference to affect a hegemon's trade policy, the notion of a lag has been introduced to account for this.[25] A rising hegemon may fail to appreciate its own significance, while a declining one may fail to understand its weakness and need for closure. This difference may account for dissimilarities between the two periods. But why such a lag occurs is obscure.

Second, the monetary systems operating at the two times differed. In the 1920s, the system shifted from a controlled flexible exchange rate system before 1925 to a fixed, gold standard system until 1931. In the 1970s, the opposite movement occurred: from a fixed, dollar-gold standard to a managed flexible rate system by 1973. The consequences of these two different systems for trade policy are unclear, however. The effects of different exchange rate systems on trade are not well understood. Many have claimed that flexible rates should hinder protectionism because such barriers are nullified by exchange rate changes.[26] Others maintain that flexible rates augment protectionist pressures by increasing risk and that fixed rates are best for ensuring free trade.[27] At best it seems fair to say that the exchange rate systems operating in both periods did little to provide a stable environment for international trade.

A related issue is whether the value of U.S. exchange rates affected trade policy differentially in the two periods. The claim is that the level of exchange rates was driving trade policy, especially in the 1970s. Thus the relative undervaluation of the dollar in the late 1970s weakened protectionist pressures, while its overvaluation in the early 1980s led to new pressures for barriers.[28] The problem with this argument is that the 1920s look similar. The

---

24. I differ with Lake's interpretation of these two structures and their differences. See Lake 1984, figures 5 and 6.

25. Kindleberger 1973; Krasner 1976.

26. Grubel 1977, chap. 22; Kindleberger and Lindert 1978, chap. 21; Baldwin and Richardson 1986, chap. 21.

27. Bergsten and Cline 1983.

28. Kindleberger and Lindert 1978, chap. 21, esp. figure 21.5.

U.S. dollar appears undervalued in general after World War I, once again supposedly mitigating protectionist pressures. But by the late 1920s the dollar seems overvalued relative to the mark, lira, franc, and gold, although under-valued relative to sterling.[29] Differences in exchange rate levels then do *not* seem to differentiate the two periods.

Despite these differences, the similarities between the 1920s and 1970s in terms of economic difficulties and the U.S.'s relative economic position might lead one to expect U.S. trade policy in the 1970s would look like that of the 1920s. The 1970s, however, were not marked by the extensive closure of the U.S. market that occurred in the 1920s. American trade policy remained oriented toward a relatively open market in this period. While it is commonly believed that protectionism grew substantially in the 1970s and early 1980s, U.S. trade policy actually had mixed currents. Overall a small net increase in trade barriers relative to the 1960s probably occurred, but these new barriers were nowhere near the levels of the 1920s. Moreover these barriers had little effect on the volume of trade, unlike in the 1930s; global and U.S. trade continued to grow throughout the decade of the 1970s, and to grow faster than production. In addition tariffs were further reduced to their lowest levels, about 5 percent on average, through the GATT Tokyo Round negotiations.[30]

On the other hand, some nontariff barriers (NTBs) grew. While these barriers remained difficult to measure and were generally not measured while tariffs remained high, their relative importance increased in the late 1970s. By that time nearly 30 percent of all categories (not values) of American man-ufactured imports were affected by them.[31] But one empirical study concludes that these new NTBs have had only limited protectionist effects; as the authors point out, ". . . on average over a full range of manufactured products, the protection given by NTBs that may limit or reduce imports . . . is not nearly as large as the protection afforded by tariffs . . . or natural barriers to trade. . .".[32] Further they project that "if the United States continues on its present policy course, the U.S. economy will be considerably more open in 1985 than it was in 1976."[33] Thus the erection of NTBs in the 1970s and 1980s may have produced a small net increase in protection. But this increase did not approach the levels of the 1920s even though two key preconditions— serious economic distress and declining hegemony—characterized both peri-ods. Given the fertile ground of the late 1970s protectionism could have grown like a weed, as it did in the 1920s. For some reason it did not.

---

29. Kindleberger and Lindert 1978, chap. 21, figure 21.3. Note how all other currencies rise in value against the dollar after the 1931 change.
30. U.S. Tariff Commission 1974, 81–82.
31. Reich 1983, 786.
32. Morici and Megna 1983, 103.
33. Morici and Megna 1983, 103.

Other Explanations

The puzzle then is why trade policy was different in the 1920s and 1970s
when key pressures influencing it in one direction were similar. This puzzle
has been addressed by a number of other studies. Three other answers, all of
which focus on aspects of the international or domestic system different from
the one central to this study, require examination. These arguments should be
seen less as competing ones than as arguments pitched at different levels of
analysis. I argue only that the argument developed in this study has been
neglected and that it is more basic than these other arguments.

One type of explanation looks at the international distribution of power,
usually in terms of economic capabilities. These explanations involve modifications of the hegemonic stability thesis, which, as has been shown, cannot in
its original form explain the different policy outcomes in the 1920s and
1970s.[34] Three modified arguments have been presented. First, some have
argued that American hegemony has not declined enough to set off the expected protectionist response.[35] Even though other countries have caught up
with the United States, it still remains the strongest, especially when its
military might is included. This argument then depends on the U.S.'s military
capabilities being an important factor in its trade policy considerations. The
fungibility of these power resources, however, is questionable.[36] A second
type of hegemonic stability argument in fact denies this fungibility. By considering only trade-related power resources, these arguments suggest also that
U.S. hegemony has not declined enough to evoke extensive protectionism.[37]
However, relative to its trade position in the 1920s, the United States held a
similar, or even less dominant, position in the 1970s. One explanation for this
disparity is the lag phenomenon discussed earlier. A third argument, which
modifies the hegemonic stability thesis, argues that different configurations of
states in terms of their relative economic power lead to different trade policy
outcomes. But this argument has trouble explaining the differences between
the 1920s and 1970s since the configuration of states at those two points (1929
and 1977) was very similar.[38]

---

34. Krasner 1976, 317–47.
35. Russett 1985; Strange 1982.
36. Baldwin 1979; Keohane and Nye 1977, chap. 2.
37. Keohane and Nye 1977, chap. 3; Keohane 1984, chap. 4,9; Aggarwal 1985, chaps.
2,7.
38. Lake 1983; Lake 1988; Lake 1984. To overcome this difficulty, he makes two arguments. One is that due to the disruption caused by World War I, much greater uncertainty existed
in the 1920s, which prompted more protectionist activity. As a second point, he implies that the
height of protectionism globally was in the 1930s, not the 1920s, when the structure was
somewhat different. Protectionism, however, was rising worldwide throughout the 1920s; it hit its

A second type of explanation focuses on the existence of an international regime in trade. In this view the creation and continuation of the GATT system in the postwar period has been partially responsible for the maintenance of a relatively open international economy. The lack of any such regime in the 1920s helped protectionism spread. The ways GATT is seen as working against protectionism are numerous. Some claim it operates through the externalization of a norm—that is, "embedded liberalism"—which promotes trade but also minimizes its domestic costs and hence protectionist demands.[39] Others suggest that the regime and its norms are embodied in domestic policies and practices; that the regime has its effect by constraining and shaping domestic behavior.[40] Others see the regime as encouraging international commerce itself by increasing its efficiency.[41] Differences thus exist over exactly how the regime has abated protectionist pressures, but generally it is seen as exerting a brake on domestic pressures for protection.

In all of these views, however, regimes play only an intermediate role. They are acknowledged as an intervening variable, influencing the preferences, pressures, and practices already established at the domestic and international levels.[42] Examination of these preexisting factors seems necessary for one to judge what effect the regime had. Regime analysis needs then to be supplemented with analysis of other domestic and international forces, analysis that this study provides.

A third type of explanation focuses on the structure of the domestic policy-making system. The argument here is that despite the pressures for protection in the 1970s a different policy structure existed which helped defuse these pressures. This structure insulated political actors, especially Congress, from societal pressures for protection. Hence the state was able to resist these pressures in the 1970s but not in the 1920s. The specific way this insulation occurred differs. Most acknowledge the importance of the shift in tariff-making authority from Congress to the President as being central.[43] Others point to the nature of the relationship between Congress and the executive[44]: some to the way trade policy is made within the executive branch,[45] some to the lessons of the 1930s and the norms and ideology now

---

peak in the United States in 1930 and elsewhere by 1933 or 1934. His argument gives a more sophisticated and perhaps accurate explanation of trade policy outcomes than do other hegemonic stability arguments, but it still has difficulty accounting for the 1920s and 1970s differences.

39. Ruggie 1982.
40. Lipson 1982; Lenway 1985.
41. Lipson 1982.
42. See *International Organization* 36:2, esp. introduction by Stephen Krasner.
43. Pastor 1980; Goldstein 1986; Destler 1986.
44. Pastor 1980.
45. Porter 1980; Winham 1980.

surrounding those lessons,[46] and others to the way Congress functions and responds to societal pressures.[47]

This proliferation of domestic policy "structures" points out an interesting aspect of the trade policy process. Trade policy is not made within one structure. Many economic actors are involved in trade matters, and they bring their complaints and pressures to bear on different political actors. Moreover no single, coherent national trade policy exists. Policy relating to one sector of the economy may differ completely from that concerning another. Thus the policy toward autos may differ greatly from that toward wheat, textiles, or telecommunications equipment. Moreover, for each of these industries, the influence of Congress, the executive, and the ITC varies. All this is to say that no one trade policy "structure" exists. Knowing who the relevant domestic actors are and what their trade preferences are is essential in understanding the influence of the particular policy "structure" for that sector on the policy outcome.

The Argument

The argument here operates on a different level of analysis from these three. I argue that the increased international economic interdependence of the post–World War II period has been a major reason why protectionism did not spread widely in the 1970s and early 1980s. Aspects of the U.S.'s much greater integration into the international economy worked against recourse to protectionism by altering domestic actors' preferences. Specifically, while increased interdependence has subjected areas of the economy to new foreign competition, it has also meant greatly augmented international economic ties for some firms in the form of exports, imports of critical inputs, multinational production, and global intrafirm trade. The growth of these international ties by American firms between the 1920s and 1970s then is seen as a major reason for the maintenance of a relatively open market in the 1970s, despite other pressures for closure.

Evidence for the growth of these international ties is abundant. In general the magnitude of American trade grew phenomenally over these fifty years.[48] More goods and more different types of goods were traded. More specifically America's trade dependence grew substantially. United States export dependence rose from about 2 percent in 1923 to 9 percent in 1960 and to about 20 percent by the late 1970s.[49] Likewise its import dependence climbed from 2.5

---

46. Goldstein 1986; Goldstein 1983.

47. Schattschneider 1935; Bauer, Sola Pool, and Dexter 1972.

48. Ratner, Soltow, and Sylla 1976, 463–66.

49. For the 1920s, see Lipsey 1963, 434–35; for the period from 1960 on, see Report of the President's Commission on Industrial Competitiveness 1985, 36.

percent in 1921 to 5 percent in 1960 and to over 20 percent in 1980.[50] The multinationality of American firms also rose substantially over these five decades. The total of American direct foreign investment abroad grew from about $5.5 billion in 1923 to $11.8 billion in 1950 and to over $86 billion in 1970.[51] Moreover the internationalization of American industry grew in relative terms. Foreign assets of U.S. industry accounted for only 2.5 percent of total industrial assets in 1929, but over 20 percent by the 1970s.[52] Additionally the global operations of these firms intensified, leading to the creation of webs of international trade flows within firms. Exports by U.S. multinationals from foreign production sites back to the U.S. market have grown immensely. From an almost unknown practice before the 1940s, these types of transfers now account for somewhere between 15 and 50 percent of all U.S. industrial imports.[53] In sum the U.S.'s integration into the international economy through both trade and multinationality has deepened considerably since the 1920s.

This aspect of increased interdependence, I maintain, has lessened pressures for protection in domestic industries. I hypothesize then that firms with greater international ties in the form of exports, multinationality, and global intrafirm trade will be less interested in protection than more domestically oriented firms. These internationally oriented firms will view protection as undesirable because of its costs. Protection will be more costly to these firms than to more domestically oriented ones for five reasons. First, firms that export and/or produce abroad and trade will be concerned about foreign retaliation and its costs. Demanding protection at home may prompt greater protection abroad, reducing one's exports; or it may lead to new restrictions on foreign operations and their trade flows, thus reducing their profitability. Second, protection in one market may hurt a firm's exports to third markets as other exporters divert their products to these markets to compensate for market closure elsewhere.

Third, firms with a global web of production and trade will view trade barriers, even at home, as a new cost, one that may undermine their competitiveness. For these firms protection will be very disruptive and costly. Fourth, for firms dependent on imports—whether from their subsidiaries,

---

50. Ibid.

51. Dunn 1926, 182; Hughes 1979, 94. Ratner, Soltow, and Sylla (1979, 464) show it grew in the 1920s to $17.2 billion and then retreated to $11.5 billion by the end of the 1930s. Pollard 1985, 205, shows U.S. DFI dropped to its lowest point in the century so far in 1946.

52. For the 1920s, see U.S. Congress 1931, 27, for the value of U.S. direct foreign investment in manufacturing; and Lipsey 1963, 424, for the value of U.S. manufacturing GNP. For the 1970s, see U.S. Department of Commerce 1981.

53. Figures for this vary widely. See Grunwald and Flamm 1985, 7; Helleiner and Lavergne 1979; and Helleiner 1979.

subcontractors, or foreign firms—new trade barriers will increase their costs and thus erode their competitiveness. Finally, intra-industry rivalries will create opposition to protectionism. Internationally oriented firms will find that trade barriers put them at a disadvantage relative to their domestically oriented competitors. They impose new costs on the international firm, while providing benefits to the domestic-centered firm. Consequently these different relative costs and benefits of protection to firms within an industry may lead the international firms to oppose it. For these reasons then firms with strong international ties will find protection of the home market very costly and will be likely to resist appeals for it, even when faced with severe import competition.

While containing an international element, this argument shares similarities with domestic interest group arguments made mainly by economists. Most interest group analyses, however, focus on the forces pushing *for* protection.[54] One reason for this is the assumption of a collective action problem in trade politics. Small groups of producers (management and labor) facing import competition are seen as more likely to press actively for help since it will bring them concentrated and substantial benefits, while larger groups (other industries, consumers) opposing protection will be less likely to act since the benefits of openness will be diffuse and less tangible.[55] But some small groups may also feel high costs from protection and receive important tangible benefits from openness.

Increasingly the interest group literature has focused on the international variables examined here. Several aggregate-level studies of U.S. industries by economists have shown that high levels of export dependence reduce industries' preferences for protection and lead to lower trade barriers for these industries.[56] Other nonquantitative studies also reveal that in the 1920s the growth of an export sector contributed to attempts to open the American and foreign markets.[57] Some have also linked the adoption of the RTAA in 1934 with its anti-protectionist bent to the influence of American exporters and multinationals.[58] These studies have lent credence to the idea that export dependent industries may not prefer protection and may even advocate the dismantling of trade barriers.

Other studies have examined how multinationality and its related intra-firm trade affect trade policy. The idea that the spread of multinational firms

---

54. Examples are Caves 1976; Brock and Magee 1978; Baldwin 1986; Pincus 1977; Ray 1981; and Lavergne 1983.
55. See Olson 1965 for the classic treatment; also see Brock and Magee 1978.
56. Fong 1982 supports this strongly. Baldwin 1986 also supports it. Lavergne 1983 and Goldstein 1983 show more mixed evidence for this claim.
57. Wilson 1971; Becker 1982.
58. Ferguson 1984.

would reduce trade barriers has been discounted to some extent, because these firms often enter a market to circumvent such barriers and thus come to see them as a way to keep out other foreign competitors. Instead the growth of global intrafirm trading has led to the view that firms with such trade would be against protection of their markets.[59] Analysis at the aggregate industry level has produced mixed evidence for both the multinational and the intrafirm trade variables.[60]

Overall these empirical tests are plagued by two problems. First, these tests look only at the industry and not at the firms within them. Firms are central because they develop international ties, anticipate the costs of protection, and formulate trade preferences; yet most of these studies examine international ties at the industry level. In addition, since these ties are usually unevenly distributed among the firms in an industry, the influence of these ties on preferences is often obscured in industry-level analysis. Examination of both international ties and preferences at the firm level is thus likely to yield better results about what conditions corporate preferences. Second, these theories about industry preferences are embedded in models that explain actual trade outcomes. The intermediate step of explaining industry demands is rarely taken. Empirical tests of these theories thus suffer because they are only indirect tests of theories of demand. In other words, factors influencing demand may be obscured when examining outcomes since certain variables may prompt trade policy demands that are not satisfied in the policy process. Looking at demands by firms is essential. The analysis here avoids both of these problems by focusing on firms and their actual demands.

This focus also corrects for one of the problems encountered by others considering the puzzle posed here. Unlike international system, regime, or domestic structure arguments, my argument can account for differences in trade policy outcomes among industries in the same period. Why at one time some industries demand and receive protection while others do not is hard to explain parsimoniously with these other arguments. For example, the fact that 60 percent of all imports entered the United States duty-free in the 1920s is not easily explicable if one claims that the international structure, the lack of any regime, or the domestic political structure all encouraged the adoption of widespread protectionism at this time.[61] The argument here, and interest group arguments in general, is much better able to address such differences among industries at any one time, as well as being able to account for dif-

---

59. Helleiner 1977; Helleiner 1979. See Lipson 1982 for discussion of the effect of intra-industry trade on industry trade preferences.

60. Baldwin (1986) and Lavergne (1983) do not find much influence exercised by these variables, but Pugel and Walter (1985) do find multinationality to be an important brake on protectionist preferences.

61. Lake 1988, chap. 5, 8, and table 5.1.

ferences over time. The argument here should not be seen as directly competing with these other explanations. These arguments operate at different levels of analysis and may all be valid. The fact that my argument can explain differences within the periods as well as across them suggests its greater explanatory power. But the claim here is that examinations of trade politics have missed anti-protectionist interests and that a domestic politics view of the pressures for and against trade barriers is the place where one should start to understand trade policy.

The Case Studies

The industries examined in this article were those experiencing the greatest growth in import penetration among those already having high levels of import penetration in the two decades.[62] These industries also had to show evidence of other economic difficulty: unemployment, profit problems, overcapacity, etc. Since studies have shown that high levels of import penetration are strongly associated with demands for protection and high levels of actual protection, the industries selected should be the least likely to confirm my argument.[63] Given their situation, they should have been very likely to desire protection. It would be surprising to find that these import-threatened industries did *not* prefer new trade barriers.

Once these "hard" cases were chosen, I explored the extent of their integration into the international economy and their trade policy preferences. Data on their export dependence, import requirements, multinationality, and global intrafirm trade were collected for both the industry and the individual firms. To understand their preferences, their activities in a number of political arenas were surveyed. In the 1920s, the main arenas were (1) the U.S. Congress, which handled most issues related to tariff levels; (2) the U.S. Tariff Commission, which investigated industry complaints about trade matters; and (3) industry trade associations, whose internal deliberations over trade issues were reported in various newspapers and industry trade journals. For the 1970s, four slightly different arenas were surveyed: (1) the U.S. Congress, which authorized general tariff changes and introduced bills to help particular industries; (2) the U.S. International Trade Commission (ITC), which investigated industry trade complaints; (3) the U.S. Special Trade Representative (STR) and other executive agencies, who decided on and implemented solutions to industry trade complaints while also managing the U.S.'s activities in the GATT negotiations; and (4) the industry trade associations, which developed industry-wide positions on trade.

---

62. Eighteen industries were examined in detail in Milner 1988.

63. Many studies have found that high levels or high rates of increase in import penetration are strongly correlated with high levels of demand for protection and high actual levels of protection. See, for example, Baldwin 1986; Lavergne 1983; Goldstein 1983.

The investigation of the industries chosen in the 1920s and 1970s revealed a strong correlation between their firms' international ties and their trade policy preferences. (See table 2.) For firms lacking ties to the international economy, mounting import competition produced rising demands for extensive protection. In sharp contrast firms with well-developed multinational operations including integrated global production and trade flows and strong exports did *not* seek protection even when imports rose to high levels. In fact these firms often desired that markets at home and abroad be further opened. For firms possessing substantial export dependence but no multinational production, protection was also not desired as long as import competition did not swamp their exports. Finally, for those firms with some foreign production but no U.S. exports or intrafirm trade, rising import competition often brought a limited protectionist response. These firms sometimes sought selective protection; that is, they attempted to curb their strongest competitors through limited protection against one country or one product line, while leaving the main foreign markets they were involved in undisturbed. Overall the cases revealed that the more integrated the firm was into the international economy, the less likely it was to seek import restraints even when imports rose significantly.

The U.S. woolen goods manufacturers in the 1920s and the footwear producers in the 1970s were typical of industries lacking international economic ties. The vast majority of the many small firms in the woolens goods sector were domestically oriented, with few exports and no multinationality. After World War I when import competition resumed and other difficulties set in, the majority of firms in this industry began lobbying for closure of the U.S. market.[64] They demanded and received increased tariffs during the 1921 Emergency Tariff bill debate, and later they called for a 130 percent increase in their duties during the Fordney-McCumber tariff hearings and were granted a sizable increase. Problems in the late 1920s evoked new demands for protection as they lobbied for even higher tariffs before and during the Smoot-Hawley hearings. Their success with Congress did not placate them, however. In addition the producers fought against changes in tariff-making rules that could have made tariff reductions easier. They also pressured the U.S. Tariff Commission for greater protection. Thus the woolens manufacturers' preferences for protection were voiced in all possible political arenas and were focused on obtaining global protection for all segments of the industry. Their intense and unified advocacy for closure of the home market was not unexpected, given their similar economic problems and lack of international ties.

Like the woolen goods manufacturers, the American (nonrubber) footwear producers were largely domestic in their operations in the 1970s. Beginning in the late 1960s when shoe imports began flooding the U.S. market, the

---

64. For the full story, see Milner 1988.

TABLE 2. The Industries, Their Preferences, and Policy Outcomes

International Ties				
Export Dependence	Multinational and Global Intrafirm Trade	Industry	Expected Preferences	Actual Preferences	Policy Outcomes
Low	Low	Woolens, 1920s	Protectionist	Protectionist	High, increasing tarrifs
		Watches and Clocks, 1920s	Protectionist	Protectionist	High, rising tariffs
		Footwear, 1970s	Protectionist	Protectionist	Some protection via voluntary export restraints in mid-1970s
High	Low	Textile Machinery, 1920s	Open markets, esp. abroad	Divided; some free trade and some moderate protection	Low tariffs in early 1920s; some increases later
		Machine Tools, 1970s	Open markets, esp. abroad	Free trade in 1970s; Protectionist in early 1980s	Tariff reductions in 1970s; voluntary export restraints in mid-1980s

Low	Newsprint, 1920s	Selective protection, if any	Free trade	Duty-free
	Tires, 1970s	Selective protection, if any	Free trade, some complaints of unfair trade	Tariff reductions
	Watches & Clocks, 1970s	Selective protection, if any	Divided; some free trade, some selective protection	Some tariff reductions
	Radios & Television sets, 1970s	Selective protection	Some selective protection; some free trade	Some tariff reductions; voluntary export restraints in mid-1970s
High	Fertilizer, 1920s	Free trade	Free trade	Duty-free
	Photo Equipment, 1920s	Free trade	Moderate protection; increasing free trade	Some tariff increases in early 1920s; some decreases in late 1920s
High	Semiconductors, 1970s	Free trade	Free trade in 1970s; strategic trade demands in 1980s	Tariff reductions, but export pricing agreement with Japan in mid-1980s

industry association, backed by almost all of the producers, launched a campaign to obtain tariff protection.[65] After the early 1970s, the association and the firms pursued this goal with increasing intensity. The association filed numerous trade complaints with the ITC, lobbied Congress for help and formed a coalition of Congressmen to promote the industry cause, and launched a public relations campaign to generate public support. These activities forced President Carter in the late 1970s to negotiate voluntary export restraints with several East Asian competitors; however, even these restraints were not restrictive enough for many of the firms who sought global quotas. By the early 1980s, industry unity over trade matters began declining. At this time a growing number of producers began opposing renewed protection as they began importing or producing offshore. This opposition weakened the association's appeals for help and contributed to its more limited political success since then. Overall the firms' waxing and waning protectionist demands were related to the level of their international economic ties.

In contrast large multinationals with extensive international trade flows and exports from the United States avoided protection as a solution to their import problems largely because of the costly effects it would produce for the firms' global operations. The American fertilizer producers in the 1920s and the semiconductor producers in the 1970s were characteristic. The large fertilizer producers by the early 1920s were highly export dependent and multinational. These producers preferred freer trade, despite their economic problems.[66] In the 1921 tariff hearings, they requested and received the retention of the duty-free status of their products. In the Smoot-Hawley hearings, this preference prevailed among most of the firms, although some sought a more strategic position. Certain producers advocated a strategy of demanding protection on certain goods unless they received tariff reductions on others. This strategy was aimed at, and resulted in, greater openness of the U.S. market since so new tariffs were imposed on fertilizers and some were reduced. Finally, throughout the decade, the major producers—that is, those with international operations—opposed the attempts of some small domestic producers to have tariffs on various fertilizer products increased. In general the internationally-oriented fertilizer manufacturers wanted to preserve the U.S. market's openness, while opposing attempts to erect new barriers around it despite mounting foreign competition.

During the 1970s, the American semiconductor industry faced serious competition for the first time. The largest firms in this industry—IBM, Texas Instruments, and Motorola—were quite internationally-oriented, possessing

---

65. Milner 1988.
66. Milner 1988.

widespread foreign production operations and intrafirm trade flows, while the remainder were much more domestically oriented. Most of the firms favored trade liberalization throughout the 1970s; demands for aid or protection were nonexistent before the late 1970s despite mounting foreign competition.[67] In the late 1970s, the smaller firms, united in the new Semiconductor Industry Association (SIA), began formulating a trade complaint against the Japanese. Due to the opposition of the large firms, mainly IBM and TI, this complaint was not formalized at the time. Instead IBM joined the SIA and helped turn its attention toward negotiations with Japan over further tariff *reductions*. These negotiations, impelled by the industry, resulted in lower semiconductor tariffs; other negotiations to further open the Japanese market continued as well. In the early 1980s, however, the SIA and some firms within the industry filed several trade complaints against the Japanese, as did the Reagan administration.[68] These complaints resulted in intensified efforts to open the Japanese market and in a pact to regulate Japanese semiconductor export prices, which was intended to alleviate illegal dumping. On the whole the American firms resisted the strong pressures for demanding protection; their important international economic ties made protection less desirable than further opening of markets at home and abroad.

Much like these trade-oriented multinationals, firms with extensive export dependence (but not multinationality) also tended to avoid protectionist demands in times of difficulty. The U.S. textile machinery builders in the 1920s and the machine tool manufacturers in the 1970s provide examples. While having significant export dependence in the aggregate, the American textile machinery manufacturers were divided in two: the cotton machinery producers had become substantial exporters since World War I, while the woolen machinery producers were domestically oriented.[69] This division, as well as the novelty and volatility of the producers' exports, rendered the industry unable to develop a single trade policy preference. Thus, in the early 1920s when exports were most significant, the producers did not lobby Congress for any change in their tariffs during the 1921 hearings. Severe economic distress and rising imports at the time did not drive these producers to seek protection. Rather the export interests of some firms divided the industry, muting preferences for tariff increases. Over the decade these export interests declined and so did the capacity of these firms to forestall protectionist demands. In the 1929 Smoot-Hawley hearings, firms from the woolen machinery sector pressed for and received moderate tariff increases on their ma-

---

67. Milner 1988.
68. *Boston Globe* 1986; *Wall Street Journal* 1986a; *Wall Street Journal* 1986b.
69. Milner 1988.

chines; the more export-oriented firms remained silent. Despite being besieged by imports, these producers refrained from demanding protection for much of the decade and remained moderate and divided in their later requests.

The American machine tool builders in the 1970s were sizable, although declining exporters as well. During this decade these producers lost major market shares to imports and experienced other economic difficulties. Their response, however, was not a resort to demands for protection but rather pressure for help in promoting their exports.[70] In the 1970s, in addition to favoring tariff reductions during the GATT negotiations, the industry association, backed by most producers, lobbied Congress to obtain aid for their exports. In particular the builders wanted major foreign markets—especially the Soviet Union and other Eastern bloc countries—to be opened to their exports. By the late 1970s, the failure of these export initiatives, the continuing decline of its export trade, and the rising import tide pushed groups in the industry to seek some aid from imports. Pressure for protection rose in the late 1970s but was not formalized into a public complaint until the early 1980s. At this point, as the tide of imports overwhelmed the firms' exports, a trade complaint against several countries' imports—mainly Japan's—was made. The Reagan administration responded to this by negotiating a set of voluntary export restraints with several countries.[71] The case of the machine tool builders thus shows again how sizable export dependence may promote an interest in freer trade and damp pressures for protection when imports surge. Moreover, as the firms' export orientation declined, their trade preferences shifted as well.

For industries with firms having some foreign production but no intrafirm trade or U.S. exports, their resistance to protection when imports grew was evident in some cases, although it was often weaker than for export-oriented industries. In many of these industries, growing foreign competition was met by calls for limited protection since the costs of this protection could be minimized. Two examples of this were the American newsprint producers in the 1920s and the U.S. television makers in the 1970s. Newsprint producers in the 1920s were multinational but only minor U.S. exporters. Furthermore their foreign operations were concentrated almost exclusively in Canada, and from there they exported heavily back to the United States. This industry then possessed substantial intrafirm trade. Throughout the 1920s, the newsprint producers actively supported freer trade in their products.[72] In neither the 1921 nor the 1929 tariff revisions did they try to have the duty-free status of newsprint altered. In 1921, several firms did attempt to make this status

---

70. Milner 1988.
71. *New York Times* 1986a; *New York Times* 1986b.
72. Milner 1988.

conditional on other countries' treatment of imports and exports. But this strategic maneuver was distasteful to many firms and was never adopted as part of U.S. policy. As the U.S. producers' trade between the United States and Canada grew in the 1920s, interest in protection waned even more. During the Smoot-Hawley tariff revision, when most tariffs reached their highest levels ever, the newsprint manufacturers uniformly supported the continuing duty-free status of their products. For these international producers, not even rising imports could induce them to think about protection.

The U.S. television makers in the 1970s had some foreign operations but, unlike the newsprint producers, were not very trade-oriented. The industry was, in fact, divided in two: the largest producers, RCA and GE, were multinationals with global trading operations; while the rest, including Zenith, Magnavox, and GTE-Sylvania, were domestic producers. In the 1970s, imports poured into the United States, and the domestically oriented firms led by Zenith initiated a series of trade complaints targeted against a few East Asian countries and on several specific products.[73] These complaints met with varying success, but they were opposed by RCA, the industry's giant multinational. By the late 1970s and early 1980s, much of this protectionist activity had abated as the domestically oriented American firms either moved production abroad, left the industry, or were bought by foreign interests. This international adjustment process eroded support for even the limited, selective protection desired by some earlier.

In all of these cases then, the existence, or creation, of extensive international economic ties prompted firms to resist seeking protection even in times of severe import competition. Conversely the lack or loss of these ties was associated with rising demands for protection. This pattern of results occurred in both the 1920s and 1970s. Increased integration into the international economy was experienced similarly by firms in both decades in spite of their different historical contexts. This pattern then helps explain the varied nature of trade policy *within* each time period. At each point in time, industries dominated by firms with extensive international ties were less protectionist than more domestically oriented ones.

In addition to accounting for variation in preferences *within* each period, the argument and the cases suggest why trade policy varied *between* the two periods. On a macro level, the evidence here implies that, in periods like the 1970s when such international economic ties are widespread and well-developed, pressure for protection by industries should be reduced. As noted earlier, the U.S.'s trade dependence, multinationality, and global intrafirm trade grew much over the years between the 1920s and 1970s.

While arguing that this growth of international ties contributed to the

---

73. Milner 1988.

maintenance of free trade in the 1970s and early 1980s, it must be noted that this internationalization of U.S. industry went hand-in-hand with trade liberalization in the postwar period. Clearly the liberalization of trade in the 1950s and 1960s was one factor promoting the growth of these international ties. But much of this expansion occurred before the two most significant reductions in trade barriers. United States export dependence and especially U.S. multinationality grew significantly before the phasing in of the Kennedy Round tariff cuts in the early 1970s. United States industrial export dependence rose 33 percent between 1960 and 1970, while the value of U.S. direct foreign investment in manufacturing increased nearly 800 percent between 1950 and 1970.[74] The growth of these international ties cannot be separated from the liberalization of trade occurring at the same time. But the expansion of these ties prior to the 1970s suggests that forces for trade liberalization—for example, industries with international ties—were in place prior to the 1970s and were factors in the liberalization which occurred during that decade. The growth of the international ties meant that by the 1970s many more firms were more willing to resist protectionist pressures. Despite higher import penetration levels, demands for protection were less widespread than in the 1920s. This reduced demand then provides a partial answer to our central puzzle.

Other Explanations

Do these case studies shed light on economists' explanations of firms' trade policy preferences? Although the preferences of industries have been less studied than other factors affecting trade policy outcomes, several different explanations do exist. These have focused on predicting firms' demands for protection; much less has been written about firms' preferences for further trade liberalization.[75] Despite these limitations, the cases here provide new evidence for these other theories by economists.

In part firms' preferences for protection have been accounted for by their competitive position. That is, indicators of competitive disadvantage have been used to predict protectionist demands. One factor indicating disadvantage that is linked to demands for protection is an industry's labor intensity.[76] The claim is that the more labor-intensive (especially unskilled labor) an industry in a developed country is, the more disadvantaged it is and the more

---

74. Consistent data series on export dependence and multinationality as a percent of GNP for the period from 1945 on are not to my knowledge available. The export dependence data come from Report of the President's Commission on Industrial Competitiveness 1985, 1:36. The data on direct foreign investment come from Feldstein 1980, 240, table 3.30.

75. See note 54.

76. For example, see Caves 1976; Ray 1981; Baldwin 1986, 150–72; and Lavergne 1983, 75–87.

likely it is to seek protection. The cases here support this argument to an extent. The most labor-intensive industries among the cases were usually domestic-oriented industries, and hence ones preferring protection. The cases also suggest that the movement of labor-intensive segments of firms' production abroad can enhance firms' willingness to resist protection. As this movement further internationalizes their operations, it thereby increases the costs of protection. Examples of this abounded: the semiconductor producers, watch and clock manufacturers, radio and television producers, and newsprint firms. This migration of labor-intensive production abroad has been an important force in the internationalization of production occurring in the past several decades. It also has been a major reason for the growing divergence between the trade preferences of labor unions and multinationals in developed countries.

Other economic explanations of an industry's preferences on trade focus on the characteristics that enhance the rents obtained from trade barriers.[77] This line of inquiry has pointed to the degree of industry concentration—as a proxy for its monopoly power—as a determinant of protectionist demand. One economist explains:

> Ceteris paribus, monopolistic industries can be expected to have a relatively larger stake in tariffs than competitive industries since the latter can enjoy only ephemeral excess quasi-rents before increased investment by the industry and the consequent expansion of supply sends excess capital returns back to zero. . . . Certainly industries which also enjoy monopoly rents are in a better position to exploit the advantages of tariff protection and could be expected, therefore, to lobby relatively intensely.[78]

Tests of this hypothesis have generally not supported it, and the cases here also cast some doubt on it.[79] Many concentrated industries, like semiconductors, were much less protectionist than more competitive industries, like footwear in the 1970s and woolens and watches and clocks in the 1920s. On the other hand, one case strongly supports this argument. Of all the cases studied, the photographic industry was the most dominated by one firm. In the 1920s, Kodak's photographic equipment sector was a monopolist, using trade barriers to increase its profits. Indeed Kodak's interest in protection was largely attributable to its monopoly position. This case suggests that only very high levels of concentration may induce firms to seek protection and that more oligopolistic structures may have mixed effects on firms' preferences.

---

77. Krueger 1974; Brock and Magee 1978; Lavergne 1983, 164–66.
78. Lavergne 1983, 92.
79. Lavergne 1983, 152–56; Baldwin 1986, 150–72.

The amount of protection previously supplied has also been seen as influencing firms' later trade preferences. In general past protection is expected to have a consistent, positive effect on future demands.[80] Past protection is seen as leading to future demands for protection.[81] The cases provide mixed support for this argument. In some, high levels of protection did not seem to influence industries' later preferences. For example, watches and clocks, semiconductors, and machine tools all had relatively high levels of protection prior to the 1970s.[82] During much of the decade, however, these industries favored tariff reductions. For other industries, past protection did engender further demands for it. For instance, the woolens industry and the footwear industry in the 1920s and the 1970s were all highly protected before the period examined and remained protectionist throughout it. In these cases, past protection appeared unsuccessful; that is, the industry's problems continued and/or intensified. This unsuccessful past protection then led to demands for new protection.

This brings us to a final set of factors that economists have seen as influencing firms' trade preferences—their international ties. First, export dependence, it is claimed, affects firms' trade preferences.[83] Various studies show that demands for protective measures are much less common among firms that export a substantial part of their production. This study confirms this observation. Export-dependent firms were likely to resist protectionist urges even in times of increasing imports.

In addition economists have argued that multinationals have an interest in reduced trade barriers as a result of concerns about their foreign operations and global intrafirm trade.[84] But in earlier studies the industry's degree of multinationality has often not been a significant determinant of its preferences, and this finding is supported here.[85] Industry-wide levels of multinationality are not good predictors of firms' trade preferences. One must look both at the individual firms' multinational relations and at the character of that multinationality. Industry-level data obscure the distribution of international ties among firms. In a highly multinational industry, some firms may have few, if any, international ties and may thus be protectionist. Because of this uneven distribution, data on individual firms may give a more accurate picture of their trade preferences. Indeed firm-level analysis elsewhere strongly con-

80. On outcomes, see Lavergne 1983, 164–66.
81. Baldwin 1981, 194.
82. U.S. Tariff Commission 1974, 56–58.
83. Fong 1982, chap. 2; Baldwin 1986, 150–72; Lavergne 1983, 160–64; Becker 1982; Wilson 1971; Destler and Odell 1987.
84. Vernon 1982; Baldwin 1986, 145–51; Fong 1982, chap. 2; Helleiner 1979; Lavergne 1983, 166–67.
85. For example, Baldwin 1986, 166–67.

firms the importance of multinational ties as a brake on protectionist demands, as this study also does.[86]

Multinational firms organized in different ways may also have distinct preferences. As pointed out multinationals without global trade networks may be selectively protectionist; multinationals with extensive global networks are likely to be ardent opponents of protectionism. It is not simply multinationality but the character of this foreign involvement that is crucial to understanding firms' trade preferences. The impact of multinationals' trade relations on their trade preferences has also been examined by economists. Lavergne has tested the hypothesis that the growth of U.S. multinationals with large trade flows from abroad has altered the structure of U.S. protection. He finds little evidence for such a claim but realizes that his dependent variable may not capture their influence. Noting that multinational affiliates' exports to the United States are of "a modest proportion," or about 12 percent of all nonauto, nonpetroleum manufactured imports, he queries whether "it is legitimate to ask if such a proportion is sufficient to have an important impact in determining the *structure* of barriers to trade in the U.S.," and points out that "it is quite possible that such imports have had an impact of importance in selected sectors" (emphasis added).[87] Our case studies support this latter point; for highly internationally oriented firms, resistance to protection was widespread.

The industries focused on in this study lend credence to economists' assertions that high levels of labor intensity, concentration, export dependence, and multinationality influence firms' trade policy preferences. The cases also imply that the influence of past policies on later demands may be complicated since the industries reveal varying effects exercised by the past. The case study approach thus helps shed light on more aggregate examinations of firms' trade preferences by economists and can provide a more detailed understanding of how some key factors may actually operate to affect firms' preferences.

Industry Divisions, Context, and Policy Outcomes

Three further issues are raised by the argument. The first of these deals with intra-industry divisions on trade issues. One notable feature of the growing internationalization of U.S. industries has been its uneven character. Within an industry some firms, usually the largest, have become international, while the smaller ones have often remained dependent on the domestic market. This uneven process has tended to divide industries in two on trade politics with the

---

86. Pugel and Walter 1985.
87. Lavergne 1983, 106.

large multinationals opposing the more numerous but smaller domestic-centered firms, a pattern evident in the cases.

Two consequences of this political division stand out. First, it has made developing an industry-wide position difficult. As seen in the textile machinery case, internal divisions created by different international interests can leave an industry without the capacity to develop a political position on trade. Second, the attempt to create an "industry" position in a divided industry may lead to the fashioning of compromises that are less protectionist than the majority of firms may prefer. This process was evident in the semi-conductor case. Both of these results may reduce protectionist demands even more than the extent of internationalization of the industry would suggest. Thus the creation of these intra-industry divisions through unevenly rising interdependence may further dampen pressures for protection.

In the 1920s and 1970s, the extent of these intra-industry divisions varied. In the 1920s, these internal divisions were less apparent than in the later period since internationalization was less widespread then. Moreover the existing divisions tended to be incipient, often the initial breach in an industry's unity as a consequence of its recent internationalization. Having developed only in the 1920s as certain producers began exporting, the divisions in the textile machinery industry were exemplary. This difference between the two periods meant that another counterweight—that is, intra-industry divisions—to protectionist pressures was also weaker in the 1920s.

Second, contextual differences between the two periods have been alleged to undercut any comparison between them.[88] But contextual differences did not override the powerful influence that a firm's international position exerted on its trade preferences. In both periods internationally oriented firms opposed protectionist solutions to their problems. This finding is especially interesting since it suggests that the broad differences—for example, in macroeconomic circumstances, political structures, and economic ideology—between the two periods did not greatly affect the way firms calculated their preferences. The similarities in firms' preferences in the two periods implies that factors differentiating the times may have only a minor impact on demands for protection by industries at any time.

Moreover firms often did not take these contextual features as given. In particular, some firms worked in both periods to alter domestic political structures responsible for trade policy. In the 1920s, for example, several industries promoted attempts intended to make U.S. procedures more free-trade oriented, opposing the American valuation plan and supporting the flexible tariff provisions; other industries, including the domestically oriented woolen goods one, acted contrarily. In the 1970s, those footwear and televi-

---

88. For example, see Oye 1985, 199.

sion manufacturers who pursued protection lobbied to change U.S. procedures in order to make them more amenable to protectionist outcomes. This involved efforts—most of which were successful—to loosen U.S. trade laws and to shift their enforcement to agencies more favorable to domestic industry. Certain contextual features, such as the domestic political process for trade issues, thus may not be exogenous; rather, these structures in which firms are assumed to operate may be amenable to the influence of firms.

A final issue involves the question of trade policy outcomes. I have focused mostly on explaining firm's preferences and less so on policy decisions. That such preferences influence outcomes has been largely assumed. The cases here and elsewhere, however, provide some support for this assumption. In almost all of the cases, the industry's demands for protection or freer trade had some eventual effect upon policy. First, in none of the cases were industries accorded protection when they did not demand it. This suggests that the issue of protection was usually placed on the political agenda by the industries themselves. Second, industries desiring the maintenance of low barriers or reductions of restraints were successful in all cases in the 1920s and 1970s, as the fertilizer, newsprint, and semiconductor cases show. Thus, even in the 1920s, no systematic bias against low or reduced trade barriers appeared to exist.

Finally, industries seeking increases in these barriers also tended to be successful. Cases where the industry was divided reduced their capacity for effective political influence, however. The limited success of the domestically oriented television makers in the 1970s exemplified this. In contrast where industries were united in favor of protection, they generally received it. This was true for all cases in the 1920s and for all but two in the 1970s. The footwear producers failed throughout the early 1970s to have new trade barriers erected, but in the late 1970s their efforts met with some success as the Carter administration negotiated voluntary export restraints for them. Likewise, the early efforts of the machine tool builders in the late 1970s and early 1980s failed to produce any response from the government. By the mid-1980s, however, the Reagan administration was pressing the industry's case and negotiating export restraints with foreign governments.

In neither period did industries always get exactly what they wanted when they wanted it. But their demands tended in time to move policy in the desired direction. The greater difficulty of industries to obtain their demands for protection in the 1970s may reflect both the greater awareness of the international problems caused by protection among industry and government officials and the more limited responsiveness of the executive—now in control of more trade issues—as opposed to Congress, who played a larger role in the 1920s, vis-à-vis domestic pressures. Some bias in the trade policy system against protection appears evident in the 1970s. Unlike the determination of firms' preferences then, the fashioning of trade policy outcomes may depend more on factors that differed in the two contexts, such as policy-making structures and economic ideology.

In general industries in both periods were able over time to realize trade policies close to the ones they desired. Thus their preferences seemed to count in the policy process. Other influences on trade policy, such as the interests of labor or decision-makers' ideologies, were likely to be important in both periods. But the evidence here simply shows that reduced interest in protection by internationally oriented industries in the 1970s by itself was one, but not the sole, reason for the resistance to protection in the United States.

Conclusion

Why did trade policy outcomes differ between the 1920s and 1970s when a number of conditions influencing trade politics were similar? Why was protectionism resisted in the 1970s when economic difficulties were severe and U.S. hegemony was in decline? While noting other answers to this puzzle, involving the international distribution of power, international regimes, and domestic political structures, I maintained that aspects of rising international economic interdependence in the post–World War II period led to changes in the trade policy preferences of domestic actors. Rising interdependence meant in part the growth of firms' ties to the international economy through exports, multinationality, and global intrafirm trade; and these ties in turn made protectionism a more costly policy for these firms. In brief the new interdependence made protectionism a less viable option for many firms facing serious import competition. Consequently, it dampened the demand for protection.

This argument was evaluated by examining a set of industries from the 1920s and 1970s. These cases supported the contention that internationally-oriented firms were less likely to demand protection than were domestically-oriented ones, *even* if they faced the high levels of import penetration. The cases also pointed out the importance of firm-level analysis. International ties conditioned firms' preferences, and divergences in these ties among firms in an industry created important political divisions over trade *within* the industry. These intra-industry divisions also helped damp pressures for protectionism.

Differences in the historical context between the 1920s and 1970s did not override the argument. Internationally oriented firms in both periods were less protectionist than their domestic-centered counterparts, despite differences in the international and domestic political structures at the two times. In fact features often considered contextual were amenable to influence by firms. Moreover, among the firms examined, their trade preferences mattered. Policy outcomes often reflected the desires of firms. Reduced demand for protection then by firms in the 1970s, as compared to the 1920s, may be one central, but not the only, reason why trade policy in the two periods differed.

REFERENCES

Aggarwal, Vinod. 1985. *Liberal Protectionism: The International Politics of Organized Textile Trade.* Berkeley: University of California Press.

Baldwin, David. 1979. "Power Analysis and World Politics." *World Politics* 31:161–94.

Baldwin, Robert. 1981. "Political Economy of U.S. Import Policy." Typescript. Madison, Wis.: University of Wisconsin, Department of Economics.

Baldwin, Robert. 1986. *The Political Economy of U.S. Import Policy.* Cambridge, Mass.: MIT Press.

Baldwin, Robert, and J. David Richardson. 1986. *International Trade and Finance.* 3d ed. Boston: Little, Brown.

Bauer, Raymond, Ithiel de Sola Pool, and Lewis Dexter. 1972. *American Business and Public Policy.* Chicago: Aldine-Atherton.

Becker, William. 1982. *The Dynamics of Business-Government Relations.* Chicago: University of Chicago Press.

Bergsten, C. Fred. 1971. "The Crisis in U.S. Trade Policy." *Foreign Affairs* 49:619–35.

Bergsten, C. Fred, and William Cline. 1983. "Overview." In *Trade Policy in the 1980's,* ed. William Cline. Washington, D.C.: Institute for International Economics.

Boston Globe. 1986. April 13.

Brock, William, and Stephen Magee. 1978. "The Economics of Special Interest Politics: Case of the Tariff." *American Economic Review Papers and Proceedings* 68:246–50.

Caves, Richard. 1976. "Economic Models of Political Choice: Canada's Tariff Structure." *Canada Journal of Economy* 9:278–300.

Destler, I. M. 1986. *American Trade Politics: System Under Stress.* Washington, D.C.: Institute for International Economics.

Destler, I. M., and John Odell. 1987. *Anti-Protection: Changing Forces in United States Trade Politics.* Washington, D.C.: Institute for International Economics.

Dunn, Robert. 1926. *American Foreign Investments.* New York: Viking.

Feldstein, Martin, ed. 1980. *The American Economy in Transition.* Chicago: NBER.

Ferguson, Thomas. 1984. "From Normalcy to New Deal." *International Organization* 38:40–94.

Fong, Glenn. 1982. "Export Dependence and the New Protectionism." Ph.D. diss., Cornell University.

Gallarotti, Giulio. 1985. "Toward a Business Cycle Model of Tariffs." *International Organization* 39:155–87.

Gerschenkron, Alexander. 1962. *Economic Backwardness in Historical Perspective.* Cambridge, Mass.: Harvard University Press.

Gilpin, Robert. 1975. *U.S. Power and the Multinational Corporation.* New York: Basic.

Goldstein, Judith. 1983. "A Reexamination of American Commercial Policy" Ph.D. diss., UCLA.

Goldstein, Judith. 1986. "The Political Economy of Trade." *American Political Science Review* 80:161–84.

Grubel, Herbert. 1977. *International Economics.* Homewood, Ill.: Irwin.

Grunwald, Joseph, and Kenneth Flamm. 1985. *Global Factory.* Washington, D.C.: Brookings.

Hays, Samuel. 1957. *The Response to Industrialism, 1885–1914.* Chicago: University of Chicago.

Helleiner, Gerald. 1977. "Transnational Enterprise and the New Political Economy of U.S. Trade Policy." *Oxford Economic Papers* 29:102–16.

Helleiner, Gerald. 1979. "Transnational Corporations and the Trade Structure." In *On the Economics of Intra-Firm Trade,* ed. H. Giersch. Tubingen: Mohr.

Helleiner, Gerald, and Real Lavergne. 1979. "Intra-Firm Trade and Industrial Exports to the U.S." *Oxford Bulletin of Economics and Statistics* 41:297–312.

Hughes, K. 1979. *Trade, Taxes, and Transnationals.* New York: Praeger.

Keohane, Robert. 1980. "The Theory of Hegemonic Stability and Changes in International Economic Regimes." In *Change in the International System,* ed. Ole Holsti, Randolph Siverson, and Alexander George, Boulder, Colo.: Westview.

Keohane, Robert. 1984. *After Hegemony: Cooperation and Discord in the World Political Economy.* Princeton: Princeton University Press.

Keohane, Robert, and Joseph Nye. 1977. *Power and Interdependence: World Politics in Transition.* Boston: Little, Brown.

Kindleberger, Charles. 1973. *The World in Depression, 1929–1939.* Berkeley: University of California Press.

Kindleberger, Charles, and Peter Lindert. 1978. *International Economics,* 6th ed. Homewood, Ill.: Irwin.

Krasner, Stephen. 1976. "State Power and the Structure of International Trade." *World Politics* 28:317–47.

Krueger, Anne. 1974. "Political Economy of the Rent-Seeking Society." *American Economic Review* 64:291–303.

Kronholz, J. 1979. "Trade and Currency Wars Deepen the Depression." *Wall Street Journal,* Oct. 23, 1979.

Lake, David. 1983. "International Economic Structures and American Foreign Policy, 1887–1934." *World Politics* 35:517–43.

Lake, David. 1984. "Beneath the Commerce of Nations." *International Studies Quarterly* 28:143–70.

Lake, David. 1988. *Power, Protection, and Free Trade.* Ithaca: Cornell University Press.

Lavergne, Real. 1983. *The Political Economy of U.S. Tariffs.* Toronto: Academic Press.

League of Nations. 1942. *Economic Fluctuations in the U.S. and U.K., 1918–1942.* Geneva: League of Nations.

Lenway, Stephanie. 1985. *The Politics of U.S. International Trade.* Boston: Pitman.

Lewis, W. Arthur. 1949. *Economic Survey, 1919–1939.* London: Allen, Unwin.

Lipsey, Robert. 1963. *Price and Quantity Trends in the Foreign Trade of the U.S.* Princeton: Princeton University Press.

Lipson, Charles. 1982. "The Transformation of Trade." *International Organization* 36:417–56.

Malmgren, Harald. 1970. "Coming Trade Wars?" *Foreign Policy* 1:115–43.

McKeown, Timothy. 1984. "Firms and Tariff Regime Change." *World Politics* 36:215–33.

Milner, Helen. 1988. *Resisting Protectionism: Global Industries and the Politics of International Trade.* Princeton: Princeton University Press.

Morici, Peter, and Laura Megna. 1983. *U.S. Economic Policies Affecting Industrial Trade: A Quantitative Assessment.* Washington, D.C.: National Planning Association.

New York Times. 1986a. February 3.

New York Times. 1986b. March 6.

Odell, John. 1982. *U.S. International Monetary Policy: Markets, Power, and Ideas as Sources of Change.* Princeton: Princeton University Press.

Olson, Mancur. 1965. *The Logic of Collective Action.* Cambridge, Mass.: Harvard University Press.

Oye, Kenneth. 1985. "The Sterling-Dollar-Franc Triangle: Monetary Diplomacy, 1929–1937." *World Politics* 38:173–99.

Pastor, Robert. 1980. *Congress and the Politics of U.S. Foreign Economic Policy.* Berkeley: University of California Press.

Pincus, Jonathan. 1977. *Pressure Groups and Politics in Antebellum Tariffs.* New York: Columbia University Press.

Pollard, Robert. 1985. *Economic Security and the Origins of the Cold War.* New York: Columbia University Press.

Porter, Roger. 1980. *Presidential Decision Making.* Cambridge: Cambridge University Press.

Presidents Commission on Industrial Competitiveness. 1985. *Global Competition: The New Reality.* vol.1.

Pugel, Thomas, and Ingo Walter. 1985. "U.S. Corporate Interests and the Political Economy of Trade Policy." *Review of Economics and Statistics* 67:465–73.

Ratner, Sidney, James Soltow, and Richard Sylla. 1979. *The Evolution of the American Economy.* New York: Basic Books.

Ray, Edward. 1981. "Determinants of Tariff and Nontariff Trade Restrictions in the U.S." *Journal of Political Economy* 81:105–21.

Reich, Robert. 1983. "Beyond Free Trade." *Foreign Affairs* 61:4.

Ruggie, John. 1982. "International Regimes, Transactions, and Change." *International Organization* 36:379–415.

Russett, Bruce. 1985. "The Mysterious Case of Vanishing Hegemony." *International Organization* 39:207–32.

Schnattschneider, E. E. 1935. *Politics, Pressure and the Tariff.* Englewood Cliffs, N.J.: Prentice-Hall.

Strange, Susan. 1982. "Still an Extraordinary Power." In *Political Economy of International and Domestic Monetary Relations,* ed. Raymond Lombra and Willard Witte. Ames, Iowa: Iowa State University.

Strange, Susan, and Roger Tooze, eds. 1980. *The International Politics of Surplus Capacity.* London: Butterworth.

Takacs, Wendy. 1981. "Pressures for Protectionism: An Empirical Analysis." *Economic Inquiry* 19:687–93.

U.S., Department of Commerce. 1919–30. *Survey of Current Business,* various issues.

U.S., Department of Commerce, Census Bureau. 1975. *Historical Statistics of the U.S., Colonial Times to the Present.*

U.S., Department of Commerce. 1981. *1977 Enterprise Statistics.*

U.S., Senate. 1931. *American Branch Factories Abroad.* S. Doc. no. 258, 71st Cong., 3d sess.

U.S., Tariff Commission. 1974. *Trade Barriers: An Overview.* Doc. no. 665.

Vernon, Raymond. 1982. "International Trade Policy in the 1980s." *International Studies Quarterly* 26:483–510.

Wall Street Journal. 1986a. March 12, 7.

Wall Street Journal. 1986b. March 31, 2.

Wilson, Joan H. 1971. *American Business and Foreign Policy, 1920–33.* Boston: Beacon.

Winham, Gilbert. 1980. "Robert Strauss, the MTN, and the Control of Faction." *Journal of World Trade Law* 14:377–97.

CHAPTER 7

Analyzing Economic Sanctions: Toward a Public Choice Framework

William H. Kaempfer and Anton D. Lowenberg

1. Introduction

The issue of international economic sanctions falls within the broader scope of international political economy in general and, as such, has traditionally occupied the interests of political scientists and international relations specialists. A few economists have written in depth on the subject, but they have been relatively recent entrants into the field. Even more recently, a smaller subset of economists has applied public choice theory to the study of international political economy and economic sanctions in particular. The purpose of the present essay is to argue that the public choice approach contributes a positive analysis of the process of foreign economic policy formation (including economic sanctions), and of the effects of foreign economic policy, which, while consistent with some explanations developed by political scientists, also adds insights that are unique to the public choice approach. Policy implications generated from public choice models are the product of the specific methodology of public choice.

The broadest conception of an economic sanction is the use of economic measures as penalties imposed in order to ensure the target country's compliance with a law, an accepted norm of international conduct, or a mode of behavior regarded as desirable by an international organization, group of nations, or a single sanctioning nation (Losman 1979, 1; Doxey 1980, 1–9; Renwick 1981, 2). In modern practice, sanctions have often been linked with policies of collective security and the prevention of war, or aggression on the part of either global or regional international organizations (Doxey 1980, 3;

An earlier version of this essay was presented at the Claremont-U.S.C. Conference on Blending Political and Economic Analysis of International Trade Policies, March 5–7, 1987. The authors are grateful to John Odell, Thomas Willett, and other conference participants for helpful comments and suggestions. Funding, in the form of a Faculty Research Grant for released time for Lowenberg, was provided by California State University, Northridge.

Knorr 1975, 160). The economic measures directed by the League of Nations against Italy in retaliation for the latter's occupation of Abyssinia in 1935 are usually cited as the first elaboration of the modern notion of economic sanctions (Renwick 1981, 4), although historical precedents are generally identified in the Continental Blockade and the countermeasures adopted by Britain during the Napoleonic Wars, as well as in Jefferson's retaliatory embargo on trade with Britain (Doxey 1980, 10; Losman 1979, 2; Renwick 1981, 4–8).

Both economists and political scientists have tended to follow a case study or historical approach to the sanctions issue. In fact, there is now a well-established history of "classic cases" that has developed in the literature. Certainly the League comprised the first modern experiment with the notion of collective security, and it provided the blueprint for subsequent multilateral applications of sanctions such as those of the United Nations against Rhodesia; the Arab League against Israel; OPEC against the United States, Japan, and the Netherlands; and the OAS against Cuba. Frequently analyzed modern episodes of bilateral sanctions include the United States against the Soviet Union (in retaliation for the latter's intervention in Afghanistan), the United States against Iran initiated by the hostage crisis, the United States against Cuba, the United States against Japan when the latter was at war with China in 1940–41, the United States against the Trujillo regime in the Dominican Republic, the Soviet Union's reprisals against China and Yugoslavia, the British boycott of Iran in 1952, and French sanctions against Algeria in 1970.

We believe that public choice theory provides a valuable approach to analyzing both market and nonmarket channels of influence which characterize economic tools of foreign policy. In order to illustrate this point, an example will be presented with reference to a recent major episode of international economic sanctions—namely, those applied against South Africa.

Section 2 discusses traditional approaches to the issue of international economic sanctions that lie outside the boundaries of public choice theory per se. Section 3 briefly outlines some definitive features of the public choice method, and the application of public choice to the realm of international political economy. A public choice model of the impact of sanctions on South African apartheid policy is presented in section 4. Section 5 concludes with an evaluation of the fruitfulness of the public choice approach as an explanation of foreign economic policy, and economic sanctions in particular.

2. The Received Wisdom on Sanctions: Political Scientists and Economists

The purpose of this section is to review the traditional literature on sanctions in order to provide a background against which to evaluate the contribution of the public choice approach. Within the international relations literature, several schools of thought may be identified (Willett 1980; Keohane and Nye 1977; Katzenstein 1976). In the aftermath of World War II and the breakup of the League of Nations, there was a strong feeling of pessimism regarding the likelihood of successful international cooperation and integration among nation states. Competing nationalisms were seen as the norm and the possibilities for maintaining peace through international organization and supranational government appeared remote. The school of thought in international relations most closely associated with this approach has been variously labeled the "realist," "statist," or "mercantilist" school (D. Baldwin 1985, 155; Willett 1980, 15–16). According to these proponents of realpolitik, foreign policy is designed to promote the national interests of sovereign states and there is no inherent tendency toward increased cooperation or integration that would involve the subsuming of individual states' sovereignties to global or even regional interests. The successful application of sanctions requires collective action by a sufficiently large group of nations to ensure that the target country would find it difficult to circumvent the restrictions imposed upon it (Losman 1979, 126; Knorr 1975, 87). Such subordination of individual profit opportunities by sovereign states to the collective interests of the group would be hard to achieve in a world of virulently competitive sovereignties. Related to this idea is the notion of "hegemonic states," according to which concerted collective action against a violator of international norms is only likely to occur under the auspices of a world hegemon, or dominant power, which leads an hierarchical alliance. Since hegemonic systems have apparently broken down in the twentieth century, the possibilities for successful multilateral sanctions have likewise diminished (McKeown 1986, 9–10).

In contrast to the mercantilist school, there is a group of "optimists" whose views derive from the ideals underlying the Charter of the League and later the Covenant of the United Nations. This school of so-called "interdependence theorists," who are exponents of the "sovereignty-at-bay" idea, subscribes to the view that the development of the international division of labor and the pursuit of free trade will automatically promote the breakdown of nationalist barriers and the growth of supranational cooperation (Willett 1980; Vaubel 1986, 40). Richard Cooper (1986) defines economic interdependence as a situation in which economic transactions between two or more countries are highly sensitive to domestic economic developments within any single country. According to Cooper, growing interdependence in the world economy will inevitably create pressures for international coordination of economic policies, but will also greatly complicate the management of each nation's foreign policy (14, 19). Some international relations theorists treat the formation of foreign policy as an endogenous outcome of interactions between domestic interest groups and competing factions within domestic bureaucracies (Katzenstein 1976, 1978), and in this respect, as we shall see, they are not far removed from the public choice approach. Others—the practitioners of "comparative politics"—abandon the rigid "liberal pluralism" of the public choice approach in favor of the belief that each country's ability to exert economic power in an interdependent world depends crucially on the unique set of domestic political structures which evolved according to each nation's special historical experiences with modernization and industrialization (Ilgen 1985, 4–5).

The postwar literature on economic sanctions displays a "realist" skepticism about the efficacy of cooperative international experiments with sanctions. "Whereas military force symbolized hard-headed 'realism,' economic sanctions symbolized fuzzy-minded 'idealism' and unwillingness to face up to the hard facts of international life" (D. Baldwin 1985, 155). The realists tend to draw, at least implicitly, a distinction between "high politics"—which includes military strategy and diplomacy—and "low politics"—which comprises the mundane, humdrum, and not spectacularly effective pursuit of foreign economic policy (including sanctions). A careful reading of the most effective exponents of this school—which include Margaret Doxey (1980), Johan Galtung (1967), Klaus Knorr (1975), Donald Losman (1979), and Robin Renwick (1981)—reveals their chief conclusion to be that, while most cases of international economic sanctions which where sustained over a sufficiently long period of time did produce at least some economic hardship in the target countries, in no instance were the economic sanctions themselves primarily responsible for inducing changes in the political behavior of the target regimes (Knorr 1975, 140, 146, 165; Losman 1979, 125; Doxey 1980, 125, 131).

For example, in the case of the League's sanctions against Italy, the latter country was forced to bear painful shortages of raw materials and consumer goods, but adjustments were made by means of civilian rationing, development of substitutes, and use of nonsanctioning neighbors, such as Austria and Hungary as third party conduits to circumvent boycotts. The sanctions did not induce Mussolini to withdraw from Abyssinia. Similarly, it is pointed out that the U.N.'s sanctions against Rhodesia placed a real resource cost on that country's economy but were not the prime cause of the ultimate capitulation of the Smith regime to majority rule. The guerrilla war, which intensified after the attainment of independence by Angola and Mozambique in 1974, and general worldwide recession, due to high energy prices after 1973, are the two factors most often cited as causing the downfall of the Rhodesian rebellion (Doxey 1980, 79; Renwick 1981, 57; Losman 1979, 122–23, 136). As a further example, the U.S. and OAS sanctions against Cuba are depicted as placing a heavy burden on the Soviet Union, but as singularly unsuccessful in bringing about an insurrection within Cuba against the Castro government (Knorr 1975, 149; Losman 1979, 46). In all of these cases, and in almost all of the other classic case studies examined in the international relations literature, economic sanctions are held up as a glaring failure in the sense that they did not effect the desired change in domestic policy within the target country.

David Baldwin (1985) is one of the few political scientists of the postwar era who paints a more positive picture of the effectiveness of economic statecraft, broadly defined. Baldwin, adopting the theoretical framework of modern social power analysis, argues in favor of treating "economic state-craft" broadly as any "influence attempt" by a single state or group of states that relies primarily on economic policy instruments (1985, 13–14). According to Baldwin, economic statecraft is exercised whenever normal market interactions are manipulated by one party as a means to exert power over another party. In this view, *any* use of economic policy instruments that causes another party to do something it would not otherwise do falls under the aegis of economic statecraft. Thus even an act of exchange qualifies. Offering to buy or sell something is one way to induce an actor in the sphere of international relations to change his behavior. In other words, economic statecraft is not limited to a zero-sum game in which one party gains and the other loses. Both parties typically gain from exchange, but the distribution of the gain between the two depends partly upon relative bargaining power. Furthermore, as Hirschman (1980, 18) points out, the total gain from trade bestowed on one country simply reflects the power of its trading partners to induce economic hardship in that country in the event that they were to cut off trade. Even the deliberate promotion of free trade as a foreign policy strategy represents an important instance of economic statecraft (D. Baldwin 1985, 44–46). In contrast, Knorr offers a more standard view of the exercise of economic power, which will sound more familiar to economists: " . . . strictly commercial or quasi-commercial exchanges do not . . . involve economic power, unless they are affected by monopolist market power" (1975, 81). Economists typically start from the premise that voluntary exchange and mutually beneficial contracting necessarily preclude coercive power relationships. The notion that exchange—because it involves alterations in the behavior of the contracting parties—represents an instance of power exertion is based upon a set of premises which is alien to the economic approach.

Political scientists often point out that power is multidimensional, which means that there are numerous bases of power possessed by an actor in international relations (Knorr 1975, 6–26). These bases of power include not just military might, economic strength, or wealth; but also more nebulous and nevertheless important characteristics such as prestige, respect, and ideological or moral leadership. This implies that any "influence attempt" or exercise of power can and usually does have multiple objectives. The application of economic sanctions by a particular state might have as its goal not just a change in the political behavior of its adversary, but also, and perhaps more importantly, the promotion of an image or reputation in the eyes of allies and enemies alike that it will not tolerate certain actions within its sphere of influence.

David Baldwin's (1985) definition of economic statecraft subsumes a wide range of activities that other authors have categorized separately from sanctions as "economic warfare," "economic coercion," "economic diplomacy," or "foreign economic policy." Most writers in the field of international relations have treated the manipulation of tariffs and quotas or the promotion of antiprotectionist ideals as part of normal trade policy, having nothing to do with economic sanctions. Similarly, interruptions in flows of goods and services designed to reinforce military actions against an enemy nation are typically regarded as an adjunct to military warfare and not as an exercise in sanctions (Knorr 1975, 135, 138). Economic sanctions are thus viewed as something special—namely, the application of economic measures to bring about a change in the domestic policy of the target country. At times, however, as Knorr points out, the debate on the effectiveness of sanctions does seem to hinge on fairly trivial quibbling about causality and time frames (1975, 152). For example, after sanctions were applied against Rhodesia for fourteen years, the Smith regime finally gave up and handed over the reins of government to a black majority cabinet. Although the guerrilla war and high world energy prices were proximate causes of this reversal by Smith, economic sanctions must have exacerbated these. Baldwin argues that this is prima facie evidence for the success of sanctions, while Doxey, Losman, and Renwick argue that sanctions against Rhodesia were a failure.

Economists, like their counterparts in political science, have also tended to conclude that sanctions are ineffective in bringing about their stated political goals within the target country. The logic used by economists to arrive at this conclusion is somewhat different, however, and is based on what Brock (1986) refers to as the "elasticity approach." It is typically pointed out by economists that as long as both the demand for and the supply of internationally traded goods is sufficiently elastic, little economic hardship will be induced in the target country by sanctions (Kaempfer and Lowenberg 1988b; Black and Cooper 1987; H. Cooper 1986; Bayard, Pelzman, and Perez-Lopez 1983). If markets operate efficiently, it is likely that alternative sources of supply, transshipment of boycotted goods, and substitution possibilities on the demand side will ensure that the target nation can circumscribe the sanctions with relatively low transaction costs (Kaempfer and Moffett 1988; Willett and Jalalighajar 1983–84). Only if the sanctions are universal, in the sense that all potential trading partners are united in a binding cartel agreement to refuse to sell to or buy from the target country, will boycotts have a severe wealth-reducing effect (Bernholz 1985, 134). But it is generally pointed out that the incentives to free ride on cartel agreements are notoriously alluring. Hufbauer and Schott (1985, 80) conclude that sanctions have been "successful" in only 36 percent of the 103 cases that they examine.

Rigorous general equilibrium models of the target economies have revealed that the impact of sanctions is far from clear-cut. Interruptions in investment flows and trade boycotts might have real wealth or scale effects that impinge upon the owners of different factors of production in different directions—not necessarily the ones most conducive to bringing about the desired political changes (C. Becker 1987; Lundahl 1984; Porter 1979). For example, Charles Becker (1987, 163n) shows that a ban on the sale to South Africa of those manufactured goods which could easily be produced in that country might well cause a shift in the structure of the economy from relatively unskilled, labor-intensive activities to skilled, capital-intensive sectors. This would hurt unskilled black workers and benefit the owners of human and physical capital.

Most economists writing about sanctions have thus emphasized a weak link existing between the application of sanctions and the perception of severe economic dislocation in the target country. This weak link logically precedes that which political scientists have identified between economic hardship and the desired change in political behavior (Renwick 1981, 24, 89, 91). Economists have shown that, given the fungibility and efficiency of world commodity and capital markets, the conditions under which sanctions would be successful in bringing about economic hardship are limited at best. But if sanctions are ineffective, why are they used? In section 4 it will be argued that public choice and political analyses are able to provide reasons for the use of sanctions as instruments of foreign policy, even when their economic effects are minimal.

3. The Public Choice Approach to International Political Economy

Numerous applications of the "economic approach" to the explanation and prediction of human behavior outside of narrow market contexts have yielded interesting results (G. Becker 1976; Radnitzky and Bernholz 1987). Public choice is a subset of this field of endeavor, which some have labeled "the new institutional economics" (Heijdra, Lowenberg, and Mallick, 1988; Langlois 1986; Coase 1984; North 1984). It represents the extension of axioms of voluntary exchange to the subject matter of political science, and derives its impetus from the seminal work of Arrow, Black, Downs, Breton, Buchanan, Tullock, and others of the "Virginia School" of political economy (Mueller 1979).

The method of public choice is inherently individualist (Buchanan 1987; Gray 1987; Frey 1984). The starting point for public choice, like that of the "economic approach" more generally, is the individual value-maximizing agent. The ontological entity known as "the economy" or "the market" is really nothing other than the end product or outcome of a process of individual profit seeking in which each value-maximizing agent, with given preferences and endowments, strives to exhaust all perceived gains from trade. To the extent that individuals are not constrained in their ability to enter into voluntary exchanges and contracts, this process will yield an "efficient" outcome, where the normative benchmark of efficiency is defined essentially as the attainment of mutual agreement on the part of all participating agents that they have done as well for themselves as possible (Buchanan 1987). The technical requirement for this notion of efficiency is that no further Pareto-improvements be attainable in the framework of the existing set of transaction costs which constrain the individual agents.

The premise of public choice theory is that the same value-maximizing agents who comprise "the economy" also comprise "the polity." The only difference concerns the nature of the institutional constraints that condition the agents' profit-seeking behavior. Because the "goods" that are distributed through the polity are collective, the institutions of market exchange are replaced by the institutions of political interaction. The central problem for public choice theory is to show how individual rationality is transformed into collective action. Often the most preferred outcome of the median voter is not the one that emerges out of the political market process. Divergences from the median voter result are usually explained with reference to the actions of interest groups, vote trading (logrolling) by politicians, and the decisions of bureaucrats whose objective is to maximize the size of their budgets.

Applications of public choice theory to international political economy have mainly focused on attempts to explain trade policy, protectionism, and international monetary coordination as endogenous outcomes of the interplay of domestic interest group pressures within countries (Frey 1984; Willett 1980; Amacher, Tollison, and Willett 1979; R. Baldwin 1985; Kaempfer 1987; Marks 1987). Strictly speaking, the relevant unit of analysis for public choice theory, as in economics generally, is the individual rational agent (Bernholz 1985, 10). Institutions such as nation states are essentially human artifacts; they are endogenous products of human action, and, as such, they can have no ends of their own. State policy—including foreign economic policy—is therefore comprehensible only if viewed as the consequence of competing influences exerted by interest groups.[1] Nevertheless, the study of international politics sometimes requires simplification, which involves reducing the number of agents to a few collective actors—usually nation states. This is legitimate on the grounds that human beings are often severely constrained in their behavior by the existence of social artifacts like the state, and

---

1. These interest groups might include not only domestic groups seeking income gains, but also foreign interest groups and groups pursuing ideological goals (Kaempfer and Lowenberg 1988a).

their interests are sometimes indistinguishable from those of the state (Bernholz 1985, 10–13, 101). Thus, although the methodological individualism of the public choice approach generally casts the individual as the primary unit of analysis, some theorists argue that it is not necessarily inconsistent with the logic of the public choice approach to treat the state or other collective entity as an autonomous actor in the context of international political economy.[2] Furthermore, state bureaucracies themselves play an important role in determining policy outcomes.[3]

Frey (1984) describes public choice as being synonymous with formal, precise modeling. However, much work in public choice is more descriptive and less formal than Frey's characterization would suggest. There is a trade-off here: the descriptive approach produces many insights but is less rigorous, while the formal method yields a narrower range of predictions each of which is more precise. There is a place for both in the overall research program of political economy (Willett 1980).

One of the most important insights to emerge out of models of rent-seeking, regulation, and interest group competition is that individual interest groups will seek wealth redistributions and will expend resources to bring these about, even if the total costs to society of such redistributions exceed the amount redistributed (Krueger 1974; Stigler 1971; Peltzman 1976; Olson 1982; Colander 1984). Politicians seeking to maximize political support will supply regulation up to the point where the marginal benefit of additional regulation to beneficiary interest groups equals its marginal cost to those who are hurt by regulation. For example, Bernholz (1985, 117) shows that political support maximizing politicians in a democracy will enforce regulation designed to encourage exports and restrict imports of goods produced in declining sectors of the economy. However, they will prefer measures that reduce imports over those that promote exports because the former are the most efficient means to win the support of voters who are dependent on the favored industries (Bernholz 1966, 66). Those political scientists who have followed a "bureaucracy theory" approach to foreign policy have adopted an orientation which is consistent with that of public choice. Thus, Katzenstein (1976, 1978) emphasizes the importance for the conduct of foreign policy of domestic political considerations (Willett 1980, 29).

The kinds of issues that arise in considering the motives and content of the push for economic sanctions in the sanctioning countries have a close resemblance to those issues involved in studies of protectionist or anti–free trade movements in general (R. Baldwin 1985; Destler 1986; Rowe 1987). Therefore, since sanctions represent a particular type of foreign policy out-

---

2. See, for example, Willett 1980 and Kaempfer 1989.
3. See Katzenstein 1976, 1978.

come which is not dissimilar to other protectionist trade interventions, it is clear that sanctions also should be amenable to analysis using public choice theory. Indeed, public choice does provide a unified framework within which it is possible to develop positive theories to explain the types of international economic sanctions that are likely to be applied (Kaempfer and Lowenberg 1988a, 1989).

A fully fledged public choice theory of international sanctions can be used not only to model the configuration of interest group politics within the sanctioning country or countries in order to determine what forms of economic statecraft will emerge out of the political market process, but also to model the configuration of interest groups within the target country in order to predict the political—as well as economic—effects of sanctions. In the next section, we will illustrate the fruitfulness of this approach by developing a public choice model of the impact of international sanctions directed against South Africa.

4. A Public Choice Model of the Impact of International Sanctions Against South Africa

In general most analysts proceed on the assumption that external economic sanctions have been brought to bear against South Africa because of the apartheid policies of that nation. This section presents a model to explain the "level" of apartheid in South Africa that incorporates international economic sanctions as an exogenous variable.[4] The effects of sanctions on the application of apartheid policy are therefore endogenized. However, as opposed to more traditional economic approaches which examine the market effects of sanctions, the approach taken here is to build a public choice model in order to determine the political changes in South Africa that might be induced by different types of sanctions. The analysis is not intended to comprise an explanation of international relations, but is a first step in that direction since it focuses on the impact of foreign policy on the target nation.

In keeping with the economic approach to human behavior, the motives for apartheid are explained in terms of the responses of rational agents to perceived situational constraints. Essentially, apartheid is treated as a state policy that redistributes wealth in accordance with the relative strengths of interest groups within the polity. An alternative type of explanation might attribute apartheid to the existence of psychological propensities such as racism or bigotry on the part of whites. The economic model used in this section does not deny the importance of racism as an explanation of discriminatory

---

4. In a pair of recent articles, we discuss the extent to which self-interest in the sanctioning country may also shape the sanctions that are imposed (Kaempfer and Lowenberg, 1988a, 1989).

policy. However, the purpose of the analysis is to explain apartheid not as a product of taste, but as a function of the objective constraints faced by agents with given tastes.[5] Changes in the level of apartheid can then be accounted for in terms of changing constraints, not changes in preferences. Furthermore, apartheid policy is viewed as changing along a continuum, abstracting from sudden revolutionary changes in the political institutional framework. This facilitates the use of a comparative static technique to analyze the way in which race policy in South Africa responds to changing pressures brought to bear in the political system by interest groups of differing motives.

From the public choice perspective, political influence is produced as a result of the actions of private utility-maximizing individual members of interest groups. While the groups are defined by commonality of interests, the political participation of any group member, and hence the political effectiveness of the group, is tempered by a desire to free ride on the contributions of others in the group.

Following the interpretation of Lowenberg (1989), apartheid, in our model, consists of a series of regulations that effect redistributions between domestic interest groups in South Africa. In aggregate these regulations are wealth decreasing, but some groups benefit at the expense of others because of apartheid. Specifically, white workers and some employers in the agriculture sector will be the beneficiaries of apartheid regulations restricting the employability of black workers in certain jobs, while black workers and to some extent other employers will be penalized by the regulations.

The structure of our model is depicted in figure 1.[6] The "level of apartheid," or the extent of enforcement of apartheid laws, is represented by the variable A, measured on the horizontal axis. The downward sloping demand curves and the upward sloping supply curves are marginal utility and disutility schedules. The curve labelled D in figure 1 shows the marginal utility, to those interest groups that benefit from apartheid, associated with increased levels of A. The curve labelled S is the marginal utility to opponents of apartheid from reduced levels of A. The height of the D curve reflects the amount of resources that the proponents of apartheid policy are willing to spend on the margin to generate political influence in order to secure one more "unit" of apartheid. Similarly, the height of the S curve is the marginal willingness to pay on the part of opponents of apartheid in order to prevent one more unit from being supplied.

Demanders of apartheid are willing to pay for additional increments of the policy because the discrimination against others that ensues from apart-

---

5. This is consistent with the economic approach to human behavior. See Becker 1976 and Radnitzky and Bernholz 1987.

6. The model presented here is based on the more general model developed by Kaempfer and Lowenberg (1988a).

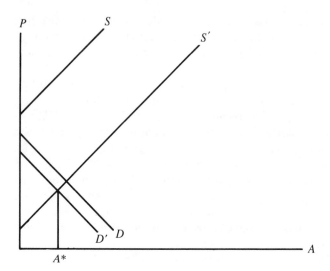

Fig. 1. Equilibrium level of policy A

heid raises the real incomes of the demanders or beneficiaries. This willingness to pay is represented in a political market where the demanders "pay" for apartheid in a variety of ways. Payment might take the form of political contributions to candidates or volunteer work for those candidates who support apartheid policies, or it might represent a willingness to accept higher taxes in order to enforce apartheid or to make side payments to groups not otherwise involved in the issue.[7] The demand curve has the traditional negative slope because, as the level of apartheid rises, additional benefits to the demanders decrease at the margin. For instance, a low level of discrimination will increase the demand for white workers and raise their wages, but more intense discrimination may cause employers to substitute other factors of production, like capital, or cease production in South Africa.

The supply curve of apartheid shows the ability of the government to implement discriminatory policies. Those who are hurt by apartheid are made worse off in the sense that their real income is reduced. This creates an incentive for the losers to engage in political activity that imposes costs on the government. These costs can come in the form of increased support for opposition candidates or various forms of protest ranging from nonviolent dissent to armed revolution. The justification for the upward sloping supply curve comes from the realization that increased apartheid will cause increasing income losses at the margin for those made worse off.

---

7. For instance, subsidies could be paid to employers to partially offset the costs to them of more apartheid in order to get them to abstain in the political process.

In this model, the government supplies apartheid policy, A, up to the point where the marginal utility to the beneficiaries is equal to the marginal disutility to the losers (Stigler 1971; Peltzman 1976; Becker 1983). Since apartheid is wealth decreasing in aggregate, it follows that, if the pro-apartheid groups and the anti-apartheid groups are equally effective in translating their preferences into political pressure, no positive amount of A will be supplied (Becker 1983). Thus the demand curve, D, and the supply curve, S, in figure 1 fail to intersect at a positive quantity of apartheid.

The political market for apartheid must be tempered by the public good nature of apartheid regulation. Individual actors in the political market may find their participation constrained by existing institutions and may under-represent their true benefits or costs due to the tendency to free ride in the provision of nonexcludable public goods. Under the South African constitution, political participation by the opponents of apartheid is severely limited and costly. Most of them are excluded from formal participation in the political process. As a result they must resort to much more costly forms of participation like demonstration and violence. This rise in the cost of participation will increase the incentive to free ride and reduce the political effectiveness of anti-apartheid interest groups. Free riding diminishes the extent to which individual members of anti-apartheid groups are willing to allocate resources to political opposition, thus reducing the "supply price" of apartheid. In figure 1, this translates into a downward shift of the supply curve of apartheid from S to S'. Of course, some free riding will be expected on the part of the demanders of apartheid as well, but because of their access to the political system and their greater political effectiveness, the shift to D' is smaller, and a positive equilibrium level of apartheid, A^*, comes about through the political market interaction.

At this juncture, suppose external economic sanctions are levied against South Africa. The impact of such sanctions is presented in figure 2. We assume that sanctions imposed on South Africa by other nations are income reducing for all South Africans, whether they are beneficiaries or losers from apartheid.[8] With a fall in income due to sanctions, however, demanders of apartheid will be less willing to pay for this public good and the demand curve for apartheid in figure 2 will shift down from D' to D''. However, the political costs to the government in supplying apartheid will also fall due to the negative income effect suffered by opponents of apartheid policies. A decrease in

---

8. In general, this need not be true. For instance, see Porter 1979 for a more detailed examination of the differential effects of sanctions on income groups within South Africa. Sanctions restricting the imports of South Africa might increase the market power of producers of import substitutes. So too, disinvestment sanctions can bring about a fire-sale sell-off of foreign-owned assets in South Africa, leading to a wealth transfer to those South Africans who acquire them at depressed prices (Kaempfer and Lowenberg 1986).

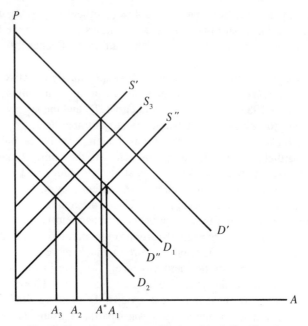

Fig. 2. Changes in the equilibrium level of policy A

incomes of individual members of anti-apartheid interest groups reduces their ability to allocate resources to resistance activities. This fall in the costs of supplying apartheid lowers the supply curve from S' to S''.

The effect on the level of apartheid due to the income effects of external sanctions is indeterminate and depends on the relative magnitudes of the shifts in demand and supply. In figure 2, the level of apartheid, A^*, is unchanged. Clearly, however, it is conceivable that the income effect of sanctions might well entail an *increase* in apartheid if opponents experience a greater reduction in income than proponents. This implies that, in order to be successful in producing a diminution of apartheid in South Africa, sanctions should be designed by the sanctioning nations so as to hurt the prime beneficiaries of apartheid to a greater extent than those groups opposing apartheid.[9]

Sanctions can also have indirect effects in the political market for

---

9. However, apartheid could be an inferior good to its beneficiaries, and lower incomes might mean a greater demand for apartheid. In other words, sanctions that reduce the incomes of white workers in South Africa might lead them to demand more regulations to protect them from competition in the labor market from blacks (Kaempfer, Lehman, and Lowenberg 1987).

apartheid in a variety of different ways. Supporters of the apartheid regime might regard sanctions as a foreign interference with national sovereignty, in which case they will "rally around the flag," and the group as a whole will expend more resources on the production of political influence in favor of apartheid. This would lead to a shift to the right of the demand curve for apartheid from D'' to D_1 and a rise in the resulting level of apartheid to A_1.

Alternatively, if sanctions are applied by increments, holding out the threat of further sanctions in the future if the level of apartheid is not reduced or promising that existing sanctions will be lifted in the future if the level of apartheid is retrenched, then a "discouraged rent seeker" effect on members of the interest group supporting apartheid might more than offset the "rally around the flag" effect.[10] This will lead to a decrease in the willingness to pay for apartheid and a consequent downward shift of the demand curve from D'' to D_2, which causes the equilibrium level of apartheid supplied by the government to fall to A_2.

A final indirect effect of sanctions on the level of apartheid comes through changes in the political effectiveness of groups opposed to apartheid. As Tullock (1971) has pointed out, anything that increases the probability of successful political resistance or lowers the expected costs to individuals of political participation will lead to an increase in resistance activities. Sanctions might serve to transmit a signal to the opposition group that they have the support of foreign governments and individuals and therefore reduce their incentive to free ride in the collective production of political pressure against apartheid. This could lead to an increase in the costs to the government of supplying its apartheid policies, a rise in the supply curve to S_3 and a fall in the level of apartheid from A_2 to A_3.

The implication of the analytical framework outlined above is that international economic sanctions applied against South Africa can have an effect on the level of apartheid regulation in South Africa, even if their economic effects are weak. The signal and threat effects of sanctions operate to bring about a change in the level of apartheid that is quite independent of the economic impacts of sanctions on income and wealth in South Africa. Furthermore, these economic impacts of sanctions have an ambiguous and potentially perverse effect on the level of apartheid. Optimally, sanctions against South Africa should be designed to have selective and differential income effects on members of groups supporting and opposing apartheid, as well as conveying appropriate signals and threats to those groups.

---

10. An example is provided by Findlay and Lundahl (1987, 148) who argue that white South African workers might respond to divestment pressure from shareholder groups abroad by conceding to a diminution of apartheid in order to prevent erosion of their standard of living.

5. Conclusion: The Contribution of Public Choice Theory

Many of the substantive predictions of public choice theory follow inevitably from its individualist methodology. For example, one implication of the assumption that political agents are rational value maximizers is that the government is not a beneficent *deus ex machina,* but rather an institution whose form can be explained as an endogenous outcome of competitive rent-seeking and interest group pressures. Similarly, the public choice approach treats the regulatory actions of the government as the end product of a political market process in which regulations are demanded by interest groups and supplied by politicians. A well-known corollary to this approach is that the quantity of public goods supplied through the political system will tend to exceed the efficient level.[11] While particular regulations might increase the wealth of some groups at the expense of others, total societal wealth is reduced by such interventions. This emphasis on the *process* of policy formation within the polity facilitates an understanding of the political economy of foreign economic policy that extends to both the sanctioning country (where the impetus for particular strategies of economic statecraft can be explained) and the target country (where the impact of sanctions is endogenized).

Political scientists, particularly those writing within the "social power theory" paradigm (D. Baldwin 1985) have shown that the political impact of sanctions can operate quite independently of market effects. Sanctioning countries have numerous bases of power upon which they can rely to alter the behavior of target nations, and economic power (narrowly defined) is only one dimension of this. Equally important is the capacity of a sanctioning country to elicit respect, prestige, and impose credible threats on other countries. Even if a particular exercise of economic statecraft (sanctions) is not successful in causing severe economic damage in the target country, it might still transmit signals or threats to the relevant interest groups in that country which are effective in bringing about alterations in political behavior. Thus, for example, even though the economic effects of disinvestment and trade sanctions against South Africa are ambiguous at best, political reform has occurred as a result of the signal and threat effects of sanctions as communicated both to the white ruling group and to black workers in the industrial sector (Kaempfer and Lowenberg 1986; Kaempfer, Lehman, and Lowenberg 1987). Doxey (1980, 128) points out that "the pressure governments exert behind the scenes to impel others to adopt sanctions may be more persuasive than the sanctions themselves." A public choice model, such as that used in section 4 above, is able to shed some analytical light on the mechanisms whereby

---

11. See Buchanan and Tullock 1962, chap. 14.

foreign economic policy can have effects on political decisions through such nonmarket channels. While the predictions of this model are a direct outgrowth of the public choice method, they are also fully consistent with David Baldwin's (1985) conclusions and add support to his findings on the effectiveness of sanctions.

Public choice and non–public choice methods are not necessarily mutually exclusive, but the public choice focus on endogenous policy in a competitive environment adds insights to the study of political economy that derive from its individualist methodology. As pointed out earlier, the public choice approach to foreign policy formation is quite compatible with that of political scientists who emphasize the structure of domestic interests.

The public choice perspective has the advantage of enabling the formalization of the process through which policy making in the target country might respond to particular types of sanctions. Furthermore, we have seen that public choice models are able to accommodate an alternative "logic" for the effectiveness of sanctions which has little to do with their direct market impact and which has occupied the attention of political scientists for some time. By modeling explicitly the configuration of interest groups within the target country, the public choice approach contributes further understanding of the channels through which the use of economic tools of foreign policy can sometimes achieve their ends largely by inflicting noneconomic or nonmarket repercussions.

REFERENCES

Amacher, Ryan C., Robert D. Tollison, and Thomas D. Willett. 1979. "The Divergence Between Trade Theory and Practice." In *Tariffs, Quotas and Trade: The Politics of Protectionism,* ed. Walter Adams et al. San Francisco: Institute for Contemporary Studies.

Baldwin, David A. 1985. *Economic Statecraft*. Princeton: Princeton University Press.

Baldwin, Robert E. 1985. *The Political Economy of U.S. Import Policy*. Cambridge, Mass.: MIT Press.

Bayard, Thomas O., Joseph Pelzman, and Jorge Perez-Lopez. 1983. "Stakes and Risks in Economic Sanctions." *World Economy* 6:73–87.

Becker, Charles M. 1987. "Economic Sanctions Against South Africa." *World Politics* 39:147–73.

Becker, Gary S. 1976. *The Economic Approach to Human Behavior*. Chicago: University of Chicago Press.

Becker, Gary S. 1983. "A Theory of Competition Among Pressure Groups for Political Influence." *Quarterly Journal of Economics* 98:371–400.

Bernholz, Peter. 1966. "Economic Policies in a Democracy." *Kyklos* 19:48–80.

Bernholz, Peter. 1985. *The International Game of Power*. Berlin: Mouton Publishers.

Black, P. A., and H. Cooper. 1987. "On the Welfare and Employment Effects of Economic Sanctions." *South African Journal of Economics* 55:1–15.

Brock, William W. 1986. "Economic Sanctions: An Eclectic Approach." Working Paper, University of Wisconsin.

Buchanan, James M. 1987. "The Constitution of Economic Policy." *American Economic Review* 77:243–50.

Buchanan, James M., and Gordon Tullock. 1962. *The Calculus of Consent.* Ann Arbor: University of Michigan Press.

Coase, Ronald H. 1984. "The New Institutional Economics." *Zeitschrift fur die gesamte Staatswissenschaft* 140:229–31.

Colander, David C. 1984. "Introduction." In *Neoclassical Political Economy: The Analysis of Rent-Seeking and DUP Activities,* ed. David C. Colander. Cambridge, Mass.: Ballinger.

Cooper, H. 1986. "The Welfare Effects of Sanctions." *Journal for Studies in Economics and Econometrics* 25:3–11.

Cooper, Richard N. 1986. *Economic Policy in an Interdependent World.* Cambridge, Mass.: MIT Press.

Destler, I. M. 1986. *American Trade Policies: System under Stress.* Washington, D.C.: Institute for International Economics.

Doxey, Margaret P. 1980. *Economic Sanctions and International Enforcement.* 2d ed. New York: Oxford University Press.

Findlay, Ronald, and Mats Lundahl. 1987. "Racial Discrimination, Dualistic Labor Markets and Foreign Investment." *Journal of Development Economics* 27:139–48.

Frey, Bruno S. 1984. "The Public Choice View of International Political Economy." *International Organization* 38:199–223.

Galtung, Johan. 1967. "On the Effects of International Economic Sanctions with Examples from the Case of Rhodesia." *World Politics* 19:378–416.

Gray, John H. 1987. "The Economic Approach to Human Behavior: Its Prospects and Limitations." In *Economic Imperialism: The Economic Approach Applied Outside the Field of Economics,* ed. Gerard Radnitzky and Peter Bernholz. New York: Paragon House.

Heijdra, Ben J., Anton D. Lowenberg, and Robert J. Mallick. 1988. "Marxism, Methodological Individualism, and the New Institutional Economics." *Journal of Institutional and Theoretical Economics* 144:296–317.

Hirschman, Albert O. 1980. *National Power and the Structure of Foreign Trade.* Berkeley and Los Angeles: University of California Press.

Hufbauer, Gary Clyde, and Jeffrey J. Schott. 1985. *Economic Sanctions Reconsidered: History and Current Policy.* Washington, D.C.: Institute for International Economics.

Ilgen, Thomas L. 1985. *Autonomy and Interdependence: U.S.–Western European Monetary and Trade Relations, 1958–1984.* Totowa, N.J.: Rowman and Allanheld.

Kaempfer, William H. 1987. "Explaining the Forms of Protectionist Policies: A Public Choice Perspective." Working Paper, Claremont Center for Economic Policy Studies.

Kaempfer, William H. 1989. "Immiserizing Growth with Globally Optimal Policies." *Journal of Economic Studies* 38:54–60.

Kaempfer, William H., James A. Lehman, and Anton D. Lowenberg. 1987. "Divestment, Investment Sanctions, and Disinvestment: An Evaluation of Anti-Apartheid Policy Instruments." *International Organization* 41:457–73.

Kaempfer, William H., and Anton D. Lowenberg. 1986. "A Model of the Political Economy of International Investment Sanctions: The Case of South Africa." *Kyklos* 39:377–96.

Kaempfer, William H., and Anton D. Lowenberg. 1988a. "The Theory of International Economic Sanctions: A Public Choice Approach." *American Economic Review* 78:786–93.

Kaempfer, William H., and Anton D. Lowenberg. 1988b. "Determinants of the Economic and Political Effects of Trade Sanctions." *South African Journal of Economics* 56:270–77.

Kaempfer, William H., and Anton D. Lowenberg. 1989. "Sanctioning South Africa: The Politics Behind the Policies." *Cato Journal* 8:713–27.

Kaempfer, William H., and Michael H. Moffett. 1988. "Impact of Anti-Apartheid Sanctions on South Africa: Some Trade and Financial Evidence." *Contemporary Policy Issues* 6:118–29.

Katzenstein, Peter J. 1976. "International Relations and Domestic Structures: Foreign Economic Policies of Advanced Industrial States." *International Organization* 30:1–45.

Katzenstein, Peter J. 1978. "Introduction: Domestic and International Forces and Strategies of Foreign Economic Policy." In *Between Power and Plenty: Foreign Economic Policies of Advanced Industrial States,* ed. Peter J. Katzenstein. Madison: University of Wisconsin Press.

Keohane, Robert D., and Joseph S. Nye. 1977. *Power and Interdependence: World Politics in Transition.* Boston: Little, Brown and Company.

Knorr, Klaus. 1975. *The Power of Nations: The Political Economy of International Relations.* New York: Basic Books.

Krueger, Anne O. 1974. "The Political Economy of Rent Seeking." *American Economic Review* 64:291–303.

Langlois, Richard N. 1986. "The New Institutional Economics: An Introductory Essay." In *Economics as a Process: Essays in the New Institutional Economics,* ed. Richard N. Langlois. Cambridge: Cambridge University Press.

Losman, Donald L. 1979. *International Economic Sanctions: The Cases of Cuba, Israel, and Rhodesia.* Albuquerque: University of New Mexico Press.

Lowenberg, Anton D. 1989. "An Economic Theory of Apartheid." *Economic Inquiry* 27:57–74.

Lundahl, Mats. 1984. "Economic Effects of a Trade and Investment Boycott Against South Africa." *Scandinavian Journal of Economics* 86:68–83.

Marks, Stephen V. 1987. "Quantitative Analysis of the Determinants of Congressional Voting on Trade Policy Issues." Working Paper, Claremont Center for Economic Policy Studies.

McKeown, Timothy. 1986. "Thoughts on Sanctions." Working Paper, University of North Carolina.

Mueller, Dennis C. 1979. *Public Choice*. Cambridge: Cambridge University Press.

North, Douglass C. 1984. "Transaction Costs, Institutions, and Economic History." *Zeitschrift fur die gesamte Staatswissenschaft* 140:7–17.

Olson, Mancur. 1982. *The Rise and Decline of Nations: Economic Growth, Stagflation, and Social Rigidities*. New Haven, Conn.: Yale University Press.

Peltzman, Sam. 1976. "Toward a More General Theory of Regulation." *Journal of Law and Economics* 19:211–40.

Porter, Richard C. 1979. "International Trade and Investment Sanctions: Potential Impact on the South African Economy." *Journal of Conflict Resolution* 23:579–612.

Radnitzky, Gerard, and Peter Bernholz, eds. 1987. *Economic Imperialism: The Economic Approach Applied Outside the Field of Economics*. New York: Paragon House.

Renwick, Robin. 1981. *Economic Sanctions*. Cambridge, Mass.: Harvard University Center for International Affairs.

Rowe, David M. 1987. "The Symmetry of Tariffs and Sanctions." Working Paper, Duke University.

Stigler, George J. 1971. "The Theory of Economic Regulation." *The Bell Journal of Economics and Management Science* 2:3–21.

Tullock, Gordon. 1971. "The Paradox of Revolution." *Public Choice* 11:89–99.

Vaubel, Roland. 1986. "A Public Choice Approach to International Organization." *Public Choice* 51:39–57.

Willett, Thomas D. 1980. "Some Aspects of the Public Choice Approach to International Economic Relations." Working Paper, Claremont Center for Economic Policy Studies.

Willett, Thomas D., and Mehrdad Jalalighajar. 1983–84. "U.S. Trade Policy and National Security." *Cato Journal* 3:717–27.

CHAPTER 8

Domestic Institutions and Shifts in Trade and Development Policy: Colombia 1951–68

David R. Mares

Two issues dominate the study of international political economy. One involves the relationship between economic and political approaches to the study of trade policies. Both disciplines now recognize that trade issues include economic and political dimensions, and there is an active debate about the political economy of trade policy. Another issue is the relationship between state and societal forces in the making of foreign economic policy. A decade ago, in an edited volume on the foreign economic policies of advanced industrial states, Katzenstein (1978) postulated that domestic structure was the key variable determining how foreign economic policy would respond to international crisis.

In this study I use the Colombian case to address these issues. Incorporating insights from a public choice perspective, I explain why and how state actors were able to use state and societal institutions to make significant changes in trade and development policy, *changes that had not been possible previous to the creation of those institutions.*

The Colombian case is a particularly apt one for exploring these concerns. The orientation of its shift in trade and development strategy, from inward to outward, was relatively unique in Latin America at that time. The development failures in the region have been well documented and lead many Latin American analysts to stress perceived irreproducible factors in the East Asian success stories (for example, level of U.S. aid, dynamic growth in international trade, Asian peculiarities, etc.). But Colombia underwent a transition similar to the East Asian with very positive, though less spectacular,

I would like to thank John Odell, Thomas Willett, Jeff Nugent, Gary Cox, and Jane Milner-Mares for helpful comments; responsibility for views presented here is mine alone. Support was provided by a University of California Pacific Rim Research Grant, the Center for Advanced Studies in the Behavioral Sciences, and the National Science Foundation (BNS-84-11738). This essay was originally prepared for the conference, "Blending Political and Economic Analysis of International Trade Policies," University of Southern California, March 1987.

results. After fifteen years of failed attempts, during 1966–68 Colombia succeeded in liberalizing exports, instituting export promotion incentives, and placing its multiple foreign exchange rates under a consistent and systematic mini-devaluation program (crawling peg regime). Partly as a result of these policies, the value of nontraditional exports expanded at an average annual rate of 28 percent from 1968–74 and GDP per capita experienced historic highs (average annual rates of 6.1 percent, up from 4.6 percent during 1956–67).[1]

The policy success draws attention mainly to one question: Why did Colombia look outward when most of Latin America was focusing inward? That question is only partly answered by explaining why Colombian policy makers wanted to make such a change. This paper accepts that policy preference by state actors and focuses instead on explaining the second part of the answer: why it took sixteen years for this state policy preference to actually become policy.

My explanation of the Colombian experience highlights institutional factors as intervening variables.[2] Institutions do not "choose" policies; state and societal actors interact to produce policy choices. But state-societal bargaining over policy takes place within an institutional context, with actors' resources and strategies influenced by their own institutions. In addition, institutions may facilitate cooperation among actors facing potential losses in the short run, but greater benefits in the medium to longer run. Without institutions these actors may not have been willing to make those bargains.[3] Consequently, institutions emerge as major intervening variables between the state-societal policy struggle and the policy outcome.

In brief, since 1951, unstable coffee export earnings and import-substitution demands on foreign exchange had created a major international constraint on the development process: recurring balance of payments problems. State actors believed that the primary export/import-substitution industrialization emphasis of Colombian development strategy was no longer viable and that Colombia must make a transition to a development strategy based on a more diversified export base. This transition was to occur even at the expense of the "deepening" of import-substitution industrialization.

State actors sought to use trade policy to stimulate this transition. Trade policy consisted of a number of policies including tariffs, licensing, prior deposits, subsidies, and even a variety of exchange rates that might have been

---

1. Diaz-Alejandro 1976, 2.

2. For a similar treatment, see two special issues of *International Organization* 1988, 36, no. 2., 42, no. 1.

3. Institutions have been argued to be important in understanding the international political economy at both its structural level and responses by its units. On the former, see Keohane 1984; for an example of the latter, see Katzenstein 1985.

used in support of these goals. General macroeconomic policy, however, was dominated by societal forces seeking to safeguard their own short-run interests.

Faced with these strong societal pressures, state actors attempted to manage the domestic economy by using trade policies. But the use of trade policy for nontrade considerations frustrated state efforts to change the old trade and development strategies.[4] In the 1960s, this scenario changed, largely as a result of institutional innovations both within the party system and in the Executive-Legislative relationship. These institutional changes altered the incentives structuring societal behavior and increasingly insulated economic policy making within the Executive. Largely as a result of these institutional changes, state actors could transform initial societal opposition to shifts in trade and development policy into support for state-preferred policies.

This essay is organized into four sections. First, I briefly review economic explanations of trade policy in developing countries. The purpose of this section is to demonstrate that strictly economic explanations fail because (1) economists disagree on what constitute optimal trade and development policies in the international political economy, and (2) inefficient allocation of resources is not punishment enough to force policy makers to forego all of their other goals. The second section examines political economy explanations. Here I present my argument about the way in which institutions affect the relationship between state and societal forces on trade and development policy. The third section examines the actors in the Colombian story as well as the evolution of Colombian trade and development policy up to 1966. Particular attention is paid to Presidents' repeated failures to adopt and implement policy to which societal forces were opposed. In addition, institutional changes during this period at both the level of society and the state are analyzed. A fourth section analyzes the successful policy shift in 1966–67. The institutional changes of the previous period are demonstrated to have played fundamental roles in this explanation. The conclusion speculates on the relevant conditions for a successful shift in trade and development policy.

Economic Explanations

Economic thought contributes to the analysis of trade policy in developing countries in two ways. First, economists have sought to define optimal trade and development policies for a country according to its level of development

---

4. For example, because the reserve requirements on bank deposits could not be enforced, state efforts to control the money supply frequently relied upon prior deposits for imports. But by forcing importers to deposit money for up to six months and receive no interest, the cost of producing with imported goods could be increased substantially. Diaz-Alejandro 1976, 20 and passim, provides other examples.

and international payments situation. As important as such knowledge might be, however, before economic analysis could purport to explain trade policies, a causal argument about why those policies would or would not be adopted is necessary. Economic thought can provide answers to this issue as well. It can postulate that market forces directly determine policy or it can propose reasons (for example, the existence of economic rents) why policy makers choose suboptimal policies. In this section, I examine the former explanation of policy, and turn to economists' arguments about why optimal and actual policies may diverge in the following section.

Let's begin with optimal trade and development policies. Tariffs are a popular subject of international trade theorists. Tariff theory suggests two circumstances in which a country seeking to maximize its real income should impose tariffs: when it has a large enough share in its international markets to influence its terms of trade and/or when it faces market distortions that can be remedied through taxes or subsidies.[5] Of course, trade and development policies include policies other than tariffs.

Trade theory is less helpful when we consider this wider arena. The theoretical links between alternative trade policies and growth are underdeveloped. Empirical analysis has suggested the superiority of an export promotion orientation ("meant as a general bias toward exports and not as a package of specific measures to encourage selective exports of particular items themselves induced by a bias toward import substitution") over import substitution strategies. But the reasons for this superiority are not clear. They could be due to technological-economic factors ("minimum efficient size of plant, increasing returns to scale, indivisibilities in the production process, and the necessity for competition"), policy implementation, or because export promotion strategies allow the market to function as a constraint upon public and private economic behavior.[6]

Nevertheless, most developing countries followed an import substitution industrialization strategy. In the early phases of the import substitution process, an "unorthodox combination of inflation, overvaluation of the currency, tight quantitative import controls, and some foreign finance in the form of both aid and private capital" transferred income from the traditional exporting sector to the rapidly growing industrial sector. But the necessary conditions for this strategy (continued traditional exports, avoidance of runaway inflation, limited state expenditures and continued foreign investment and aid) gradually disappeared. Industrial growth ran into difficulties and there came a need for a transition to a more outward-oriented strategy.[7]

5. Caves 1976, 280.
6. Krueger 1980b, 511.
7. Hirschman 1979, 73.

Thus we have agreement on the need for more open, and therefore more market-oriented trade and development strategies. The question then becomes one of explaining the transition process from a closed to a more open trade and development strategy. An elaborate classificatory scheme has been developed to track the transition process of exchange control regimes (of which trade policy is only one component). Five phases have been identified, leading from "systematic and significant imposition of quantitative restrictions" to "full convertibility on current account and (in which) quantitative restrictions are not employed as a means of regulating the balance of payments." Intermediate steps move from increased complexity of the control system to a rationalization of the restrictions to continued liberalization.[8]

Despite agreement on goals, controversy arises with respect to the actual process by which to reach the last phase. Bhagwati (1978, 60–62) notes that progress is not necessarily unidirectional, as economic or political shocks may lead to backtracking. But there is disagreement over whether or not changes in the direction or pace of the transition are beneficial. For one group it is important to get to the fifth phase quickly because "getting prices right" signals the most efficient allocation of resources. An important implication of this group's policy is that the government must stay out of the economy and allow the invisible hand to work. To a large degree, countries in the southern cone of Latin America (Chile, Argentina, and Uruguay) followed such a strategy for nearly a decade.[9] A second group of development economists notes that merely getting prices right may not lead to optimal outcomes. In developing countries in particular, there are many forms and sources of market failure.[10] Consequently, public policy needs to address the sources of market failure. In terms of the phases of exchange control regimes described above, transitions will take time.

Assuming the optimal policy, one still confronts the relationship between the optimal and the actual policy chosen. The economic determinants of policy perspective emphasize international economic conditions and market behavior. "In general, a market explanation for policy change claims that international market conditions changed so as to make it economically irrational for a government to continue prevailing policy, and it was for this reason that the government yielded and adopted a new policy more in conformity with market signals. Market conditions would have made such a change likely, regardless of other conditions also present (Odell 1982, 18).

In terms of trade policy, two economic variables could be highlighted by this argument. One considers the balance of payments situation as determinate

---

8. Bhagwati 1978, 56–59.
9. Ramos 1986; Foxley 1983.
10. Meier 1983, 137–38, as cited in Timmer 1986, 142–43; Ramos 1986, 10–11.

of policy change. Among developing countries with an import-substitution development strategy, the prediction would be that the foreign exchange bottleneck would force adoption of a trade and development strategy which is both more outward-oriented and less interventionist at home. Although a quick look at the Korean and Taiwanese experiences might seem to support this argument, many more cases from Latin America, Africa, and even Asia (Philippines) demonstrate that a balance of payments crisis is not a sufficient determinant of policy.

A second international economic explanation of trade policy change focuses on the level of development attained by the country in question. Level of development is usually conceived of in terms of GDP per capita, but Conybeare's (1983, 450–51) recent study found that inclusion of growth rates of GDP and export instability contributed to the ability of this perspective to explain tariff levels. For our purposes, this argument is significantly limited for three reasons. First, tariff policies are only one part of trade strategies, which also include fiscal and nonfiscal incentives, licenses, etc. Consequently, tariff levels, guided by an international regime,[11] may not necessarily represent important shifts in trade and development strategies, which are not guided by international regimes.[12] Second, the predictability of level of development in Conybeare's model appears to be strong only at very broadly defined levels of development since some newly industrializing countries (Brazil, Singapore, and Taiwan) were found to have tariff levels similar to less industrialized developing countries.[13] And third, Colombia is interesting precisely because it adopted a trade and development strategy significantly more outward-oriented than that in most every other Latin American country, even in those at higher levels of development.

In sum, economic analysis is fundamental for understanding the costs, benefits, and trade-offs associated with different policy choices. But an emphasis on the most efficient trade and development strategy for growth, even if economists could agree on its composition, is insufficient to explain actual policy choices. For that we need a political-economy analysis.

Political Economy Explanations

Analysts of foreign economic policy are generally in agreement that both international and domestic factors are fundamental to explanation. International elements include both the nation state system and the international economy. By integrating state system and international economic variables,

---

11. Lipson 1982.
12. At least not until the IMF is called in. For a discussion of IMF policy preferences, see Williamson 1983.
13. Williamson 1983, 461.

we determine a range of policy responses to the question of how a country will relate to the international political economy. Each of the potential policy choices has distinct political and economic costs and benefits. But that policy range and the variation in acceptance of costs and benefits are both sufficiently great to draw our attention to domestic determinants of policy choice.[14]

Once again we confront a basic dichotomy in the analysis. The major debate in the domestic determinants of foreign economic policy literature is between those whose analyses are societal- (social classes, production groups, etc.) or state-centered (bureaucratic politics, central decision makers, etc.). Each group recognizes the existence of the other group's variable(s), but disagrees over their interrelationships. The question of the particulars of that relationship revolves around the conceptualization of "state" and the historical evolution of the nation in question.[15]

The societal-centered analyst views state actors as severely constrained by the need to meet societal demands. Consequently, one begins with societal preferences. Analysis then focuses on the political struggles to fashion a coalition of societal groups that can implement its preferred policies. Within this societal focus there are two general perspectives for explaining the degree of openness of national economies. One begins with microeconomic principles, the other with macro historical-sociological foundations.

Public choice economists seeking to understand why actual tariffs vary from theoretically optimal tariffs represent one variant of the microeconomic approach. Public choice analyses of tariff levels suggest the need to distinguish between the incentive for groups to seek tariffs and their ability to engage in collective action to bring them about. Caves (1976, 288) notes that incentives for tariffs can be thought of in terms of a net increase in profits and a perceived responsiveness of the political process to such pleas. While it is common to expect that sectors facing economic adversity as a result of their position in the international division of labor will be partial to government action,[16] Krueger (1980a) and Buchanan (1980) argue that domestic factors (that is, an interventionist government at home) can provide incentives for even efficient firms to become "rent-seekers." Rent-seeking behavior should be particularly evident in a developing economy because of the aforementioned prevalence of market failures, as well as extensive state intervention. Whatever the incentives for tariffs, the microeconomic approach emphasizes that actors confront collective action and "free rider" problems because tariffs have public goods properties.[17]

---

14. Katzenstein 1978; Gourevitch 1986; Mares 1985.
15. For example, Katzenstein 1978, 297, explains the difference in domestic structures of six advanced industrial states in terms of their experience with the elimination of feudalism, the Industrial Revolution, and the process of state building.
16. Kurth 1979; Strange 1979.
17. Pincus 1975, 758.

This public choice approach is useful for analyzing the transition from an internally to an externally oriented trade and development strategy, but a few modifications are necessary. First, the econometric models that support these public choice tariff theories suffer from the use of proxies for the desired variables, measurement errors, and statistically weak results.[18] Consequently, I will pursue a qualitative approach. Second, my concern is broader than that of tariff levels. The demand for nontariff barriers has been found to correlate with that for tariffs, so presumably the same arguments would hold.[19] But I am also concerned with the provision of export incentives, including favorable exchange rates, and side payments (for example, favorable credit) to those losing out in the transition, which may or may not be explained by the same factors.[20] Despite the fact that these other policy decisions can violate the nonexcludability and jointness of supply characteristics of public goods, the collective action perspective is still relevant because I am concerned with the provision of goods that are provided collectively.[21]

A third and fundamental modification results from the fact that change in tariff levels over time is inadequately treated in both Pincus and Caves. Since Pincus (1975) is concerned with variations in duties from the average, he cautions that his model does not address variations in the height of the average duty. In short, "[g]eneral political circumstances can invalidate the theory proposed here" (763), when there is a significant shift in general tariff policy. Caves (1976) also confronts a major problem in explaining a key variable in his discussion of the costs and benefits of organizing for, or successfully achieving, tariff changes. The receptivity of government to societal pleas is important for incentive calculations and he explains it in terms of equity considerations for those "whose reasonable expectations have been frustrated (and penalizing those who enjoy unearned windfalls)" (288). But without explanations of (1) the criteria for deciding equity and (2) variations in government's application of the criteria, we cannot know why governments receptivity to interest groups demands vary over time. Because Colombian changes in trade and development policy took place fifteen years after they had initially been proposed, this particular issue is extremely important for this study.

The macro historical-sociological approach to societal interests attempts to explain government responsiveness in terms of the social coalitions behind them. The historical-sociological approach takes broad social groups or classes as the prime actors: farmers, industrialists, bankers, and labor. These

---

18. Caves 1976, 287–91, 293, 296.
19. Conybeare 1983 assumes so. On page 445, he cites Ray 1981a and Ray 1981b.
20. Caves (1976, 289) raises the issue of "choice among various plums on the public tree," which is omitted from his model.
21. Hardin 1982, 5.

analysts derive societal interests internationally from their positions in the international division of labor; that is, efficient firms and their workers want open economies, while their inefficient counterparts seek protection. Investigation then turns to the political contests to create governing coalitions. International crises represent opportunities for the creation of new, or the modification of old, dominant coalitions. A successful coalition gains control of government, and government chooses those policies that meet the terms on which its coalition formed.[22] Government receptivity to interest groups' demands for protection, therefore, is not necessarily consistent over time. Rather it varies with the composition of the dominant social coalition.

There is another approach to the question of government receptivity to societal demands. It claims the question is misformulated and backward. It is not a government of societal representatives that responds, so much as a "bureaucratic apparatus and institutionalized legal order in its totality" denominated by the term "state"[23] and most usefully operationalized in terms of the key decision makers on any particular issue.[24] State-centered analysts do not dispute the existence of social coalitions that support governments. Rather, they find it difficult to test the degree to which social coalitions are determinants of policy because "the approach tends to lack theoretical rigor and predictive value, largely because it lacks an independent measure of group power."[25] Instead, these analysts emphasize that state actors, irrespective of their societal support base, have interests that derive from being part of the state and that are consistent over time and across coalitions.

If one uses a statist approach to analyzing policy, it is imperative to define these national interests. This can be done through either a logical-deductive or empirical-inductive approach. The former is the most popular approach among political scientists, but its utility in explaining foreign economic policy in developing countries has been limited. For example, one of the most prevalent logical-deductive paradigms for explaining Latin American trade and development policy is Gerschenkron's analysis of late developers. State interests in Latin America are assumed to lie in stimulating industrialization via a protected and publicly subsidized import substitution process.[26] But while this route has provided benefits, it has done so at greater costs to national sovereignty (recurrent need for IMF financing, private bankers and debt rescheduling, and transnational corporation penetration of the industrial sector) than in the more market-oriented East Asian cases.

Not only does this approach to state interests fare poorly in a regional

---

22. Gourevitch 1986; Kurth 1979; Strange 1979; Ruggie 1982.
23. Krasner (1984) reviews some of the recent literature.
24. Such a definition mitigates the possibility of reification of the state.
25. Ikenberry, Lake, and Mastanduno 1988, 8.
26. Bennett and Sharpe 1982.

context, it does not help us with Colombia's decision to avoid the modal Latin American pattern. Here the adoption of import-substitution was never as complete. Consequently, it appears more promising to derive state interests inductively, by examining actual state policy preferences across ruling coalitions and individual presidencies.[27] Diaz-Alejandro's (1976, chap. 1) study documents a consistent effort since 1951 to liberalize imports and promote noncoffee and nonpetroleum exports.

We now have societal interests and state interests and we need a way to conceive of how they relate to one another. A focus on institutions can be helpful. Institutions are "a set of rules, compliance procedures, and moral and ethical norms designed to constrain the behavior of individuals in the interests of maximizing the wealth or utility of principals" (North 1981, 201–2). Institutions determine the relevant actors in a policy issue, and thus can be used to insulate policy making from particular groups or link issues to build particular policy coalitions.[28] Institutions can also affect the incentives for collective action among relevant actors.[29] So what determines institutional characteristics and innovation?

There are societal, as well as state, institutions and studies which have demonstrated that explanation of foreign economic policy outcomes is best served by an incorporation of institutions at both levels of analysis.[30] In the Colombian case, a fundamental change in the way in which political parties contested elections (the National Front agreement) facilitated institutional change within the state (in particular the creation of planning and monetary commissions, and constitutional reforms increasing the Executive's ability to make policy). North (1981, 32) argues that the free-rider problem means that "institutional innovation will come from the rulers rather than constituents. . . ." The same free-rider problems apply to the study of state and societal institutions, but in the latter case the small numbers belong not to governmental "rulers" but to the party elites.

What are the conditions under which institutional innovation occurs? North (1981, 208–9), taking a much longer view, notes that time and changes in population and knowledge (the capital stock) induce changes in institutions via changes in relative prices, military technology, and ideology. Taking the shorter perspective (15–20 years in the present case) and for the case of foreign economic policy, changes in relative prices and ideology are most appropriate to the analysis.[31] The result of dramatic changes in these two elements is to produce a crisis that calls into question the old order and its institutions. Alliances develop a certain fluidity although constrained by pre-

27. This approach is adopted from Krasner 1978a, 35–54.
28. Orloff and Skocpol 1984; Skocpol 1980; Krasner 1978b.
29. Keohane 1984, part 2.
30. Katzenstein 1978.
31. On ideology, see Odell 1982.

vious solutions to previous crises,[32] and political entrepreneurs emerge to build new coalitions and new institutions.[33]

In short, political economy analysts disagree broadly over whether society or the state sets the constraints under which the other acts, as well as over the latitude within them. Both state- and societal-centered analysts have been receptive to the collective action and institutional foci that the application of economic analysis to political issues has spawned. But actual transaction costs and institutional make-up will be historically contingent, and so we come to the Colombian case.

My approach to the debate on foreign economic policy determinants is very conventional: begin with the international constraints and opportunities. In Colombia the key international constraint on foreign economic policy was an economic one, a recurring balance of payments disequilibrium as a result of a sustained decline in the price of its only generator of foreign exchange, coffee. International political constraints, however, such as the approach to international payments problems favored by the United States in its Agency for International Development (AID), the International Monetary Fund (IMF), and the World Bank were inadequate to keep Colombia from adopting its preferred strategy for dealing with the international economic constraints.[34] Actually, the IMF provided state leaders with an opportunity to mobilize an ideological incentive (nationalism) behind state policies.

A second step is to lay out the distribution of societal and state interests in trade and development strategies. But rather than follow economists who limit their tariff explanations to direct interests, I pay particular attention to nontrade interests as potential side payments or threats that state actors might use in structuring the context within which societal actors "choose" to support or oppose trade and development policy. The third part of the analysis then concentrates on explaining the evolution of state and societal institutions during the time state actors were consistently frustrated by societal pressures.

Colombia: From Import Substitution to Export Promotion

Colombia stands out in Latin America as having achieved sustained export growth after a period of ISI and with political costs far short of those paid, with less return, in the southern cone of the region. This dramatic shift can be

---

32. Both societal- and state-centered analysts agree on the impact of previous choices. See Gourevitch 1986 and Krasner 1984.

33. Hardin (1982, 35–37) discusses political entrepreneurs in a collective action framework. Hirschman (1963, chaps. 4 and 5) provides a fascinating analysis in his discussion of reform mongering.

34. The U.S. approach is not the only possible one. For the debate between the United States and Great Britain over the approach the postwar international monetary authorities should take, see Block 1977, 32–69.

appreciated with some figures. From 1948–50, coffee and petroleum accounted for 91 percent (coffee alone was 75 percent) of total export revenue, and industry was heavily protected. By 1970–72, this figure had declined to 66 percent for both, with coffee falling below 50 percent by the 1980s.[35] Noncoffee and nonpetroleum exports (known as "minor exports") grew at rates of over 25 percent per year (in current dollars) from 1965–74. Exports of manufactures accounted for 15–20 percent of the growth in manufacturing output from 1968–74.[36]

Trade policy underwent a significant change over this period. Despite an emphasis on ISI, import liberalization was often adopted. From 1959–65, Colombian trade policy experienced wide fluctuations in protection, from total regulation of imports to 60–65 percent of imports falling into the free list. The major factor determining the degree of openness was the balance of payments situation. International financial and aid authorities insisted on rapid liberalization as part of agreements to help stabilize international payments crises. At least in the Colombian context, in which private interests dominated fiscal, monetary, and trade policy, following this advice produced a vicious cycle.[37] Given the falling coffee price and limited minor exports in this period, import liberalization contributed to pressures on foreign reserves and devaluation ensued, leading to stringent control of imports. Since 1967, however, the consistent trend has been toward greater liberalization and the promotion of exports.[38]

Although one can explain the success of sustained import liberalization after 1967 by the easing of the balance of payments constraint, we are left with explaining the shift in that constraint and why export promotion continued after the immediate international payments crisis was overcome. From 1967–74, coffee prices did rise steadily (1973 was the highest in the postwar years to that date) and the Eurocurrency market began to expand. But Colombia did not use foreign debt to finance growth and coffee income was insufficient by itself (the little information available on the drug trade does not suggest it was fundamental to the changes up through the 1970s). Analysts have demonstrated that it was the growth in minor exports which proved key for Colombia. Interestingly, import liberalization contributed little to export diversification and growth; exchange rate reforms and export promotion policies were more important.[39] In short, had Colombia wanted to abandon the

---

35. Diaz-Alejandro (1976, 6–8) for the earlier two periods; Bagely (1984, 143) for coffee in the 1980s.

36. Berry and Thoumi 1977, 99.

37. This criticism is a popular one in the literature on IMF stabilization programs in developing countries. See the introduction to Thorp and Whitehead 1979, 12–17.

38. Diaz-Alejandro 1976, Appendix B, 262–69.

39. Diaz-Alejandro 1976, 13, 208, 224.

outward shift in trade and development policy, short-run justifications were available.

Before seeking to explain this sustained change in trade and development policy, it is necessary to recognize what the shift was and was not. Most analysts go so far as to argue that the country made a transition from an ISI development strategy to an export-led one.[40] But liberalization and export promotion were not undertaken at the expense of protection for most import-substituting industries. Rather, as in South Korea and Taiwan, protection for import-substituting industries was not eliminated.[41] To explain change in trade and development strategy, and its limits, we now turn to the interaction between state and societal forces within Colombia.

Development of Modern State Institutions

The modern Colombian state developed in the 1930s, partly as a result of the Depression and the inability of the Conservative party to offer solutions. The Liberal party gained control of government and undertook policies to increase political participation and enhance the role of the state. Universal male suffrage was established, education was secularized, labor was organized and protected, and tax and land reforms were implemented. Because these reforms were carried out by an upperclass-led established party, mobilization and state intervention did not immediately provoke an anti-system movement either by the reformers or the Conservatives.[42]

These structural and political reforms unraveled in the 1940s as groups on both ends of the political spectrum sought control of this newly interventionist state. A new reformist faction within the Liberals, headed by Jorge Eliecer Gaitan, mobilized new urban workers to gain control of the Liberal party. His social-democratic orientation made him appear very radical within the context of the elite dominated Colombian society. Among the Conservatives, Laureano Gomez, an admirer of Franco's Falange, represented the radical right. Gomez engaged in his own mobilization of groups outside traditional party politics and, like Gaitan, he also criticized party collaboration in government. The closed political system could not deal with these new demands and civil war (known as *La Violencia*) broke out in 1946. Gaitan was assassinated in 1948 and Gomez engineered a political coup in 1950 to install his fascist government. But Gomez' new politics threatened the traditional party system and a Liberal-Conservative alliance supported General Gustavo Rojas Pinilla's military coup in 1953.[43]

---

40. Diaz-Alejandro 1976, 3, 208, 224; Morawetz 1981 39.
41. Haggard and Moon 1983, 136–37.
42. Solaun 1980, 20–21; Bailey 1977, 266.
43. This quick summary of a very complex history is drawn from Solaun 1980.

In this environment of great political violence a process of decentraliza-
tion of state functions ensued. Bailey (1977) argues persuasively that de-
centralization constituted an effort to protect the gains of the 1930s by de-
politicizing the new interventionist state and turning it into a technocratic
state. This process was virtually uncontrolled; in 1963 the government did not
even know how many decentralized agencies existed. Their claim to
autonomy from the executive branch lay in their purported technical rather
than political approach to policy. But the lack of a technical bureaucracy
allowed them to become captured by the private economic enterprises they
were supposed to regulate.[44] Consequently, state actors' abilities to use the
modern state to manipulate the incentives confronting societal actors diminished after 1946.

Sources of Societal Opposition to State Policy
Autonomy in the Late 1950s

Economic Interests. Given the fact of governmental regulation of private
activity and societal dominance of those institutions and of the distribution of
the rents that public intervention produces, private economic actors could be
expected to oppose efforts by state actors to regain control of state institutions
and their economic functions. Following Caves's (1976) approach, we need to
examine the incentive and abilities of interest groups to pursue collective
action in Colombia's trade and development policies.

Coffee growers (almost 200,000) were among the most important societal actors at this time because they had earlier joined with the state to solve
their collective action problems.[45] Their common interests arose because the
international coffee market is characterized by frequent and dramatic price
fluctuations. Coffee prices began a dramatic and prolonged downturn in 1957
and Colombia joined other Latin American countries in an effort to mitigate
the decline. The chief policy concerns of coffee growers in this period, therefore, were international controls on supply, the level of the coffee exchange
rate, and state funding of the guaranteed price when the coffee export tax
proved inadequate. The latter meant that coffee growers had a direct and
independent impact on the money supply, as the government was committed
to funding the domestic coffee program.[46] Because of this periodic need to
utilize noncoffee sector resources and because coffee prices are denominated
in dollars, coffee growers were reticent to advocate exporter interests in avoid-

---

44. Bailey 1977, 276, 287, 291–93.
45. Although many analysts mention this state action, no one explains it. Compare
Palacios 1983, 511–12.
46. Bird 1968, 76.

ing overvaluation of the exchange rate. Rather than contradict importer interests in keeping the nominal rate low, coffee growers attempted to separate discussion of the main exchange rate from the coffee rate and domestic support price. As long as they were successful, coffee growers could not be counted on to support exporter interests outside of their sector.[47]

Agricultural diversification programs were already contributing to increasing output of bananas (once very important), cotton, sugar, and tobacco by the end of the 1950s. This production was mainly for a protected domestic market and at times exports were subject to state-imposed controls to guarantee adequate domestic supply. Banana, cotton, sugar, and tobacco growers all suffered from unstable international prices, just as coffee growers, and faced foreign demand, which was "rather" price elastic.[48] These growers represented a potential constituent for export promotion policies but not at the expense of a protected domestic market.

The manufacturing sector was developing under the protection of import substitution, but ISI had not progressed very far. In 1958, value added in manufacturing as a percent of total manufacturing value added was 66 percent for consumer goods, 26.6 percent for intermediate goods, and 7.4 percent for capital goods.[49] Since manufacturers used only a relatively small proportion of inputs produced by Colombian firms, there was little opposition to tariff dispersion (high tariffs for consumer goods, low tariffs for all others). In fact, it was preferred because manufacturers could support an overvalued exchange rate to lower the cost of their imports without increasing competition from foreign competitors.[50]

There were no clear-cut export-oriented interests in Colombian manufacturing since, given its ISI orientation, it was largely noncompetitive. In 1957, manufactured exports accounted for only $11 million, were quite heterogeneous in their economic characteristics, and consisted mainly of excess production for the domestic market.[51] Direct foreign investment in manufacturing was also domestically oriented.[52]

The manufacturing sector was organized into two national associations. The National Association of Industrialists (ANDI) represented the major firms, estimated at 540 in 1963.[53] Although it is generally perceived as a

---

47. Nelson, Schultz, and Slighton 1971, 252–53.
48. Diaz-Alejandro 1976, 44. He notes that the evidence does not allow him to be more precise than "rather price-elastic."
49. Thoumi 1980, 329; Berry and Thoumi 1977, 93.
50. Nelson, Schultz, and Slighton 1971, 245, 249.
51. Diaz-Alejandro 1976, 38–39, 45–46. In addition to labor-intensive products, they include fuel oil, chemicals, and cement.
52. Diaz-Alejandro 1976, 47.
53. Bailey 1977, 282–83.

powerful organization by both Colombians and foreign analysts,[54] case studies suggest otherwise.[55] Its weakness can be explained in terms of collective action problems caused by competitive rent seeking at the firm level. As largely inefficient industrialists producing for a highly protected domestic market, they all have a common interest in preventing a shift in trade and development strategy toward a more outward orientation. But the extent of tariff dispersion and the vast array of government regulations and decentralized agencies provide firms with an opportunity to meet their needs on an individual basis, thereby avoiding the costs of collective action and perhaps gaining vis-à-vis domestic competitors. ANDI thus seems to have been relegated by the industrialists to a public relations champion of broad interests, such as "efficiency," which are not in their short-run interests.[56] Small industrialists, organized into ACOPI, would seem to face similar constraints on collective action, but a detailed study of this group could not be located.

Merchants were also organized (FENALCO) but there is little evidence of their preferences or policy action. Bankers were organized (Asociacion Bancaria) but none of the studies on interest groups in Colombia includes them on their lists.[57] The explanation for their weak organization appears to be that they were individually powerful enough, so discouraging government regulation of their sector was possible without collective action. Private bankers dominated the board of directors of the Central Bank and were able to effectively disregard attempts by the state to control the money supply via manipulation of reserve requirements.[58]

Liberals (1930s) and Conservatives (1940s) organized a small segment of the labor force. In 1963, the 6–20 percent of the unionized urban labor force were found in the industrial, petroleum, textile, and transport sectors, as well as in commercial agriculture plantations, such as sugar. The two main unions were loosely affiliated with the Liberal (CTC) and Conservative (UTC, which is larger than the CTC) parties. The CTC organized a rural labor union, the National Agricultural Federation, in 1959. The looseness of the ties, as well as its economic orientation, are suggested by the fact that the CTC called for a one-day general strike in 1963 against the wishes of the Liberal leadership. They were among the chief opponents of devaluation because of its effects on inflation.[59]

---

54. Bailey 1977, 278; Kline 1974, 295.
55. See, for example, the analysis of the Colombian automobile industry by Fleet (1982).
56. Nelson, Schultz, and Slighton 1971, 231.
57. De Santamaria 1965, 209.
58. De Santamaria 1965, 207–9; Diaz-Alejandro 1976, 20; Nelson, Schultz, and Slighton 1971, 257.
59. Dix 1967, 330–41; Kaufmann 1977, 128–29; on societal concerns over devaluation, see Nelson, Schultz, and Slighton 1971, 243.

In sum, during the late 1950s, a shift in Colombian trade and development policy toward export promotion was not on the agenda of any economic interest groups. This can be explained by the rent-seeking behavior of import-substituting entrepreneurs and their labor force, as well as by coffee growers faced with an unstable international market. But protectionist interests confronted potentially serious collective action problems because of the decentralized and disaggregated structure of protectionist policy.

Party Interests. A political institution, the two-party system, has been a fundamental factor in Colombian political life since 1849. The Liberal and Conservative parties are multiclass but virtually ignored large segments of society until the 1940s.[60] Party conflict reached civil war levels in the late 1940s when factions on the extreme of both parties sought to gain command of the new modern Colombian state.

There were attempts to resolve these disputes as in the past, with national unity governments (half of the years between 1900 and 1953 had been governed by coalitions). Cooperative efforts failed, mainly because the radical factions in both parties believed they could control the new political forces they were mobilizing. Despite initial gains in controlling the rural violence, even a military government proved unable to prevent a renewed challenge to the traditional elite. General Rojas Pinilla himself became a threat to the political elite when he began mobilizing new political forces in order to perpetuate himself in power. Confronted with successive challenges to their social and political dominance, Liberal and Conservative party leaders called a truce to their competition and, with the support of the Catholic church, persuaded the military to oust Rojas Pinilla in 1957.

The failures of the 1940s national unity attempts and the enormity of the threats in the 1950s stimulated the two parties to make a truly innovative change in their institutional relationship. Party leaders found themselves in a prisoner's dilemma game.[61] The defect-defect cell was represented by the situation of 1953–1957. The parties had been out of power as a result of the military coup. Counterelite mobilization by the *Violencia* and Rojas Pinilla threatened to end Liberal and Conservative domination of Colombian society and politics. The parties thus had an incentive to cooperate in controlling the *Violencia* and convincing the military that civilian control of politics was viable once again.

The problem was that the defect strategy had become the preferred choice of the parties. The polarized political environment since the late 1940s had made it both possible and probable that the party in power would use the

---

60. Solaun 1980, 5.
61. For a discussion of this game and the conditions under which cooperative solutions are possible, see Axelrod 1984.

increased interventionist capacity of the state to consolidate its hold on power. Gaitan's mobilization efforts were intended to do so, and Gomez' presidency (1949–53) actually did so. A truce among the parties and cooperation in defeating the counterelite challenges, therefore, raised the likelihood of one party contributing to its own demise (the "sucker" payoff). Consequently, the defect strategy dominated party politics. The solution in 1957, which changed the nature of the game, was to create a societal institution to enforce agreements and turn a single-shot play into an iterated game.

The National Front coalition government was unique in Colombian history because it was significantly more institutionalized than any of its predecessors. It was approved by a plebiscite (95 percent in favor) and written into the Constitution.[62] It contained a number of provisions designed to meet the counterelite challenge and avoid any "sucker" payoffs.

The counterelite threat was handled in two ways. First, the political pact between the two parties gave the military an opportunity to return to its preferred place, the barracks (1953–57 was the only military government in this century). As a result, military officials would not be able to use their institution to challenge civilian control of politics.[63] Second, counterelites were forced into the traditional party structure by a stipulation that only the Liberal and Conservative parties could compete in the elections. Party factions could compete with different electoral lists, but in this way counterelites could be watched, diluted, and hopefully reformed.

To diminish the possibility of defection from the agreement, it was necessary to ensure that the state was not "captured" by one party and used to its advantage during this period of relegitimation of the system and socialization of counterelites and their followers. A variety of safeguards were introduced. All elected positions, as well as Cabinet posts and Supreme Court positions, were to be evenly divided between the two parties. The presidency would alternate between the two parties for sixteen years. And a century old trend was reversed with increased congressional independence of and veto power over (legislation required a two-thirds majority) presidential policies.

It is alleged that this political arrangement eliminated political competition and made economic policy very conservative.[64] I shall argue below that important changes in economic policy were actually facilitated by this societal institution. But political dynamics were not frozen either. De facto third parties, linked to the Liberal and Conservative parties in order to meet legal

---

62. Angell 1966, 64.

63. National Front presidents would dismiss the Minister of War (1965) and the Commander of the Army (1969) for publicly criticizing government policy, and place General Rojas Pinilla and some military officers under house arrest (1970) for subversive behavior, without provoking a crisis in military-civilian relations. Corr 1971, 71–72.

64. Bagely 1984, passim.

requirements but opposed to the National Front, gained 23 percent of the presidential vote in 1962, 28 percent in 1966, and almost won with 39 percent in a four-way race in 1970.[65] Each party also experienced significant electoral competition among its own members at the local level.[66] In the context of ten years of civil war and a military coup, party leaders came to highly value this institution. Consequently, state actors were not insulated from a broad range of societal pressures, but the National Front itself provided an important bargaining chip with the parties.

The Shift in Trade Policy

Trade policy during the years before the transition to export promotion was made in this context of interest group control of state agencies and congressional dominance of legislation. Since 1951 state actors had recognized a need to stimulate exports as well as industrialize via import substitution. Export promotion was understood to require import liberalization and export incentives, including favorable exchange rates. But as a result of falling coffee prices and a lack of control over fiscal and monetary policy, Colombia had been caught in a devaluation-inflation-devaluation cycle, which forced restraints on imports, trade taxes to finance the federal budget, and left few funds with which to stimulate exports. The story of the shift in trade and development policy after 1966 thus begins with fiscal and monetary reform.

Economic policy under the National Front began conservatively, drawing heavily upon past policies, especially import substitution. Nevertheless, both the Lleras Camargo (1958–62) and Valencia (1962–66) administrations began to reclaim control over state functions from interest groups and Congress. Some of these steps merely entailed making use of provisions in the Constitution. The Colombian constitution provided for a declaration of state of siege, during which the President could make policy by decree and Congress was limited only to asking the Supreme Court to rule on constitutional issues. From 1958–74, Colombia was under partial or total state of siege 75 percent of the time, as presidents responded to legislative stalemate in economic policy, as well as sporadic outbursts of political violence.[67]

But major changes would require freeing the state (that is, enhancing Executive discretion) from the constraints created by the political solutions to La Violencia (private control of state functions and congressional domination of the Executive through the National Front arrangements). Congress and interest groups were initially successful in blocking these statist efforts but,

---

65. For 1962 and 1966, Ruhl 1981, 59, fn. 11; for 1970, Dix 1980, 140.

66. Kline 1980, 76–77; in the same volume, Hoskin (122–23) disputes Kline's claim that national party leaders could control local party lists or congressmen.

67. Rothlisberger 1974, 38, as cited in Hoskin 1980. Most analysts cite only rural violence, especially guerrilla activity, when noting Colombian states of siege.

over the course of a decade, found themselves outmaneuvered by the Executive.

One of the important early steps for state actors was the development of a technocratic bureaucracy. A Planning Department and a National Council of Economic Policy and Planning were created during Lleras Camargo's tenure. Congress accepted these institutional innovations because the President had no control over them and Congress expected to use them for its purposes. Congress appointed two of the four members on the Council and diminished the Planning Department's effectiveness by constantly feuding with it.[68] As a further hedge against presidential use of these departments to increase his bargaining power with Congress, they reported directly to the relevant Ministries, and under the National Front arrangements the President had minimal authority over his cabinet.[69]

And when Congress could not influence Ministers' preferences, it had its veto power. The most important example occurred when the Finance Minister proposed responding to the deteriorating international payments situation in 1961 by preempting the standard IMF austerity package by adopting a much needed tax reform and adopting a crawling exchange rate. Congress rejected these measures in both 1961 and 1962. Ironically, Carlos Lleras Restrepo reportedly led the congressional veto (as President, he himself would force congressional acceptance of the exchange rate measures in 1967).[70] The legislature actually made things more difficult by responding to interest group needs without providing the federal government with additional funds to finance those projects.[71]

Unable to avoid the balance of payments crisis with domestic measures, Lleras Camargo and his successor Valencia sought help from the U.S. government, through its Agency for International Development (AID). But the U.S. government refused to lend Colombia the funds that would allow it to stave off the IMF for a while longer. Valencia was forced to devalue in November 1962. He presented Congress with an alternative to the IMF program, which included using differential exchange rates to finance both the federal budget and export incentives. But Congress rejected the reforms that threatened to give the Executive more independence and adopted the IMF program, with minor modifications.[72]

Although at a high cost (acceptance of a standard IMF stabilization

---

68. Berry 1980, 297.

69. De Santamaria 1965, 150.

70. Diaz-Alejandro 1976, 190; de Santamaria 1965, 55–115, never mentions Lleras Restrepo in his retelling of those events.

71. Congress eliminated the export tax on coffee and also provided budgetary relief to Departmental (state) governments by nationalizing the police force and teachers. de Santamaria 1965, 58.

72. De Santamaria 1965, 55–56, 79, 114–16.

program), Valencia was able to utilize this setback to increase Executive autonomy. The Economic Planning Council had resigned because they were not consulted about the devaluation. Valencia replaced the Council with a Cabinet group, increased the Planning Department's role and made it report directly to him. Foreign support (studies by the Organization of American States, IMF, and the Alliance for Progress) was sought to sway Congress to adopt legislation that would increase the national finances and the Executive's policy independence. But it was the unprecedented levels of inflation that followed the devaluation of 1962 which convinced Congress to approve creation of a Monetary Council. The Executive then stacked the council's membership in favor of the state and gave it a number of administrative powers to control interest rates, direct credit, and limit rediscounting. Congress objected to the Executive's alleged usurpation of its legislative powers and the bankers accused the President of attacking the private sector, but the Executive stood by its constitutional faculties.[73]

Inflationary pressures from societal forces proved unmanageable and thwarted state actors' attempts to promote exports. Congress went beyond Executive recommendations for modification of the hourly wage rates and raised them 7 percent in real terms. Even though they fell in 1964, real wages remained 2 percent higher than in 1962. The coffee support price could not be funded by the tax on the coffee exchange rate and federal subsidies increased. Private banks frustrated efforts to restrain credit by ignoring central bank imposed reserve requirements.[74]

To cope with inflation, the Monetary Council suggested a devaluation. But Valencia, also confronting preelectoral political violence and coup rumors, believed the political price of devaluation too high.[75] He turned to policy tools whose societal impact could be managed more easily.[76] By late 1965, however, it became clear that import licensing and prior import deposits could not defend the current exchange rate. In a desperate hope of combating inflation and restoring confidence in the President and the Colombian peso, the Monetary Council convinced the President to adopt a dramatic liberalization program.

The liberalization effort was financed by the weaker societal interests who had gained in the early 1960s when Congress refused to make any

---

73. De Santamaria (1965, 58) on taxes; information on the monetary council creation is fragmentary, see de Santamaria 1965, 201–30; Berry 1980, 298–300; Nelson, Schultz, and Slighton 1971, 297; Holguin 1966, 142–47.

74. De Santamaria 1965, 229–30; see also Diaz-Alejandro 1976, 190–201.

75. Diaz-Alejandro 1976, 196; de Santamaria 1965, 59.

76. Through 1964, imports on the free list as a percent of total registered imports declined, finally being eliminated by December. The length of time for application review reached three months, prior deposits were held for over ten months, and over a third of applications were rejected. Diaz-Alejandro 1976, 190–97.

choices. Exporters were increasingly taxed via the exchange rate for minor exports and real wages fell. Foreigners were also asked to contribute via a new loan agreement with the IMF. But import liberalization proceeded faster than anticipated, leading to a drain on the country's foreign exchange holdings. When coffee prices began a new fall in April 1966, the antidevaluation strategy was doomed.

International financial authorities (IMF, the World Bank, and AID) called for a devaluation. Carlos Lleras Restrepo, newly elected president, once again opposed a devaluation because of its political consequences (as he had earlier while in Congress). This time the finance minister apparently opposed it for its inflationary impact and questionable structural value. State actors overrode their own technical advisers, who could see no alternatives, and rejected devaluation. In a televised national address, President Lleras Restrepo informed Colombia that policy sovereignty remained in national hands and announced his own stabilization program without devaluation. He declared a state of siege and, among other policies, linked the coffee rate to the main rate.[77]

At this point, Lleras Restrepo had no real alternative plan. But his advisors reexamined the proposals that Congress had rejected during the 1957–63 attempts to break the devaluation-inflation-devaluation cycle. Between December 1966 to March 1967, a program was put together that combined liberalization, export promotion, and a crawling peg exchange rate (Law 444 of March 1967). This program significantly stimulated exports without dismantling import substitution. A constitutional amendment was passed by Congress which gave the Executive the initiative on budgetary matters and diminished Congress' ability to oppose the Executive by requiring only a simple majority (it had been two thirds).[78] The results were impressive:

> Higher growth rates in foreign-exchange receipts, primarily derived from merchandise exports, allowed the government systematically to follow more expansionary fiscal and monetary policies than had been possible during 1956–67. Such stimuli, and the positive reactions they triggered in private expenditure, led to a higher level of resource utilization almost across the board within the Colombian economy. Widespread pockets of underutilized labor, capital, and land were gradually brought into production without any major sector being required to contract so as to release resources for better use elsewhere.[79]

---

77. Maullin 1967 is the most complete treatment of the episode.

78. Every discussion of Colombia's political economy in the last twenty years contains a description of the program. The best summary is in Diaz-Alejandro (1976, chaps. 2 and 7). For similarities with previous failed attempts, see Nelson, Shultz, and Slighton (1971, 256) and de Santamaria (1965, 79).

79. Diaz-Alejandro 1976, 224.

Explaining the Policy Shift

But why was this Executive successful in getting his program past Congress while his predecessors failed? Did the societal actors that Congress represented suddenly decide to turn economic policy over to the state? As we shall see, Congress continued trying to thwart these economic reforms and there were not any societal actors clamoring for these policies. Was this a case of individual brilliance? As a former leader of Congress, Lleras Restrepo certainly knew the system well and he appears to have taken full advantage of his opportunities. But the understanding and motivation necessary to be a "Master Reformmonger" (as Hirschman called him)[80] were not lacking in Lleras Camargo, his finance minister, or Valencia. The presence of Hirschman's other criteria (crisis and the emergence of a new problem as an impetus to creating new alliances by interrelating the various problems) was also not unique to 1966–68.

The difference between 1957–65 and 1966 was Lleras Restrepo's ability to take advantage of the economic crisis and change the terms of the trade and development policy alliance. What gave him that ability were institutional changes in both state and society that occurred before he took office. Because Lleras Camargo defeated Congress' attempt to control the newly created Planning Department and Valencia expanded its scope, Lleras Restrepo had a bureaucracy that responded to his needs, rather than those of Congress or of special interests. Lleras Restrepo could develop credible (domestically and internationally) policy alternatives, but he still faced the problem of getting them accepted by the relevant societal and congressional actors. Building a new policy alliance meant changing the incentives of those with whom he needed to strike a deal (coffee growers and Congress), while not alienating those whose interests would be too costly to meet (import-substituting industrialists who wanted cheap foreign inputs).

To get early national and favorable attention for his new policy, Lleras Restrepo created an international crisis for Colombia with his rejection of a typical devaluation/austerity IMF program. In the absence of other factors, the nationalist appeal would not have been enough to create a winning alliance domestically, but in the short run it increased the political costs to any group that opposed him. Potential allies were thus "softened up" to his appeals, demands, and side payments.

Given the weight of the coffee sector in Colombia, coffee growers were very important to any policy coalition. As noted above, FEDECAFE had a defensive interest in separating discussion of the coffee exchange rate from the main rate. As such they were not part of an export coalition. Lleras Restrepo

---

80. Hirschman 1963. The dedication lists both Lleras Restrepo and Celso Furtado. His analysis of reform mongering is found in the last two chapters.

began to change these interests with his emergency measures linking the coffee and main exchange rates in November 1966. In 1967, the Monetary Council (created by Valencia, who subsequently gave it expanded powers by administrative fiat), undertook an exchange rate reform, which not only continued the link of the coffee exchange rate to the main rate but reincorporated an export tax to reduce Federation borrowing to support the domestic price.[81] These two steps gave coffee growers an incentive to support a mini-devaluation strategy that would give them more pesos to support domestic prices. With this move state actors were able to eliminate the competition between coffee and minor exports, and create a powerful societal coalition to support a favorable minor export exchange rate.

Industrialists constituted a second necessary societal pillar of support for the policy shift. As a result, the limited import substitution gains were safeguarded in the liberalization component of the 1967 reforms. Liberalization would take place mainly in the intermediate and capital goods sectors, where Colombian industrialists were only minimally represented. To facilitate domestic adjustment, the liberalization process was to be carried out at a significantly slower pace than in 1965. Unlike the Chilean shift in the late 1970s, in Colombia export promotion was to be built upon a minimal industrial base, rather than at its expense.[82]

Congress also represented a severe threat to the policy shift. Under the National Front agreements, Congress had important veto power over economic policy. In defense of both societal and its own organizational interests, Congress had vetoed Executive efforts to undertake a similar shift in trade and development policy during the previous decade. Once the nationalist euphoria dissipated and the harsh realities of the development process were re-exposed, Congress could be expected to attack the new reforms.

Lleras Restrepo attempted to weaken this obstacle to Executive policy making by presenting Congress with a Constitutional reform package while nationalist sentiment ran high. The reform gave the Executive the initiative on budgetary matters, watered down Congress' ability to oppose the Executive by requiring only a majority vote to pass legislation, and called for a reduction in the size of Congress.

Congress seems to have acquiesced to the amendment because of the current political climate and the opportunity to easily rescind its vote when things quieted down. In an effort to defend the status quo, the Colombian constitution required that an amendment to it had to be passed in two con-

---

81. Bird 1968, 79–80.
82. In Colombia, value added in manufacturing (millions of 1980 dollars) rose from 3,297 in 1970 to 5,787 in 1984; the comparable Chilean figures are 5,275 to 5,422. The World Bank 1987, 215, table 7.

secutive years by the Congress. By late 1968, Congress refused to second its affirmative vote of 1967. The nationalist crisis atmosphere of the fight with the international monetary authorities had diminished when they accepted Lleras Restrepo's adjustment program and domestic interests refocused their opposition to the costs of that program. Lleras Restrepo thus precipitated a domestic political crisis by firing all of his ministers and governors and threatening to resign if Congress rejected the amendment.[83]

The president was essentially playing a game of chicken with the National Front parties. Resignation was a severe threat only because it put at risk a societal institution (the National Front) believed fundamental to maintaining elite rule. By taking such dramatic steps, he convinced Congress that he had bound himself to the decision to resign if his demands were not met.[84] In the process, he transformed the vote from an Executive-Legislative issue with Congress the loser, to a referendum on the National Front, with the National Front parties the potential losers. Framed in this context, members of the National Front parties voted 134 to 3 to support the amendment; the Independent Conservatives, which opposed the National Front agreement, voted 32 to 1 against it.[85]

The general shift to trade and development policy provided by Lleras Restrepo endured after he left office although he did not solve all of the Legislative-Executive tensions. (In 1974, the president declared a state of siege in order to implement a major tax reform that came down particularly hard on nonproductive assets.[86]) Some slackening occurred, particularly with respect to the exchange rate, and export incentives were diminished.[87]

But none of these changes signaled a return to an inward orientation for trade and development policy. Rather they represented a move toward more market allocation because many of the export incentives under Lleras Restrepo were biased toward capital-intensive products. The adjustments in 1974–78 removed that bias, thus stimulating agricultural and labor-intensive exports. Outward orientation was consequently reaffirmed and made more efficient.[88]

---

83. Nelson, Schultz, and Slighton 1971, 227.

84. Schelling 1980, 22–28.

85. Kline 1970, 274; Kline 1974, 276. He interprets this bargain as evidence of Congress' strength, but analysis of the previous decade of Legislative-Executive relations refutes that perception.

86. Bagely 1984, 140.

87. The most critical study of this change in Colombia is Morawetz 1981.

88. The development of the Colombian motor vehicle industry (perceived a key sector in any import-substitution strategy because of its forward and backward linkages) during the 1970s illustrates the continued outward orientation quite nicely. See Fleet 1982.

Conclusion: Institutions and Trade Policymaking

This essay proposed that a societal focus would be significantly insufficient to explain shifts in trade and development policy. State actors were expected to play an important role. Incorporation of collective action problems and the rent-seeking behavior of societal groups was expected to contribute to a better appreciation of the state-societal relationship in foreign economic policy. I used the Colombian shift in trade and development policy after 1966 to illustrate the argument.

In the 1950s, the Colombian state was decentralized. Given the prevalence of market failure in a developing economy like Colombia's, monopolists and oligopolists were able to demand that a weak state intervene to protect their rents (coffee growers and import-substituting industrialists) or seize control of state functions (private bankers). Consequently, the societal explanation of foreign economic policy does quite well at explaining the failure of state attempts to shift trade and development policy.

But the societal focus began to have less explanatory power in the 1960s. State actors were able to utilize institutional innovations within the political party system and, between the Executive and Legislative branches, to alter the incentives structuring societal behavior and to increasingly insulate some areas of economic policy making within the Executive. As a result, policies previously opposed by domestic societal actors authorities could be adopted.

Without incorporating a statist perspective into our analysis, the 1960s changes in Colombian trade and development strategies would be incomprehensible. Of course, arguing that state actors could influence societal preferences does not mean that building a basis of support within society is a foregone conclusion. The Colombian case supports the view that the particulars of the state-societal relationship cannot be specified a priori but are a product of time, place, and issue.[89] We must, therefore, examine the preconditions for state actors to guide foreign economic policy. The Colombian case suggests three.

First are the economic preconditions. Joan Nelson's (1984) comparative analysis of Sri Lanka, Jamaica, Ghana, Zambia, and Kenya pointed out the importance of quick results from stabilization efforts if social actors were to support them. The immediate growth, trade, and balance of payments benefits accruing from the 1966–67 Colombian reforms thus probably helped convince reluctant social actors that they could live with the new policies. Without them, Lleras Restrepo's policy success might have been quickly undone. The question then becomes, why was there such an immediate response?

From an economic perspective Colombia suffered from, among others,

---

89. For example, Katzenstein 1978, 297.

two development problems: widespread pockets of underutilized resources, and a small and unintegrated industrial base (mainly focusing on producing consumer goods and with little use of inputs produced in Colombia).[90] But policy makers could reap substantial benefits from this situation. The prevalence of imported industrial inputs made it possible for first stage import substitution industrialists and their labor to support liberalization in the intermediate and capital goods sector, as long as their own stage was protected.[91] In addition, economic growth could follow relatively quickly after the adoption of incentives to utilize those resources. Societal groups, which had reluctantly joined the reform, found that the new policies did provide benefits. To the degree that both of these economic characteristics were important in diminishing societal opposition during and after the policy shift, countries further along the process of import-substitution industrialization can take little solace from the Colombian experience.

A second point concerns the relationship between crises and policy change. Many analysts have pointed out the importance of crises to both institutional change and policy shifts. This study demonstrates that there is no automatic link between economic crisis and new institutions or policy. Colombia experienced three balance of payments crises before 1966 (1957–58, 1961–63, and 1965) but responded to each with the same policies. It was not until a political crisis coincided with the economic one that Colombia was able to abandon the old responses. In short, economic crisis appears to be a necessary but not sufficient condition for important changes in foreign economic policy.

A third point is that the existence of institutional innovation as a response to societal collective action problems does not necessarily increase state autonomy. In the Colombian case, the creation of the National Front initially severely constrained state policy autonomy. When Congress acquiesced in the creation of planning departments, it was to facilitate its own impact on national policy. The proliferation of new state regulatory institutions during the 1950s likewise served to increase private interest groups' influence over public policy. Without state actors seeking to increase their relative autonomy from Congress and the private sector, institutions could only serve to decrease the transaction costs for the principal's (society) enforcement of its contract with the agent (the state).

A final word should address the issue of policy outcome. In the Colombian case, societal collective action problems and institutional innovation facilitated a state-led shift away from inward-oriented strategies. But state

---

90. Nelson, Schultz, and Slighton 1971, 245.
91. This was not a costless policy, as Colombian textile exporters who had to use overpriced and poor quality yarn discovered. Morawetz 1981.

guidance of foreign economic policy is not policy specific; the actual policy chosen depends upon what determines the preferences of state actors, as well as the outcome of state-societal bargaining. In Mexico, because of historical experience, the stage of its industrialization by 1970, and the availability of foreign financing via debt and petroleum, the institutions used by state actors to influence societal preferences or insulate economic policy making from direct societal pressures were used to re-invigorate the inward orientation of trade and development policy.[92] Nelson's (1984) comparative analysis of stabilization experiences also found political leaders' commitment to stabilization and adjustment policies (and therefore to the trade and development policies for pursuing those goals) to be an important variable.

REFERENCES

Angell, Alan. 1966. "Co-operation and Conflict in Colombian Party Politics." *Political Studies* 14:1.
Axelrod, Robert. 1984. *The Evolution of Cooperation.* New York: Basic Books.
Bagely, Bruce Michael. 1984. "Colombia: National Front and Economic Development." In *Politics, Policies, & Economic Development in Latin America,* ed. Robert Wesson. Stanford: Hoover Press.
Bailey, John J. 1977. "Pluralist and Corporatist Dimensions of Interest Representation in Colombia." In *Authoritarianism and Corporatism in Latin America,* ed. James M. Malloy. Pittsburgh: University of Pittsburgh Press.
Bennett, Douglas, and Kenneth Sharpe. 1982. "The State as Banker and Entrepreneur: The Last Resort Character of the Mexican State's Economic Intervention, 1917–1970." In *Brazil and Mexico,* ed. Sylvia A. Hewlett and Richard Weinert. Philadelphia: ISHI.
Berry, R. Albert. 1980. "The National Front and Colombia's Economic Development." In Berry, Hellman, and Solaun 1980.
Berry, R. Albert, and Francisco Thoumi. 1977. "Import Substitution and Beyond: Columbia." *World Development* 5, nos. 1/2:89–109.
Berry, R. Albert, Ronald G. Hellman, and Mauricio Solaun, eds. 1980. *Politics of Compromise.* New Brunswick, N.J.: Transaction Books.
Bhagwati, Jagdish. 1978. *Foreign Trade Regimes and Economic Development: Anatomy and Consequences of Exchange Control Regimes.* New York: Columbia University Press.
Bird, Richard M. 1968. "Coffee Tax Policy in Colombia." *Inter-American Economic Affairs* 22, no. 1:75–86.
Block, Fred L. 1977. *The Origins of the International Monetary Disorder.* Berkeley: University of California Press.
Buchanan, James M. 1980. "Rent Seeking and Profit Seeking." In *Toward a Theory of*

---

92. Mares 1985.

the Rent-Seeking Society, ed. James M. Buchanan, Robert D. Tollison, and Gordon Tulluck. College Station: Texas A & M University Press.

Caves, Richard E. 1976. "Economic Models of Political Choice: Canada's Tariff Structure." *Canadian Journal of Economics* 9, no. 2:278–300.

Conybeare, John A. C. 1983. "Tariff Protection in Developed and Developing Countries: A Cross-Sectional and Longitudinal Analysis." *International Organization* 37, no. 3:441–63.

Corr, Edwin G. 1971. *The Political Process in Colombia.* Monograph in World Affairs, 1971–72. Denver: University of Denver.

de Santamaria, Sanz. 1965. *Una Epoca Difícil.* Bogota: Ediciones Tercer Mundo.

Diaz-Alejandro, Carlos. 1976. *Foreign Trade Regimes and Development.* Vol. 9, *Colombia.* New York: Columbia University Press.

Dix, Robert. 1967. *Colombia: The Political Dimensions of Change.* New Haven: Yale University Press.

Dix, Robert. 1980. "Political Oppositions under the National Front." In Berry, Hellman, and Solaun 1980.

Fleet, Michael. 1982. "The Politics of Automobile Industry Development in Colombia." *Journal of Interamerican Studies and World Affairs* 24:211–39.

Foxley, Alejandro. 1983. *Latin American Experiments in Neoconservative Economics.* Berkeley: University of California Press.

Gourevitch, Peter. 1986. *Politics in Hard Times.* Ithaca: Cornell University Press.

Haggard, Stephen, and Chung-in Moon. 1983. "The South Korean State in the International Economy: Liberal, Dependent, or Mercantile." In *The Antimonies of Interdependence,* ed. John Gerard Ruggie. New York: Columbia University Press.

Hardin, Russell. 1982. *Collective Action.* Baltimore: Johns Hopkins University Press.

Hirschman, Albert O. 1963. *Journeys toward Progress.* New York: W. W. Norton.

Hirschman, Albert O. 1979. "The Turn to Authoritarianism in Latin America and the Search for Its Economic Determinants." In *The New Authoritarianism in Latin America,* ed. David Collier. Princeton: Princeton University Press.

Holguin, Jorge Franco. 1966. *Evolucion de las Instituciones Financieras en Colombia.* Mexico: CEMLA.

Hoskin, Gary. 1980. "The Impact of the National Front on Congressional Behavior: The Attempted Restoration of El Pais Politico." In Berry, Hellman, and Solaun 1980.

Ikenberry, G. John, David A. Lake, and Michael Mastanduno. 1988. "Introduction: Approaches to Explaining American Foreign Economic Policy." *International Organization* 42:1–8.

International Organization. 1982. 36, no. 2.

International Organization. 1988. 42, no. 1.

Katzenstein, Peter J., ed. 1978. *Between Power and Plenty.* Madison: University of Wisconsin Press. Originally published as a special edition of *International Organization* 31, no. 4.

Katzenstein, Peter J. 1985. *Small States in World Markets.* Ithaca: Cornell University Press.

Kaufmann, Robert R. 1977. "Corporatism, Clientelism, and Partisan Conflict: A Study of Seven Latin American Countries." In *Authoritarianism and Corporatism in Latin America*. ed. James M. Malloy. Pittsburgh: University of Pittsburgh Press.

Keohane, Robert O. 1984. *After Hegemony*. Princeton: Princeton University Press.

Kline, Harvey F. 1980. "The National Front: Historical Perspective and Overview." In Berry, Hellman, and Solaun 1980.

Kline, Harvey F. 1974. "Interest Groups in the Colombian Congress." *Journal of Inter-American Studies and World Affairs* 16:274–300.

Kline, Harvey F. 1970. "The Cohesion of Political Parties." Ph.D. diss. University of Texas.

Krasner, Stephen D. 1978a. *Defending the National Interest*. Princeton: Princeton University Press.

Krasner, Stephen D. 1978b. "United States Commercial and Monetary Policy: Unraveling the Paradox of External Strength and Internal Weakness." In Katzenstein 1978.

Krasner, Stephen D. 1984. "Approaches to the State: Historical Contingencies and Alternative Conceptions." *Comparative Politics* 16:223–46.

Krueger, Anne O. 1980a. "The Political Economy of the Rent-Seeking Society." In *Toward a Theory of the Rent-Seeking Society,* ed. James M. Buchanan, Robert D. Tollison, and Gordon Tulluck. College Station: Texas A & M University Press.

Krueger, Anne O. 1980b. "Trade Policy as an Input to Development." *American Economic Review* Papers and Proceedings, 288–92. Reprinted in Gerald M. Meier, ed., *Leading Issues in Economic Development*. 4th ed. New York: Oxford University Press, 1984.

Kurth, James R. 1979. "The Political Consequences of the Product Cycle." *International Organization* 33:1–35.

Lipson, Charles. 1982. "The Transformation of Trade." *International Organization* 36, no. 2:417–55.

Mares, David R. 1985. "Explaining Choice of Development Strategy: Suggestions From Mexico, 1970–1982." *International Organization* 39, no. 4:667–97.

Maullin, Richard L. 1967. *The Colombia-IMF Disagreement of November-December 1966: An Interpretation of its Place in Colombian Politics*. Santa Monica: RAND Memorandum, RM-5314-RC.

Meier, Gerald M., ed. 1983. *Pricing Policy for Development Management*. EDI Series in Economic Development. Baltimore: Johns Hopkins University Press for the Economic Development Institute of the World Bank.

Morawetz, David. 1981. *Why the Emperor's New Clothes Are Not Made in Colombia*. New York: Oxford University Press for the World Bank.

Nelson, Joan. 1984. "The Political Economy of Stabilization." *World Development* 12, no. 10:983–1006.

Nelson, Richard, T. Paul Schultz, and Robert L. Slighton. 1971. *Structural Change in a Developing Economy*. Princeton: Princeton University Press.

North, Douglass C. 1981. *Structure and Change in Economic History*. New York: Norton.

Odell, John S. 1982. *U.S. International Monetary Policy: Markets, Power, and Ideas as Sources of Change.* Princeton: Princeton University Press.

Orloff, Ann Shola, and Theda Skocpol. 1984. "Why Not Equal Protection? Explaining the Politics of Public Social Spending in Britain, 1900–1901, and the United States, 1880–1920." *American Sociological Review* 49:726–50.

Palacios, Marco. 1983. *El Cafe en Colombia.* Rev. ed. Mexico: El Colegio de Mexico.

Pincus, J. J. 1975. "Pressure Groups and the Pattern of Tariffs." *Journal of Political Economy* 83, no. 4:757–78.

Ramos, Joseph. 1986. *Neoconservatives in the Southern Cone of Latin America, 1973–1983.* Baltimore: Johns Hopkins University Press.

Ray, E. J. 1981a. "Tariff and Nontariff Barriers in the United States and Abroad." *Review of Economics and Statistics* 63:161–68.

Ray, E. J. 1981b. "The Determinants of Tariff and Nontariff Trade Restrictions in the United States." *Journal of Political Economy* 89:105–21.

Rothlisberger, Dora. 1974. "Esbozo de la Realidad Colombiana con Referencia al Pacto Andino." Bogota.

Ruggie, John Gerard. 1982. "International Regimes, Transactions and Embedded Liberalism in the Postwar Era." *International Organization* 36:379–415.

Ruhl, J. Mark. 1981. "An Alternative to the Bureaucratic-Authoritarian Regime: The Case of Colombian Modernization." *Journal of Inter-American Economic Affairs* 35:43–69.

Schelling, Thomas. 1980. *Strategy of Conflict.* Cambridge, Mass.: Harvard University Press.

Skocpol, Theda. 1980. "Political Response to Capitalist Crisis: Neo-Marxist Theories of the State and the Case of the New Deal." *Politics and Society* 10:155–201.

Solaun, Mauricio. 1980. "Colombian Politics: Historical Characteristics and Problems." In Berry, Hellman, and Solaun 1980.

Strange, Susan. 1979. "The Management of Surplus Capacity: Or How Does Theory Stand Up to Protectionism 1970s Style." *International Organization* 33:303–33.

Thorp, Rosemary, and Laurence Whitehead, eds. 1979. *Inflation and Stabilization in Latin America.* New York: Holmes and Meier.

Thoumi, Francisco E. 1980. "Industrial Development Policies During the National Front Years." In Berry, Hellman, and Solaun 1980.

Timmer, Peter C. 1986. *Getting Prices Right: The Scope and Limits of Agricultural Price Policy.* Ithaca: Cornell University Press.

Williamson, John, ed. 1983. *IMF Conditionality.* Cambridge, Mass.: MIT Press for Institute of International Economics.

The World Bank. 1987. *World Development Report 1987.* New York: Oxford University Press.

CHAPTER 9

"States" and "Politics" in American Foreign Economic Policy

Peter F. Cowhey

This essay critically examines the "statist" theory of the formulation of foreign economic policy that has dominated much of the literature in international relations over the past decade. Briefly put, statist theory holds that an elite group of Executive Branch institutions and officials tries to steer foreign policy in accord with the dictates of the competitive environment of international relations. Domestic politics may sometimes thwart their efforts but the dynamics of these institutional guardians of foreign policy provide the continuity and direction of the heart of foreign economic policy. Statist theory usefully focused scholars' attention on how institutional dynamics shape foreign policy outcomes. At the same time, it saved foreign policy analysis from the mistake of believing that turf wars and bureaucratic inertia are the most import components of institutional behavior. However, statist theory itself is flawed because it has no theory of the politics of foreign policy choices. This paper proposes one variant of the "new institutionalism," political choice theory, to correct these shortcomings.[1] A theory of political choice stresses how electoral politics condition all other influences on foreign policy choices and it shows how foreign policy institutions are designed to serve strategic goals of electoral politics.

A second theme of this essay is that the politics of both international trade and international regulatory policy are closely akin to those of domestic regulatory policy because all three depend on the allocation of market advan-

My thanks to Jonathan Aronson and Gary Jacobson for letting me build on work done jointly with them. I also thank Matthew McCubbins and Gary Cox for several important ideas. John Odell and Tom Willett offered extremely helpful comments on prior drafts, as did Steve Krasner and Jeff Frieden.
    1. This essay uses the term "political choice" to distinguish its approach from earlier work on "public choice" on which it builds. Political scientists rightly criticized the early literature on public choice for failing to take account of how political institutions shaped policy outcomes. Political choice theory marries public choice theory to what is now called the "new institutionalism" in political science journals (March and Olsen 1984).

tages by government control over the terms of entry and pricing. Scholars interested in each area (economists and political scientists alike) can learn much from each other. Moreover, international trade policy is becoming increasingly intermeshed with international regulatory policy simply because trade in goods is becoming intertwined in international trade in services, and services were traditionally subject to extensive domestic and international regulation. For example, the sales of such high technology hardware as jet aircraft, telephone switches, and supercomputers are intimately tied to competitive policies governing the service industries for airlines and telecommunications.

This essay offers a number of brief examples drawn from U.S. trade and regulatory policy for telecommunications and petroleum to illustrate its argument.[2] Both are particularly good cases for exploring the merits of statist and political choice theories. As highly regulated domestic markets, one might expect strong political influence. As industries with a long history of linkage to national security priorities, a strong degree of intergovernmental supervision of the world market, and roles as leading economic sectors, one might expect statist forces to be at work. Perhaps most importantly, the prominent degree of regulation of the two markets makes it easier to spot the linkages between government policies influencing the domestic organization of the market and policies designed to advance international economic competitiveness. An accurate understanding of foreign economic policy depends crucially on this linkage, and a good theory of foreign economic policy should permit a general explanation of the total domestic and international policy.

The first section critically reviews the claims of statist theory about foreign policy. The second explains how a theory of political choice would examine American foreign economic policy.

The State of the Literature

Is there a theory of foreign economic policy that can account for the shift in the U.S. telecommunications strategy and for that strategy's subsequent evolution? This section critically reviews the contribution of statist theorizing.

The Statist Theory

The theory of international relations has deep roots in the concept of balance of power diplomacy. Balance of power theorists argue that anarchy among states (that is, the absence of an authoritative central power for the world)

---

2. Much of the evidence and details of the telecommunications cases is set forth in Cowhey 1989b.

forces states to look out for themselves and to constantly strive to check the expansion of power of other states. States do so either by unilateral action or by forming alliances with others. In short, states have to follow policies that adjust steadily to the demands of competition in a world with no assured guarantee of survival or prosperity.

Hand in hand with balance of power theorizing came the idea that each state acted in regard to foreign policy as if it was steered by a single rational unified actor responding deftly to the demands of international rivalry and opportunity. "Washington" responded to a crisis, not President Bush or a State Department bickering with the Congress. This simplifying assumption long troubled analysts and led some to counterattack by stressing how bureaucratic politics and organizational inertia structured much of foreign policy. In response, other scholars proposed to formulate a more precise theory of how a country responded to the demands of international competition without simply saying that it was all undirected bureaucratic adventurism or sombulence. Quite sensibly, this latter group of scholars argued that the White House (for example) did try to give direction to foreign policy and the executive bureaucratic politics suggested. Thus, statist theories grew up as a way of giving analytic content to the rational unified actor posited by balance of power theory.

As one might expect, there are many varieties of statist theorizing. This essay simplifies the task by sticking to the most recent contributions modeling the case of U.S. foreign economic policy. This work argues that the "state" consists of the enduring institutions of government (particularly the central norms and organizational characteristics of the executive branch) and the goal-oriented behavior of the President and administrators in the executive branch of government, particularly the elite parts of the national security bureaucracy.[3] In keeping with the tradition stressing the primacy of international constraints on foreign policy (such as balance of power diplomacy), statists emphasize how the state permits rational responses to the perils of the international system.[4]

---

3. Ikenberry 1988a, 10. Other influential statist analyses have included Katzenstein 1978, Krasner 1978, and Skocpol 1985.

4. " . . . politicians and executive officials, embracing a distinctive set of policy objectives, may be of decisive importance in shaping outcomes. State officials may be instrumental in interpreting the nature of international pressures or imperatives" (Ikenberry 1988b, 220). But not every theorist interested in how international anarchy and competition shapes foreign policy is inherently a statist. For example, in broad terms, one could posit the world of international conflict and cooperation depicted by Robert Keohane without assuming that individual countries conform to the statist model. One would assume that domestic political processes set much of the diplomatic agenda, change the enforceability of international agreements, and change the amount of information available to states involved in diplomacy. However, Keohane (1984) might assume that international competition limits national options more than would political choice theorists discussed in the second section.

The first generation of statist theorizing also tried to test macropolitical comparisons about the degree to which governments, especially the professional bureaucrats, differed in their ability to direct the nation's response to challenges of the world economy. Thus, a strong state, such as Japan, had much stronger central governmental guidance of responses to the world economy than a weak state like the United States. This argument meant that statist theory tried to account for the forms of "industrial policy" deployed by a country in support of its foreign economic policy objectives.

The strong state argument ran into trouble because analysts showed that politicians can and do reverse the judgment of the state officials in ways not easily squared with the original theory.[5] Nonetheless, the agenda of linking industrial policies with the study of foreign economic policy remains in statist theorizing. Today, most analysts look to more sensitive distinctions about the capacity of governments to shape the future of their societies in regard to specific issues. The recent literature is the focus of this essay.

Statist literature emphasizes that examinations of popular political pressures do not suffice to explain foreign economic policy. State institutions have their own logic and consequences that do not bend completely to current exigencies. The President and the national security bureaucracy have some ideas about the public good in the world system that are not reducible to politics as usual.[6] Indeed, not only do states resist purely interest-driven policies, they can reshape the game of interest politics around them. For example, the Pentagon can try to rally support for an indirect industrial policy for high technology if it fears that U.S. military leadership is endangered by Japanese technological challenges.

Statists also argue that the state is not simply a conveyor for moving imperatives derived from the international system to appropriate national policy responses. Statists note that institutions shaping foreign policy take on a life of their own, or at least do not rapidly change in response to short-term political incentives. Institutions, they argue, reinforce normative limits on the range of political dialogue and they raise the stakes for political challengers to

---

5. As a regulated industry, telecommunications is also similar to petroleum, an industry often used in studies of foreign economic policy that also was marked by strenuous (albeit unsuccessful) efforts to emphasize autarky. Krasner (1978) established oil as a benchmark industry. Subsequent detailed studies of the energy industries in Japan (Samuels 1987) and France (Nowell 1983) have revealed severe limits on the degree of state leadership. Comparisons of trade policies for industrial sectors in the United States and France have shown that the strength of state apparently does little to explain the major patterns of outcomes (Milner 1988).

6. The current generation of statists emphasize that these claims are a far cry from the original discussion of strong and weak states in Katzenstein (1978). Strong states, like Japan and France, supposedly had executive bureaucracies with less accountability to politicians and interest groups, while nurturing strong traditions of independent state visions for advancing international competitiveness.

the status quo embodied by institutions. By virtue of their command over expertise, strong sensitivity to the international environment, and agenda-setting powers (as active proponents of policy initiatives), state actors produce a bargaining path that begins and ends at points others than those derived solely from an examination of domestic or international politics. Presidents can use their bully pulpit in diplomacy to influence legislation as foreign policy issues, and new policies and bureaucracies can reshape interest group behavior either by spurring transnational coalitions or new participants in the policy process.[7] For example, Ikenberry argues that the price controls on oil divided the oil industry (thus weakening its power), while the President used economic summit diplomacy to jawbone Congress.[8]

Flaws of Statist Theory

The analytic middle ground between reducing foreign policy to bureaucratic politics and simply assuming a unified rational government taken by statist theory has usefully advanced the study of foreign policy, but it also is a flawed vehicle for future analytic progress. Four problems with the statist theory deserve special attention.

One problem is that the state is a sweeping analytic invention without any clear empirical content. (A demand curve is also an analytic invention, but it is easier to create a clear and sensible empirical interpretation.) After all of the writing about the state, it is still hard to know what it is.

When is a policy merely the outcome of epiphenomenal bureaucratic politics and when is it a product of the state? For example, when the State Department's international communications bureau abandoned most prior commitments on international satellite policy to promote President Reagan's policy of deregulation in the 1980s, was this a grab for power by a weak bureau or was it a redefinition of the state's priorities?

Which bureaucracies are part of the state? Which norms and laws reflect the state, which reflect electoral pressures? For example, when the Federal Communications Commission works on international communications policy is it part of the state? No one would claim that it is especially attuned to the international system, and it is highly political.

Recent definitions of the state further extend the sweep of the concept without giving it clear content by embracing two analytic traditions that largely redefine the state in an open-ended way. (The state consists of long-standing organizations and efforts of senior officials to promote the public interest according to professional norms rather than requiring a major mission

---

7. Lake 1988, 39.
8. Ikenberry 1988a.

in foreign affairs.)[9] Certainly, in the case of foreign economic policy, this means that a statist theory must explain the behavior of agencies ranging from the Nuclear Regulatory Commission to the Federal Trade Commission, and this means that the theory has to provide a general theory of regulatory behavior even though these agencies characteristically spend relatively little time on their international policy missions.

In short, the state is an analytic shell. It is hard to define operationally, and most of its content concerning institutional dynamics has to be filled in from other theoretical inspirations. Such an analytic invention is perfectly acceptable if it is necessary. But most statist theories are too sweeping to guide detailed examination of the individual cases of foreign economic policy that they explore.[10] In short, there is a mismatch between the sweep of the theoretical concepts and the cases under investigation.

The domain of the state is fuzzy. Still, statists are right to argue that international incentives influence national politics and policies. The questions are when and how? A second problem with statist theory is its ill-defined answers to these questions. After abandoning its initial efforts to show how the distribution of international power could predict central attributes of American foreign economic policy, statist theory cannot decide how the international system drives the state. For example, does one begin with an idea about international structure (however defined), deduce a proper national response, and test to see if the United States fulfilled it?[11] Or does the international system matter only in an ad hoc manner?[12]

9. Ikenberry (1988b) sets forth this definition. The two major elements of the definition point to yet another problem. One of the earliest points of the literature on organizations is that large organizations often breed the displacement of the goals of its professionals.

10. In my view the concept of the state is necessary for certain types of research. For example, Haggard (1988) usefully restates how the state can be coded as a multidimensional category for the purposes of analytic simplification. This simplification makes sense for certain purposes of macro-political comparisons, a traditional objective in the field of comparative politics. In addition, the state can also be a proxy variable for certain constants in the political landscape. This usage is acceptable if the analyst can demonstrate the invariability of the assumed constant, and if the analyst can show that the explanation of the constant requires variables that are different than those used in more micro-analytic theories. Recent reworkings of the earlier generation of scholarship on political cleavages may fit this bill. See the work of David Laitin (1985). Alt (1987) likens institutions and ideas to fixed capital investments that are often hard to change rapidly. Therefore, he treats them as quasi-permanent givens for any individual case. This approach has the problem of not asking why they remain fixed in the given case.

11. Lake (1988) ingeniously refines the model of international systemic restraints so as to deduce how these restraints should shape presidential policy agendas. See the critiques of Haggard (1988) and Frieden (1988) of Lake's solution.

12. Haggard (1988) makes the case for why a loose interpretation of systemic imperatives is the maximum possible. Ikenberry's imaginative efforts to work out the links to the international system illustrate the dilemma faced by statists. He has offered two analytic variants. On one hand, he argues that the American state's weakness forces its leaders to advocate changes in the

A third difficulty with the literature is its treatment of domestic politics. Statists largely test their theory against interest group theories in the tradition of Schnatsneider and Bentley that the field of American politics has rejected.[13] Statists have not seriously addressed explanations based on the "electoral imperative." Electoral theories argue that interest group politics are one part of the broader political game, so interest group theorizing alone would fail as a predictor of policy.[14] When statists discuss electoral influences, they do so primarily by asking if policy "x" was directly demanded by the incumbent party's constituency.[15] Unsurprisingly, the answer often is no. But, as the next section explains, this does not mean that elections do not drive policies.

A fourth problem for statists is their treatment of the origins and latitude of powers granted to officials and institutions (the state). As noted above, statists argue that public institutions have their own dynamics which can substantively influence the outcome of policies. For example, foreign policy bureaucracies often raise unpopular concerns over good relations with Japan when Congress wants action to end "unfair" trade quickly. The statist intuition is certainly reasonable, but the logic is largely ad hoc and finesses the larger political and policy question—in a constitutional democracy, how do institutions (such as the State Department) gain and maintain their powers?[16]

---

international regime (in order to impose many of the costs of change on other countries) rather than imposing painful discipline at home. (In contrast, other states will move to adjustment at home much faster.) Ikenberry 1986. On the other hand, he argues that the President's control over diplomacy gives him the leverage to make international deals that will permit him to impose painful adjustment at home (Ikenberry 1988a).

13. Political scientists have also criticized the latest bearers of the old interest group models, regulatory economists such as Pelzman (1976), for ignoring electoral factors. A good example of the new literature in political science is McCubbins, Noll, and Weingast 1987.

14. Gowa (1988) makes telling observations about how institutions change the role of interest groups (which could easily fit within a political choice theory). Her own explanations, however, then treat most domestic politics as if it were interest group politics. Lake (1988, 36) recognizes the electoral imperative, but then does not recognize that electoral politics necessarily require more than pork barrel politics. Indeed by identifying Congress, for example, with societal interests he has to argue that its leadership must differ from the strategic perspective on foreign economic policy of the President.

15. Statists have done little to analyze the impact of electoral incentives in any systematic form even though many of them have noted that crises (a major source of electoral shifts) are conducive to policy change. One exception is Haggard 1988.

16. A similar point can be made about the hegemony of ideas. Goldstein (1988) and Odell (1982) have rightly pointed out the staying power of ideas in shaping policy. But ideas are the product of policy communities that are given access to power by politicians seeking broader goals. They then become part of the "brand name" identity of parties discussed earlier. See, for example, Gourevitch's 1986 enlightening discussion of the treatment of Keynesian ideas in the Great Depression.

A better theory of policy would incorporate a theory of institutional change into a broader theory of politics.[17]

In sum, statism has become a patchwork of ad hoc theorizing whose critical claim is that one should expect special concern for international systemic considerations in the foreign affairs bureaucracy and the White House, an attempt to convert domestic policy into foreign policy when advantageous (and mobilize transnational actors outside the United States), active attempts to shape agenda and selectively mobilize constituencies, and some impact of institutional processes on substantive outcomes. The next section suggests a political choice model is superior because it is more general in what it can explain. While it can account for cases where outcomes coincide with the predictions of statists, it can also identify the limits of power of statist institutions and set up systematic analysis of the specific preferences worked out by the policy process that drives U.S. responses to international economic challenges.

Political Choice Theory

What alternative exists to statist arguments in regard to domestic variables? This paper builds on one variant of the "new institutionalism" that emphasizes the primacy of politics in resolving collective choice problems. The new institutionalists look for ways in which collective choice problems are resolved by the creation of procedures and hierarchies. These institutional solutions for collective action problems in turn shape the substance of outcomes. While there are many variants on the new institutionalism, this section emphasizes models deriving from the ways in which politicians structure government institutions and policies to further their electoral goals. The exposition concentrates on the United States in order to simplify discussion, but the theory is applicable elsewhere.

Choice theory begins with politicians because they are the "principals" (the superiors who are the ultimate holders of power in day to day life) of the political system.[18] The United States is unusual in that both Congress and the President are the principals of political power. The theory addresses the

---

17. Katzenstein's 1984 work on small nations reworked the argument on strong states into a thesis about how political bargaining can be organized to maximize international economic competitiveness. He argued that dependence on trade in small states has bred corporatist arrangements capable of inducing quick domestic adjustment to global competitive challenges. A theory of political choice would not quarrel with this finding.

18. Principal-agent theory in economics often looks to stockholders as the principals, and by analogy one might argue that voters are the ultimate principals. But work in the tradition discussed here makes the simplifying assumption that the operational principals are politicians who are motivated by electoral ambitions.

demand and supply side of the political process as well as its "production functions" (the institutional arrangements used to resolve collective choice problems). A theory of political choice emphasizes that: (1) electoral politics, not just interest group politics, dominate the calculus of political leaders; (2) electoral incentives set predictable parameters for choosing among competing bundles of collective goods and the key features of the programs to implement these policies; and (3) the political leadership determines the amount and types of discretion granted to executive foreign affairs bureaucracies in a manner consistent with electoral calculations and the anticipated problems of overseeing delegated powers. The following sections spell out these points and highlight some of the propositions that flow from them.

Electoral Politics

Political choice theory holds that politicians control the policy game and constantly act as entrepreneurs on behalf of their political goals. This search for political gain by rewarding supporters with policy instruments is the motive of the entrepreneurial political process. Both the President and Congress put top priority on electoral considerations, followed by building political power within government, and then fulfilling substantive goals of public policy.[19]

Politicians respond to the "demand side" of the political equation, the demands made by voters and interest groups in politics. Interest groups matter as a source of financial support and votes in elections, and also as important resources in the search for the secondary and tertiary goals of building power and pursuing policy goals. But political choice theory argues that interest group politics are only one subordinate part of the broader political game of building electoral strength.[20] Interest groups only dominate the formulation of the policy agenda when (at a minimum) they can demonstrate that they can articulate a winning political position for most interested politicians on a repeated basis and on a more reliable basis than other sources of policy advice. For example, a recent study of U.S. agricultural policy concluded that

19. This formulation follows Arnold (1981). More formally put, the politician puts highest priority on maximizing electoral support based on the mix of interests in his electoral district. Presidents may have a more permissive view of their room for maneuver because any solution acceptable to Congress as a whole is likely to have a winning coalition of national support.
20. Noll (1983) makes the case about the importance of political structures on interest group dynamics. The broader political game includes the strengthening of the party. Although national political parties do not operate as tightly disciplined units, the White House has an interest in the state of its political party and congressional party membership (through its caucus system) does impose important elements of a party approach to structuring legislation. Kiewet and McCubbins 1990.

farm lobbying organizations declined in influence when their advice was no longer a secure guide to local voters' preferences for both Republicans and Democrats.[21] In short, the influence of interest groups is variable and contingent on broader electoral incentives and processes.

The difference between political choice and interest group theories is illustrated by how they predict the influence of groups. Economists refurbished interest group theory by arguing that the groups of producers or consumers with the most concentrated costs or benefits would triumph in regulatory affairs because they are the easiest to organize for collective action.[22] For example, one would predict that the unusual concentration of benefits for large consumers in the telecommunications market fundamentally drove its politics in the past twenty years. (In most industrial countries about five percent of the users constitute half of the long distance market.)

In contrast to conventional interest group hypotheses, the electoral connection suggests interest groups' influence also depends on how many voters they employ, where they do business, and the degree to which interests convince politicians that they have successfully identified a broader political payoff. For these reasons Congress often goes to unusual lengths to make it easier for geographically diverse and numerous small businesses to become politically influential even though they are not concentrated. For example, concern over small businesses and households led Congress to insist on continued cross-subsidies for local phone service even after the breakup of AT&T.[23]

Perhaps most markedly, Congress and the executive branch have designed policy channels to bolster the influence of voting (and interest group) constituencies who might otherwise find it hard to compete for attention. This has made small business much more important in shaping policy than most interest group models would suggest. Congress has done so, for example, by redesigning procedures to simplify administrative appeals against executive branch decisions, making it easier for small firms to launch private antitrust actions and bolstering the political visibility of newcomers through the use of showcase congressional hearings.

A good example of how electoral inspiration influences the dance of private interests is in telecommunications. Congress and the executive branch both instituted procedures to cater to the concerns of smaller innovative firms in high technology in part because these firms employ large numbers of more educated voters whose political loyalty is considered contestable. Moreover,

---

21. Hansen 1988.
22. Peltzman 1976.
23. Ferejohn and Shipan 1989.

large corporate customers of communications and information systems spoke favorably of these smaller suppliers because the newcomers opened up new pricing, service, and equipment options for customers. Thus, Representative (now Senator) Timothy Wirth, an Atari Democrat from a Republican high technology district originally, strongly skewed the role of his key House subcommittee on telecommunications to favor smaller entrants in the telecommunications industry during the crucial congressional considerations about the demise of the AT&T monopoly.

Demand-side reasoning also suggests that if markets are subject to intense political organization domestically, domestic political bargains set the parameters for foreign economic policy. Domestic economics are more salient to voters unless there is a foreign policy debacle. International constraints drive policy indirectly. Interested actors anticipate the constraints imposed by the international system in their working out of domestic policies.[24] In many cases the discounted expected value of international constraints is so low that foreign economic considerations matter little in the choice. For example, most companies simply did not care if the unilateral opening of the U.S. telephone market to telecommunications equipment imports would increase the role of foreign companies greatly. They cared only about establishing an opening of the domestic market.[25] In other markets foreign economic stakes will loom large.

The evolution of United States policy concerning international satellite communications nicely illustrates many of the demand-side factors of a political choice model. If the foreign economic policy of telecommunications ever became part of the White House agenda, it occurred early in the Kennedy administration. The Democratic leadership in Congress had selected space policy in the late 1950s as a major avenue for attacking Eisenhower Re-

---

24. In many cases the constraints imposed by the international system are so ambiguous as to make them unreliable as a guide to action. When foreign policy does take primacy, a choice theorist would assume one of two things—either the foreign policy move fits within the parameters of domestic policy (so there is no issue to activate domestic policy actors) or the politician is taking a risk in the short-term in regard to foreign policy in order to protect his long-term domestic political base. The latter, and more interesting case, would then predict that short-term risk taking will be strongly conditioned by the nature of the domestic coalition backing political leaders.

25. Congress had promoted competition as a way to boost U.S. innovation and international competitiveness but largely focused on domestic issues. The executive branch also calculated the impact largely in terms of domestic economic and political performance. But its overall responsibility for foreign trade performance did make it anxious to keep AT&T intact (albeit subject to competition) to boost its global competitiveness in such areas as central office switching. It is important to note that the United States suffered no trade deficit in such big ticket items. Its losses were in smaller systems where no one proposed halting the movement to unilateral opening of the U.S. market because of the benefits to consumers.

publicanism and shoring up Democratic presidential prospects. NASA as an organization was a direct result of this congressional policy.[26]

Kennedy subsequently elevated leadership in space into a major political theme of his New Frontier, and the commercial opening of international communications through satellite communications was one of its central thrusts.[27] Kennedy proposed a new International Telecommunications Satellite Organization (Intelsat), which would have a monopoly on international satellite communications and be owned by the national telephone authorities of the world.

The high priority assigned to satellite policy and much of the detailed design of the policy came out of political considerations. Kennedy's choice of policy was not simply a clearcut response to the international system. First, although Kennedy warned darkly of Soviet incursions in the space arena if the United States did not act vigorously, a fair amount of this rhetoric was straight electoral politics.[28] Second, monopoly on the U.S. side was not a self-evident choice.[29] Third, in terms of the international regime for telecommunications, the U.S. approach challenged much of the regional and national basis for organizing the investment in and deployment of the physical facilities needed for the international communications network. Ultimately, the United States had to threaten to deploy its satellite technology on a unilateral international basis in order to win the day diplomatically with European authorities who preferred more traditional approaches to deploying the new technology.

A political choice theory suggests that the international innovation could not break the parameters of domestic bargains involving communications. This meant that a monopoly system was assumed unless one was willing to fight a long political battle to change the system. But speed was of the essence to reap the political benefits envisioned by Kennedy. At the same time, creating an extension of the monopoly system for telecommunications to outer space gave traditional champions of antitrust policy (still a powerful political theme in the early 1960s) and some of AT&T's new critics (such as television networks which disliked its prices and terms of service) a political opening.

---

26. The Democratic leadership's strategy is also a telling rejoinder to those who think that Congress cannot think about the U.S. strategic position. McDougall (1985) describes the Democratic strategy.

27. The emphasis on space also reflected a larger belief in the ability of technology to constructively reshape the international system. McDougall 1985, 344.

28. Weber and Drell (1988) give more credence to the role of strategic thinking to Kennedy's changing views about Soviet space strategy. My approach looks to the interplay of electoral incentives (and constraints) with judgments about international systemic constraints. For evidence on the political dimension, see, for example, McDougall 1985, 219–20, and Kinsley 1976.

29. Eisenhower apparently favored competition among U.S. international carriers to create more than one new satellite carrier. McDougall 1985, 353.

This meant that Kennedy had to invent an institutional formula that put some distance between the commercial interests of AT&T and the new satellite organization even if the new approach ran afoul of European nations. (Even after creating a new institutional framework, the passage of the Intelsat legislation required one of the most bitter floor fights in Senate history to break the antitrust lobby's filibuster.) Luckily for Kennedy, all the parties (ranging from liberal critics of monopoly systems to commercial rivals of AT&T) agreed that the United States ultimately needed commercial support from the Europeans. So, they acquiesced to provisions that made the Intelsat proposal, however unorthodox, more appealing to other nations.

As political choice theory would predict, the United States pushed for the international regime that most strongly reinforced the dominant political coalition at home. Domestic politics tilted policy toward institutional innovation that also created international controversy.[30] International constraints were salient to the extent that the political participants recognized the end game depended on winning foreign partners. Thus, after domestic politics set the fundamental policy path, all the U.S. actors recognized that it was a good idea to make some concessions to other nations' sensibilities in fine tuning the policy.

A theory of political choice's emphasis on how political strategy can elevate the power of smaller firms also nicely illuminates the subsequent U.S. attack on its own diplomatic creation, Intelsat, in the Reagan years. In the 1980s, the U.S. government elevated a small satellite communications company (Orion Satellite Corporation) with no known customers and limited finances into a centerpiece of U.S. international communications policy. It did so even though it meant creating a diplomatic confrontation by challenging the monopoly jurisdiction of Intelsat.

The Reagan administration saw Orion as an innovative forerunner of a larger number of would-be entrants in the international communications market. It was eager to show that its new domestic policy of telecommunications deregulation could yield new international commercial advantages at a time when it was being severely criticized for its passive stance on foreign trade. Therefore, it made the approval of Orion's application for international service agreements with other countries (and the campaign to win Intelsat's bitter acquiescence to these agreements) into a significant trade issue. The United States argued that the high speed data and video networks proposed by Orion

---

30. These are the instances that are most interesting for Putnam's (1988) two level game analysis. For example, political choice would lead us to expect Presidents will use summit diplomacy to challenge domestic arrangements when short-term political constraints challenge longer term electoral viability. This outcome also fits statist theory. But political choice would argue that the President will only win this game if Congress agrees about the domestic political calculus, not because it is defined as a foreign policy issue!

fell under the U.S. claim that free trade agreements should apply to the provision of services across national frontiers.[31] Just as importantly, U.S. trade negotiators believed that the Democratic Congress might make political capital from protectionist trade legislation if the Republican administration could be blamed for inaction on opening foreign telecommunications markets.

Later, another company (PanAmSat) proved to be the first of the newcomers to be operational. As the French government put it in a press conference announcing its acceptance of entry by PanAmSat: "This is a very sensitive issue for your government. Our government knows this, and this shows its willingness to cooperate."[32] Throughout the entire process, it was the Democratic House of Representatives that worried far more than the State Department about the effect of U.S. tactics on broader American diplomatic relations.[33] But, then again, Intelsat was the legacy of the last popular Democratic president.

The satellite case shows how a political choice theory can illuminate the incentives for policy innovation. But, unlike many discussions of domestic politics that focus solely on demand, the theory also looks at the supply side of the political equation.[34]

The Supply Side: Choosing Collective Goods

The supply side to politics is the costs and benefits of the policies themselves. An emphasis on political calculations does not restrict the analyst to discussing only distributional (or pork barrel) politics. Political choice theory also illuminates how governments will select public goods.[35] As Gowa (1988) has

---

31. The general principle of making services subject to free trade rules was subsequently accepted in 1989 by the mid-term review of the Uruguay Round of GATT negotiations.

32. *Telecommunications Reports*, December 12, 1988, 12. A more comprehensive account of this policy is in Colino (1986) and Cowhey and Aronson (1985).

33. Many countries viewed the U.S. case for competition with Intelsat as part of an American assault on international organizations in general and any international economic institution concerned with the welfare of developing nations in particular. Congressional action especially came from the House Foreign Affairs Committee that was very concerned about declining U.S. relations with the developing nations and the possibility that some executive branch officials wanted to pull the United States out of Intelsat (as it had exited from the International Labor Organization).

34. Cassing, McKeown, and Ochs (1986) represent a sophisticated work in the tradition of public choice theory that essentially treats trade policy solely as a product of varying competing demands.

35. A classic public good (like clean air) is in joint supply and it is hard to exclude any individual from the good. Many goods characterized by joint supply (for example, navigation signals from an outer space satellite) may provide opportunities for exclusion (for example, by the use of a scrambler on the signal). Many other permutations of the classic public good exist. For the purposes of this essay, it is not necessary to distinguish among them very closely.

pointed out, doing good can produce positive rewards to pass out to voters and interest groups. (Avoiding international debacles is a political constraint with positive policy consequences.) But politics mean that determining the "public interest" is somewhat volatile. For example, market allocation and government allocation of resources may both offer public goods and bads, but different mixes of each.[36] Politics shape the mix, and the attendant distribution of costs and benefits.[37]

The supply-side costs and the electoral connection lead politicians to emphasize the distributional side of politics even when packaging collective goods.[38] Simply put, politicians prefer policies that impose fewer visible costs, or distribute major side payments to balance new costs, or impose a small penalty (to use as a side payment to pay off protesters) on recipients of a controversial public benefit, or spread out the costs of adjustment to a new policy over time. They prefer this packaging even if it detracts from total economic or policy efficiency.[39] These distributional mechanisms are driven by politics, and they substantially influence many of the important dimensions of economic policies even when politicians are trying to produce public goods. Yet statists often miss them as the basis for key political bargains.[40]

---

36. More technically put, most policy choices involving public goods are the result of a nonzero-sum, noncooperative game. Its outcome, the Nash equilibrium, exists "when each agent does the best he can given his rational expectations of the other agents' actions" (McMillan 1987, 7). In all likelihood the equilibrium solution will leave some dissatisfied. When played repeatedly the game may result in better than the least efficient equilibrium outcome, but it will not necessarily achieve maximum efficiency. Moreover, there are multiple efficient outcomes where a war over spoils may still be fought.

37. Political choice theorists probably view the delegation of resource allocations to markets more frequently as a "public interest" solution than do statists. The literature on law and economics explores how economic reasoning can guide the design of efficient legal systems or other institutional arrangements for mediating economic disputes. It shows how government intervention can contribute to the creation of more efficient social outcomes (even when redistributing rents), yet government leadership is only one of several alternative solutions for collective action problems. Thus, unlike the versions of pluralism that so disturbed the statists, this approach can show how the rules of bargaining/social choice lead to the redefinition of private interests in a way consistent with greater social welfare. North 1981. But, unlike statists, it does not have to posit a set of institutional bureaucracies as the source of the public good and it can more easily look at courts and other mechanisms for decentralized bargaining as a way to increase efficiency and reshape societal interests. For a balanced coverage of its political implications, see the collection of essays in Kuperberg and Beitz 1983. The broader formulation of the theory is in Williamson 1985.

38. By implication, successful regulatory policies essentially roll over costs and benefits for winners and losers; both sides view the political arena primarily as a form of insurance against risks in the marketplace. Owen and Braeutigam 1978. Wilson 1980.

39. Weingast, Shepsle, and Johnson 1981. Cohen and Noll 1983.

40. For example, Haggard's (1988) fine paper on trade policy in the New Deal concludes that the electoral interests of the New Deal were too ambiguous to predict trade policy. He then provides ample detail on why a set of mixed political incentives would lead politicians to hedge

For example, traditional regulatory policies and protectionist trade policies, such as domestic regulation of the level of U.S. oil production and oil import quotas until 1970, favored some specialized economic interests (plus their workers and local economies) at the expense of the rest of the economy. But the costs of regulation and protection were very low to the average voter and only slightly higher for other specialized economic interests. Moreover, these policies were important for delivering the "oil patch" in presidential and congressional elections.

When would a political choice theory expect a major reversal in policy for a regulated market? Politicians rarely make a major shift in regulatory policy if the costs of regulation for losers are constant or declining.[41] When the costs imposed by regulation rise steeply, there is an opportunity to reverse the regulations. The reversal will depend first on how it affects voters and secondarily on how it affects other special interests. Foreign economic policy would be a tertiary influence on the process.

To understand the logic of political choice theories, consider the case of oil policy, a favorite of statist theories.[42] When oil prices rose steeply in 1970, the White House reversed traditional oil policy and imposed price controls on oil in order to lower the cost of oil for the average household and reduce the high inflation rate, a dangerous liability for a President facing reelection. Congress then made the program into law in 1974 as a way to provide a period of temporary relief during adjustment to another sharp jump in prices in 1973 (there were expiration dates on the controls).[43] Divisions within the oil industry may have helped to reinforce the staying power of controls, but the power of smaller refineries supporting controls came precisely because it coincided with regional economic and consumer household demands. (The small refiners positioned themselves as the champions of households in the industrial Northeast, for example.) Moreover, the President (a key figure in statist theory) could have vetoed the renewal of controls in 1975, but chose to keep them so as to not cripple his chances for reelection.

By 1979, the staggering economic costs imposed by controls (higher oil imports and world oil prices, plus enormous deadweight losses in efficiency)

---

their bets. His fundamental finding that the New Deal introduced a policy of small practical impact in the short term (thus imposing few immediate costs) but larger impact in the long term exactly fits what an electoral theory of policy reversal would expect.

41. This hypothesis is from Joskow and Noll 1981. Distributional politics could also lead government to deal with demands for entry into regulated markets by opening up quickly growing segments of the market rather than redistributing market shares. (Or policy entrepreneurs look for loopholes in the coverage of regulated markets because there are no existing property rights to market shares.)

42. Ikenberry 1988a. Krasner 1978.

43. The controls also were politically popular because they seemingly punished "Big Oil," which many people blamed for the price hikes.

were so high that virtually everyone could be paid off by redistributing the gains from a more rational program.[44] Even then President Carter was not prepared to act against controls because he was more concerned about inflation. Only the new jump in oil prices and a supply shortage led Carter and large parts of Congress to decide to act on oil.[45]

More fundamentally, the economic ills imposed by price controls were part of the overall phenonomon of stagflation that posed a crippling political threat to the Democratic Party (a legacy still exploited in the 1988 Presidential campaign). Statists have argued that Carter succeeded in deregulating prices only when he successfully linked it to his foreign policy credibility, especially his leadership in the Western alliance. Political choice would acknowledge the effort at linkage but argue that Helmut Schmidt's scorn of Jimmy Carter was unfortunate but not life threatening to the Democratic party. Indeed, the Democratic Congress had been unmoved previously by arguments about alliance politics. Congress acted when it concluded that voter scorn of Democratic incompetence on the economy was a serious threat.[46] Deregulation of several key industries (of which oil was one) was one policy and political response to the electoral problem.

Political choice theory would predict that the drive to win voters (not to balance interest groups) explained the primary thrust of policy. It would also predict that such high political stakes would lead to fine tuning the economic consequences of decontrol to put the most favorable face on the program to key electoral constituencies. Political leaders would substantially reduce the total economic gains from decontrol in order to cater to key constituents. As predicted, to make decontrol of oil more palatable, Congress and the White House also agreed to impose a windfall profits tax on oil companies whose staggering proceeds of $227 billion were earmarked for a huge windfall of

44. The Phase Four price controls discouraged conservation and boosted the amount of imported oil by holding down the price of oil. It also reduced domestic production by reducing profits from the industry. At the same time, it used an elaborate "rebate" system to encourage stepped up production of domestic oil even under controls (higher production levels could be sold at world prices, and the amount of production earned decontrol for a matching barrel of base level production). The system also effectively kept regional oil prices equal by allocating cheaper oil among refineries in such a way as to equal the crude oil costs for refiners. It also offered special economic benefits to the numerous and geographically well-distributed small refiners and oil producers of the United States.

45. Congress had left room for administrative decontrol of oil prices. Once Carter took the initiative, there was an apparent majority in Congress to sustain him (Vietor 1984, 262–65).

46. Ikenberry's account of the linkage to economic summitry is unpersuasive. To be sure, proponents of decontrol within the White House pushed the summit deal as a reason for decontrol. But he produces little evidence that Congress gave this a major weighting in its reasoning, and the advocates of decontrol already held that position prior to the summit. A better view of the matter would follow Putnam's (1988) observation that presidents can use international diplomacy to ease the costs of domestic political choices.

cross-subsidies to voters and interest groups. The tax nullified many of the economic gains from decontrol.[47]

Production Functions and the Design of Institutions

The demand and supply sides of political choice are incomplete because they assume that preferences can be aggregated into collective decisions. In fact, politicians also face the now familiar hazards of collective choices—the difficulty of achieving stable policies due to Arrow's paradox, and the problems of achieving agreement due to problems concerning the enforcement and monitoring of collective agreements.[48] Thus, the "production function" side of political choice is the study of institutional arrangements to resolve collective choice problems.[49] These range from parliamentary rules of procedure to the delegation of power. In the study of foreign economic policy, it is especially important to look at how Congress structures the work of the executive branch because the Constitution gives Congress strong powers over foreign economic policy.

The delegation of power to an agent is a particularly important way of resolving collective choice problems. Delegation limits who can make decisions on behalf of the political principals but it also sets implicit boundaries on the scope of subsequent actions. Delegation is an important phenomenon within Congress and within the executive branch, and between Congress and the executive branch. For example, Democratic congressmen delegate authority to party leadership.

Cox and McCubbins have argued that the delegation of power to party leadership in Congress creates incentives for leadership to look at the "big picture": ". . . by creating a leadership post which is both attractive and elective [for example, the Speaker of the House], a party can induce its leader to internalize the collective electoral fate of the party. In Olsonian terms, this creation of a position whose occupant is personally motivated to pursue collective interests serves to make the party a privileged group. . . . Electoral inefficiencies that can potentially accumulate because of the free rider problems inherent in legislation (of both the particularistic-benefits and collective-

---

47. Vietor 1984, 270.

48. One could, of course, assume that in domestic politics the problem of enforcement is solved; therefore, the political bargaining problem is much easier. But times of political contention make prior mechanisms to assure good faith questionable. Thus, we are back to the situation described by Nash. Cooperating without assured enforcement is implausible in most cases because it is easier to build new institutional solutions to solve the contract problem.

49. A production function represents an entrepreneur's calculation of what output is possible from a given mix of inputs. Technology is often a key factor in determining production functions. Similarly, this paper views political institutions as the social technology that allows varying mixes of policy output given a particular set of political demands. Institutions improve efficiency in resolving collective action problems for political entrepreneurs.

benefits kind) are prevented because party leaders have a personal incentive to prevent them."[50] The congressional party leadership has an incentive to look for policy mixes that provide an attractive profile for the party as a whole and the individual electoral goals of its members. The motives begin in domestic politics but the calculations are not solely particularistic. The leadership uses its control over membership on committees and over committee jurisdictions to make sure that committees reflect this balance. The purpose is to protect the value of its electoral identity, still the most important single factor driving a federal election contest.[51] Thus, delegation means that the congressional leadership, not just the President, has an incentive to look at both the national strategic picture and local particularistic politics. Statists have missed this dynamic.[52]

Political choice theory also permits more systematic thinking about the statists' observation that institutions are not malleable to the whim of the moment. While the claim is generally true, the demise of the War Department and the Civil Aeronautics Board should show that radical change is possible even without a policy disaster if politicians push hard.

In general, politicians make the barriers to major new policy initiatives especially high because the political costs of such innovation may be great and highly uncertain. Once contemplating major innovation, politicians often delegate power to new (or reformulated) institutions to embody the political bargains that permit the change. These institutions are a form of political promise to those who must defer some benefits today for other benefits in the future. For example, the Congress created the United States Trade Representative and foisted the office on the executive office of the President in order to assure critics of free trade that trade grievances would receive more political attention from the White House and remain subject to detailed congressional oversight. The White House and Congress agreed to make the Communications Satellite Corporation (Comsat), which held the U.S. franchise for membership in Intelsat, into a public corporation with private stock holdings on the open market in order to assure the public (and commercial rivals to AT&T) that AT&T would not exploit this new commercial opportunity.[53] In short,

50. Cox and McCubbins 1989, 15–16.

51. Ferejohn and Shipan (1989) rely somewhat less on the party leadership to reach largely compatible predictions. The elaborate system of delegation to congressional committees balances a decision to allow the most intensely committed subpublics to shape the initial agenda for action (a way to resolve collective choice problems) against letting the majority party and congressional chamber as a whole review the decision to assure that it is more broadly acceptable.

52. The party identity is akin to a national brand name in consumer markets. Cox and McCubbins 1989.

53. The Federal Communications Commission originally proposed to form Comsat as a common carriers' consortium to be owned exclusively by the major U.S. international telecommunications carriers. Political skepticism of this cozy commercial setup assured that it became a corporation with stock held by telephone companies and the general public.

institutions make it harder to reverse the fundamental priorities of prior political bargains embodied in the institution. Unlike statist theory, political choice theory has a consistent theoretical basis for predicting when and for what end institutions are created.

Institutions are more than extraordinary safeguards to guarantee the credibility of current promises. Politicians often delegate power to specialized institutions and agents (the state) in order to deal with collective action problems. One purpose of delegation may be to lower direct political accountability for a tough decision. For example, Congress and the White House might firmly favor giving greater protection to consumers but wish to avoid the risk of writing protective legislation that is so complex that it is unworkable. An alternative is to rewrite the laws to make it easier to sue firms for product defects. This will certainly make the courts more influential, but politicians can defend this as merely assuring people of their day in court.[54] Delegation to bureaucracies (which gives the bureaucracy "first mover" advantages) allows many problems to be resolved after passing less formidable hurdles than passing a new law. Thus changing ideology, internal bureaucratic politics and other developments in the executive bureaucracy may influence policy. This is where statists focus their attention, especially when looking at foreign affairs bureaucracies. However, a theory of political choice also predicts that principals will not relinquish ultimate control over these institutions. Choice theorists look at the power of the State Department as a specialized check and balance on the policy process created by political principals to serve their general purposes. If the agents fail to suit those needs over time, the delegation of power will be modified. The reshuffling of jurisdictions over trade policy and arms control talks show what can be done by political leaders.[55]

Political choice theory holds that major initiatives out of executive branch institutions do not exist outside of some broader political equilibrium. As in any formal institution, politicians know that they confront problems of hidden information and action by their agents, as well as oligopolistic collusion among agents.[56] This is particularly so because there are two sets of principals in the U.S. government.

Politicians use a combination of a careful scrutiny during the appoint-

---

54. Usually the institutional rules make it very hard to reverse prior bargains (which is why "reform" is often difficult); the same barriers make it easier to compromise because bargains will be kept. Another purpose of delegation is to permit agencies to acquire the expertise necessary to build a case for further action. This is a primary reason for creating new agencies.

55. By the same token, this theory suggests that principals anticipate and discount the discretion and "cheating" by agents. Therefore, bureaucratic politics per se are not an important explanation of outcomes. But one can specify selected conditions where the degree of discretion of agents will be greater. See Bendor, Taylor, and Van Gaalen 1987.

56. Hart and Holmstrom 1986.

ment process, monitoring (for example, congressional oversight hearings), checks and balances (giving more than one bureaucracy a say over policy), management by exception (the bureaucracy can act fairly freely so long as there is not bitter opposition), and incentives (for example, agencies get larger budgets and key individuals get promoted if they anticipate the preferences of politicians correctly) to overcome the problems of delegation.[57]

For example, the White House shows the executive agencies that their ability to control policies and expand budgets depends on finding ideas that will win attention in the White House.[58] Conversely, Congress often controls the power of the President over an executive agency by giving the agency a strong "professional identity" and then using specialized oversight to reinforce the idea that professional ethics should override identity with the White House. This is precisely what happened in the case of the Justice Department when it handled the AT&T antitrust case.[59]

The Congress had long held the Justice Department up to tough criticism over its supposed caving in to President Eisenhower on the terms of settlement of an earlier antitrust suit against AT&T in 1956. During the critical negotiations over possible dismissal of the AT&T antitrust suit under Reagan, the professionals of the Justice Department bitterly objected to any action that smacked of bowing to political pressure. This forced the political leadership of the Reagan administration to take full responsibility to end the law suit. Despite protests about national security from the Defense Department and foreign trade policy from Commerce, the White House senior staff refused to act to end the antitrust case for fear of unpleasant political repercussions.[60]

---

57. The formal proof of the power of appointment in particular is found in Calvert, McCubbins, and Weingast 1988. In general, one would expect that the more politically sensitive is the policy, the greater will be the effectiveness of these controls. Moreover, one would expect the power of Congress in control of agencies would vary according to the degree of division in Congress over the issue. Ferejohn and Shipan 1989.

58. The time and attention of the White House is limited. Therefore, the White House's control over the executive agencies largely depends on having the agencies choose programs that they hope will win the support of the White House if the White House ever looked. Each branch of government also has incentives to specialize on policy. Only the White House has a national constituency and easy access to a bully pulpit. It has a comparative advantage is dealing with the politics of new ideas for broad collective goods, such as foreign economic policy (and especially security policy). (It is also more likely to be held accountable by voters for diffuse collective bads.)

59. Moe (1985) has pointed out this also means that neither the President nor Congress can demand detailed micro management of such an agency.

60. As the Justice Department pro who fought off the other departments explained about the White House in retrospect: "If you're a White House staffer, you want to deliver to the President the best result, the least damage, and the best policy—sometimes in that order. . . . They want to get it [the AT&T antitrust settlement] out of there [the White House] and take it on over to Defense or Justice or OMB or wherever—just get it away from the President" (Coll 1986,

In short, political choice theory examines the question of which agency has been delegated power to discover the political roots of policy. Statists usually note only the delegated power. Moreover, the executive agencies can fulfill the broad wishes of the Congress and the White House while providing "deniability" to the politicians on unpopular issues so long as there is no law or White House mandate that needs reversal. Congress often uses legislative hearings to indicate its preferences to the executive branch. It has also empowered the courts to expand their review of choices of executive agencies in light of presumed congressional intent.[61]

There can be major shifts in policy so long as agencies build on informal precedent and bargains between the executive and legislative branches. For example, political leaders shied from granting a formal monopoly on long-distance services to AT&T. However, Congress did nothing to clearly bar the FCC from taking this action; the executive and legislative branches had made a tacit bargain. In contrast, the controls on oil prices in the United States after 1973 were a matter of public law. It took an explicit act of Congress or a veto of the law by the President to reverse them.

The breaking up of AT&T, one of the major decisions on industrial organization in recent U.S. history, which led ultimately to many disputes over fair competition in world trade, is an excellent example of how institutional design and delegation of power can combine to permit outcomes that no political principals would risk on their own.

The final form of the approach taken by the United States to make the communications market competitive—namely, divesting local phone companies from AT&T—was a result of the dynamics of delegated power. The courts (arguably) could not have achieved divestiture of the local phone operations of the Bell Operating Companies, nor could Congress—but politics plus the courts could do so.

As just explained, congressional political pressure paralyzed the White House and cabinet and left policy in the hands of an Assistant Attorney General, who believed that only separating AT&T's long distance business from local phone operations would be efficient. His position had considerable

---

227–28). Judge Green reinforced Justice's will whenever it wavered by indirectly invoking Congress's attention. Also see the accounts of divestiture of Shooshan (1984) and Wiley (1984) for a clear picture of how Congress used hearings and the introduction of legislation to shape the deregulation of telecommunications.

61. For example, Congress uses the hearings process to allow interest groups to raise problems and demonstrate their potential political appeal. McCubbins 1985. Hearings on draft legislation also allow Congress to signal the range of acceptable action to the executive agencies. It has also aggressively changed the mandate of the courts through rewriting administrative law in order to expand oversight and organize potential constituents. Thus, Congress can steer policy indirectly in the name of procedural fairness rather than taking substantive policy positions. McCubbins, Noll, and Weingast 1987.

support in Congress. But he feared a trial would most likely only divest Western Electric (the equipment manufacturing arm of AT&T). AT&T calculated that the appeals court might also support divesting Western Electric even though there was otherwise limited political support for this action. However, AT&T preferred divestiture of its local phone services to the chance of an antitrust decision divesting it of Western Electric. AT&T also conjectured that it would win an appeal of any order to divest local phone operations but a successful appeal would not satisfy its critics in the political arena (thereby still leaving AT&T open to new attacks). Therefore, AT&T chose to divest its local phone operations as the price for settling the suit, ending the threat to Western Electric and assuring its right to compete in the computer and computer communications markets. It also meant that the newly independent Bell Operating Companies became independent customers for the purchase of foreign telecommunications equipment.

The AT&T consent decree had many critics in Congress. But Congress declined to intervene legislatively to change the outcome. Some say that this was due to congressional paralysis. Political choice theory leads one to look for why politicians tolerate a controversial policy, and therefore how the specific choice fits a broader political equilibrium.

In the case of divestiture, Congress had long ago made three calculations. First, the politics of long-distance services had changed irrevocably. The problems of stagflation made regulatory reform very attractive and telecommunications fit the profile of an industry where increased competition could battle inflation, lower prices for large corporate customers, and reduce rates for the middle class who were both the most active voters and the largest residential users of long distance. Second, once a decision had been made on long-distance competition, a single integrated phone company for local and long-distance services would not offer local households (and voters) much lower prices than a system where long-distance companies had to pay an access fee (that is, a subsidy) to local phone companies for the right to interconnect to local residences. Third, congressional leaders on telecommunications policy, as noted earlier, wanted to court high technology industry, much of which consisted of smaller communications and computer firms who mistrusted AT&T. A basic problem rooted in bargaining costs eventually became clear to everyone.

Simply put, AT&T's rivals and most experts had little confidence in their ability to monitor AT&T under a finely tuned settlement designed to keep AT&T in one piece (that is, in local and long-distance services plus retaining manufacturing and the right to enter the computer industry).[62] Indeed, a

---

62. Temin (1987) criticizes other analysts for not recognizing the importance of this phenomenon.

significant effect of letting small upstarts like MCI carry the political ball on pressing competition at an earlier date was to create a long history illustrating the messiness of any efforts to make AT&T a "fair" competitor against newcomers.[63] As long as AT&T remained essentially in one piece, even with a structurally separated subsidiary for such markets as computers and long distance services, its would-be competitors feared AT&T's integrated control of the national network and enormous financial resources could discriminate against newcomers and cross-subsidize new computer ventures. An integrated AT&T was only acceptable on one of two conditions: either it could be subject to rigid controls on its conduct (which might cripple AT&T as a competitor) or AT&T could be subject to competition in both local and long-distance services. Viewed from the broader viewpoint of shaping American competitive capabilities in the world market, this solution let AT&T compete in computer and information services for the first time, encouraged entry by new domestic firms, and made it easier for foreign firms to find customers among major U.S. phone companies.

In summary, political choice theory looks at domestic electoral politics first. It incorporates international considerations as part of the strategic calculus of actors who are usually more attuned to domestic politics and markets. Because political solutions always pose collective action problems and usually impose costs on some parties, political choice theory looks for how distributional considerations influence the design of collective goods and for the impact on policy of institutional designs that were designed to serve a broader political agenda than any one issue raises. Sometimes political entrepreneurs and the bureaucracies act like the statesmen of the statist textbook. But usually, as in a pointillist painting by Seurat, the picture breaks down into a thousand strokes of political maneuver that have strongly shaped the diplomatic package. It is far safer to estimate possible changes in foreign economic policy by thinking about the everyday politics of coping with the international system than to guess what a determined statesman in pursuit of the balance of power would attempt.

BIBLIOGRAPHY

Alt, James E. 1987. "Crude Politics: Oil and the Political Economy of Unemployment in Britain and Norway, 1970–85." *British Journal of Political Science* 17:149–99.
Arnold, Douglas. 1981. "The Local Roots of Domestic Policy." In *The New Congress,* ed. Thomas Mann and Norman Ornstein. Washington, D.C.: American Enterprise Institute.

---

63. See the telling passage in Temin 1987, 104–7. Extensive interviews with several of the key lobbyists have also confirmed this point.

Aronson, Jonathan D., and Peter F. Cowhey. 1988. *When Countries Talk: International Trade in Telecommunications Services.* Cambridge, Mass.: Ballinger.

Bendor, Jonathan, J. Serge Taylor, and Ronald Van Gaalen. 1987. "Stacking the Deck: Bureaucratic Missions and Policy Design." *American Political Science Review* 81:873–96.

Calvert, Randall L., Mathew D. McCubbins, and Barry R. Weingast. 1988. "A Theory of Political Control and Agency Discretion." Working paper, University of California, San Diego.

Cassing, J., T. J. McKeown, and J. Ochs. 1986. "The Political Economy of the Tariff Cycle." *American Political Science Review* 80:843–62.

Coase, Ronald H. 1960. "The Problem of Social Cost." *Journal of Law and Economics* 3:1–44.

Cohen, Linda, and Roger Noll. 1983. "The Political Economy of Government Programs to Promote New Technology." Paper delivered to the annual meeting of the American Political Science Association. Washington, D.C.

Colino, Richard A. 1986. "A Chronicle of Policy and Procedure: The Formulation of the Reagan Administration Policy on International Satellite Telecommunications." *Journal of Space Law* 13:103–56.

Coll, Steve. 1986. *The Deal of the Century—The Breakup of AT&T.* New York: Atheneum.

Cowhey, Peter F. 1989a. "Telecommunications and Foreign Economic Policy." In *New Directions in Communications Policy,* vol. 2, ed. Paula Newburg. Durham: Duke University Press.

Cowhey, Peter F. 1989b. "Bringing the Politician Back In: Political Choice and American Foreign Economic Policy." Working paper, University of California, San Diego.

Cowhey, Peter F., and Jonathan D. Aronson. 1985. "The Great Satellite Shootout." *Regulation* (May/June): 27–35.

Cox, Gary W., and Mathew D. McCubbins. 1989. "Political Parties and the Appointment of Committees." Paper for a Conference on Congressional Structure and Elections, University of California, San Diego.

Ferejohn, John, and Charles Shipan. 1989. "Congressional Influence on Telecommunications Policy." In *New Directions in Communications Policy,* vol. 1, ed. Paula Newburg. Durham: Duke University Press.

Frieden, Jeff. 1988. "Sectoral Conflict and U.S. Foreign Economic Policy, 1914–1940." *International Organization* 42:59–90.

Fiorina, Morris P. 1982. "Legislative Choice of Regulatory Forms: Legal Process or Administrative Process?" *Public Choice* 39:33–66.

Gilligan, Thomas W., William J. Marshall, and Barry R. Weingast. 1988. "Regulation and the Theory of Legislative Choice: The Interstate Commerce Act of 1887." Working paper, Hoover Institution, Stanford University.

Goldstein, Judith. 1988. "Ideas, Institutions, and American Trade Policy." *International Organization* 42:179–219.

Gowa, Joanne. 1988. "Public Goods and Political Institutions: Trade and Monetary Policy Processes in the United States." *International Organization* 42:15–32.

Gourevitch, Peter A. 1986. *Politics in Hard Times.* Ithaca: Cornell University Press.

Haggard, Stephan. 1988. "The Institutional Foundations of Hegemony: Explaining the Reciprocal Trade Agreements Act of 1934." *International Organization* 42:91–120.

Hansen, John Mark. 1988. "Creating a New Politics: The Evolution of an Agricultural Policy Network in Congress, 1919–1980." Ph.D. diss., Department of Political Science, Yale University.

Hart, Oliver, and Bengt Holmstrom. 1986. "The Theory of Contracts." Working Paper No. 418, Department of Economics, MIT.

Hills, Jill. 1988. *Deregulating Telecoms.* London: Quantum Books.

Ikenberry, G. John. 1986. "The State and Strategies of International Adjustment." *World Politics* 34:53–77.

Ikenberry, G. John. 1988a. "Market Solutions for State Problems: The International and Domestic Politics of American Oil Decontrol." *International Organization* 42:151–78.

Ikenberry, G. John. 1988b. "Conclusion: An Institutional Approach to American Foreign Economic Policy." *International Organization* 42:219–43.

Joskow, Paul L., and Roger G. Noll. 1981. "Regulation in Theory and Practice: An Overview." In *Studies in Public Regulation,* ed. Gary Fromm. Cambridge: Cambridge University Press.

Katzenstein, Peter J. 1978. "Conclusion: Domestic-Structures and Strategies of Foreign Economic Policy." In *Between Power and Plenty,* ed. Peter J. Katzenstein. Madison: University of Wisconsin Press.

Katzenstein, Peter J. 1984. *Corporatism and Change: Switzerland, Austria, and the Politics of Industry.* Ithaca: Cornell University Press.

Keohane, Robert O. 1984. *After Hegemony.* Princeton: Princeton University Press.

Kiewet, Rod, and Matthew McCubbins. 1990. *The Spending Power: The Congress, President and Appropriations.* Chicago: University of Chicago Press.

Kinsley, Michael. 1976. *Outer Space and Inner Sanctums: Government, Business, and Satellite Communication.* New York: Wiley.

Krasner, Stephen. 1978. *Defending the National Interest: Raw Materials Investments and U.S. Foreign Policy.* Berkeley: University of California Press.

Kuperberg, Mark, and Charles Beitz, eds. 1983. *Law, Economics, and Philosophy: A Critical Introduction with Applications to the Law of Torts.* Towata, N.J.: Rowman and Allanheld.

Lake, David A. 1988. "The State and American Trade Strategy in the Pre-Hegemonic Era." *International Organization* 42:33–58.

Laitin, David D. 1985. "Hegemony and Religious Conflict: British Imperial Control and Political Cleavages in Yorubaland." In *Bringing the State Back In,* ed. Peter B. Evans, Dietrich Rueschemeyer, and Theda Skocpol. Cambridge: Cambridge University Press.

March, James, and Johan Olsen. 1984. "The New Institutionalism: Organizational Factors in Political Life." *American Political Science Review* 78:734–50.

McCubbins, Matthew. 1985. "Regulating the Regulators: A Theory of Legislative Delegation." *American Journal of Political Science* 29:721–48.

McCubbins, Mathew, Roger Noll, and Barry R. Weingast. 1987. "Administrative Procedures as Instruments of Political Control." *Journal of Law, Economics, and Organization* 3:243–77.

McDougall, Walter A. 1985. *The Heavens and the Earth: A Political History of the Space Age*. New York: Basic.

McMillan, John. 1987. "International Trade Negotiations: A Game-Theoretic View." Paper prepared for the Ford Foundation project on Trade Policy and the Developing World, New York City.

Milner, Helen. 1988. *Resisting Protectionism*. Princeton: Princeton University Press.

Moe, Terry. 1985. "Control and Feedback in Economic Regulation: The Case of the NLRB." *American Political Science Review* 79:1094–116.

Noll, Roger. 1983. "The Political Foundations of Regulatory Policy." *Journal of Institutional and Theoretical Economics* 139:377–404.

North, Douglass C. 1981. *Structure and Change in Economic History*. New York: W. W. Norton.

Nowell, Gregory P. 1983. "The French State and Developing World Oil Market: Domestic, International and Environmental Constraints, 1864–1928." *Research in Political Economy* 6:225–76.

Odell, John S. 1982. *U.S. International Monetary Policy: Markets, Power, and Ideas as Sources of Change*. Princeton: Princeton University Press.

Owen, Bruce, and Ronald Braeutigam. 1978. *The Regulation Game: Strategic Use of the Administrative Process*. Cambridge, Mass.: Ballinger.

Peltzman, Samuel. 1976. "Toward a More General Theory of Regulation." *Journal of Law and Economics* 14:109–48.

Posner, Richard. 1983. *The Economics of Justice*. Cambridge, Mass.: Harvard University Press.

Putnam, Robert. 1988. "Diplomacy and Domestic Politics: The Logic of Two Level Games." *International Organization* 43:427–60.

Samuels, Richard. 1987. *The Business of the Japanese State*. Ithaca: Cornell University Press.

Shapiro, Martin. 1985. *Courts*. Chicago: University of Chicago Press.

Skocpol, Theda. 1985. "Bringing the State Back In: Strategies of Analysis in Current Research." In *Bringing the State Back In*, ed. Peter B. Evans, Dietrich Rueschemeyer, and Theda Skocpol. Cambridge: Cambridge University Press.

Shooshan, Harry M., III. 1984. "The Bell Breakup: Putting It in Perspective." In *Disconnecting Bell*, ed. Harry M. Shooshan, III, 8–22. New York: Pergamon.

Temin, Peter. 1987. *The Fall of the Bell System—A Study of Prices and Politics*. Cambridge: Cambridge University Press.

Vietor, Richard. 1984. *Energy Policy in America Since 1945*. New York: Cambridge University Press.

Webber, Stephen, and Sidney Drell. 1988. In *U.S.-Soviet Cooperation*, ed. Alexander George, Philip Farley, and Alexander Dallin. Cambridge: Cambridge University Press.

Weingast, Barry, Kenneth Shepsle, and Christopher Johnson. 1981. "The Political Economy of Costs and Benefits: A Neoclassical Approach to Distributive Politics." *The Journal of Political Economy* 89:642–64.

Wiley, Richard E. 1984. "The End of Monopoly: Regulatory Change and the Promotion of Competition." In *Disconnecting Bell*, ed. Harry M. Shoosan. 23–46.

Williamson, Oliver. 1985. *The Economics of Capitalism*. New York: The Free Press.

Wilson, James Q. 1980. *The Politics of Regulation*. New York: Basic Books.

CHAPTER 10

Political Exchange and Government Policy Toward the Canadian Automotive Industry

Keith Acheson

1. Introduction

In this essay, policy evolution and industry developments are viewed as the result of an exchange process between the government and organized groups in the industry. The power of this approach is demonstrated with examples of its application to the automotive industry in North America, an important industry in international trade that has been frequently examined from other perspectives.[1] The political exchange perspective emphasizes the importance of industrial interest groups, but differs from much of the traditional public choice theory in characterizing the government as an efficient arbiter of conflicting interests. The theory focuses on the realization of exchange opportunities over a wider domain than traditionally considered as a mechanism for improving the welfare of individuals who belong to the different groups. This view has its roots in the writing of Knight[2] and has been recently strongly

    I would like to thank Katherine Acheson, Tom Borcherding, Richard Brecher, Stephen Ferris, Jeff Frieden, Frank Mathewson, Chris Maule, Don McFetridge, John Odell, David Richardson, and Tom Willett for helpful comments.
    1. A selective list includes a study by the tariff board, a Royal Commission (Bladen 1961), a number of special task forces and reports initiated by governments or the industry (United States International Trade Commission 1976; Automotive Task Force 1977; Dykes 1978; Ontario 1978; Reisman 1978; Department of Regional Industrial Expansion 1985, 1987; Grey, Clark, Shih and Associates, Limited 1986; Automotive Industry's Human Resource Task Force 1986) and studies by academic observers (Helmers 1967; Beigie 1970; Fuss and Waverman 1985).
    2. In 1947, Knight stated:
        For a genuine understanding of social phenomena and problems we "obviously" have to use the methods and concepts of various sciences, physical, biological, and "psychological" in a broad interpretation; but, in addition, we have to enter other universes of discourse. Whether "adaptive response" can be interpreted mechanically is a disputed question; but human beings engage in *rational manipulation,* which certainly involves

endorsed by Becker (1983). Different writers in Canada have been applying variants of this approach to various problems over the past two decades.[3]

The exchanges between government and industry involve adaptation of industry decisions to produce political outputs in return for modifications in policy treatment of the industry. The political outputs may be improved environmental impacts, plant locations in lagging regions, research and development activities, jobs, hiring of disadvantaged groups—actions which make the government more popular at a cost to the industry. Management and organized labor in the industry have an incentive to coordinate their activities to provide a better package of political outputs. Before the 1965 Canada-U.S. auto pact, the Canadian automotive industry was substantially insulated from events abroad by tariffs and other trade barriers, and political exchange in each country mainly involved the national industry and its government. After the 1965 Canada-U.S. auto pact, the automotive industry became integrated on a North American basis and one industry interacted with two governments.

The trading nexus for the North American industry under the pact is shown in figure 1. The political output flows shown by the two arrows emanating from the industry and ending in the box for each national government differ from each other; the flow to the Canadian government is tailored to its tastes, while that to the American government is affected by a different set of evaluations.

In the next section, this political exchange framework is explained in more detail. In section 3 examples of exchange involving political dimensions under the umbrella of the Canada-U.S. auto pact are analyzed. The first two that are summarized—one involving the private initiatives with respect to labor contracts in the United States and Canada, and the second examining the differences between the Canadian and American governments' bailout offers to Chrysler when it was flirting with bankruptcy—have been examined in detail in a companion piece (Acheson 1989). The third example is the process of interaction between the Canadian and American government that determined the path of adjustment in prices of automobiles in Canada relative to those in the United States during the first decade of the pact. Finally, the policy reactions in Canada over a longer period of time than that covered by the auto pact are examined briefly to discern whether policy provided "insurance" against hard times through tailoring of policy to affect individual firms.

---

more than either or both. And, apart from various forms of quasi-mechanical interaction and one-sided "control" among themselves, they to some extent reach a consensus through discussion, which cannot be conceived in terms either of mechanics or of the use of given means to achieve given ends. (1956, 247, italics in original)

3. Some examples are McManus 1972, Acheson 1977, Borcherding 1981, and Breton and Wintrobe 1986.

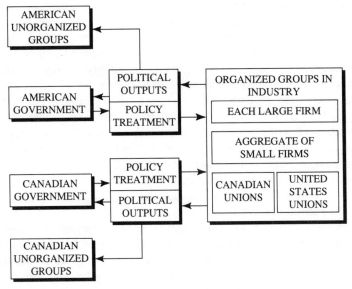

Fig. 1. Political trading flows

2. The Political Exchange Framework

The Social System

The analysis integrates political objectives and economic effects. Policy is assumed to be created within a competitive political system, defined by an explicit or implicit constitution. The economic constitution is a set of rules and enforcement mechanisms determined by custom and policies developed within the political system. Under the umbrella of the economic constitution, contracts and transactions take place and private institutions develop or wither. Together the economic and political constitutions define a social system.

Information, Institutions, Political, and Economic Outputs

Information assumptions affect how any prescribed social system will operate. Organizational forms, institutional practices, and contracts are mechanisms by which individuals reduce the dissipations caused by imperfect and asymmetrically distributed information.[4] Examples of organizational responses in the current social system are firms, unions, cooperatives, trading exchanges, franchises, chain stores, shopping centers, parties, interest groups, task forces, polls, and think tanks. Some of these institutions perform predominantly economic functions, but their viability usually depends on effectiveness in both the political and economic domains.

In equilibrium, organizational diversity generally prevails. For example, in an industry in which small firms and large firms both survive, the two organizational types are revealed to be of equal commercial competence at the margin of their "reach." This balance at the margin often involves different and offsetting political and economic advantages. For instance, the small firm may receive certain regulatory and tax concessions that offset higher production costs, or vice versa. More importantly, inframarginal differences will exist.[5] As various traditional inframarginal economic rents may arise because of economies of scale and the internalizing of economic activities, inframarginal rents earned because of politically oriented behavior also vary with size. Different incentives at the margin lead to different politically directed behavior. A large firm may lobby on its own and receive firm-specific concessions, whereas small firms may not. The large firm's participation and influence in a trade association may also differ substantially from that of a set of small firms of equivalent economic weight. To summarize, profit is enhanced if an organization is efficient politically, just as it is enhanced by better marketing and quality control.

In a political equilibrium, some voters are more informed than others, and the policies adopted reflect both these informational asymmetries and the political decision-making process. The informational problems dictate that government interacts differently with interest groups and organizations (such as firms, large cooperatives, trade unions, and professional organizations) than with unorganized interests.

---

4. Uncertainty that is symmetric does not adversely affect exchange as a means of coordinating resources and allocating products. It is asymmetries in information that cause problems for exchange. Better-informed traders can exploit less-informed ones. Anticipation of exploitation leads uninformed traders to eschew traditional price-taking trade and seek alternatives. Different trading practices (for example, all-or-nothing offers, tie-ins, resale restrictions) or arranged coordination within an institutional structure emerge as mechanisms for reducing the losses caused by informational asymmetry. See, among others, McManus 1975, Williamson 1979, and Barzel 1985.

5. In equilibrium, each institution will be equally efficient at the margin. A marginal transaction can be switched from one supplier to another and not affect efficiency. On the other transactions (the inframarginal transactions), each firm may receive more in revenue than the unit costs incurred. The amount and source of these economic rents will differ among firms.

Exchange Between Government and Organized Groups

The interactions between government and organized and unorganized interest groups are modeled as different types of exchange relationships. Implicit and explicit commitments by the government to alter policy are exchanged with organized groups in return for politically valued outputs or actions. In contrast, the interaction of the government with unorganized groups (for example consumers) involves commitments by the government as to the type of society it will pursue, in part by mobilizing political outputs from the organized sector, in anticipation of direct electoral support. It is the government/organized group relationship that is most relevant to this essay.

Campaign contributions and an organization's official support for a party at election time are important aspects of the interaction between government and organized groups, but organizations and the government also interact frequently between elections. This continuous exchange activity differs in important ways from the periodic support granted during an election campaign.[6] In these interactions, economic organizations "pay for" the implementation of favorable policy adaptations by generating more politically valuable characteristics from their operating and strategic decisions. For instance, a firm's investment, location, product quality, research, hiring, training, job environment, and other decisions have political dimensions. The placement of a plant in a depressed region, the construction of a prestigious research complex in the jurisdiction, the generation of jobs, the hiring of groups that are disadvantaged or perceived to be, and the sensitivity of management to ethnic and language differences in the society are examples of political outputs of economic institutions that affect the government's success in "providing" the type of society which strengthens its support among unorganized voters. In providing political outputs, a firm or industry typically incurs lower gross commercial revenues or higher production costs. Such costs will be voluntarily incurred if the profit increase from favorable policy changes is greater.

The Shifting Terms of Trade in Political Exchange

In economic exchange, shocks are constantly affecting the terms and volume of exchange in markets. With imperfect information and uncertainty, nominal prices may be constant over protracted periods of time with adjustment occurring in some other way. The shifting terms of trade, masked by the constant nominal price, will be reflected in the length of queues, the amount of com-

---

6. Continuous exchange as an important phenomenon within an organization has been stressed in the work of Breton and Wintrobe (1982, 1986).

plementary services offered, the terms of financing, prices of tied products, disguised discounts, or some mix of these. Whether a product is sold in a continuing price auction or with posted prices is an endogenous institutional practice subject to the discipline of competition. The assumption made here is that the incumbent institution generates more joint wealth than alternatives. Otherwise it would be changed.

The same process holds for political exchange between the government and economic organizations. The political terms of trade change constantly in response to shocks in technology, demographics, and perceptions of scarcity. The forms of the adjustment to these changes depend on the costs of adaptation along different dimensions of the political arrangement. For example, with respect to commercial policy, adaptations can occur in tariff rates, tariff categories, changes in classification procedures, evaluations for ad valorem tariffs, conditions of qualification for favorable rates and interpretations of whether those conditions have been met, speed of clearance, imposed quotas, voluntary quotas, and treatment of international intracompany transfer prices for calculating corporate tax. Commercial policy may be changing significantly with a constant tariff, just as the generalized price of a product or service may be changing despite the nominal price being fixed.

Rationality of Public Policy

That policies are constantly in flux is not interpreted here as evidence that authorities are "tinkering" in a nonpurposeful way. On the contrary, if the opportunities for exchange alter, policy stability would signal either lethargy and an absence of commitment or prohibitively high costs of adaptation. In circumstances where the costs of adaptation are low, constant policy accommodation is to be expected.

It is assumed that these policy adjustments are rational responses to new information, just as changes in price or quantity offers in commercial markets are assumed to be in traditional economics. As compared to a world in which every voter had the same accurate view of causal relations in society, the policies chosen by an imperfectly informed electorate are suboptimal in some ideal sense, but optimal when compared to feasible alternatives. In this sense, the evolving situation is perceived as an optimum. Within existing institutions, individuals develop appropriate responses to new problems and devise better schemes for coping with old ones.

This approach does not claim that surviving government institutions are efficient in any ideal sense. The coordination of legislature, government departments, and factions within the bureaucracy may be very imperfect. Citizens may line up for hours to be told that they are in the wrong queue or have the wrong form. Survival in a competitive setting does reveal that no better method of delivery can be economically introduced. As the costly resolution of conflicting interests between the corporate planning, production, and sales divisions of General Motors is ignored and the company considered a single behavioral entity, the same assumption is made for the government.[7]

Three further caveats with respect to the approach need to be kept in mind. First, societies are affected by the cumulative political, institutional, and individual decisions that create "framework" constraints, policies that are part of the basic infrastructure of the society. These frameworks display institutional stickiness. Changing frameworks, part of the social capital, can be very costly. For example, the language policy adopted in the polity, the educational system embraced, the legal structure, or the terms of amending the political constitution are assumed to be ex ante rational but ex post may be ill-suited to the course of events. In hindsight, wealth is lower than it would have been if some feasible alternative had been chosen, but introducing the alternative now may make wealth even lower. Ex post regret is irrelevant to efficiency, which reflects rationality at the time that a path was chosen. Bad luck differs conceptually from inefficiency.

Second, efficiency refers to the absence of opportunities to make someone better off without damaging others. As is well known, Pareto efficiency has no moral connotation. The equilibrium may be efficient in this sense and still be disgusting.[8]

Third, legislation and administrative decisions may redistribute wealth as well as reallocate resources. It is assumed here that the democratic process has been legitimized as a choice mechanism among feasible Pareto-efficient options. Again, this mechanism may not reflect any individual's conception of the ideal but reflects what the society has been able to implement, given its cultural, intellectual, and institutional history.

Predictions about the Political Terms of Trade

The conditions of political exchange will be altered by exogenous shocks that change the industry's capacity to deliver political output. For example, tech-

---

7. In some contexts, this level of aggregation is inappropriate. For a review of two decades of literature discussing economic approaches to the theory of bureaucracy, see Acheson 1988 and Borcherding 1988.

8. Breton and Wintrobe (1986) provide a grisly example in their persuasive argument that Adolf Eichmann was responsible for his actions:

We do not accept that subordinates in large organizations obey orders. Instead, we argue, they are placed in a competitive framework in which they are rewarded for entrepreneurial initiatives that promote the interests and objectives of their superiors. The more useful they are to their superiors, the larger the rewards. We have sought to show that the bureaucratic structure of Nazi Germany was extremely competitive, that the bureaucrats—SS officers, heads of concentration camps, and so forth—active in the bureaucracy were energetic, entrepreneurial, and competitive and that, except at the end, subordinates were intensely loyal to their superiors. (925)

nological change may alter locational economies for the industry and make it a more or less suitable instrument for regional development. In addition, if the political process acts to insure groups against the effects of exogenous factors, policies will be altered as a means of delivering the insurance. That a political process of the type envisaged here will act to share the gain and to share the pain has been predicted by Peltzman (1976). With respect to the automotive industry one would expect the general incidence of policy to favor producer interests when sales and profits were low and consumer interests when they were high. If policy can be tailored to the firm level, firm insurance would be provided rather than industry insurance.

Self-Enforcing Exchanges

Generally, agreements between government and industry cannot be enforced legally.[9] Enforcement depends on each party being able to punish the other for failure to comply. In these transactions, the principal sanction available to industry is not delivering on its side of the bargain. On the other hand, the risk to the industry is that it will make irreversible investments and the government will not deliver the promised relaxation in policy, or will withdraw the concession. The government's risk is that an individual firm may "free ride" and enjoy the benefits of a policy change, but not deliver the politically valued action. If the government can impose only industry-wide sanctions, it may have to punish the many for the sins of a few. Political entrepreneurs have an incentive to search for means to reduce the dissipation arising from these "political" transacting costs.

The free-rider problem can be avoided if the government can marshall a sufficient portfolio of instruments to discipline delinquent firms and reward complying ones, by tailoring policy to the firm level. The scope for fine tuning policy is enhanced if the industry is concentrated and the major firms differ substantially in characteristics. The North American automotive industry fits this mold.[10] Another defense against opportunism and a consequent contraction in trade is the prospect of continuous dealings. Past experience builds trust, and (perhaps more importantly) the anticipation of future gains from trading can impose discipline on the parties.

---

9. Subject to constitutional constraints, the government can legally enforce compliance to the agreed "terms" but private parties cannot. Election or subsequent promises to introduce new laws (or not to) by a government are disciplined only by the political cost of reneging. Even if the government fulfills its promises, a future government can reverse existing legislation.

10. In 1980, there were a total of 83 Canadian firms listed as bona fide manufacturers eligible for special duty treatment under the auto pact, while the equivalent list of manufacturers eligible to import original equipment parts into the U.S. contained 214 manufacturers in 1981.

Political Exchange in an International Setting

International trade and investment allow traditional economic gains from exploiting specialization, different factor endowments, and technological capital. They also change the opportunities to produce politically valued outputs. For example, the costs of generating economic activity and relieving regional unemployment may be lowered because of greater access to contiguous markets in another country; or a sophisticated research and development project can be enticed as part of the terms of access to foreign multinationals. Since the political demand for political outputs reflects the country's interest structure, demand prices will also be affected by the introduction of new players in domestic politics. In particular, if the trade regime encourages large inflows of foreign capital, the influence of owners in domestic politics will fall as the proportion of foreign ownership rises, because the foreign owners have less political impact. Ceteris paribus, policies that repatriate ownership will receive stronger political support.

Specifically, with respect to Canada and the United States, political demands in the two countries differ because of resource, climatic, and geographical differences.[11] Canada has lower wealth per capita, a higher natural rate of unemployment, a larger natural resource endowment per capita, and greater regional disparities. In addition, the ownership of the Canadian automobile industry is predominantly foreign,[12] making labor employed in the industry a relatively more important factor politically in Canada than in the United States.[13]

A trade regime that permits the tailoring of its effects to the evaluation of political attributes in participating countries will be superior to one that does not. If the trade regime mainly involves two countries, two effects will be perceived. Arrangements by the private organizations involved—firms, trade associations, and labor unions—will respond to the political demand prices (constraints) in each country. In addition, there will be a discretionary and continuous adaptation of the policy structure for the industry in the block as a whole, a structure that is jointly produced by the two countries. This adaptation will be influenced by the value of political outputs in both countries.

In the automotive case, since the introduction of the Canada-U.S. auto

---

11. For an elaboration of these differences, see Acheson 1989.

12. Chrysler, Ford, and General Motors, all American firms, dominate motor vehicle manufacturing in Canada. In parts manufacturing, production is less concentrated; but only one-seventh of the industry was Canadian owned in 1984.

13. It is a commonly held view that the Canadian polity is more "socialist" than the American—that majority opinion in Canada is more favorable to the interests of labor than in the United States. The view taken here is that the difference is due to differences in setting and not to ideology. If there is a different set of tastes for political and social arrangements in Canada, then that will just reinforce the potential for political exchange in the shaping of a trade regime.

pact in 1965, tax, subsidy, commercial, and other policies in Canada and the United States have taken into account political prices in the other jurisdiction as well as those in its own. The balance of payments between the pact partners, the distribution of employment, the purchase of intermediate inputs,[14] the location of production and research activities, the level of wages, and the purchase of inputs from offshore are monitored and have become political outputs affecting the support of individual governments. The auto pact permits an integration of the industry on a North American basis that is responsive to both economic and political imperatives. Two governments jointly create the policy environment for firms in the integrated industry. Coordination of policy is enhanced by a long history of consultation and resolution of disputes between the two governments. The expected policy responses of Canadian and American governments have also become an important part of the political trading environment within which private initiatives are taken.

3. Examples of Political Exchange[15]

Summary of Labor Contracts and Chrysler Bailout

Under the auto pact, the North American industry became integrated compared to the earlier structure in which a miniature replica of the American industry had developed within a protected Canadian market. In this new commercial environment, the vehicle manufacturers shifted specialized production to Canada and raised profits since comparably trained labor was cheaper and the plants were contiguously located. Profits to American owners rose as activity was shifted; but after some point, opposition by American labor threatened to counter the political effect in the United States of the profit increase. Additional expansion in Canada faced this American political constraint.

Further shifts of jobs to Canada were achieved, however, by relaxing this constraint through the companies "spending" some of the profit increase to compensate the adversely affected party, American labor. These "side payments" defused political opposition to the change because American unions were prepared to accept a reduction in members if the pay of each member

---

14. In 1977, it was estimated that 12 percent of the aluminum, 21 percent of the steel, and 64 percent of synthetic rubber consumed annually in Canada was used by the industry (Automotive Task Force 1977, 15).

15. Further examples (discussed in a related working paper [Acheson 1987]) are the coordination of conservation, safety and emission controls, and the ongoing development of a process establishing ground rules for government grants subsidizing the establishment of plants in the different national, state, and provincial jurisdictions.

increased sufficiently. Labor settlements with the American union, which granted increasingly higher wage equivalent packages than were being agreed to in negotiations with Canadian workers, would be consistent with such a complex implicit contract.

In contrast to the political exchange dynamic, the standard economic view of integration would result in the remuneration of labor being equalized in the two jurisdictions.[16] If political considerations were not creating the need for side payments, locational arbitrage based only on the cost of production would equalize money wage offers.

The evidence is consistent with the political exchange view. The difference in hourly compensation has widened, accompanying a substantial shift of jobs from the United States to Canada. In addition, American labor contracts have incorporated profit-sharing clauses, while Canadian contracts have typically eschewed them. (See Acheson 1989, 9–11.)

The response of the American and Canadian governments to the financial difficulties experienced by Chrysler in the late 1970s and early 1980s illustrates different evaluations of political outputs. Labor in this industry has more political clout in Canada than in the United States, where the ownership interest resides and acts as a countervailing force. As a result, there were predictably different political responses by the two governments to the plight of a firm operating in both jurisdictions. The governments of Canada and Ontario, the province in which Chrysler's plants were located, made a series of offers of aid to the stricken company in 1980 and 1981. These offers of financial assistance were conditional on the company maintaining specified levels of employment in Canada, not closing any Canadian plants without the permission of the relevant Canadian cabinet minister, and investing a specified amount in Canadian facilities during its five-year reconstruction program. No concession from Canadian labor was required for access to this financing and none was offered. The Canadian and provincial governments' suggested terms changed in detail as Chrysler's fortunes altered over the period of negotiation, but the general structure was maintained. Chrysler's fortunes improved and it did not have to draw on financing from the governments.[17] In contrast, the American government moved more quickly to initiate loan guarantees. In the American rescue package, concessions from labor and suppliers were required rather than assurances of expanding employment opportunities from the company.

---

16. With the same technology available to the companies on both sides of the border, with borrowing costs to the firms unaffected by the location of plants, with no locational advantage of being on one side or the other of the Detroit River, and with equal quality labor available in both countries, the value of the marginal product of labor would be the same in a Canadian plant as in an American plant.

17. For more details of the bailout, see Trebilcock et al. 1985.

Controlling the Producer-Consumer Price Differential

Freight[18] and the "lemon"[19] distinction between new and old cars offer limited scope for price discrimination on a North American basis in the automobile industry. Government-enforced separation of the Canadian consumer market from the American substantially expanded the scope for price discrimination.[20] Wholesale and retail prices can differ between the two countries, within a range determined by the Canadian tariff, and dealers or customers cannot arbitrage into Canada. The ability of the companies to discriminate within this band depended on the joint management of the industry by the two governments.

Both governments realized that the adjustments to free trade for manufacturers—developing new administrative systems, rationalizing existing plants, and building new plants—would have to be financed. The profits from price discrimination, the temporary collection of a "private" customs duty, provided a flexible tool to achieve this. Payment could be metered and adjusted to the performance of the industry. After the pact became operative, a substantial price differential developed.

Both governments anticipated "a narrowing differential between Canadian and United States prices,"[21] but opinion on the appropriate time profile

---

18. In the past spatial discrimination in the industry was reflected in the practice of charging "phantom freight." White (1971, 159) described the situation:

> Cars that were assembled in regional assembly plants and which, therefore, incurred only the stacked freight costs to the assembly plant were nevertheless carrying a freight charge as if the assembled car had been shipped all the way from Detroit to the customer. Freight charges to Los Angeles ran $365 for a Buick and $279 for a Chevrolet; the actual shipping costs were approximately $194 for the former and $124 for the latter. More importantly, tow-bar, drive-away, and even small scale trucking costs were significantly under the company-charged freight costs.

"Bootlegging," the practice of dealers selling cars for $50 over cost as long as they were resold in a different area, became big business and illustrated the limits that arbitrage put on discrimination. Specialized wholesalers emerged and White (160) reports one estimate that 20 percent of the cars in California were bootleg sales. With the growth of Japanese competitiveness, the elasticities of demand on the west coast were dramatically increased and the phantom freight charges swung in the other direction. Testimony by Bennett, then President and CEO of Ford Canada, indicated that, in the mid-seventies, the price charged by Ford for shipping a Pinto from St. Thomas to Vancouver was $50, whereas the true cost of the transportation was $250.

19. The lemon attribute is that the resale value of a new car is far less than its cost from the dealer because the buyer rationally suspects that only lemons are immediately offered for resale. This margin prevents someone who has low-cost access to cars from arbitraging to those who would pay more (see Akerlof 1970).

20. The agreement is not symmetric. American consumers can drive a car across the border duty free, as long as it has 50 percent North American content. Only bona fide manufacturers can bring cars from the United States into Canada.

21. From the 1965 press release of the Canadian Minister of Industry, Bud Drury, announcing the agreement.

differed. The United States government was concerned that the differential not be too large and extend for too long; too much capacity would then be shifted to Canada, resulting in too large a political backlash by American labor. The companies were principally concerned in gauging what the net price would be when American policy reaction was factored into the decision. To be left with plants specialized to North American requirements that no longer had duty-free access to the American market would be costly.

As a result, the Canadian consumer interest found itself a surprising champion, the American government. The annual reports of the President to the Congress on the operation of the pact provided statistics on the price differences, emphasised their temporary role, and encouraged their disappearance. The American "voice" on the price differential steadily became louder; finally in 1975, ten years after the pact became operative, the stick was flourished and

> . . . The U.S. Treasury Department launched a series of inquiries as a result of allegations that motor vehicles were being dumped in the United States at less than fair market value. (Reisman 1978, 46)

These investigations were discontinued after the Treasury and the companies reached an accord whereby the dumping charges would not be pressed, but the companies would act to remove the wholesale price differences.

The Pattern of Policy Interaction Over Time

A continuous process of adjusting policy to the shifting conditions of the industry, predictable from the theory of regulation or from the need to keep a self-enforcing agreement together, is descriptive of the history of Canadian automotive policy.[22] An aspect of this government-industry exchange, which is clearly reflected in the automotive industry, is that the gains from exchange between an oligopolistic industry and the government are enhanced if the government can tailor policies to have a differential effect on at least the large firms. Differences in the major automotive companies in their degree of vertical integration, the breadth of their product line, their presence in other industries, their ownership patterns, their financing, their locational characteristics, and their research and development activities, make discrimination possible while maintaining a common policy for the industry.

Discrimination among the companies is not a new phenomenon. In the

---

22. For a chronology of the multiple dimensions of Canadian automotive policy, see the working paper (Acheson 1987). Change occurs frequently in the formal structure of the tariff, the sales tax along many dimensions, and continuously in discretionary administrative and enforcement decisions.

early 1920s, the Ford Motor Company was the dominant firm in the Canadian industry. In 1926, Ford of Canada produced 100,614 vehicles, mostly Model T's (Marshall, Southard, and Taylor 1976, 64), almost 50 percent of total Canadian output in that year. Ford was extremely profitable.[23] In the tariff reductions of 1926, the tariffs on cars in the price range of the Model T were reduced from 35 percent to 20 percent while the tariff on more expensive cars, produced by Ford's rivals, was held at 27.5 percent. Ford's sales fell after 1926 and the level of sales of that year were not again realized until after World War II. Although scale economies are pronounced in the auto industry, incumbent small firms were given favorable policy treatment, despite the deterring effect on the expansion of more efficient units. The tariff and content conditions have had many features favoring smaller units.[24]

The auto pact includes a number of individual commitments of the major vehicle manufacturers to the Canadian government. Distinct promises of investment in the early years of the pact were contained in letters from the individual companies.[25] Subsequent correspondence from each major manufacturer concerning its expansion plans was tabled in the House of Commons on September 16, 1978. Because of the discretionary power to grant bona fide manufacturer status, the Canadian government has been able to bargain separately with each entrant into the Canadian market. The duty remission agreements represent an extension of this discretionary scope since the firm may receive privileges that are tailored directly to its situation.

Under the auto pact, any company not complying with the requirements for duty-free entry of parts and vehicles must pay the full tariff on all of its imports. Only GM has always been in compliance, but no company has ever

---

23. As witnessed by the story in the *Financial Post* of February 12, 1926, which presents a litany of financial statistics and concludes that the net earnings on paid-up capital of the company were approximately 87.5 percent.

24. The point is well illustrated by the details of the extended content plan proposed by Bladen (1961, 40).

If the number of passenger automobiles produced in Canada and imported under the "extended content" plan is as follows,		then the percentage of Canadian content required to qualify for duty-free entry shall be:
up to	5,000	30 percent
on the next	15,000	50 percent
on the next	30,000	60 percent
on the next	50,000	65 percent
on the next	100,000	70 percent
on the excess over	200,000	75 percent

25. The letters also included a commitment that the growth in the value added in Canada would be at least 60 percent of the growth in the value of sales of cars and 50 percent for trucks.

had to pay duty for not meeting its requirements. For example, Ford was cited for being in default in the Auditor General of Canada's report for 1967–68.[26] Mr. Pepin, the government minister responsible for the pact, justified giving Ford a waiver:

> The Ford company has acted openly, honestly and quite sincerely through Mr. Scott and his executives in all its dealings with the Government on this matter. The company did indeed offset its shortfall of "in-vehicle content" and also generated an additional $200 million Canadian content. This represents new production over and above the company's promise and includes considerable new employment that would not otherwise have developed.[27]

The United States International Trade Commission (1976, 40) reported that Chrysler failed to meet its assembly-to-sales ratio for trucks in 1973, 1974, and 1975, but instead of being fined was required to establish a facility for the production of trucks in Canada. The Automotive Task Force of 1977[28] explicitly advised the Canadian government to craft regulations with the impact on individual firms in mind.[29]

Conclusion

The political exchange process adapts aspects of traditional economics, the economic theory of organizations, and public choice theory to examine the

---

26. The auditor-general's report discussed the uncollected duties in general terms and did not name the firms; in hearings of the public accounts committee it was disclosed that Ford was one of the firms and that it owed over $75 million. The president of Ford denied that his company had not met the pact requirements; the government passed an order in council formally forgiving the duties in January 1969. American Motors was listed as having been forgiven $3,049,708 in duties, but it also denied being in default. It also received absolution by order in council. *Globe and Mail*, June 13, 1969.

27. Public Accounts Committee of the House of Commons, cited in Dykes 1978, 68.

28. In December 1974, Prime Minister Trudeau and President Ford met and initiated a joint study of the automotive industry in North America. Representatives of the two governments met and separate studies were commissioned in each country on an agreed-upon set of topics. Similar methodologies were to be used in both countries. The Canadian task force report of 1977 was conducted by the Office of Special Advisor (Automotive) of the Department of Industry, Trade, and Commerce and summarized information in reports written by other government departments.

29. "In developing government policies relating to nonautomotive requirements, the governments should not only endeavor to effectively balance the sometimes "conflicting" objectives of reduced energy consumption, increased safety, and improved environmental quality, but also take into account the impact of these requirements on the competitive prospects for the individual companies and the social and economic consequences of changes in the structure of the industry." (67)

interplay between the government and private organizations. Unlike the idealized view of the Pigovian and optimal policy literature, it explicitly recognizes the costs of making political decisions, as the modern theory of transacting and organization does with respect to private economic decisions. Characteristics of voting mechanisms—that they fail to order alternatives consistently and can generate paradoxical results, that the potency of interest groups in influencing democratic decisions is not perfectly correlated with the impact of a governmental decision on the wealth of those groups, and that voting systems frequently fail to generate incentives for accurate revelations of information and valuations by voters—are incorporated as determinants of the costs of using political methods. The institutional equilibrium reflects the comparative advantages of different private and public organizations. In a dynamic similar to that stressed in Austrian economics, existing and emerging institutions exchange along many dimensions in response to shifting perceptions of the gains from cooperation and the ability to enforce arrangements about mutually agreed-upon responsibilities.[30] Individuals from industry, labor groups, consumer groups, political parties, or the bureaucracy, who recognize opportunities and organize responses to them, are the engine of constructive change.

This examination of the evolution of the North American automotive industry has documented that:

1. Economic and political outputs are not separable but are jointly produced;[31]
2. Varied "coinage" is exchanged between the industry participants and the government;
3. The interaction between industry firms and labor unions and the government with respect to the evolving letter and enforcement of policy is continuous, with diverse shocks generating an opportunity for beneficial adjustments;[32]

---

30. Political exchange is more in the spirit of dynamic models of the regulatory process, such as those developed by Goldberg (1976) and Williamson (1976). This dynamic element and greater symmetry distinguish it from hegemony explanations. Hegemony theory is asymmetric with the hegemon controlling events and bestowing benefits (or grief) on other countries. For the weaknesses of hegemony theory in a dynamic setting, see Eichengreen 1987, 5. For its application to the automotive industry, see Cowhey and Long 1983. See also the analysis and references by Gowa in this volume.

31. The ignoring of political outputs altogether in industry studies is common in empirical research on costs and productivity of an industry. For example, Fuss and Waverman (1988) have done a comprehensive study of productivity in the North American automotive industry and report some "surprising" results. A possibility suggested by the approach taken in this paper is that the surprising results may arise from a specification error due to ignoring the jointly produced political outputs.

32. Some theories, such as the surplus capacity theory (see Cowhey and Long 1983) of the industry, concentrate on a single type of shock.

4. The terms at which government and producing institutions (large firms in the automotive case) "trade" systematically alter with economic circumstances;

5. There are many interesting political exchange opportunities created when an industry is "internationalized" and "regulated" by a number of different governments.

Other approaches may explain phenomena not captured by the political exchange approach, but the insights from its application are sufficient to warrant adding it to our tool bag for political economy analysis.

REFERENCES

Acheson, K. 1977. "Revenue versus Protection: The Pricing of Wine by the Liquor Control Board of Ontario." *Canadian Journal of Economics* 10:246–62.

Acheson, K. 1987. "Power Steering the Canadian Automotive Industry: Political Exchange and Trade Regime Evolution." Carleton Industrial Working Paper Series 87-05. Ottawa: Carleton University Industrial Organization Research Unit.

Acheson, K. 1988. "Bureaucratic Theory: Retrospect and Prospect." *European Journal of Political Economy*, extra issue 4:17–46.

Acheson, K. 1989. "Power Steering the Canadian Automotive Industry: The 1965 Canada-USA Auto Pact and Political Exchange." *Journal of Economic Behavior and Organization* 11:237–51.

Akerlof, G. A. 1970. "The Market for "Lemons": Quality Uncertainty and the Market Mechanism." *Quarterly Journal of Economics* 84:488–500.

Automotive Industry Human Resource Task Force. 1986. *Report,* Canada: Employment and Immigration.

Automotive Task Force. 1977. *Review of the North American Automotive Industry.* Canada: Department of Industry, Trade and Commerce.

Barzel, Y. 1985. "Transaction Costs: Are They Just Costs?" *Journal of Institutional and Theoretical Economics,* 4–16.

Becker, G. S. 1983. "A Theory of Competition Among Pressure Groups for Political Influence." *Quarterly Journal of Economics* 98:371–400.

Beigie, C. 1970. *Canada-U.S. Automotive Agreement: An Evaluation.* Montreal: Canadian-American Committee.

Bladen V. 1961. *Report.* Canada: Royal Commission on the Automotive Industry.

Borcherding, T. 1981. *The Egg Marketing Board.* Vancouver: Fraser Institute.

Borcherding, T. 1988. "Some Revisionist Thoughts on the Theory of Public Bureaucracy. *European Journal of Political Economy,* extra issue 4:47–64.

Breton, A., and R. Wintrobe. 1982. *The Logic of Bureaucratic Conduct: An Economic Analysis of Competition, Exchange, and Efficiency in Private and Public Organizations.* Cambridge: Cambridge University Press.

Breton, A., and R. Wintrobe 1986. The Bureaucracy of Murder Revisited." *Journal of Political Economy* 94:905–26.

Cowhey, P. F., and E. Long. 1983. "Testing Theories of Regime Change: Hegemonic Decline or Surplus Capacity?" *International Organization* 37:157–88.

Department of Regional Industrial Expansion. 1985. *Report on the Canadian Automotive Industry in 1984.* Canada: Regional Industrial Expansion.

Department of Regional Industrial Expansion. 1987. *Report on the Canadian Automotive Industry in 1985.* Canada: Regional Industrial Expansion.

Dykes, J. G. 1978. *Background on the Canada-United States Automotive Products Trade Agreement.* N.p.: Motor Vehicle Manufacturers' Association.

Eichengreen, B. 1987. "Hegemonic Stability Theories of the International Monetary System." Harvard Institute of Economic Research, Discussion Paper 1305. Cambridge, Mass.: Harvard University.

Fuss, M., and L. Waverman. 1985. "Productivity Growth in the Automobile Industry, 1970–1980: A Comparison of Canada, Japan, and the United States." NBER Working Paper 1735. New York: National Bureau of Economic Research.

Goldberg, V. 1976. "Regulation and Administered Contracts." *Bell Journal of Economics* 7:426–48.

Grey, Clark, Shih and Associates, Limited. 1986. *The Automotive Agreement in a Canada-United States Comprehensive Trade Arrangement.* Ottawa: Department of External Affairs.

Helmers, H. O. 1967. *The United States–Canadian Automobile Agreement: A Study in Industry Adjustment.* Ann Arbor: Institute for International Commerce.

Knight, F. H. 1956. *On the History and Method of Economics.* Chicago: University of Chicago Press.

Marshall, H., F. Southard, and K. Taylor. 1976. *Canadian-American Industry.* Ottawa: Carleton Library.

McManus, J. 1972. "An Economic Analysis of Indian Behaviour in the North American Fur Trade." *Journal of Economic History* 32:36–53.

McManus, J. 1975. "The Costs of Alternative Economic Organizations." *Canadian Journal of Economics* 8:334–50.

Ontario, Ministry of Treasury, Economics and Intergovernmental Affairs. 1978. *Canada's Share of the North American Automotive Industry: An Ontario Perspective.* Ontario: Ministry of Treasury, Economics and Intergovernmental Affairs.

Peltzman, S. 1976. "Toward a Theory of Economic Regulation." *Journal of Law and Economics* 19:211–44.

Reisman, S. 1978. *Canadian Automotive Industry: Performance and Proposals for Progress.* Canada: Commission of Inquiry into the Automotive Industry.

Safarian, A. 1970. *The Canadian Economy in the Great Depression.* Ottawa: Carleton Library.

Telser, L. 1980. "A Theory of Self-Enforcing Agreements." *Journal of Business* 53:27–44.

Trebilcock, M., M. Chandler, M. Gunderson, P. Halpern, and J. Quinn. 1985. *The Political Economy of Business Bailouts,* vol. 2. Toronto: Ontario Economic Council.

United States International Trade Commission. 1976. *Report on the United States–Canadian Automotive Agreement: Its History, Terms and Impact.* Washington, D.C.: International Trade Commission.

White, L. 1971. *The Automobile Industry Since 1945.* Cambridge, Mass.: Harvard University Press.

Williamson, O. 1976. "Franchise Bidding for Natural Monopolies—In General and With Respect To CATV." *Bell Journal of Economics* 7:73–104.

Williamson, O. 1979. "Transaction Cost Economics: The Governance of Contractual Relations." *Journal of Law and Economics* 22:233–61.

CHAPTER 11

Future Directions in the Political Economy of Trade Policies

Patricia Dillon, John S. Odell, and Thomas D. Willett

Introduction

For a century the sibling disciplines of political science and economics kept their distance from one another, but during the last generation a political economy revival has been underway. It is no longer accurate to think that economists are not concerned with explaining the formation of trade and other economic policies, nor to charge that most political scientists misunderstand or reject the use of economic insights or techniques. Gains from exchange are being realized.

There is considerable scope for the disciplines to work with rather than against each other. Indeed, on closer inspection, differences within each discipline loom nearly as large as divisions between them. For example, some political scientists base their analyses on the assumption that actors are rational utility maximizers.[1] Likewise, some make considerable use of formal modeling and statistical testing, though they are fewer than in economics. Within economics, a number of scholars have recognized that in attempting to explain government behavior one must often focus on motivations that go beyond maximization of actors' narrowly defined economic interests in income or wealth (see, for example, Baldwin 1985 and the contribution by Marks and McArthur in this volume). As traditional political science writings have emphasized, ideology and concerns with power and security can be powerful motivators of government actions. In addition, some economists have contributed important studies utilizing qualitative, less formal methods.[2]

The authors are grateful to Keith Acheson, Ian Bell, Thomas Biersteker, James Caporaso, Benjamin J. Cohen, Jeffry Frieden, Joanne Gowa, Stephen Marks, John McArthur, and colleagues at the Claremont political economy seminar for comments on a previous draft of this essay. None of them is responsible for any weaknesses that remain.
    1. For a characterization of and extensive references to the literature on the economic approach to policy issues, see Amacher, Tollison, and Willett 1976.
    2. See, for example, Cooper 1989, Ekelund and Tollison 1981, Eichengreen 1985, Kindleberger 1973, North 1981, and Olson 1965.

Efforts at better integration are still in their infancy. The political economy revival to date has still left many differences unresolved; no single unified theory of trade policy has established its dominance. In the absence of such a theory, this book suggests that several different theories and approaches can all be productive for improving our understanding of international trade and other economic policies. Each of these approaches should be pursued for the deeper insights it promises to reveal. At the same time, advocates of each should attempt to incorporate, rather than ignore, interesting findings developed in neighboring camps.

Consider again some of the main analytical points made in this volume using these ideas:

- First, trade theory is a sound but incomplete basis for analyzing trade policy. Only at their peril can political scientists sidestep study of market trends and consequences such as those illuminated by trade theory, or treat them as exogenous. A deeper understanding of policy will follow from delving into the market forces behind observed trade flows and output losses and gains. Trade theory itself also continues to evolve in response to trade developments. Theorists are paying increased attention to various types of market imperfections and to political considerations, recognizing that trade policy cannot be understood without explicit attention to the political channels through which policies are adopted. Economic efficiency is not the only consideration influencing this process.

- International power structures almost certainly drive and constrain trade policies as well, most obviously with smaller states hemmed in by large ones. Economists attempting to explain those policies while ignoring hegemonic or other international power distributions and goals risk producing misspecifed models. We still do not understand these effects with much precision, however. For instance, hegemony and power-related hypotheses need to specify better the sources of power, how much power is needed for hegemony, when it will express itself via bearing costs of collective goods and when in a more coercive manner, what alternatives can substitute for it and under what conditions.

- Nations' international security and human rights objectives, among others, affect trade policies in some cases. Moreover, we can go beyond informal assertions about these linkages. Security and foreign policy dimensions can be integrated with economic variables into formal models.

- Trade policies obviously reflect material interests of specific sectors. Public choice and interest group studies have documented industries' rent seeking and its effects, and have given us insight into how small, well-organized minorities may have more political influence at times than do unorganized majorities. But not all affected sectors favor protection or work for it through politics. "Domestic politics" is not identical to "protectionism"; it includes active opposition from organized trade beneficiaries as well. Moreover, political leaders' and businessmen's ideologies may affect policies independently, as well as shaping how industries see their interests.

- Politicians are not merely passive registers for sectoral pressures. Trade and other regulatory policies depend, for example in both North and South America, on inherited institutional structures and on leadership choices made by active heads of government and other politicians, choices that will be determined partly but not entirely by the internal political constellation of forces.
- "Domestic" regulatory decisions change international trade and investment flows and related negotiations. Political science and economics literatures on the politics of regulation offer additional insights that may aid the analysis of trade policy formation, and help integrate our views of domestic and international phenomena.

What should a reader new to the political economy of international economic relations make of the contributions to this volume? Given that there are a number of productive approaches to analyzing international trade policies, or economic policies more generally, what is the best way to go about analyzing a specific question? Which approaches should be used? Part of the answer lies in recognizing that applied analysis is at present as much an art as a science. Theoretical frameworks are essential, but they cannot substitute completely for the careful study of a particular situation with the aim of developing a view of its core elements. In this regard, the variety of available approaches provides a checklist of considerations the analyst should review, at least in a preliminary fashion.

From the theoretical standpoint, however, it is important to attempt to provide more than a rich tool kit from which applied analysts may choose. At the extreme, too much pluralism can undercut the value of theory itself. To be useful, theory must help simplify the complexity of raw data in order to focus on key elements and search for important patterns.

This concluding essay reflects on the perennial dilemma of empirical richness versus theoretical abstraction and parsimony. Our central argument is that at the current stage of development, our primary need is not for new attempts at grand theory but rather efforts to develop a better synthesis of the theories that have already been offered. How do these approaches relate to one another and what are the comparative advantages and disadvantages of each approach as applied to different types of questions? We need to bring greater order to our political-economic knowledge, but not by confining ourselves to any particular narrow theory that excludes significant findings developed by other schools of thought.

This essay offers suggestions toward these ends. We have argued, first, that further work in each of the major traditions should be pursued. Second, attempts to move directly to one simple theory for unifying all our knowledge are probably premature. Third, we nevertheless could strengthen and simplify theory by seeking to develop conditional hypotheses, to be explained below. Each of these three points concerning theoretical choices cuts across a fourth dimension, namely, the research methods used to express the theoretical ideas and test or apply them empirically. This chapter suggests both greater experimentation with less familiar methods by each discipline, and greater use of multiple methods to answer the same theoretical question.

Dealing with Complexity: The Case for Conditional Hypotheses

Each of these analytical angles is likely to yield further valuable insights in the future, particularly if each is pursued with an eye on the others as well. And yet if we work in separate tracks, in the end we risk producing only a checklist of variables. If complexity is ultimately the enemy of theory, how should we deal with this multiplicity of findings?

Looking to the long term, one suggestion arises at the level of metatheory or broad theoretical strategy. It is to postpone efforts to move directly to a simple grand theory of trade policy or political economy; we have tried this direct approach and it has not been adequate. Studies working within the framework of methodological individualism and economic rationality have certainly contributed valuable findings, but some parsimonious versions of this theory exclude too much that we know is valuable. Analogously, attempts to explain trade policies by concentrating on institutions and ideology alone and by excluding insights of rational choice reasoning are also unlikely to be adequate over the long term. To be sure, competition among ideas, stated starkly and defended vigorously, can be stimulating and valuable heuristically. In this field, however, we also know from experience that such debates can become largely ideological, thus diverting energy away from activity that generates scientific progress.

The contributions to this volume illustrate a number of different approaches to policy issues. No contributor lays claim to a singularly superior method of analysis; the policy process is far too complex to attempt to deal rigorously with all of it at one time. Treating particular parts of reality as a "black box" may be an essential element in the productive study of other parts. Our knowledge will progress more rapidly, however, if this is done with a degree of humility. Today one scholar's black box is another scholar's central issue. What is needed, and what we see many encouraging signs of developing, is a genuinely scientific as opposed to a debating spirit. This is not to say that we should not subject each other's (and our own) work to critical scrutiny, but rather that we should recognize that the world is complex and that theoretical simplification should always be considered provisional.

The crucial point with such limited or partial approaches is that they be treated with their partial nature in mind. Much unnecessary heat has been generated in debates among both economists and political scientists by failures to clarify initially whether particular hypotheses or theoretical views were intended to try to provide a useful explanation of some nontrivial aspect of behavior, or whether they were essentially the whole story, with other considerations being of only minor importance. The search for all-encompassing simple theory is appealing in principle but its likelihood of success seems low. As Strange (1983, 338) has said, seeking "an all-pervasive pattern of behavior in world politics, a 'general theory' that will provide a nice, neat, and above all simple explanation of the past and an easy means to predict the future" is "a vain search for an El Dorado."[3]

Even if we cannot move directly to such a powerful theoretical solution, however, we might proceed in that direction over the long term by attempting to construct conditional hypotheses. Present research seems to be inconsistent on many issues, one study confirming a given hypothesis while another casts doubt on it. We could strengthen and possibly also simplify our knowledge by sorting out the conditions under which a given functional relationship holds more or less strongly, or not at all. This strategy may be employed in either formal modeling or informal theorizing, and by political scientists and economists alike.

Say, for example, we are concerned with the determinants of the behavior of X. Existing research has identified several variables, A, B, and C, as possible determinants of X; but results are inconsistent and it seems unlikely that A, B, and C are equally powerful under all circumstances. The strategy calls for identifying variable M such that variable A has stronger effects on X when M is present than when M is absent. If such contingencies could be specified, we could "thin out" our larger theoretical structure at least when referring to circumstances when M is absent. These conditioning M variables might be located within the menu of existing findings, and if so, this strategy

---

3. We do not fully agree, however, with Strange's characterization of international regime theory as seeking this goal. See, for example, the more modest objectives indicated by Krasner (1983a and 1983b) and by Keohane (1983) in the same volume.

would build links between A, B, and C. If one variable conditions the effects of others and is not dependent on them, it might be thought of as having a "higher" theoretical status.

To take an illustration, X might represent the degree of import protection, A might be the degree to which the government has a security or foreign policy interest in import liberalization, and B might be the distribution of domestic interest group pressures for and against protection. In the case of the United States, it could be argued that the 1934 change in institutional arrangements for setting tariffs conditioned the effects of B and perhaps A as well. By moving decisions on particular products largely to the executive branch, the Congress made it more difficult for interest groups to penetrate the decision-making process, and also allowed the president greater discretion to link tariff decisions to other international negotiations. After this institutional change, A was freed to have a greater effect on tariffs and B's effects were dampened (see Destler 1986 and Haggard 1988).

In a different application, C might represent policymakers' ideologies. While some have argued strongly that they do not exert any independent influence, Marks and McArthur (in this volume) offer empirical evidence from the area of international trade policy that ideology does matter, but that its influence responds to opportunity costs. Their study of Congressional voting on the auto domestic content bill is consistent with the hypothesis that a free trade ideology is prevalent in Congress, but that legislators face trade-offs between constituent group interests and voting in support of their free trade beliefs. Lame duck legislators freed from the reelection constraint displayed a significantly higher tendency to vote against this piece of protectionist legislation.

Hypotheses can be conditioned in more than one way. As another example, consider the proposition that changes in the distribution of interests in society or increased lobbying (B) may lead to changes in policy on some issues, such as product-specific trade protection (X), but not on others, such as aggregate monetary policy (Y). Gowa (1988) proposes that the importance of such interest group propositions varies with the degree of publicness of the government good being provided or not provided (M). Across-the-board changes in tariff rates or monetary policy display much greater publicness than special protection for a particular industry; they raise greater free-rider problems for interest groups; therefore the importance of the corresponding political variable, interest group struggle, for policy change will be much reduced (see also Ikenberry 1988). To be sure, as Gowa notes, an issue's degree of publicness may also be influenced by legislation and institutional structures. For that matter, a changing composition of society's interests could also work its way into changed institutions over the longer term.

In general, we are saying that simple formulations may be misspecified and a higher level of analysis is required. This is somewhat akin to the problem in econometrics of using reduced-form equations when the estimation of a structural model is required. If it yields stable empirical results, there is much to be said for the simplicity of the reduced-form approach. But often the estimated relationship will not be stable. Consider, for example, the correlation between changes in interest rates (A) and exchange rates (Y). We have discovered that these correlations tend to be variable over time; if higher interest rates are caused by tight monetary policies (M), then standard theory predicts currency appreciation, while if higher interest rates are due to an increase in expected inflation (N), then we would expect currency depreciation. Thus our prediction of the direction of exchange rate change accompanying a change in interest rates needs to be conditioned on the cause of the change in interest rates.

Another specification issue is that the relationships between different explanatory factors may not all take a simple additive form. For example, rent seeking by powerful industries may also be insufficient to produce protection unless the industry is facing hard times, and can therefore make a claim on the public's sense of obligation to help fellow citizens in distress. At the same time, industries facing hard times but lacking political clout are seldom successful in moving trade policy in their favor. Though the two hypotheses are sometimes posed as substitute explanations (e.g., Hillman 1989), it may be that each condition is necessary and neither is sufficient alone. It may be their combination that is powerful (Willett 1989).

As these examples illustrate, the careful construction and application of conditional hypotheses can give us some sense of why a theory seems confirmed in some studies and disconfirmed in others. What are we to make of one study which finds that Congressional committees have an important influence on one regulatory agency, while another equally excellent study has concluded that Congressional committees have little influence on another one? Instead of debating which view by itself has the greater explanatory power, it would seem wise (and intellectually satisfying) to see whether it is possible to develop some type of explanation for the differences in results, relying for example on different types of regulatory agencies, some of which Congress has incentives to attempt to control and others which it does not. If such an explanation or theory were forthcoming, it could then be tested against studies of other regulatory agencies.

In sum, both theoretical and empirical studies can help produce a more consistent and ultimately more parsimonious body of knowledge if we seek to identify conditional hypotheses. This strategy can be implemented through both formal deduction and more informal and inductive methods. The key is to move beyond single-factor interpretations by seeking contingencies that influence the effects of each important explanatory variable.

Research Methods

Research methods, like theories, traditionally divided the two disciplines, but this division is breaking down. Today members of both groups use each of the following methods: (1) formal or mathematical deduction; (2) qualitative concepts and hypotheses; (3) statistical testing; and (4) case study analysis, usually historical and inductive. While types 1 and 3 are more common in economics and types 2 and 4 more frequent in political science, differences between the fields are actually matters of degree.

In general, both economists and political scientists could benefit from greater experimentation with methods more common in the other's discipline. Political science could probably gain by exploring deductive analysis more fully, and greater attention to historical and case study analysis would strengthen economics.

Economists should recognize that rigorous analysis need not take only the forms of mathematical modeling and econometric testing. Case study methods need not mean mere "storytelling." The most useful case studies derive from a concern for theory development and testing, which guides the selection of cases. Comparative analysis of even a small number of cases can contribute to the development of generalizations.[4] Such comparative case analysis can suggest (or help disconfirm) interesting hypotheses concerning dimensions that are omitted by quantitative studies. Indeed the skilled analyst can advance theory even with a single case study, if it is well chosen (Eckstein 1975). Of course small-n comparisons and case studies seldom produce definitive conclusions by themselves, but econometric exercises rarely do so either. In order to yield their maximum value, case studies should be designed with these theoretical considerations in mind. Researchers' sensitivity to this broader framework will make it easier for readers to interpret their studies and will contribute to successful creation of empirically supported conditional generalizations.

Likewise it would be unfortunate if political scientists succumbed to the temptation to toss out deductive methods and modeling with the bathwater. Formal and statistical research can be done in mundane fashion, but it can also express great imagination and power. The very problem of complexity is after all a central reason to turn to formal analysis. By the same token, in order to yield their own maximum value, models could attempt to incorporate to a greater extent the significant insights contributed by less formal research. Econometric work can also benefit from efforts to go beyond reliance on

---

4. Such studies can focus on explicit general propositions, and cases can be selected, for example, to illustrate variation while "holding constant" other potential influences. See guidelines in George 1974, and examples in Katzenstein 1978, Milner 1988, and Odell 1988.

easily available statistical proxies to the collection of more direct evidence of political activity.

These different methods are most usefully seen as complements rather than substitutes. The natural tendency is to defend the most familiar method and dismiss the alternatives, but we need to resist this loss of perspective on the relative contributions and limitations of each. As with theoretical approaches, different research methods will have particular comparative advantages and disadvantages. For example, it seems likely that a good deal more knowledge of historical development will be needed when uncovering the causes of major changes in institutional structure than when analyzing the effects of different institutions. Likewise there may be more formal modeling and statistical testing in the latter than in the former application. Economists and political scientists may well continue to specialize as to their respective research methods, but we could all become more frequent consumers of the results of methods we do not use ourselves.

Methodological diversity need not mean perpetual fragmentation of our knowledge. By attacking the same problem from different methodological angles, we may confirm previous findings, or reveal how they need to be refined or rejected. This volume illustrates several types of methodological convergence, despite the overall picture of great diversity. Chapters 4 and 7, which address linkages between security and trade policy—in NATO and the European gas trade and in sanctions against South Africa—attempt to show that informal propositions about these linkages and effects can be accommodated and made more precise in formal models. In general, doing so may also raise logical possibilities and questions not considered previously, and may also reveal inconsistencies in the looser chain of reasoning. As another example, the investigation in chapter 6 of industry interests in antiprotection politics, based on industry and firm case studies, confirms some results of cross-sectional statistical testing, and better reveals the social processes through which those relationships operate. Generally, formal and informal methods can be used to enrich development across disciplines, and they can be deployed in some ways that will enhance the unity of our enterprise.

In conclusion, we believe that this volume has amply demonstrated the gains from exchange between and within economics and political science in analyzing international trade policies. Increasing trade between the disciplines is unlikely to put particular approaches out of business. Instead, greater attention to the results from other theories offers the prospect of enhancing the productivity of each.

The world is complex and we must recognize this in our research. In expanding beyond overly narrow analysis, however, we should not lose sight of the ultimate goal of developing powerful simplifications. While each of the major approaches has an important agenda for further research within its own tradition, we believe that efforts to understand the interrelationships among these approaches are likely to be particularly fruitful.

REFERENCES

Amacher, Ryan, Robert D. Tollison, and Thomas D. Willett, eds. 1976. *The Economic Approach to Public Policy*. Ithaca: Cornell University Press.
Baldwin, Robert. 1985. *The Political Economy of U.S. Import Policy*. Cambridge, Mass.: MIT Press.
Cooper, Richard N. 1989. "International Cooperation in Public Health as a Prologue to Macroeconomic Cooperation." In *Can Nations Agree?* by Richard N. Cooper, Barry Eichengreen, C. Randall Henning, Gerald Holtham, and Robert D. Putnam. Washington: Brookings Institution.
Destler, I. M. 1986. *American Trade Politics: System under Stress*. Washington, D.C., and New York: Institute for International Economics and Twentieth Century Fund.
Eckstein, Harry. 1975. "Case Study and Theory in Political Science." In *Handbook of Political Science*, vol. 7, ed. Fred I. Greenstein and Nelson W. Polsby. Reading, Mass.: Addison-Wesley.
Eichengreen, Barry. 1985. "International Economic Policy Coordination in Historical Perspective: A View from the Interwar Years." In *International Economic Policy Coordination*, ed. Willem H. Buiter and Richard C. Marston. Cambridge: Cambridge University Press.
Ekelund, R. B., and Robert D. Tollison. 1981. *Mercantilism as a Rent-seeking Society*. College Station, Tex.: Texas A & M University Press.
George, Alexander L. 1974. "Case Studies and Theory Development: The Method of Structured, Focused Comparison." In *Diplomacy: New Approaches in History, Theory, and Policy*, ed. Paul G. Gordon. New York: Free Press.
Gowa, Joanne. 1988. "Public Goods and Political Institutions: Trade and Monetary Policy Processes in the United States." In *The State and American Foreign Economic Policy*, ed. G. John Ikenberry, David A. Lake, and Michael Mastanduno. Ithaca: Cornell University Press.
Haggard, Stephan. 1988. "The Institutional Foundations of Hegemony: Explaining the Reciprocal Trade Agreements Act of 1934." In *The State and American Foreign Economic Policy*, ed. G. John Ikenberry, David A. Lake, and Michael Mastanduno. Ithaca: Cornell University Press.
Hillman, Arye L. 1989. "Policy Motives and International Trade Restrictions." In *New Institutional Arrangements for the World Economy*, ed. H. Vosgerau. Berlin: Springer-Verlag.
Ikenberry, G. John. 1988. "Conclusion: An Institutional Approach to American Foreign Economic Policy." In *The State and American Foreign Economic Policy*, ed. G. John Ikenberry, David A. Lake, and Michael Mastanduno. Ithaca: Cornell University Press.

Katzenstein, Peter, ed. 1978. *Between Power and Plenty: Foreign Economic Policies of Advanced Industrial States.* Madison: University of Wisconsin Press.

Keohane, Robert O. 1983. "The Demand for International Regimes." In *International Regimes,* ed. Stephen D. Krasner. Ithaca: Cornell University Press.

Kindleberger, Charles. 1973. *The World in Depression, 1929–1939.* Berkeley: University of California Press.

Krasner, Stephen D. 1983a. "Regimes and the Limits of Realism: Regimes as Autonomous Variables." In *International Regimes,* ed. Stephen D. Krasner. Ithaca: Cornell University Press.

Krasner, Stephen D. 1983b. "Structural Causes and Regime Consequences: Regimes as Intervening Variables." In *International Regimes,* ed. Stephen D. Krasner. Ithaca: Cornell University Press.

Milner, Helen. 1988. *Resisting Protectionism: Global Industries and the Politics of International Trade.* Princeton: Princeton University Press.

North, Douglass C. 1981. *Structure and Change in Economic History.* New York: W. W. Norton.

Odell, John S. 1988. "From London to Bretton Woods: Sources of Change in Bargaining Strategies and Outcomes." *Journal of Public Policy* 8:287–316.

Olson, Mancur. 1965. *The Logic of Collective Action.* Cambridge, Mass.: Harvard University Press.

Strange, Susan. 1983. "Cave! Hic Dragones: A Critique of Regime Analysis." In *International Regimes,* ed. Stephen D. Krasner. Ithaca: Cornell University Press.

Willett, Thomas D. 1989. "Comments." In *New Institutional Arrangements for the World Economy,* ed. H. Vosgerau. Berlin: Springer-Verlag.

Contributors

KEITH ACHESON, Department of Economics, Carleton University

JAMES E. ALT, Department of Government, Harvard University

PETER COWHEY, Department of Political Science and Graduate School of International Relations and Pacific Studies, University of California, San Diego

PATRICIA DILLON, Department of Economics, Scripps College and Claremont Graduate School

BARRY EICHENGREEN, Department of Economics, University of California at Berkeley

JOANNE GOWA, Department of Political Science, University of Pennsylvania

WILLIAM H. KAEMPFER, Department of Economics, University of Colorado (Boulder)

JAMES LEHMAN, Department of Economics, Pitzer College and Claremont Graduate School

ANTON D. LOWENBERG, Department of Economics, University of Colorado (Denver)

DAVID R. MARES, Department of Political Science, University of California, San Diego

STEPHEN V. MARKS, Department of Economics, Pomona College and Claremont Graduate School

JOHN MCARTHUR, Department of Economics, Claremont Graduate School and Claremont McKenna College

HELEN MILNER, Department of Political Science, Columbia University

JOHN S. ODELL, School of International Relations, University of Southern California

THOMAS D. WILLETT, Department of Economics, Claremont McKenna College and Claremont Graduate School